SPECIAL SYMBOLS

~P	P is denied.
~AD-R	Rhoda is not an adult member of the household.
~~AD-R	It is not true that Rhoda is not an adult member of the household.
?P	P is questioned and challenged.
?S	The basic suggestion [S] is questioned.
P:Q	P is the cause of Q.
X:STRN	External circumstances are responsible for role strain.

LOCAL PROPOSITIONS

{1} "I think I did the right thing"—Rhoda carried out the basic suggestion {S} correctly.
{2} Mother has fulfilled her secondary obligations to Household 2.
{3} Mother has neglected her primary obligations to Household 1.
{4} Rhoda requests her mother to come home immediately.
{5} Rhoda should ask Editha for help.
{6} Rhoda has requested Editha to help.
{7} Editha showed an inappropriate emotion.
{8} Rhoda doesn't like to eat alone.
{8a} Editha doesn't like to eat alone.
{9} Rhoda requests Editha to go to the store.
{10} Rhoda's sister requests Rhoda's mother to help with her children.
{11} Rhoda's family overreacted to her claims of independence in the same way that she overreacted to their claim that she ate too much.
{12} Rhoda's family complained that she ate too much.

THERAPEUTIC DISCOURSE

Psychotherapy as Conversation

THERAPEUTIC DISCOURSE

Psychotherapy as Conversation

WILLIAM LABOV
University of Pennsylvania

DAVID FANSHEL
Columbia University

ACADEMIC PRESS   New York   San Francisco   London

A Subsidiary of Harcourt Brace Jovanovich, Publishers

COPYRIGHT © 1977, BY ACADEMIC PRESS, INC.
ALL RIGHTS RESERVED.
NO PART OF THIS PUBLICATION MAY BE REPRODUCED OR
TRANSMITTED IN ANY FORM OR BY ANY MEANS, ELECTRONIC
OR MECHANICAL, INCLUDING PHOTOCOPY, RECORDING, OR ANY
INFORMATION STORAGE AND RETRIEVAL SYSTEM, WITHOUT
PERMISSION IN WRITING FROM THE PUBLISHER.

ACADEMIC PRESS, INC.
111 Fifth Avenue, New York, New York 10003

United Kingdom Edition published by
ACADEMIC PRESS, INC. (LONDON) LTD.
24/28 Oval Road, London NW1

Library of Congress Cataloging in Publication Data

Labov, William.
    Therapeutic discourse.

    Bibliography: p.
    Includes indexes.
    1.   Psychotherapy.   2.   Conversation.
I.   Fanshel, David, joint author.   II.   Title.
RC480.5.L3   616.8'914   76-30304
ISBN 0–12–432050–3

PRINTED IN THE UNITED STATES OF AMERICA

CONTENTS

Preface ix

1 ABOUT THERAPEUTIC CONVERSATIONS 1

The Background of This Study 4
The Case of Rhoda P. 8
Earlier Studies of the Therapeutic Interview 12
The General Analysis of Discourse 23
Empirical Studies of Conversation 24
Organization of This Study 27

2 COMPREHENSIVE DISCOURSE ANALYSIS 29

The Therapeutic Interview: Definition of the Situation 30
Cross-Sectional Analysis 37
Synthesis: The Flow of Conversation 69

3 RULES OF DISCOURSE 71

I. Requests 77
II. Challenges 93

III. Coherence   98
IV. Narratives   104
V. Sequencing   110

4 EPISODE ONE

I think I did the right thing.   113

5 EPISODE ONE (CONTINUED)

When do you plan t'come home?   155

6 EPISODE TWO

That looks **clean** t'you?   181

7 EPISODE THREE

I know you don't like to eat alone.   213

8 EPISODE FOUR

See, I told you so.   249

9 EPISODE FIVE

So there's a lot of anger passing back and forth.   279

10 WHAT HAS HAPPENED IN THIS SESSION   329

The Five Episodes as a Whole   330
Two Surfaces and Two Interiors   333
Masking and Resistance   334
Sources of Insight for the Therapist   337
Sources of Insight for the Patient   343
The Role of Mitigation and the Paradox of Microanalysis   345
The Outcome of the Therapy   346

11 DIRECTIONS FOR THE MICROANALYSIS OF CONVERSATION   349

The Importance of Historical and Factual Context   351
Research Sites for Microanalysis   352
Comprehensive Discourse Analysis   354
Directions   359

APPENDIX A

The Text of the Five Episodes   363

REFERENCES   373

INDEX TO DISCOURSE RULES   379

INDEX TO PARALINGUISTIC CUES   380

INDEX TO PROPOSITIONS:
   LOCAL   381
   GENERAL   381

INDEX TO INTERACTIONAL TERMS   382

INDEX TO UTTERANCES   384

AUTHOR INDEX   386

SUBJECT INDEX   389

PREFACE

This work is an investigation of psychotherapy seen as a form of conversational interaction. It explores the goals and techniques of therapy through a close examination of the linguistic forms used by a patient and a therapist in 15 minutes of one session.

Psychotherapy is an important institution of our society, and efforts to understand this practice have come from many directions. The present investigation is the result of extended collaboration of two investigators from distinctly different fields. Fanshel was drawn into the study of psychotherapy by his general interest in the delivery of social services. The activity of counselors and therapists was a prominent feature of his earlier investigations of social workers' perceptions of clients (Borgatta, Fanshel, & Meyer, 1960), services to the aging (Kutner, Fanshel, Togo, & Langner, 1956), as well as of his longitudinal study of children in foster care (Fanshel & Shinn, forthcoming). This work led to a study funded by the National Institute of Mental Health that attempted to report directly on the working styles of advanced practitioners of psychotherapy. One result of this investigation was the publication of *Playback* (1971), in which transcripts of six sessions of a family interview were analyzed by Fanshel and the therapist. Another part of this study was the more detailed investigation of a therapeutic conversation reported in this volume.

Labov's interest in conversational interaction is the result of a series of studies of linguistic change and structure on the basis of data gathered in the speech community. These studies developed linguistic interviews that approached the style of natural conversation (Labov, 1963, 1966). Later investigations turned to group interaction as an even more effective way of overcoming the constraints of the interview situation (Labov, Cohen, Robins, and Lewis, 1968; Labov, 1971). The systematic examination of these methods led to studies of narrative (Labov and Waletzky, 1967) and other speech events (Labov, 1972b).

This collaboration began in 1966 and has taken place over a 10 year period. In part, the extended period was required because the investigators could meet only for 2 or 3 days each month, but as other microanalyses of conversation have shown, the subject is open ended; the analysis presented here is the result of a long period of evolution in the understanding of this particular conversation and conversation in general. Throughout this period, many other sociologists and linguists have developed a strong interest in conversational structures, and there has been some interaction along the way. But on the whole, the course of this investigation has been relatively independent; most of the ideas we present have been formed by the character of the materials we have been examining.

One of the earliest influences on our thinking was the work of Harvey Sacks. At a small gathering in 1966, we were first able to expose some of our materials to his insightful observation.

We have noted a number of specific contributions of Sacks to our analysis throughout this volume, but the larger influence of his thinking should be acknowledged as well. Regular interchanges with Emanuel Schegloff at Columbia in the years 1966–1970 allowed us to maintain close contact with the Sacks–Schegloff way of looking at conversation.

It is hardly necessary for us to acknowledge our indebtedness to Erving Goffman since several extended quotations indicate the specific directions of his influence. Throughout this volume, one can observe the benefits of exchanges with him and other students of language and interaction at the University of Pennsylvania.

We are particularly indebted to Charles Fillmore, Bruce Fraser, Teresa Labov, and Jerry Sadock for specific comments or criticisms of major sections of this manuscript; we feel that our final version is improved by their insights.

Our greatest indebtedness must certainly be to the agency that provided the opportunity for the direct examination of therapeutic practice, the Arthur Lehman Counseling Service. We would particularly like to thank Ruth Fizdale, the executive director, for her firm support during the investigation and her continued interest after that agency was dissolved in 1969. Our investigation is also indebted to the late Mrs. Richard J. Bernhard, who, as president of the agency, encouraged the development of the research reported here. We would like to acknowledge the financial support of the National Institute of Mental Health (R01 MH 14980-04) and the Loeb Fund.

The typing of this manuscript was particularly demanding. Ann Gerlock transformed our dictation and the transcript into coherent form through many versions of the manuscript, and its final emergence owes a great deal to her. We thank her warmly.

Finally, we wish to thank the unnamed therapist who figures so largely in this volume. After many years of close involvement with this short segment of her practice, we have come to hold her work in high esteem. Our analysis of what she accomplished may fall short in many respects, but we hope that we have given the reader a view of her high expertise in a demanding calling.

1

ABOUT THERAPEUTIC CONVERSATIONS

One of the most human things that human beings do is talk to one another. We can refer to this activity as *conversation, discourse,* or *spoken interaction.* One might attempt to distinguish among these terms, using one or the other to include more or less of the use of language in social life: greetings, lectures, service exchanges, broadcasts, and so forth. Yet all three terms will refer to the everyday situation in which two or more people address each other for a period of time, communicating something about themselves and their experience in the process. Students of conversation are becoming increasingly aware that this is an extremely complex activity and that we do not yet understand many of the principles that regulate it. This book is an attempt to grasp some of the general principles of conversation as they appear in the therapeutic interview, and some of the ways in which conversation is influenced by the particular character of that event.

The therapeutic interview is a conversational activity of considerable importance. It has been observed many times that the interview is simultaneously a diagnostic device and the method of therapy (MacKinnon and Michels, 1971, pp. 6–7). Whether this conversation succeeds or fails in its goals will make a considerable difference to the patient, but attempts to see the detailed structure of this activity have not met with great success in the past. The general opinion is that interviewing is an art rather than a science, a skill that can be acquired but probably not taught. There do not seem to be any strict rules of what can and cannot be said in therapy, where free expression is encouraged. If almost anything can be said at any time, then the number of choices which are open to the speaker would create a bewildering complexity. Yet many linguists and sociologists recently have been focusing on the rule-governed character of conversation and uncovering preliminary principles which suggest that this activity may be as well formed as the production of sentences. Linguists frequently observe that there are sentence types that logically might have been produced but are forbidden by the rules of grammar. We have much less experience in constructing examples of ill-formed discourse, but patients confined to mental hospitals provide examples of discourse that seems to be incoherent:

> Dr.: *What is your name?*
> Patient: *Well, let's say you might have thought you had something from before, but you haven't got it anymore.*
> Dr.: *I'm going to call you Dean.* [From Laffal, 1965, p. 85.]

Linguists have stressed the extraordinary competence of children in learning the grammar of their language with great speed and accuracy in their early years. From 18 months to 4 years, the child learns the most important rules of syntax. He may fail to follow the adult rules of conversation in many ways, but there can be no doubt that he has also been learning some very intricate rules of conversational sequencing. Even before the child learns to pronounce individual words, he seems to engage in conversational activity—taking his turn at vocalizing with an adult, and producing intonation contours that exhibit the patterns of adult conversation.* Though the rules of conversation that connect sentences may be more abstract and more difficult to grasp than the rules of sentence grammar, there is no reason to think that they are less intricate or regular. Yet it cannot be denied that what a person says at any given moment is dictated by his own particular life history and the practices of the several speech communities in which he has learned how to talk; the most general principles of conversation provide only part of the framework in which he operates. Other principles are determined by the specific character of the social situation, and this situation must be clearly defined if therapeutic conversation is to be understood in any serious sense.

The therapeutic interview is only one of several types of interview situations whose taxonomy and distinctive features are outlined in Chapter 2. Psychiatric interviews have been the major focus of attention in the past. There is a strongly entrenched tradition among psychiatrists that students in training should observe interviews carried out by others and report on their own interviews in writing. Recently there has been an increasing emphasis on the use of tape recorders and video-recorders for self-monitoring. On the other hand, there are many well-developed fields of counseling and therapy where there has been no tradition of monitoring or

---

*Marilyn Shatz (1975) shows that 2-year-old children have the ability to interpret and respond appropriately to a number of rules of indirect discourse. This includes some of the constructions included in our Rule for Indirect Requests in Chapter 3, by which such questions as "Can you give me a pencil?" are interpreted properly as requests for action.

training through objective observation. Thus we have a wide range of practices in assembling data which might be used to answer the question: What takes place in the therapeutic interview?

The monitoring which does take place seldom focuses on the speech behavior itself. Many discussions of interviewing focus on abstract processes such as *cathexis, transference,* or *resistance,* or upon relatively superficial aspects of nonverbal behavior. Reading through manuals and texts on the therapeutic process, one seldom finds direct quotations from the speech that occurred in the interview itself.* When quotations are given, they are usually presented as large blocks without detailed analysis.†

Without a focus on the particular speech acts and particular use of language in the interview, it does not seem possible that therapeutic practice can develop as a technical skill. At the least, the therapist should learn to recognize the patterns that he follows himself as a speaker and user of the language. Students in therapeutically oriented professions openly speak of their difficulty in acquiring technical training since they never actually witness the work itself. In chemistry, students are given practice in the laboratory operations of weighing, titrating, taking melting points, and so forth, and their skill in these practices can be measured by objective techniques. It is clearly impossible and undesirable for conversational practice to be codified to this extent, but the first step is to give some accounting of what expert practitioners do.

Though many insightful studies of the therapeutic process have focused upon the diagnostic side of the matter and upon the evaluation of the outcome, very few authors have addressed the question of what is actually done in the therapeutic interview. Many therapists are concerned with the phenomenon of resistance, and pose the question: Why does therapy take so long? But in attempting to answer this question, they do not examine what the patient actually says when he shows resistance to the therapist's suggestions. We do not wish to set aside or take issue with the theoretical frameworks used by psychiatrists and other therapists in evaluating their own interviews, but in focusing upon the actual language used by therapist and patient we hope to uncover principles that may be valuable for any theoretical orientation.

---

*See, for example, such varied approaches to the analysis of the clinical interview as Glover, 1955, Deutsch and Murphy, 1960, and MacKinnon and Michels, 1971. In Gottschalk and Auerbach's collection of articles in *Methods of Research and Psychotherapy* (1966), only one of the 34 chapters contains quotations from the interview, and this is a complete transcript of an interview without analysis. There are a number of chapters that quote the analyst's notes, several which discuss techniques of recording, and one by Gottschalk *et al.*, 1969, which gives many examples of isolated phrases to illustrate the coding system but no quotations from actual conversational interchange.

†See, for example, Deutsch and Murphy, 1949; Watzlawick *et al.*, 1967; Truax and Carkhuff, 1967; and Satir, 1964.

Our orientation toward the rule-governed character of conversation may lead the reader to expect that there is now available a theory and practice of discourse analysis within linguistics. This is not the case. Although the great majority of linguists are now aware of the need to develop rules relating sentences and escape from the confines of a sentence grammar, linguistics has not yet developed this field in any systematic way that is available to students in the area. Whereas there are general techniques for phonetic transcription, phonemic analysis, the isolation of morphemes, and rules for transforming sentences, there is no comparable achievement in the analysis of discourse. Linguists have recently emphasized the need for such principles because of particular problems that have arisen in sentence grammar: in accounting for the use of pronouns, the sequencing of tenses, rules of ellipsis, and the use of discourse-related particles in many languages. (See p. 72ff.) As a result, there is a strong and growing interest in discourse analysis within linguistics, but no one can claim yet that there is a codified competence in this frontier area.

THE BACKGROUND OF THIS STUDY

The initial impetus for our present investigation was the interest of Fanshel in analyzing the techniques used by seasoned workers in socially oriented psychotherapy. The research was carried on at the invitation of the Arthur Lehman Counseling Service, an agency that had been set up experimentally to offer social services on a self-supporting basis. The agency staff was selected carefully to include only individuals with extensive experience in therapeutically oriented casework. All of the therapists had undergone psychoanalysis as a part of their training and were thoroughly familiar with the psychoanalytic framework.

Four therapists agreed to tape record a series of patient interviews, with the patients' permission. In Fanshel's research design, the tapes were then replayed with the researcher, who engaged in a dialogue with the therapist inquiring into the therapist's own evaluation of what had taken place. The therapist was encouraged to take a self-critical stance, both positively and negatively. At any given point in the playback, a question would be raised by either the therapist or the researcher and the tape stopped for further discussion. The therapist would elaborate on the significance for the patient of what was taking place and would introduce material from the past history of the patient that would aid in the interpretation of what was transpiring. He would identify certain decision points, discuss the rationale for them, and evaluate the effectiveness of his intervention or criticize his own failure to intervene at a certain point. The therapist's comments illuminated the theoretical basis for his behavior and developed the philosophical implications of the therapeutic activity. All of this was captured on a stereo recording in which the original session was transferred to one channel, and the discussion to the other.

Eight case histories were recorded and reviewed in this playback procedure; some included as many as 50 sessions over a 3-year period. One series of six interviews with a married couple is presented in Fanshel and Moss, *Playback: A Marriage in Jeopardy Examined* (New York, Columbia University Press, 1971). This publication makes available the tape recordings of the sessions, transcripts, and a full presentation of the playback material. The case discussed in our present study is a different one, but here too we will be able to draw upon the therapist's discussion of the patient's progress and her approach.

The *Playback* material illuminates the therapeutic process from the subjective viewpoint of the therapist enriched by her own theoretical orientation. Fanshel was also interested in reviewing the interview procedure from a more neutral viewpoint, and he therefore initiated a detailed objective examination of several interviews. His initial consultation with Labov in this connection was stimulated by Labov's work on the social stratification of English in New York City (1966).

In Labov's New York City research, five sociolinguistic variables were studied primarily through individual interviews with a random sample of local speakers. These variables showed a regular pattern of style-shifting as well as social stratification; such shifts were governed by the topic as well as the contextual situation. It was hoped that they would illuminate also the interpersonal dynamics of the therapeutic situation and serve as markers of style shifts. The linguistic study also used intonational signals as independent markers of style shifting, and it was expected that a careful analysis of intonational patterns would serve to make more precise many of the messages being conveyed.*

While some of the New York sociolinguistic variables play a role in the therapeutic session examined in this volume, they turned out to be comparatively minor factors in the overall communicative pattern.† We found that the social dialects used by patient and therapist had reached a fairly stable state, which may reflect the established familiarity of the participants in the therapeutic situation. On the other hand, the intonational patterns proved to be of crucial interest as our work progressed, in defining fields of discourse, in identifying patterns of communication, and in clarifying contradictions that would be unresolved if we considered only the words

---

*In this respect, we followed the lead of Pittenger, Hockett, and Danehy's *The First Five Minutes* (1960), although we do not build as heavily upon interpretations of paralinguistic cues as their analysis does.

†In the "Cues" section of our analyses, Chapters 4–9, the reader will find occasional examples of sociolinguistic variables such as (ing)—the "dropping of *g*'s"—and (r)—the pronunciation of final and preconsonantal *r*.

themselves. Since changes in pitch and volume assumed such an important role in our analysis, we have utilized techniques of acoustic phonetics to make more precise measurements of these phenomena. In Chapters 4 through 9, our analyses will be illustrated by instrumental displays of pitch and volume that we believe will resolve much of the uncertainty that surrounds the impressionistic transcriptions used in earlier studies.

The major contribution of linguistic theory and practice to this work is in a more abstract area than the analysis of sounds or even of grammatical patterns. As we became increasingly impressed with the complexity of the devices that speakers use to cope with each other, our attention inevitably turned to the higher-level questions of coherence in discourse, the relation between speech and speech act, and the rules of interpretation and production which relate speech to the actions being felt and performed. To answer the question, What is taking place in this interview? we necessarily dealt with what speakers were doing to each other or felt that they were doing to each other: that is, with their interaction. As long as linguistics was confined to the analysis of isolated sentences, it was possible to ignore this level of behavior. But the development of a linguistic theory which deals with discourse must inevitably take such abstract matters into account. We found that sentences are not necessarily connected at the utterance level but that sequencing in conversation takes place between actions which may be far removed from the words as literally spoken, both in time and in degree of abstraction. This research therefore represents a convergence of the social scientist's interest in human interaction and the linguist's desire to formalize the structures that govern the use of language and eventually the production of linguistic forms.

It has been obvious to everyone who has studied conversation or the therapeutic process that this activity requires an interdisciplinary effort. We have tried to present this material in a way that will be acceptable to anyone who is interested in the therapeutic situation or conversation, no matter what his academic background may be. For those interested in the clinical situation and the particular type of case discussed here, we have attempted to provide ample documentation so that it can be related to other such cases. For those whose main interest is in the more abstract analysis of conversation, we have tried to place the clinical and therapeutic situation in perspective and indicate to what degree this conversation is specialized by its situation. The analysis is presented in such a way that it can be applied freely to other conversations, in interview situations or in everyday social interactions—including the monitoring of one's own speech in daily life.

In the initial stages of our research, we studied a number of the cases that had been recorded in Fanshel's study of therapeutic practice. These included patients quite varied in age and social background. It would have been possible to develop a general discussion of particular structural principles in conversation, drawing upon examples from a number of interviews. But as we began to realize the complexity of the behavior involved, we decided that we would have to enter deeply into the details of a particular case. It seemed best to confine our analysis to a single interview and make ourselves accountable to this data. We selected a therapeutic session with Rhoda P., a 19-year-old girl with a history of anorexia nervosa.

In this interview, the patient displayed a wide range of communicative styles, with sudden and dramatic contrasts from one section to another. Though this was the first recorded interview, it was the 25th in a series of sessions. At this point, the therapist had a good knowledge of Rhoda's background and mode of behavior, which enabled her to make a number of penetrating interpretations. Both therapist and patient had developed consistent ways of dealing with each other. We were witnessing work which was well in progress, and it was evident that the patient had absorbed some of the capacity for self-awareness that the therapist was trying to instill.

The first 15 minutes of this interview contains five segments, which are quite clearly delimited by their surface topics; these are presented as Episodes 1 through 5, Chapters 4–9. We do not have the visual record, and there are many points at which our analysis no doubt might have been improved or clarified by a video tape. We can often infer that a gesture or facial expression played an important role; but it also appears that there is a great deal of redundancy in speech alone, and from other studies we have reason to believe that audio tape recordings are sufficient to give us a coherent interpretation of what takes place in a therapeutic session. We have no doubt that an extension of our approach with video tape or film will have valuable results, but the problem of presenting it and interpreting the rich visual field has not yet been solved to anyone's satisfaction.

In addition to the record of the interview itself, we are able to draw upon the comments made by the therapist in a playback session—both for this and for subsequent taped encounters. In our analysis, we will also be drawing from other sections of the interview being analyzed. There are many parallel incidents, behaviors, and expressions which we might have taken from subsequent interviews to illustrate the same general principles. However, we have been able to draw from these five episodes enough repetitions of the same phenomena to confirm our sense of the validity of the rules and analyses presented.*

Given this research strategy, we face the problem of drawing general conclusions from a single case. While we have utilized discourse rules which are drawn from a very large number of cases, the analysis presented

---

*This general observation confirms one of the principles of recurrence in Pittenger, Hockett, and Danehy: "Anyone will tell us over and over again in our dealings with him what sort of person he is...what his likes and dislikes are and so on" (1960, p. 235).

here is founded upon an understanding of this one case. The internal consistency and replication of the principles within this interview provides considerable justification for this approach. It is true that this is a case of a relatively common and important therapeutic problem; it is also true that therapy and therapeutic sessions are an increasingly important type of conversation. But our main focus is upon this interview as an example of human conversation in general, and we explicate the specific features so that the application of the general principles can be seen. Every conversation is of course a union of particular situational factors and such general conversational principles. We find that it is not feasible to study conversation by attending to general principles alone, without attempting to grasp specific conditioning factors. This is because a reader may accept a general principle based upon its intuitive attraction for him, but he may refuse assent to the proposition that this principle is inherent in a particular case unless an effort is made to arrive at an interpretation which articulates with all of the empirical facts that are available.

There is a good precedent for an intense scrutiny of a single case, both within the history of therapy, and in the history of science in general (Davidson and Costello, 1969). We believe that such microanalysis is a necessary prelude to useful generalizations, but we do not propose that the reader judge our rules and principles by their success in "solving" this particular case. Rather it is obvious that the utility of our work will be judged when the reader turns to other cases that he is more familiar with and encounters fresh data that may be assessed within this framework.

THE CASE OF RHODA P.

Rhoda, the patient in the clinical session analyzed in this volume, is a 19-year-old Jewish girl who resides in New York City.* She was referred to the agency for help with her emotional difficulties by her physician, a specialist in internal medicine, after quite intensive medical treatment for severe loss of weight. The disease had been diagnosed by him as anorexia nervosa. Rhoda showed the classical symptoms of the disease when her weight dropped from 140 pounds to 70 pounds in a relatively short period. Her family reacted with considerable alarm and eventually had her admitted to a hospital. Rhoda also showed symptomatic amenorrhea: Her menstrual flow stopped when she reached the most extreme stage of emaciation.

After hospitalization, Rhoda continued on a program of intensive medical care with close dietary supervision and medication; the weight loss was

---
*The name is obviously a fictitious one. We have taken the caution of altering all names and some of the descriptive information contained in the material to protect the confidentiality of the patient.

stabilized, and at the end of a year she had gained 20 pounds. She was still alarmingly thin, since she was 5′ 5″ tall and still weighed only 90 pounds. She had not resumed menstruation. The weight gain that she had made seemed to represent a plateau, and there was no further increase. The physician recognized that there was a strong emotional component that had contributed to the etiology of the disease and continued to interfere with her recovery. His view of the matter is supported by the extensive professional literature that points to anorexia nervosa as a classical psychosomatic illness extremely resistant to treatment.

The most striking characteristic of anorexia nervosa is its specificity. It is a well-defined set of symptoms that affects mainly girls and young women, often beginning at puberty. The syndrome is so clear that it can be recovered easily from early literature.* Some of the most detailed descriptions in the literature are those of Lasègue, who characterized the clinical picture of "anorexia hysterica" as invariable. The regularity of the symptoms was said to be such that even a doctor who had not come across it in his practice previously could be sure to recognize it. The physical symptoms are striking and grotesque; the patients are said by some to resemble "the starved inmates of a Nazi concentration camp." (Blitzer, Rollins, and Blackwell, 1961, quoted in Lipton *et al.*, 1966.) Thomä's characterization (based on Bahner, 1954) is quite precise.

> All over the bodies of these girls, the bones jut out. The creases in the skin around the mouth and the lips are so deep that they look like hags. Every curve has disappeared, the stomach is hollow, the limbs like sticks. Even when the patient stands with her legs together, there is a yawning gap between her thighs. The skin is dry and scaly, and has a greyish tinge....

The other physical symptoms are amenorrhea, constipation, and the loss of body hair. The patients frequently continue in this state for long periods of time, in a condition of low energy and ill health sometimes termed "cachexia." Many patients die; some estimates run as high as 50%.

Although there is great agreement about the consistency of the anorexia syndrome, there are diverse points of view on the fundamental causes and the proper mode of treatment. Everyone seems to agree that in extreme

---

*The first English description is that of Morton in 1689 concerning an 18-year-old girl who "fell into a total suppression of her Monthly Courses from a multitude of Cares and Passions of her Mind... from which time her Appetite began to abate, and her Digestion to be bad;... I do not remember that I did ever in all my Practice see one, that was conversant with the Living, so much wasted with the greatest degree of a Consumption (like a Skeleton only clad with skin)... Being quickly tired with Medicines, she beg'd that the whole Affair might be committed again to Nature, whereupon consuming everday more and more, she was after three months taken with a Fainting Fit and dyed" (cited in Thomä, 1967, pp. 4–5).

cases the patient first should be hospitalized, given one of several drug regimens that serve as initial stimulants of appetite, and examined for other contributing causes of the condition.* Some physicians believe that anorexia cannot be treated successfully by psychotherapy, but in any case, everyone agrees that there is no simple way to reverse the pattern of behavior which leads to anorexia and produces these symptoms.

The general pattern characteristic of the anorexia patient's behavior is that of rejection of the therapist's efforts. Thomä's characterization of this behavior will be quite relevant to our study of the case of Rhoda P.:

> ... All the physician's prescriptions and recommendations are frustrated by the patient's rejection. From the very first moment, objective judgments and considerations are overshadowed by the sheer conflict of the situation, and it is not long before the shadows have lengthened and obscured sense and reason. One physician will try to help with kindness, another experiments with strict diet; neither does any good. It is hardly surprising that the physician soon realizes his own helplessness and the futility of all his efforts in the face of the patient's alarming cachexia. [p. 308]

The conflict referred to in this quotation is a frequent theme in the description of the family patterns of anorexia patients. In many accounts, the patient had a history of overweight, and was under pressure from her parents to eat less. Lipton *et al.* (1966) point out that there is often a generalized history of difficulty with eating.

> Not infrequently, real or imagined obesity led to a limitation of food intake which persisted in the form of anorexia nervosa. Furthermore, detailed history and close observation often reveal episodes of excessive food intake alternating with starvation. [p. 194]

In the psychoanalytic literature, there is considerable discussion of the patient's rejection of her sex, the desire for male organs, and psychodynamics which revolve about the oral intake of food. Other approaches to the emotional conflicts focus upon the daily pattern of interaction within the family. These patients have often been engaged in family situations in which there is a conflict of power relations, and their behavior can be seen as a way of arguing a point that they are not in a position to make overtly. This can be considered a classic case of communicating by bodily behavior rather than by language, in the manner outlined by Szasz (1965). The emphasis upon conflict within the family pattern makes it obvious that for an anorexia patient data on family life would be extremely

---

*"Psychoanalysis should not be attempted when the speedy removal of dangerous symptoms is required as, for example, in the case of hysterical anorexia" (Freud, 1905, p. 264, quoted in Thomä, 1967, p. 33).

relevant to thereapy. Frazier *et al.* (1935), quoted in Lipton *et al.* (1966), says:

> The hostility is so marked that the child is repelled by food because of the parents' revengeful attitude about eating. [p. 198]

To sum up, anorexia nervosa is a classic psychosomatic disease, markedly consistent in its symptoms, with clear evidence of emotional involvements that antedate the overt appearance of the disorder and continue to affect the progress of the patient and interfere with complete recovery. Many of the complex physical symptoms appear to be the result of the lowered food intake, but the underlying psychological disturbance must not be lost sight of. A single misstep on the part of the physician or therapist may result in a violent reaction on the part of the patient which in turn may cause her death. As Lasègue warned:

> Woe to the physician who, misunderstanding the peril, treats as a fancy without object or duration an obstinacy which he hopes to vanquish by medicines, friendly advice, or by the still more defective resource, intimidation. With hysterical subjects, a first medical fault is never repairable. Ever on the watch for the judgments concerning themselves, especially such as are approved by the family, they never pardon; and considering that hostilities have been commenced against them, they attribute to themselves the right of employing these with implacable tenacity. [1873, pp. 145–146, quoted in Thomä, 1967, p. 9.]

The case of Rhoda P. fits these descriptions. Her symptoms, the course of her illness, and her family history all coincide with many descriptions that we have cited here and others found in the literature.

> *But I don't eat be—their-their thing is that I don't eat—because—uh—I like the way I am, and that I'm not tryin' to help myself. But I **eat!** There's nothing I can do about it. I went away—I proved it to them—I went away for a week. I didn't do anything. I laid around and ate. And I didn' gain any weight. . . . I don't know why, but it jist bothers me when they say that—'cause they look at me as if—like my sister will say to my mother, "Oh, Rhoda should never get tired."*

Just as the symptoms are consistent, so too is the manner of behavior with the physician or therapist. The therapist engaged with Rhoda P. was fully aware of these factors; she viewed the case in a psychoanalytic perspective, in which Rhoda's rejection and resistance may be characterized as a form of countertransference. Therapists have a wide range of attitudes on the issue of a "directive" or a "nondirective" approach; but in cases of this sort, every therapist must be aware of the dangers and difficulties of making direct suggestions, particularly suggestions which align the therapist with those family members that the patient is reacting against. The reader should be aware that the nature of Rhoda's physical illness and the emotional problems surrounding it have placed constraints upon the therapist and limited the kinds of communication she can have with the patient. There is always the danger that any suggestion from the therapist about how the patient might direct herself in coping with her daily problems will create echoes for her of the treatment she has received from family members who manipulate her through cajoling, carping, and derogation.

Rhoda came to therapy under strong pressure from her family and the direction of her physician. She lived at home in New York City with her mother and a maternal aunt; her father had died some years before this time. She had an older brother, who was paying for the therapy, and a married sister who lived in her own home with her husband and children. Rhoda attended college in the city, although her family had questioned whether or not her state of health would permit her to continue. In the five episodes to be analyzed, we will find many references to the detailed social structure of her family and the conflicts between the various roles she is trying to fulfill. During these interviews, she speaks quite freely and at times expressively, using the range of dialect forms characteristic of lower middle class girls of Jewish background. Though she may have a more formal style in other contexts, the speech forms that she uses in the recorded interviews are typical of the vernacular where the minimum amount of attention is given to prestige (Labov, 1966).

The therapist is a social worker with graduate training in social work and advanced training in therapy. She has been involved in the therapeutic treatment of clients for over 20 years and has had a variety of agency experiences during her professional career. Through her general background, participation in seminars and institutes, and communication with her colleagues, she acquired a thorough familiarity with the psychoanalytic literature and viewpoint in regard to psychotherapy. This general agency viewpoint was not narrowed to any one theoretical perspective, although it did focus on theoretical writings on ego psychology (Hartman, 1964; Kris, 1951). The therapist herself enjoys an excellent reputation in her profession and was viewed by her colleagues in the agency as being highly skilled.

EARLIER STUDIES OF THE THERAPEUTIC INTERVIEW

The therapeutic interview has been the object of study under two major perspectives: first, as an element in the case history of a patient, illustrating the etiology and dynamics of a disorder as well as its treatment; second, as a communicative event, a conversation in which therapist and patient interact under the general rules, constraints, and patterns of face-to-face interaction. We will review these studies by considering first the psychotherapeutic literature, which takes the first approach, and then turn to quantitative studies and microanalyses, which take the second.

Psychotherapeutic Treatments

The theoretical perspective developed by psychiatrists and psychoanalysts forms a systematic alternative to the analysis that we will present in the chapters to follow. As we already noted, we have learned a great deal from the observations of the therapist herself during playback; these often represent specific applications of the theoretical perspective that we find in a number of texts. The psychotherapeutic literature is rich in its discussion of the issues, strategies, and theoretical applications of the events perceived in the therapeutic interview by the analysts. But the terms, units, and elements perceived are often the product of considerable analysis, and the questions raised are internal to the particular theory.

We share with analysts such as Glover a concern with the phenomenon of resistance. The reader will readily recognize resistance occurring throughout the interview as the patient explicitly endorses the point of view of the therapist but implicitly contradicts it with her actual accounts and observations. Glover's account of resistance includes phenomena which play a part in our observations as well: reluctance to attend therapy, reticence, and sharply contradictory behavior during sessions. On the other hand, Glover's only mention of the actual words spoken in the interview is a discussion of "slips" (1955, p. 51). Although he does not feel that obvious slips of the tongue should be a central focus of interpretation, some therapists seem to be disregarding what the patient says entirely in their concentration upon such phenomena.*

To illustrate the depth of the theoretical constructs in the psychoanalytic literature, it will be helpful to cite one example from Glover's discussion of counterresistance and countertransference. In this discussion, he is concerned with distinguishing analytic technique proper from the emphasis on countertransferences and resistances by the therapist. He explains that what is often called counterresistance is "more often than not a manifestation of *negative* countertransference." In order to illustrate one of the com-

---

*In one interview reported in the second chapter of Gottschalk, 1961, the patient talks for six minutes with only two responses from the therapist ("Very interesting," and "Hmm Hmm"). The patient then says, "I was already missing a few beatings—business meetings on the *first day*." After he speaks for a minute more, the therapist says, "You missed the first few beatings?" The patient replies, "Business meetings, yes. I wondered if I should comment on that slip, and decided I'm not the therapist... uh...." The other interview studied in this symposium is also focused upon a slip of the patient. The analyses of these interviews are not concerned with the specific dynamics of the slip, as the therapist is, but rather with the overall pattern of speech disturbances, interventions, and so on. (Gottschalk, 1961) For some therapists, "paying attention to the words used" may mean doing nothing except looking for such slips.

monest confusions in the use of these terms, he describes the origins of counterresistance in the following terms:

> If we assume that the anal–sadistic phase has been weathered, the stage of infantile, genital or phallic primacy established, the ego advanced from a mainly narcissistic basis to a more organized relationship with objects, the difficulties likely to be observed are those connected with the positive and negative Oedipus relation and the resolution or abandonment of that situation under the spur of castration-anxiety. [Glover, 1955, p. 100]

We find no direct quotations from interviews in the traditional approach of Glover, and most case studies present only brief "narrative accounts" in the third person. Recently, entire interviews or large sections have been presented verbatim as an approach to the teaching of psychotherapy (Gill, Newman, and Redilich, 1954; Deutsch and Murphy, 1955).

The manual of Deutsch and Murphy (1955) shows us how the therapist recognizes psychodynamic events in the midst of conversation with his patient. This text provides us with case studies that consist of brief histories and long quotations from the tape recorded interview itself. On the average page, the volume of text is much greater than the volume of observations and interpretations; these are limited to brief notes that point up the expert therapist's interpretations and reactions. The following quotation shows how the therapist's intuitions are brought to bear upon the patient's words. The patient is speaking about a friend's father:

D. *You wish you had such a father?*
P. *Sometimes it's better for a father to be that way. I guess I **envied** him in some ways. That happened to be my **boss**'s son. Remember I told you about when I was working in the book store. Well, his father's **dead** now and there's an angle about that that **bothers** me. When I see a guy like that who **died**, I think maybe it's because he lived that way he **died**.*
    [A double envy: Hank is himself, just as the boss is father. He is talking about various aspects of his own ego. The punishment for doing bad is dying (going away).]
D. *And you mean he should have led a **nice clean** life if he wanted to **live**?*
P. *Yeh, keep away from **women** and **liquor** and **things like that**. They tried to get me to work for them, that is to work for the company instead of going to Washington to school. They even went so far as to invite me to a **party** at the best **fraternity** on the campus, and that night he took me aside and asked me to work for the company, and I turned him down. But he now, Hank Martin, Jr., now he runs the company. Gee, even last year I always felt that when things came to the worst, I could always go back to Hank and he'd give me a job.*
    [*Things like that* refers to infantile pregenital elements. Adolescent asceticism demands complete renunciation.] (Deutsch and Murphy, 1955, p. 207)

In our approach, we draw the interpretation more directly from the immediately surrounding text, but we also find it necessary to consult material presented in widely scattered parts of the therapeutic series. Yet the problem of correct interpretation is the same in both cases: we recognize the therapist's ability to draw deep interpretations from the entire configuration, though we take a more analytic approach that isolates the particular utterances and signals.

There is some discussion of verbal behavior in more elementary texts, which are prepared for resident psychiatric students. The future therapist is instructed to examine the patient's remarks for particular constructions which reveal the inner psychodynamics and permit a correct diagnosis.

> On several occasions, this patient casually, but abruptly, introduced highly charged material, which is typical of hysterical behavior. Early in the interview, she gave the ages of her five children as 12, 10, 6, 5, and 1. No explanation was given when, in the next sentence, she indicated that she had been married only seven years. Later in the interview, she was asked about her relationship to her in-laws, and she replied, "Well, it is not too bad now, but at first they were not happy about Bill marrying a divorcee with two children." Dramatic remarks are made frequently during the interview. For instance, the same patient, when volunteering that she was a housewife, added, "That's a glorified term." The above description easily identifies the patient as a hysteric because the features of diagnostic significance have been abstracted from the interview. However, many interviewers do not recognize this behavior when it is mixed with non-hysterical material and the patient is not the typical pretty, seductive, young woman. [MacKinnon and Michels, 1971, pp. 131–2]

This excerpt shows the therapist extracting from the interview a small number of highly significant remarks. It further illustrates the fact that many therapists feel that there is no need for tape recording, since the most important material they receive can be analyzed as it occurs. In the extreme case, the therapist simply waits for a slip, which may happen only once in 5 or 10 minutes (see footnote on p. 13). More recently, many psychotherapists have begun to recognize the value of tape recording, and we find, for instance, that texts such as Deutsch and Murphy are richly illustrated with what must have been tape recorded data. But as we examine the text quoted above, we find very few hesitations, interruptions, or pauses of the sort that our own transcriptions indicate are quite frequent. (Compare the quotation on p. 14 with our text on p. 361.) It seems clear that these hesitations and self-interruptions have been edited out.

As a whole, the psychotherapeutic literature can be described as taking the text for granted. It is possible that the techniques which we provide here, stemming from a closer examination of the text, will be useful to those working within the psychotherapeutic tradition as a further resource and as a way of validating their intuitions. However, we also recognize that the careful study of texts may always be a secondary approach for those who must make spontaneous decisions in the clinical encounter.

It should be recognized that both theoretical interpretations and the close observation of behavior find their basis in the model of case narrative description characteristic of Freud's work. Freud's concern for the minutiae of everyday behavior was richly developed in the interview itself, and some of the principles of discourse analysis set forth below—particularly its determinism—reflect a way in which Freud's thinking contributes to close examination of everyday behavior. This will appear more clearly when we have considered the literature of microanalysis.

The Quantitative Coding of Conversational Behavior

The most carefully articulated paradigm for the study of conversational interaction is that of Bales (1950), whose Interaction Process Analysis is used extensively in the study of small group behavior. Bales' categories are applied to verbal behavior by coders working in real time. A small group typically is assembled from students who do not know each other, and are assigned an experimental work task. They are observed by trained coders who categorize the events as they unfold. Since many of Bales' categories are represented in our own analysis, it may be illuminating to present them here.

Social–Emotional Area: Positive Reactions
   1. Shows solidarity
   2. Shows tension release
   3. Agrees
Task Area: Attempted Answers
   4. Gives suggestion
   5. Gives opinion
   6. Gives orientation
Task Area: Questions
   7. Asks for orientation
   8. Asks for opinion
   9. Asks for suggestion
Social–Emotional Area: Negative Reactions
   10. Disagrees
   11. Shows tension
   12. Shows antagonism

Since Bales' observers were viewing the interactions of group members as well as listening to them, and video tape recording had not been well developed in the early 1940s, it is understandable that the coding system of

Bales was developed for instant, on-the-spot decisions. For many purposes, it may still be adequate or even desirable to force such immediate decisions in the categorization of behavior. The main focus of the Bales group was not so much on the specific categories as on the number of acts performed and their direction. It has been shown in a number of papers that the number of speech acts received and the number addressed to individuals or the group form regular patterns that rank the participants in small group behavior (Bales, Strodtbeck, Mills, and Roseborough, 1951). Furthermore, the coding system has been shown to be highly reliable for a number of purposes.

Since we are concerned with the therapeutic interview as a whole, and the actions which take place in it, we are inevitably drawn to the same kind of categories as those constructed by Bales: a set of actions which people perform on one another, each one leading to a compensating or intensifying action by the other. This interaction is described by us with a restricted vocabulary that includes such terms as *gives orientation, requests support,* and so on. These categories, however, represent only a small number of the actions which are being performed in the interview; though the Bales categories play an important part in the rules of interpretation that connect what is said with what is done, it will appear that they are not rich or elaborate enough to make the connection in full.

The reliability of the Bales coding system is impressive, but the many intuitive steps necessary to perform such a coding have not been explicated. The rich formal texture of conversation is abridged and encapsulated by this device, but there is no possibility of recovering the further structure once such categories are taken as the primitive elements. In this respect, the coding and quantitative classification of conversation is not less intuitive than the theoretical categorizations performed by the psychotherapist.

This technique of categorization and quantitative coding has been adopted to the therapeutic interview by a number of analysts. Lennard and Bernstein (1960) have applied categories very similar to Bales' to interviews between psychiatrist and patient; they present a more complex picture of the therapeutic session as a system of action involving interdependence of therapist and patient. The analysts utilize a variety of measures, including gross indices of quantity of speech and more subtle codings of propositional behavior. They follow Bales in focusing on the kinds of informational acts performed and changes in speaker roles without specific reference to the content of what is said.

Many attempts have been made to measure the processes taking place within the interview through systems of coding and content analysis richer than the interaction analysis of Bales. The system of content analysis developed by Gottschalk and Gleser (1969) includes a detailed manual of instructions that allow the coder to assemble quantitative data on a number of distinct scales (Gottschalk *et al.*, 1969). These scales include Hostility

Directed Outward, Hostility Directed Inward, and Social Alienation–Personal Disorganization (schizophrenic behavior). The Hostility Directed Inward scale, for example, is designed to "measure transient and immediate thoughts, actions, and feelings that are self-critical, self-destructive, or self-punishing" (1969, p. 93). It includes thematic categories such as *"references to feelings of deprivation, disappointment, lonesomeness."* To illustrate how feelings of lonesomeness are to be recognized and coded, 16 examples are given, such as, "It's kind of lonesome being away from home," "I get lonely at home at times," "Nobody knows how I feel," "I miss my children at times like that." The Hostility Directed Outward scale includes a large number of thematic categories; these are divided into Overt and Covert types. One example of a Covert Thematic Category under this heading is "wildlife, flora, inanimate objects injured, broken, robbed, destroyed or threatened with such (with or without mention of agent)." Instances of this category include "We had a flat tire," "The toilet overflowed," "Lightning struck the side of the house," "The paint was peeling off on the walls." As an example of how the coding is performed upon a text, we cite the following *verbal sample #1* (1969, p. 86).*

> ... *Me and a buddy stole a car* (I3: self—robbing other individuals) *but I got mad at him* (I3: self—expressing anger at other human beings) *and we split up,* (uncoded) *but the cops got both of us anyway and brought us back.* (IIc3: others blaming other human beings) *He got sent to the reform school then.* (IIc3) *I ran over a dog* (self—killing, injuring or destroying domestic animals) *while I was driving* (uncoded) *and I didn't feel so damn good about that* (Ic1: self—cursing without referent). *Then the front tire got a flat* (IIa1: inanimate object broken or destroyed without mention of agent) *and that's* (uncoded) *when they caught me* (uncoded). [1969, p. 87]

The coding of Gottschalk and Gleser shows insight in some areas, especially those dealing with Hostility Directed Inward, but it seems that many of the codings in the example given above are quite arbitrary and perhaps dictated by the coder's overall attitude toward the speaker. It also seems obvious that the coding of such atomic units without reference to context will lead to serious misinterpretations. The coder undoubtedly will take the larger contexts into account informally, implicitly and perhaps unconsciously; but as we will see, the full interpretation of any utterance might be developed better by incorporating information derived from a careful study of all available data.

Within a more objective orientation, Soskin and John (1963) developed an original set of categories for coding the spontaneous conversation of a

---

*Instead of giving the full title of the Thematic Categories, which combine a number of terms with "and" and "or," we have used only the appropriate part of the conjunction or disjunction.

husband and wife monitored by FM transmitters. These included structural units such as "subject's proportion of total talking time"; functional units, such as *"regones, signones, and metrones"*; and dynamic units such as "state," "locus–direction," and "bond."

Other quantitative coding has focused on a range of verbal phenomena which are usually considered marginal by the interactants themselves. Thus Mahl (1961) has turned his attention to speech disturbances—repetitions, stutters, false starts, tongue slips, and so forth—as a measure of anxiety. These measures allow him to construct a Speech Disturbance Ratio that can be plotted for successive 2-minute intervals throughout the interview.* More abrupt surgery is performed upon the interview text by Jaffe (1961) who replaces conventional transcripts with 25 word segments called "dyads" and presents plots for successive dyads with such measures as type–token ratio, rate of verbal output, and percent of present tense verbs. In reviewing the various methods and approaches used by investigators such as Mahl, Gottschalk, and himself, Jaffe notes that "an air of eclecticism prevails here ... but common to all is the insistence on quantitative methods of established reliability. We may argue about methodology and interpretation of results, but the basic facts are clear" (1961, p. 172).

It is clear that there are an unlimited number of facts which can be found in or drawn from the therapeutic interview, but it does not seem to us that there has been any major gain from turning away from the words actually used in the interview and the speech acts which they signal. The importance of measurement is hardly to be disparaged by the present authors, who have each engaged in extensive quantitative research in other fields; but premature quantification seems to us a major disservice to the understanding of the events we are studying. If our goal is to establish that some kind of change has taken place in a series of therapeutic interviews, then such categories may be useful. But if the goal is to understand in any substantive way the nature of conversation, we find these categorizations premature. Indeed, if our understanding of conversation were at the level that permitted us to divide all the phenomena into a closed set of 6 to 12 categories, it might be said that all the serious problems had been solved already. It seems to us, however, that we are far from that point, as the explorations of succeeding chapters will attempt to show.

Microanalysis

The studies that appear to us most promising for the understanding of conversation share one feature: They examine meticulously at least some details of recorded verbal behavior. Those who examine conversation

---

*For a detailed review of work in this domain, see Mahl and Schulze, "Psychological Research in the Extra-Linguistic Area," 1964.

closely seem to agree that it is a highly determined phenomenon, with intricate structures which have not been penetrated to any significant depth. We are not referring to any single tradition here: The studies we shall cite have many different theoretical perspectives at varying degrees of abstraction and with very different admixtures of intuition and observation. Yet they all recognize and agree in a number of fundamental principles that have been stated clearly by one of the pioneering works in the field, *The First Five Minutes*, by Pittenger, Hockett, and Danehy (1960). This work is subtitled "A Sample of Microscopic Interview Analysis"; it examines the initial portion of an initial interview published originally by Gill, Newman, and Redlich (1956). A good portion of the book is devoted to an analysis of the prosodic cues provided by the recording and the meaning they convey. The authors give a minute transcription of loudness, intonation, and voice quality, in addition to the phonemic transcription of vowels and consonants; the contextual significance of these signals is discussed in a parallel analysis. *The First Five Minutes* was the first major publication that marked the shift to direct observation of film or tape recording, and the detailed analysis of behavior. The most detailed development within this tradition is the *Natural History of an Interview* of McQuown, Bateson, Birdwhistell, Brosen, and Hockett (1971). The wealth of detail and accumulated insights in this unpublished manuscript testifies to the richness of the phenomenon being studied; but it also demonstrates the great difficulty in reducing this information to a parsimonious statement that would allow the knowledge gained to be disseminated broadly and confirmed by other researchers.

Scheflen has summarized the history of these developments in the introduction to his *Communicational Structure* (1973). His detailed analysis of a family interview develops the information from the visual record of postural shifts, gestures, and other movements that orchestrate and illustrate the actions taking place in the interview. Scheflen has continued the tradition of Birdwhistell, Hockett, and others who feel that there is more to be gained by studying the physical and social context of the speech events than by examining the words themselves. He makes this quite explicit in outlining his analysis:

> I will try to describe all of the gestures, tasks, representational and juncture behaviors which occurred, because these kinesic units are not well known and need to be characterized. But in the case of the speech units I will simply illustrate some of these in order to review their structure. The remainder will merely be reproduced in Appendix A as a traditional transcript or orthography of speech content. [1973, pp. 67–68]

Scheflen is concerned with the higher level of abstract actions taking place in the interview as well as with the tactical details of posture and gesture. In discussing the strategy used by the patients, he lists a complex series of such actions, hierarchically organized. Thus one patient is seen as engaged in *Passive Protesting*, which includes *Conceding, Lamenting,* and *Disparaging;* she also is seen as *Contending*, which includes *Appealing for Empathy, Insinuating, Challenging, Accusing,* and *Repelling*. At the same time she also engaged in *Quasi-Courting, Contacting,* and *Kleenex Play*. This rich battery of interactional terms is supported primarily by the physical behavior of the participants, with comparatively little reference to the words themselves.

Although Scheflen gives us a sensitive and searching portrait of the interaction, he shares with many of the quantitative researchers a tendency to turn away from the words used in the interview in an attempt to get at what is "really happening" between therapist and patient.

As we review the many varied and rich approaches to the study of the therapeutic interview, we are struck by the fact that none of them concentrate upon what is actually being said by the therapist and patient. It stands to reason that the primary data for the listener are the words being spoken by the other parties, and whatever interpretation he constructs will be based upon them. Paralinguistic cues, gestures, and postures may underline this verbal communication or even reverse its polarity, but they are relatively empty in themselves. All of these investigators have minimized the "meaning" of what is being said. Perhaps this is a sophisticated reaction to earlier approaches, which ignore the importance of the marginal symbolic phenomena, but are impressed above all with the complexity of the constructions which are built upon the words themselves and the complexity of response to these interpretations.

To complete our review of the studies of therapeutic interviews, we return again to *The First Five Minutes*—not so much to the detailed microanalysis as to the findings presented in the form of nine general principles. Our own experience shows that these principles represent a solid basis on which the study of conversation and therapeutic interviews can proceed: We cite them here with sufficient quotation to illustrate the authors' meaning.

1. *Immanent Reference.* "... No matter what else human beings may be communicating about, or may think they are communicating about, *they are always communicating about themselves, about one another, and about the immediate context of the communication.*" [italics added]
2. *Determinism.* "The only useful working assumption... is that any communicative act is, indeed, culturally determined: the indeterminate or 'accidental' residue is non-existent."
3. *Recurrence.* "... Anyone will tell us, over and over again, in our dealings with him, what sort of person he is, what his affiliations with cultural subgroups are, what his likes and dislikes are, and so on.... The diagnostically crucial patterns of communication will not be manifested just once."

shown a certain degree of overlap with those developed in this more philosophical approach to conversation. Earlier forms of our rules (Labov, 1970) show many parallels to the Conversational Postulates of Lakoff and Gordon (1971); relations to our own rules will be developed more fully by general discussion of discourse analysis in Chapter 3.

EMPIRICAL STUDIES OF CONVERSATION

In recent years, a number of linguists and psychologists have begun the observation of conversation, partly in response to the stimulation of the introspective work described above. The most systematic studies have been concentrated on the acquisition of conversational rules by young children, particularly on the use of requests for information or requests for action (Shatz, 1975, Shatz and Gelman, 1973). Garvey's studies of the requests of young children (1975) provide empirical evidence for the existence of preconditions for valid requests or "sincerity conditions," and show a variety of mechanisms for requesting beyond those discussed in Gordon and Lakoff (1971) and Labov (1970).

The English Language Research Group in Birmingham, England has carried out a series of empirical studies of classroom interaction which have focused on sequences of speech acts, "moves," and larger discourse units (Sinclair, Forsyth, Coulthard, and Ashby, 1972).

More recent studies of doctor–patient interviews show taxonomic structures in a more tightly constrained situation: These provide evidence for many of the discourse rules discussed in Chapter 3.

The major input to the study of natural conversation has been from sociologists rather than linguists. It appears that conversation is a strategic research site for studying the ways in which members of a society organize their social interactions. The study of sequencing in conversation has been developed with great skill and insight by Sacks (1972) and Schegloff (1968). The influence of their work can be seen in our analysis at many points, but on the whole the approach that we are taking differs from theirs in several ways. Sacks has been able to discover many structural properties of sequencing through the cross-examination of group therapy sessions and a variety of other conversations. Schegloff has studied the detailed organization of initial utterances in phone conversations in *The First Five Seconds* (1967). These authors have been searching out structural principles that may appear at any given point in a body of conversation, but they do not make themselves accountable to any given body of conversation, so it is not possible for a reader to say, "But you have not explained why X said Y here." They are not concerned with the kinds of questions which were addressed to us at the outset of this research: "What is taking place in the therapeutic interview?" or, even more to the point, "What should I, as a student, attempt to do in a therapeutic interview?" We are not critical of the strategy adopted by Sacks and Schegloff, since they have had far more success in isolating principles of sequencing than anyone else; furthermore, it is possible that conversation is so complex that is is not possible for any one approach to account for it as a whole. Still, the attempt to understand everything that we can about a given 5 or 10 minutes of a therapeutic interview has proved to be a fruitful research strategy in its own right.

In the recent studies of Sacks, Schegloff, and their associates, we find a sharp focus upon rules of sequencing in conversational interaction (see Sacks, Schegloff, and Jefferson, 1975). We agree that this sequencing is a matter of considerable importance for the understanding of what takes place in conversation, and these investigators have advanced much further into the social structure of such speech events than anyone else; but it will be helpful if we can develop a more exact characterization of the units that are sequenced. Sequencing rules do not appear to relate words, sentences, and other linguistic forms, but rather form the connections between abstract actions such as requests, compliments, challenges, and defenses. Thus sequencing rules presuppose another set of relations, those between the words spoken and the actions being performed. These rules state the possible sets of relations between an interrogative form such as "Y'got enough?" and the speech actions which it represents—a request for information, a refusal, and a challenge.

The approach of the sociologists studying conversation to this problem has been as informal or intuitive as the coding procedures of Gottschalk and Gleser. Sacks deals with a wide variety of conversations, and it is clear from statements that he makes that he is very much aware of the problems of interpretation; but these problems are not usually his explicit focus. He cites the following suicide call as an example of an account not being offered.

S1. ... May I help you?
C1. Well I don't know. My brother suggested that I call you.
S2. I see. Well, he must have had a reason for making the suggestion. Has there been some personal problem or difficulty that you're experiencing?
C2. Yes. I just lost my wife and I feel awfully depressed.
     [1972, p. 50]

Sacks uses this material to illustrate the principle that "if an account has not been offered, then as an alternative to requesting one, the recipient may... construct an account himself." In this case, since C1 has not given an "account" or explanation for his call, S2 constructs a possible account; but the formal structures that would allow one to recognize accounts and requests are not Sacks' primary concern. For example, "May I help you?" is superficially a request for information; it is easy to demonstrate that on the slightly more abstract level it is an offer to help; it takes considerably more discussion to show that it is on a yet more abstract level a request for an accounting. We can intuitively recognize that "My brother suggested that I call you" is not the accounting that is requested. This intuition recognizes the fact that the "failure to provide an account" is a sequencing phenomenon at a very abstract level; it can become a part of the theory only if the rules of interpretation for constructing these abstract events are made explicit.

In examining the many recent studies of conversation, we find that very few observers have been concerned with the level of social interaction which is the main focus of our investigation. Many profound questions have been raised about the sequencing of individual speech acts or larger units of surface organization, but comparatively little attention has been given to the actions and reactions that are dependent on the position of the speakers in the social networks of family, group, or therapeutic session. A notable exception is a study of a union meeting from the English Language Research Group in Birmingham (Stubbs, 1973). The study first is concerned with empirical evidence for question–answer sequencing in issues raised by Sacks and Schegloff, but the author then focuses on the problem of accounting for the coherence in discourse and shows how a break in the surface structure forces us to assume the simultaneous presence of speech acts at several levels of abstraction. In particular, a request for confirmation is shown to function as a *challenge,* and the analyst shows how utterances scattered through various parts of the interaction must be brought together to provide the basis for the interpretation of any one.

Our aim in studying the therapeutic interview is to lay bare as much of the scaffolding of conversational interaction as we can. It has been evident to us for some time that our concerns are parallel to those of Sacks and Schegloff, but that our approach is necessarily distinct from theirs. Our substantive commitment to the therapeutic interview leads us to search for a definition of this situation as a whole and to discover everything we can that is relevant to this particular situation. In this respect, our work is informed more by the approach of Goffman than any other. We see conversation as a type of human interaction, taking place within a social frame. In response to Goffman's insistence upon a social definition of the situation as a departure for further analysis, we attempt to define the therapeutic interview as a social occasion before we apply to it the general rules of discourse analysis. The rights, duties, and obligations of each partner must be understood if the specific discourse rules are to have any formal application. The particular *state of talk* represented by the therapeutic interview has its own configurations and expectations that allow us to interpret the word spoken and relate to them the paralinguistic cues in a consistent way. Though we are interested in microanalysis, we do not start with the small details of behavior. We recognize that their significance is often ambiguous in the abstract and can be defined only when the situation in which they are used is well known.

> The human tendency to use signs and symbols means that evidence of social worth and of mutual evaluations will be conveyed by very minor things, and these things will be witnessed, as will the fact that they have been witnessed. An unguarded glance, a momentary change in tone of voice, an ecological position taken or not taken, can drench a talk with judgmental significance. Therefore, just as there is no occasion of talk in which improper impressions could not intentionally or unintentionally arise, so there is no occasion of talk so trivial as not to require each participant to show serious concern with the way in which he handles himself and the others present. [Goffman, 1967, p. 3.]

ORGANIZATION OF THIS STUDY

If we are to be accountable to the events of the therapeutic session, or even to 15 minutes of that session, we will be faced with an extraordinary amount of detail and the problem of making that information accessible and intelligible to the reader. It is not enough to understand the conversation; it must in some way be reduced to general principles that will make other conversations easier and quicker to analyze and report. The next chapter will outline the methods we propose to accomplish that end. We will begin with a few sentences from the first episode in the interview with Rhoda; these will present certain problems of understanding and interpretation that will make it absolutely clear that we cannot remain with the most superficial interpretation of the words themselves. We will orient the reader to our approach to the interview as a whole by going step by step through the analysis of four sentences, and attempting to justify each of the analytical procedures and categories used. We will separate the paralinguistic cues from the words themselves and recombine them with information draw from other parts of the interview. In this expanded text, we will find reference to the longstanding propositions characteristic of the family interaction in which Rhoda is engaged. We will then raise the question as to what actions are being performed and what is the social significance of the propositions raised at this particular time, and make our final statement about "what is being done" in terms of interaction. This completed analysis of any given utterance forms a cross section of the discourse, and we will finally assemble these cross sections to see what we have added in terms of understanding the direction and dynamics of conversation. The intent of our analysis is to use this verbal behavior to illuminate the actions that speakers perform on each other.

The third chapter develops the formal discourse rules that we will need for a concise exposition of the larger body of text. These are the rules of interpretation and production, and the rules of sequencing that we have briefly characterized above. Though Chapter 3 appears as a self-contained whole, the full justification for many of the rules to be written will appear in detailed applications in Chapters 4 through 9. Each of these chapters will analyze an episode from the therapeutic session with Rhoda, and each attempts to synthesize a view of the course of the therapy up to that point. Though there will be many illustrations of the mechanism of discourse and the intricacies of conversational interaction, our overall focus will be on the question: What is the therapist trying to do in this conversational encounter? On the other hand, what is the patient doing or not doing that the therapist must be aware of?

In our final chapter, we will attempt to sketch the course of therapy as a whole and relate the particular interview we have analyzed to therapy in general. We will explore potential applications of our method to a much wider variety of interviews, and to conversation in general. Again, we will return to the question asked by the student first coming to therapy. Listening to the interviews carried out by others, he may ask, "How do I do it?" Monitoring his own interviews, he must ask the converse, "What have I done?" We hope that even the most experienced interviewer will gain by the examination of his own behavior.

There is no doubt in our minds that this is a serious business. The painful problems that are faced in most therapeutic sessions, which arise from the stress and strain human beings exert upon each other in daily interaction, are sufficient warrant for us to take the problem seriously. Considering the enormous number of therapeutic interviews carried out every year, any contribution to the understanding, efficiency, and skill of the therapist is an important goal to aim at. Yet the study of conversation is also an important route towards the understanding of human behavior in itself. Everyone who looks at conversation in detail finds it engrossing; the fascination of observing speakers dealing with one another is no less compelling than watching the most intricate game or contest—especially if we can approach anything like a full understanding of the rules. It increases our appreciation of the competence of our fellow human beings, even if they do not always achieve the goals that they are aiming at, for we in turn remain distant from ours.

COMPREHENSIVE DISCOURSE ANALYSIS

A first approach to conversation usually focuses on the description of particular details that seem to have been neglected by traditional grammarians. As we have seen, most microanalyses have dealt with intonation or gestures. These analysts have recognized that we have only a limited ability to describe the subtle implications of paralinguistic features; their programs have proceeded on the assumption that we must gain a clear understanding of the signals that communicate before we can analyze larger units. Progress in this undertaking has not been very great: there is still no agreement on the categorization of paralinguistic cues, and linguists still find it difficult to deal with the multiple ambiguity which these signals show in isolation.

The same general strategy appears in the recent studies of presuppositions and implications of sentence structure. The general aim seems to be to work out the possible combinations of single units, and so proceed gradually to write a grammar of discourse. Those who are studying sequencing rules in conversation also begin with the smallest units or organization at their level of interest, hoping to arrive eventually at larger structures.

Over the course of this research, we came to the conclusion that a different direction is required. At first, we began by considering individual signals. We were not surprised to find that there was a great deal of implicit communication in the form of vocal gestures—intonation, voice qualifiers, hesitations, and the like. It gradually appeared, however, that there was an even richer body of implicit communication in the form of unexpressed social and psychological propositions. In the course of many reworkings and rewritings, we came to understand that there was an even larger body of implicit activity which was not verbal at all and could not be translated into single propositions: most utterances can be seen as performing several speech acts simultaneously. The parties to a conversation appear to be understanding and reacting to these speech acts at many levels of abstraction. As we see it now, conversation is not a chain of utterances, but rather a matrix of utterances and actions bound together by a web of understandings and reactions.

In some ways, this many-layered structure is quite similar to the hierarchical organization of a grammar, but we do not see conversation as a linguistic form. We have come to understand conversation as a means that people use to deal with one another. In conversation, participants use language to interpret to each other the significance of the actual and potential events that surround them and to draw the consequences for their past and future actions.

We follow Goffman in seeing conversation as a form of interaction (1971). The great bulk of human face-to-face interaction is verbal; but unless linguistic interaction is viewed as a subspecies of the larger category it is bound to be misunderstood. We find that actions and utterances are regularly linked together in chains of exchanges. In fact, this is a fundamental proposition for the therapy we are examining here—one of the basic strategies of the therapist is to break down the common-sense view that actions are one things and words another.

In our efforts to understand therapeutic conversation as a form of interaction, we have looked for the largest context that conditions that interaction. The following chapters will become deeply involved with conversational details; but the details are seen and interpreted as they function in a series of concentric contexts, framed within the general definition of the situation.

THE THERAPEUTIC INTERVIEW: DEFINITION OF THE SITUATION

Our general approach to discourse analysis is intended to apply to a wide range of conversations, but the particular form developed here has been adapted to the therapeutic interview and contains a number of devices which follow from the definition of the therapeutic situation.

A therapeutic interview can be seen as a *speech event* (Hymes, 1962): a routinized form of behavior, delineated by well-defined boundaries and well-defined sets of expected behaviors within those boundaries. The largest class of speech events that it falls under is the *interview* in general. We may define an interview as a speech event in which one person, A, extracts information from another person, B, which was contained in B's biography.*

---

*Information contained in a person's biography has been experienced and absorbed by that person and will be given back with a certain amount of orientation and interpretation that is conditioned by the other person's experience and orientation. Thus, B can be leaning out of a

We can subdivide interviews along two dimensions: according to who initiates the event, and who is to be helped by it. In each case, we have an interviewer, A, whose vocation or avocation includes the process of extracting information from others. The interviewer may go to B himself, as in market surveys, linguistic interviews, journalistic interviews, or police interrogations. On the other hand, the client may go to the interviewer, as in medical, legal, and therapeutic interviews. The motivation for this initial step may vary. In a market survey or linguistic interview, there is usually no immediate value to B, who gives the information voluntarily out of general interest or good will. There are a number of situations where B is legally required to submit to interrogation, which may in fact injure him: passport investigations, police interrogations, driver's license examinations, and so forth. In journalistic interviews, both parties may benefit from the transmission of information, though sometimes it is only the reporter and his newspaper who will gain an advantage. In all these cases, the perceived benefit has a strong influence upon the type of verbal interaction which takes place, and so does the degree of compulsion that surrounds the event. Examinations given in school, test questions, and classroom quizzes are all kinds of interviews that produce very limited and constrained types of verbal response from the client (Labov, 1969).

Where B goes to A for help, as in medical, legal, and therapeutic interviews, it is usually understood that it is B who will benefit; he is usually paying for the service.* The benefit may be quite indirect, as in interviews that take place in confessions; in this case, though the client understands that he will be better in the long run, he knows that he must undergo immediate penalties as a result of divulging this information. In the therapeutic interview, B goes to A for help and gives him information from his biography that will be used to help him.

The distinctive character of the therapeutic interview is that this help will be given only through further talk. Unlike the lawyer or the doctor, the therapist will not give the patient advice on what to do.†

---

window watching a parade or an accident, and A can be extracting information from him on how the event is going, but this is not an interview in the commonly accepted sense of the term since this information is not in B's biography—he is merely transmitting it without digesting it.

*This is of course not the case in mental hospitals and other institutions, where therapeutic interviews are often carried out under compulsion. The character of these speech events is not necessarily the same as the ones we are discussing.

†In psychoanalysis proper (as opposed to "psychoanalytically oriented psychotherapy"), the question of whether or not the therapist should direct the patient's actions is not even considered. The therapist's *intervention* is basically limited to various types of interpretation, or reinforcement, and whether even these types of actions should be taken has been questioned (Menninger and Holzman, 1973, p. 132). Since we are characterizing the social situation generally, this understanding is given categorically. It is of course possible for a therapist to give advice to the patient about particular and immediate action—he may even prescribe

The special nature of the problem that is brought to therapy is responsible for a number of deep paradoxes within the therapeutic situation. A person who requires psychotherapy is marked by a social *stigma*.* He may be recognized as honest, dependable, and morally sound, yet his act in seeking help from the therapist is socially defined as a statement that he is not fully able to take care of himself.† On the other hand, the therapist is seen as a person who can take care of himself and, furthermore, can help others to take care of themselves. Through his training he has been able to work out his personal problems in the same way that the patient is expected to work out his.‡ This asymmetry—the weakness of the patient and the strength of the therapist—is reinforced by any direct help that the therapist gives the patient. This problem gives rise to the fundamental paradox of therapy. The most general goal of therapy is to bring the patient to the point at which he can function independently and no longer needs help; but can a person be taught not to need help by giving him help?

> If one person directs another to do a particular act, a paradox is not necessarily evident, but when one person directs another not to follow his directives, the paradox is obvious. The receiver cannot obey the directive nor disobey it. If he obeys the directive not to follow directives, then he is not following directives. [Haley, 1963, p. 17]

In response to this paradox, many therapists have gone to extremes in avoiding any directive role, even confining their remarks in therapy to purely passive, reflecting comments (Rogers, 1951).

Many aspects of the patient's behavior in the therapeutic session seem to demonstrate the need to solve this contradiction. At a relatively early point, he makes the claim that he fully understands the problem, that he no longer needs help though he once did; he then attempts to demonstrate by the history of his recent actions how well he understands the problems

---

tranquilizers or advise a depressed person to stay home for a week; but in his activity as a therapist, his main way of helping the patient will be by engaging him in conversation during the interview.

*As used by Goffman, stigma is used to refer to "an attribute that is deeply discrediting" (1963, p. 3). The type of stigma we are dealing with here is one of the "blemishes of individual character" characteristic of those with a known record of "mental disorder, imprisonment, addiction, alcoholism, homosexuality, unemployment, suicidal attempts, and radical political behavior." Society exercises many varieties of discrimination against the stigmatized person, as Goffman points out, since "by definition of course, we believe the person with a stigma is not quite human" (1963, p. 5).

†This runs counter to the generally accepted norm of American society that an adult should be able to take care of himself. Failing this, he forfeits a number of rights. For a more detailed account of how such rights are forfeited, see Goffman (1961).

‡In the case of psychoanalysts, it is explicitly required that a psychoanalyst undergo psychoanalysis; he may therefore be considered superior in one sense to any patient who may come to him.

that once existed. The need for this assertion of independence is so strong that it can appear even in the first interview. We find this behavior in an initial interview with a 42-year-old man who had a history of anxiety, depression and restlessness for the previous 8 weeks (Deutsch and Murphy, 1960, p. 29).

> Doctor: *Could you tell me how you happened to come to the hospital?*
> Patient: *Well, I felt fairly good, Doctor.* (pause) *Much better.*
> Doctor: *Much better, in what way?*
> Patient: *Well, I'm not bothered with the tightening of the head that generally accompanies* (pause) *well, what I'm trying to say is well, it is something that has—well, when you have a situation that calls for stress of mind and you, you, you, well in my condition, you feel that it assumes a greater proportion than it should, in my mind that is. It all resolves itself.*

We do not have to go very far into the substance of an interview before we find contradictions between the claim that everything is going well and other statements of the patient. From another interview:

> Patient: *Well, how are things going, Doctor?*
> Doctor: (smiles and nods) *How are things going with you?*
> Patient: *Oh, comme-ci, comme-ça, as they say—oh, so-so. Well, anyhow, I'm getting along okay, I guess. Oh, I'm anxious at times in certain situations. I understand things rather than get panicky. I catch myself every now and then doing things, you know, these compulsions.* [Deutsch and Murphy, 1960, p. 97]

We frequently encountered this phenomenon in the therapeutic sessions that we studied. Many of the patients tried to demonstrate their understanding of the therapist's message by anecdotes of their behavior in the preceding week, yet their account of their own actions failed to support the verbal understanding that they displayed. Here is the very first utterance in the therapeutic session with Rhoda:

> 1.1[a] Rhoda: *I don't .. know, whether ... I—I **think** I did—the right thing, jistalittle .. situation came up ... an' I tried to uhm ...... well, try to .... use what I—what I'ved learned here, see if it worked.*
> [b] Therapist: *Mhm.*
> [c] Rhoda: *Now, I don't know if I did the right thing.*

Rhoda then plunges into an account of an incident from the preceding week that hardly supports her claim.

The patient's tendency to claim understanding is tantamount to an assertion that she may have needed help at one time in the past, but that this is no longer the case. Since her behavior has not necessarily changed, this is equivalent to rejecting therapy, and is one of the primary forms in which resistance to therapy appears. We also find a strong tendency to mitigate the problem: the use of language which systematically downgrades each difficulty so that it no longer appears to need attention.

Doctor: *Well, how have things been going?*
Patient: *Well, about the same.*
Doctor: *How do you mean?*
Patient: *Well, I've thought this thing over carefully, and I've come to the conclusion that the only thing that really bothers me is that I'm worried about myself.*

The term *bothered* is also used by Rhoda as a euphemism for 'angry', 'worried', or 'anxious'. She denies *anger,* but admits to feeling *bothered.* (See p. 306) A more extreme form of resistance is total silence. We will come to sections of the interview where Rhoda has nothing to say at all, and resists expressing agreement or disagreement with the therapist.*

Other verbal forms of resistance are secondary responses to the fundamental paradox of the therapeutic situation. The therapeutic interview is a conversation, and it requires participation from both parties. If the patient is to speak freely, there must be some areas, topics, and so forth, on which she can speak without fear of contradiction. In ordinary conversation, we are always subject to being contradicted on matters of fact, and we may expect contradiction most often if we speak about areas where the other person is known to be expert and we are not. But a speaker can be confident that there are many areas where he himself is the undisputed expert. These are his personal and private emotions, experience, and all of the events that make up his biography. If he chooses to speak of his innermost feelings, his fatigue, his anger or guilt, the other party is not as free to contradict him as if he had spoken of the temperature or predicted an economic recession.

But in the therapeutic situation, a very large part of this area of personal expertise is removed from the patient. It is understood that the therapist is an expert on dealing with personal emotions and sometimes able to say more definitely what another person feels than that person can say himself.† The whole area of personal emotions felt by the patient has now been

---

*Reticence is widely recognized as a form of resistance. It is not unknown for a patient to say nothing at all during the course of an interview; some therapists counter this by saying nothing at all themselves. "On a varying number of occasions therefore it will be necessary for [the patient] to go through a prolonged silence unassisted" (Glover, 1958, p. 98).

†MacKinnon and Michels make this clear at the outset in introducing the interne to the technique of the psychiatric interview: "As Sullivan pointed out, the psychiatrist is considered an expert in the field of interpersonal relations and, accordingly, the patient expects to find more than a sympathetic listener" (1971, p. 5).

opened up for dispute. If a patient denies that he feels anger, the therapist may challenge him and get him to admit that he is wrong. Yet if a conversation is to continue with any degree of fluency, it wil be necessary for the patient to be able to talk upon some subject without fear of such contradiction.

One consequence of this situation is a special style of discourse in the therapeutic interview. The patient draws heavily upon the one area which she can talk about confidently without fear of contradiction: the actions of everyday life. It is common in many interviews for the patient to begin with a narrative portrayal of events during the past week: it is understood that this material will be the raw material for the therapeutic work. During this account there is usually very little intervention on the part of the therapist, but patient and therapist may differ as they begin to examine the events. One way that the patient has of defending his interpretation is to change his account of what actually happened, or to elaborate upon it.* Yet there are limits to this process of restatement, since in the course of therapy, many of these incidents are discussed again and again, and eventually the therapist herself will be able to remind the patient of the facts that are now shared between them.

The defining characteristics of the therapeutic situation have immediate effects on the stylistic patterns of the therapeutic conversation. The first step in our procedure of comprehensive discourse analysis is to recognize in the text three fields of discourse with different vocabularies and rhetorical devices.

Fields of Discourse

The contradictions and pressures that exist in the therapeutic situation are responsible for the creation of distinct fields of discourse within the therapeutic session. One is the style of everyday life, in which the patient tells about the events of the preceding days in a fairly neutral, objective, colloquial style. We will refer to this everyday style by the abbreviation EV. It is marked by the absence of emotionally colored language on the one hand, and of abstract, therapeutically oriented language on the other.†

A second field of discourse is *interview style,* IV. Some discourse is easily recognized as characteristic of the therapeutic session by special vocabu-

---

*See Episode 3 (Chapter 7) for an example of this process in the session we are studying.
†A subvariety of everyday style is *narrative style,* N. When a speaker is giving an account of actual events that occurred in the past, there is a much sharper contrast between the reported events themselves and the evaluation of them, particularly when the speaker steps out of the narrative situation and addresses the listener directly. In our cross-sectional analysis of the text, we use the symbol N for those sections of everyday style that represent the basic framework of the narrative itself.

lary: "interpretation," "relationship," "guilt," "to present oneself," "working relationship," and so on.* In the session we are studying, most of these terms are used by the therapist herself, since Rhoda has not absorbed as much of this special language as we find with other, more mature patients. A more important mark of the interview style is the overt topic: emotions and behavior are evaluated as objects in themselves. In the interview style, one does not express emotions but talks about them; all the quotations in the preceding section illustrate this style.

Neither EV nor IV are highly colored with emotion. Yet anyone familiar with therapy knows that violent emotions do burst forth, sometimes in the most dramatic fashion. In general, the expression of strong emotions is concentrated in a third style embedded in the others. In our session this is termed *family style,* F: Rhoda switches to an idiom that seems to represent the style actually used in her family situation. The intonational contours of these quotations are strongly characteristic of Rhoda's family style; they are examined in detail in Chapter 6 (see Figure 25). We also find bits of family style embedded in a narrative as an evaluation of Rhoda's own emotional state.

1.3 But—she lef' Sunday, and she's still not home (O—oh.) And . . . *I'm gettin' a little nuts a'ready.*

Here F is marked by the slang expression *gettin' a little nuts* and final *already.*†

The unemotional character of EV poses a special problem for the therapist who is interested primarily in the emotional life of the patient. The brief extracts from family style are especially valuable in an individual interview, since they offer to the therapist the possibility of viewing the interaction which takes place outside of the therapeutic context. It is of course only an inference that F represents the actual events that occurred, but an examination of the many instances cited in Chapters 4 through 9 will present a convincing case that Rhoda does give us a view of how she behaves with her mother, sister, and aunt, and how they behave towards her.

The fields of discourse form a natural part of the concentric frames in which the patient's behavior is embedded (see Figure 1). The outermost frame is the institution of psychotherapy. In the preceding section we have outlined the ways in which it affects speech behavior. Within that frame we

---

*In both IV and EV, the patient talks about himself objectively, but in EV the patient becomes an animated actor, who is put through the motions of everyday life. In IV he is a more passive object, who has lost his animation and is in a static position for detailed examination of any one action or orientation.

†This is also a widely generalized influence of Yiddish upon the general syntax of the New York City area. It is derived from the Yiddish use of *sheyn* (German *schon*).

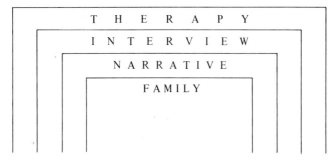

Figure 1. Embedding of fields of discourse within the therapeutic process.

find the therapeutic interview marked by a type of metalanguage—IV. Embedded within the therapeutic interview are the narratives and discussions of everyday life, conveyed in EV. More deeply embedded in accounts of everyday life, we find brief excerpts from family style, with its characteristic linguistic features.

Shifts from one frame to another are characteristic of ordinary conversation, as Goffman has shown (1974). For us, the recognition of distinct frames is particularly valuable because they determine so directly the linguistic forms that we will be examining. In our formal analysis of the therapeutic session to follow, we will identify each utterance with brackets that locate it within one of the stylistic frames outlined above.

CROSS-SECTIONAL ANALYSIS

The framework that we have provided so far indicates that the conversations to be studied will form a complex matrix of utterances, propositions, and actions. This matrix shows two kinds of relations: the vertical relations between surface utterances and deeper actions, which are united by rules of interpretation and production; the horizontal relations of sequencing between actions and utterances, which are united by sequencing rules. In order to satisfy ourselves that we have identified the correct relations, it is necessary to analyze the verbal interaction into constituent parts. This will be done by *cross sections* in which the components of the small units will be identified and their internal relations shown. A great deal of the discussion in the following chapters will be concerned with these cross sections. However, the cross sections must not be considered an end in themselves. On the contrary, the specific questions we are asking about this interview situation must direct our attention to the longitudinal character of conversation, and the assembly of the cross sections into sequences. The question "What is going on in the therapeutic interview?" (chapter 10) necessarily presupposes a longitudinal study of the sequencing of these verbal actions.

Units and Unitizing

An immediate problem is to locate units manageable enough to be subjected to analysis. A great deal of attention has been paid to the problem of segmentation in structural linguistics (Harris, 1951; Pike, 1947). Though this has been a fruitful question in some cases, it often happened that no principled basis for such unitizing could be found. It is still not possible to decide in many cases how many syllables there are in a word or how many phrases there are in a sentence. A study of the issues of segmentation may lead to interesting insights into language, but it does not seem that any single solution will be a lasting one. In linguistics, these are considered to be convenient starting points for analysis, not discoveries in their own right.

In the study of conversation, some attention has been given to finding units to be coded (Marsden, 1965); but most of the systems analysts pay much more attention to the categories than to the units to which these categories apply.* We have not concentrated upon problems of segmentation, since many of the decisions are necessarily arbitrary, and in our own treatment, there is no quantitative analysis which depends on such decisions.

The largest units that we have identified are a series of five episodes. These are based upon radical shifts in the overt topic or reference of the conversation:

Episode 1: Rhoda gives an account of how she "did the right thing" in calling up her mother and asking her to come home.

Episode 2: In response to a question from the therapist about whether her Aunt Editha might help with the housework, Rhoda gives a narrative to show how her aunt would not help clean the house when she asked her and was altogether unreasonable.

Episode 3: In response to a further question about whether Rhoda could arrive at a working relationship with her aunt, Rhoda gives another account of how her aunt would not prepare dinner even when she didn't work, and how Rhoda had to go out with her to eat.

Episode 4: Rhoda returns to the problem of her mother's being away from home and gives an account as to how it came about,

---

*One basis for arriving at a unit of analysis is that various criteria coincide at certain divisions of the speech chain. Bales (1950) discusses one case where an observer using his system found that the sentence, the utterance, and the unit for interactional analysis coincided, and noted that "the observer has thus isolated a unit of speech or process which he considers a proper unit for classification." This is certainly not the case in our analysis; we seldom find that the sentence is the most useful unit for interactional analysis.

followed by a retelling of how she asked her mother to come home.

Episode 5: The therapist offers an interpretation to explain why Rhoda and her family are behaving in this way towards each other, drawing a parallel between Rhoda's mother staying away too long, and Rhoda's refusing to eat.

These topical descriptions are at the most superficial level of organization. They give no insight into the emotional dynamics of the interview and would not prepare one at all for the bursts of emotion, alternations of feeling, and dramatic silences that characterize this session. They simply provide the gross framework in which the interaction takes place.

Each of these episodes is marked by a sudden shift of topic at its boundaries. There are also a few subepisodes; at the end of Episode 3, we have included a smaller narrative, which Rhoda adds to illustrate or reinforce her point, quite parallel to the main account. Altogether, we analyze 15 minutes of the therapeutic session.

Within each episode, we have used arabic numerals to mark the units that will be the subject of independent analysis in a cross section. In some cases, these are obvious units: they coincide with a change in speakers and an alternation of speech actions. Within each arabic numeral we indicate convenient subunits with lower-case letters. This is merely a convenience for directing the reader's attention to particular points. In many cases, the basis for such finer subdivisions is the presence of a reinforcing comment or underlining by the other party to the conversation. These may be indicated as separate acts but do not necessarily break up the surrounding utterance into distinct acts. As an example of this segmentation, we may consider 1.2:

1.2[a] R.: *Sunday.. um—my mother went to my sister's again.*
  [b] Th.: *Mm—hm.*
  [c] R.: *And she usu'lly goes for about a day or so, like if she leaves on Sunday, she'll come back Tuesday morning. So—it's nothing.*

We originally saw this segment as a unit in which Rhoda introduced her narrative of the events that led to the present situation. 1.2 might be summarized as "Rhoda gives orientation to the present problem by beginning a narrative of the event that led to her mother's being away from home...." The therapist's *Mm—hm* seems to provide general reinforcement and acknowledges the orienting information contained in Rhoda's first sentence; but a closer examination shows that there are counter-currents and subsidiary actions within 1.2 which make it desirable to analyze at least three components separately.

So—it's nothing at the end of 1.2 shows Rhoda responding to the therapist's intervention with noticeable affect. She appears to have seen the therapist's *Mm—hm* as an expression of sympathy, which she did not want at that point,* and goes on to evaluate her own account as not requiring sympathy—thus far. In fact, the next sentence suspends the narrative: it is not an account of anything that happened that week, but rather a statement of what *usually* happens. It can be understood as Rhoda's evaluative reaction to the therapist's expression, carrying out the same interactive task as *So—it's nothing*. We therefore distinguish three subsections of 1.2 as action and interaction in the final analyses:

1.2[a] Rhoda initiates a narrative from everyday life by providing orientation on time, persons, place and behavioral setting.
1.2[b] Therapist responds by giving sympathetic support.
1.2[c] Rhoda gives evaluation of narrative thus far as not requiring sympathy, thereby asserting her adult status and thereby refusing support.

We might indeed have further divided 1.2[c] into two units. The first sentence might be an action "Rhoda gives orientation to her mother's usual behavior. . . ." The second sentence would then be the evaluation and her refusal of support. But such decisions are of little interest. We do not feel that there is any profound theoretical question that depends upon how small or large a unit is selected to be described as the basis for the speech act. Here we have given only the beginning and the end of the analysis; the arbitrary nature of segmentizing will become more apparent when we expand the text into a fuller version that incorporates information from other parts of the interview, as well as intonational cues. It then will be apparent that the original sentences are not in any one-to-one relationship with the actions being performed. This *expansion* is in itself open-ended, and cannot be terminated in any nonarbitrary manner. This being the case, there always will be an arbitrary aspect to the correlation of speech units with the units of speech actions.

We will now proceed to an examination of the component parts of the cross section: the text, the paralinguistic cues, the expansion of the text with embedded propositions, and the speech actions.

The TEXT

We first present the words that are spoken together with all of the false starts, hesitation forms, and self-interruptions that we can capture. Basically, we use the same devices as a novelist. We do not attempt to show fine phonetic details in our text, though we do indicate well-recognized,

---

*Evidence for this analysis is obtained from the paralinguistic cues: See Chapter 4, pp. 134–145, and Figure 10 for the pitch contour of *Mm-hm*.

socially stereotyped dialect alternations such as *jist* for *just*, *doin'* for *doing*, *a'ready* for *already*, and so on. We also indicate tempo by occasionally putting together highly condensed phrases without word spaces in between. Since tempo and pauses play a major part in our analysis, we indicate these quite exactly by the convention of using one dot for each ½-second of pause. Hesitation forms used by these speakers are shown as *uhm*, *um*, and so on, representing various combinations of the neutral vowel [ə], nasality, and aspiration. The opening utterance indicates the range of the textual devices that we use.

> 1.1[a]   R: *I don't .. know, whether I—I **think** I did—the right thing, jistalittle .. situation came up ... an' I tried to uhm ...... well, try to .... use what I—what I've learned here, see if it worked.*

Punctuation. One of the crucial matters in our transcription is the punctuation employed. We find no difficulty whatsoever in the use of the period, question mark, and other standard punctuating devices. In transcribing this and many other conversations, we rarely find disagreement on the assignment of these symbols. The question mark indicates a syntactic question; the only place in which it specifically indicates an intonation contour is in elliptical fragments or declarative forms that have a rising intonation. Commas are used to indicate falling intonations that do not aim towards the lowest pitch level, but level off or rise slightly. A clear example of the intonation designated by a comma can be heard in counting: "1, 2, 3, ..." This contour must be sharply differentiated from that designated by the dash [—]. The dash means an abrupt termination of an utterance without change of pitch level, frequently with a glottal stop. When the sentence is continued, there is often extra heavy stress on the first syllable or upon the syllable that replaces the error in question. This is the standard *editing signal* in English, automatically and accurately identified by native speakers.* When an editing signal of this sort separates sounds that are less than a word, we use a hyphen.

> 2.3[d]   *... I—n-not—**not** that I-I run around the house cleaning ev'ry—ev'ry time,*

Here there is a full word *I* which is followed by abrupt termination and then a pronunciation of *not* with a stammering repetition of the *n* followed by another editing signal and an extra emphasis on the second *not*. The hyphen in *I-I run* indicates that the first sound does not seem to be a full pronunciation of the word *I* but a short repetition of the first part of the vowel. Contrastive stress is shown by boldface characters.

---

*For further development of a study of editing rules, see Labov, "The Grammaticality of Every-Day Speech," (forthcoming).

The symbols "x x x" indicate that the words of the text cannot be deciphered (owing to speaker overlap, and so forth).

The complete text is given as Appendix A on pp. 361–369. It is the result of many re-editings and comes as close to an accurate transcription as we have been able to achieve in many such efforts. We are aware of the fact that editing is an open-ended process: After hundreds of hearings new corrections continue to appear.

Fields of Discourse. In the text, we will indicate fields of discourse by angled brackets with subscripts as follows:

 IV = Interview Style
 EV = Everyday Style
  F = Family Style

In addition, we will indicate a subdivision of everyday style as N, indicating a continuing *narrative* structure. Such narratives have their own internal organizations, and it will be helpful to show how the structure of the narrative determines the placement of fragments of family style as evaluative devices (see Chapter 3, pp. 108–109).

Fields of discourse typically are nested within each other, reflecting the framework of Figure 1. The outermost field of discourse is always IV; if no other field of discourse is indicated by angled brackets, the text is assumed to be in IV.

Paralinguistic CUES

We have been able to limit the text to standard spelling by presenting in a parallel column the paralinguistic cues that accompany the words, phonemes, sentences, and so on, of discourse. Only one of these cues is represented in the text: tempo. As noted above, rapid, condensed speech is indicated by writing the words together without spaces, and long pauses are indicated by dots. The paralinguistic cues that we deal with in the "Cues" section are volume, pitch, and voice qualifiers (breathiness, glottalization, whine, etc.). We also record the most significant changes in breathing; the most important is obviously laughter and suppressed laughter, which is often heard as an expulsion of air at the same time that a word is pronounced. Some special idioms and lexical choices are also identified, where their expressive or nonreferential use can be separated easily from their textual significance. There is also some information to be derived from sociolinguistic variants on the phonetic level: as mentioned in Chapter 1, most of these variables have attained a constant value in the interaction between Rhoda and the therapist. Perhaps the most significant is (ing), which shows alternation between the *—in'* and the *—ing* variants.

Transcription. Unlike vowels and consonants, most paralinguistic cues are not easily coded in a discrete form. Linguists have not been able to agree upon a finite number of paralinguistic units that would form a closed set, defined by their mututal oppositions. For example, in the case of a high rising and falling intonation:

$$I\ don't\ thi^{n^k}\ s_o$$

linguists have not been able to agree on whether this is clearly opposed to a more moderate rise, a less sudden fall, and so forth. It is agreed that the physical dimensions of frequency, duration, and amplitude are realized as the subjective dimensions of pitch, length, and volume—but not in any simple way. These subjective dimensions are in turn combined to produce complex intonational contours that include the perception of "stress." As yet there is no general agreement on the overall structure of meanings conveyed by these complex contours, outside of the fundamental contours that indicate declarative sentences, interrogatives, and imperatives.* At various times, complex systems of numerical transcription have been developed to code intonation and volume discretely. We began using the numerical system of Pike (1948)—the inverse of that of Trager and Smith (1951)—which is also used in *The First Five Minutes*. The greatest expertise in this field has been developed by the authors of the unpublished *Natural History of an Interview*, where we find standard symbols for "over-loud," "over-soft"; prosodic cues and voice qualifiers are coded systematically throughout their text. Linguists have realized for some time that these methods of transcription were not very reliable, but this fact was demonstrated conclusively by Lieberman (1965), who showed that even the best-trained American linguists did not agree on their transcription of the four-step system of pitch levels. Many linguists now use the typographical devices introduced by Bolinger, which simply follow the rise and fall of the voice in an impressionistic manner in an attempt to capture the central feature of "pitch contour."

In the absence of intersubjective agreement on the coding of these intonational contours, it is important for the reader to be able to view the data directly—especially because there is often a one-to-one iconic relationship between the movement of the voice and the emotions being conveyed.† We have utilized two types of acoustic displays throughout this text; these will

---

*This is not to say that considerable progress has not been made in recent decades by analysts of intonation. See, for example, Pike (1948); Bolinger (1958, 1964); Stockwell (1960); and Bailey (1970). Our general point is that there is no general system for analyzing intonational contours that is generally accepted in linguistics in the same way that phonetic transcription is accepted.

†See Bolinger (1961) for a detailed description of the difference between such gradient signals and the all-or-none signals characteristic of vowels and consonants.

44   COMPREHENSIVE DISCOURSE ANALYSIS

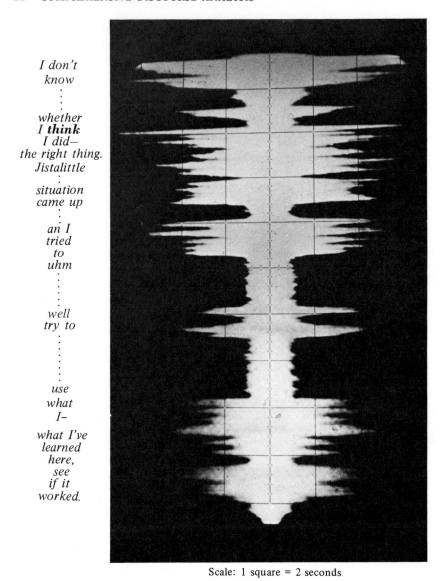

*I don't
know*
⋮
*whether
I **think**
I did—
the right thing.
Jistalittle*
⋮
*situation
came up*
⋮
*an I
tried
to
uhm*
⋮
⋮
*well
try to*
⋮
⋮
*use
what
I–*
*what I've
learned
here,
see
if it
worked.*

Scale: 1 square = 2 seconds

Figure 2. Spectographic display of Rhoda's initial hesitation in 1.1. (1 square = 2 seconds.)

give the reader a clear and immediate view of those signals that seem to play a crucial part in the conversational interaction. Hesitation, long pauses, and other forms of disruption are crucial signals in this therapeutic session, especially when contrasted with the fluent speech of everyday style. A variable-persistence oscilloscope allows us to display the overall

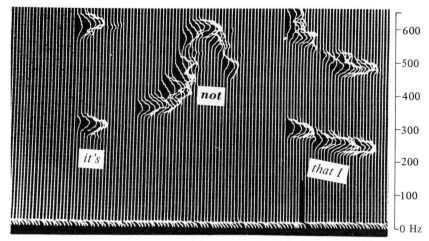

Figure 3. Pitch contour of Rhoda's emphatic negation in 1.5[a].

amplitude of the speech pattern over fairly long utterances.* The pattern of hesitations that is indicated typographically as 1.1 above is displayed more precisely in Figure 2. Each square on the grid represents 2 seconds of speech.

To show the rise and fall of the voice, we utilize a real-time spectrum analyzer.† Figure 3 shows the pitch contour display of *It's not that I*.... The horizontal axis represents time and the vertical axis, frequency. Low frequencies are at the bottom and high frequencies at the top of the diagram, ranging from 0 to 650 Hz. In this case, the phrase begins with the short word *it's* at about 300 Hz, which lasts for only about 70 msec. After a pause of 100 msec, the word *not* begins a little higher, at 345 Hz. It stays at this level for almost 100 msec, then rises sharply in the course of only 20 or 30 msec to a high point of 560 Hz. After another 100 msec at this peak, it gradually falls off to 475 Hz. There is another sizeable pause, this time about 180 msec, before the phrase *that I* begins at 300 Hz, and declines to

*A Hewlett–Packard Oscilloscope 141A with Time Base 1410.
†The instrument used here is a Spectral Dynamics Real-Time Analyzer 301C with output displayed on a Tektronix 611 storage oscilloscope. The analyzer synthesizes 500 filters every 50 milliseconds over a variety of frequency ranges; the analysis can be terminated after any given number of filters and a new sweep started immediately. The pitch contour display used throughout this volume is made with a frequency range of 5,000 Hz. Each filter has a nominal bandwidth of 10 Hz and an effective bandwidth of 15 Hz. The sweep is terminated after the first 110 filters, so that a spectrum is generated every 11 milliseconds. The display on the oscilloscope is logarithmic and cuts off at 54 db below maximum. High-pass filtering at 12 db per octave begins at 3,000 Hz, and, in addition, the roll-off of the Nagra IV-S tape recorder—LS + FA—is used. Volume is then adjusted so that only the peaks of the wave forms are visible, thus tracing the path of the fundamental frequency without the interference of other signals.

250 Hz for the second word. (In Pike's 4-level notation, this would be a 242 contour.) Note that this is a jump of almost an octave: at its peak, the fundamental in *not* is almost level with the first harmonic of *it's* and *that*, which are exactly twice the frequency of the fundamental in those words. The wide range and great flexibility of this instrument, coupled with various filtering devices and intensity control, allows us to present a fairly complete picture of the movement of the fundamental contour (and occasionally the first harmonic as well) without resorting to schematized drawings.

Interpretation. The lack of agreement on the transcription of prosodic cues is not accidental. We feel that this system of communication is utilized by speakers in conversational interaction to communicate signals that are not clear, discrete, or unambiguous. The gradience of this phenomenon has been recognized for some time (Bolinger, 1961). In our view, the lack of clarity or discreteness in the intonational signals is not an unfortunate limitation of this channel, but an essential and important aspect of it. Speakers need a form of communication which is *deniable*. It is advantageous for them to express hostility, challenge the competence of others, or express friendliness and affection in a way that can be denied if they are explicitly held to account for it. If there were not such a deniable channel of communication, and intonational contours became so well recognized and explicit that people were accountable for their intonations, then some other mode of deniable communication would undoubtedly develop. This is not to say that speakers cannot be very much aware of the significance of intonational contours, and agree about them, or even act decisively on this basis; but as we shall see, speakers are permitted to deny the communications that they have just made even though they and the hearers may be perfectly well aware of what has been done.

The problem of the interpretation of paralinguistic cues is therefore a very severe one, and we wish to stress here that many of our individual interpretations and labelings are only partly supported by agreement among linguists. We have not claimed, therefore, to produce a context-free set of interpretations of prosodic cues. Our interpretation of the cues in Rhoda's speech is greatly facilitated by the fact that they are concentrated. The effects of hesitation, choking, whining, and glottalization reinforce each other as opposed to the fluent, uninterrupted style of her everyday narrative. We use the general label *tension;* how much of this is signaled by each of the individual cues is not known. We do not assert that hesitation or glottalization would necessarily have this interpretation outside of the complex configuration we have identified.

Some of the intonational contours that we encounter here have been studied and analyzed with some success in earlier publications. One of them is the Yiddish "rise–fall" intonation analyzed by Weinreich (1956), which is an incredulous and aggressive request for confirmation (see 2.9[c] and 3.23 on pp. 205–207). More difficult are the generalized forms of indirect communications such as *heavy implication* (Pike, 1948). The use of several heavy stresses in a row, or a low falling and rising intonation frequently signals that "there is more to this than meets the eye," (see discussion of 1.9 on pp. 162–168); but there are a variety of other meanings that are signaled by similar contours, and we have not yet identified the contextual clues that would disambiguate them. In addition, we must note that every individual draws differently from the repertoire of paralinguistic devices, even when he uses the same dialect features of vowels and consonants. Though we have introduced some precision into the treatment of intonational contours, the transcription and interpretation of many such signals remains an art. We recognize the social competence of speakers and listeners in producing and interpreting such signals. Psychotherapists may be especially attuned to the significance of this mode of communication. Our mode of analysis calls attention to the existence of parallel streams of communication—the text and the paralinguistic cues—and, like *The First Five Minutes,* it tends to sensitize the listener to the more covert channel.

There is no general agreement on the terms which we might use for the major meanings communicated by paralinguistic cues. As a first step towards achieving reliability in this field, we have restricted our vocabulary to a limited set of terms. Among the most frequent are those that indicate negative emotional states:

Tension
Tension Release
Exasperation

Secondly, there is a set of terms which evaluate affectively an interactional move on the part of the speaker:

Mitigation
Aggravation

On the part of the listener:

Sympathy
Derogation
Neutrality

Thirdly, we use Formality and Informality to convey overall stylistic information related to the fields of discourse.

In addition, we record a number of prosodic signals that have been identified as "reinforcement"—contributions of the listener to the interaction, which do not interrupt the speaker's stream of speech, and which do not convey highly specific messages.

These categories label the paralinguistic cues that we have encountered in this analysis in a way that allows us to combine them with the text in a meaningful way. Such meanings are often necessary to account for the sequence of utterances that follow and precede. If we did not attribute meaning to many of these paralinguistic cues, we would find that the discourse was incoherent at many points. The way in which the text and the cues are combined forms what we call the *mode of expression*. It appears that some styles of speech rely more heavily on paralinguistic cues, while others make meanings more explicit in the text. We have not attempted to measure the balance, but we have called attention to obvious qualitative differences in these two forms of communication. It is one of the most important stylistic parameters that differentiate fields of discourse and the two speakers involved in our therapeutic session. There are many forms of indirection used in conversation. More attention has been paid to indirect modes of expression than to any other form of indirection; particular attention has been given to points where the paralinguistic cues run counter to the meaning of the text. DeGroot has pointed out that whenever paralinguistic cues contradict the text, the meaning that is understood as primary is that of the cues (1949). Bateson has been concerned with the interactional consequences of such contradictions as part of the etiology of schizophrenia (Bateson *et al.*, 1956). The *double bind* that is created by this form of contradiction is possible only when the mode of expression heavily favors the paralinguistic cues; but there is no way of stating in advance what a "normal" balance between text and cues would be, since it is highly determined by the social context of the interaction and the amount of shared knowledge between participants. In some contexts, excessive reliance upon text to the exclusion of cues can also be a form of pathology, of which the mildest form is "flattened affect." The "mode of expression" is introduced here not as a measure but as a category for registering this important stylistic dimension.

One of the clearest examples of the separation of text and paralinguistic cues is found in the first episode.*

1.8   Rhoda: *An-nd so—when—I called her t'day, I said, "Well, when do you plan t'come* **home**?"
1.9   R.: *So she said, "Oh, why?"*

In 1.8, Rhoda reports a communication to her mother that has many indirect interactional consequences, but the mode of expression is relatively direct. There are some indirect implications in *well* and in *plan,* but we do not read any special significance into the prosodic cues other than those

---

*We will use this quotation in this and the following sections to illustrate the cross-sectional analysis we use in Chapters 4–9. A fuller account is given in Chapter 5 (p. 163 ff.) together with the background information needed to justify many of these operations on the text.

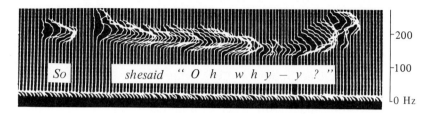

Figure 4. Pitch contour of 1.9, *Oh why-y?*

appropriate for a *when* question (see p. 156). In contrast, her mother's answer quoted in 1.9 carries a heavy prosodic load: it can be separated into the words, *"Oh, why?"* and the pitch contour (2 1 2) which starts low, falls, and rises again. Figure 4 shows a pitch contour display of this utterance, which gives us a view of an intonation pattern that moves over a smaller range than *It's **not** that I....* Directly above the fundamental is the first harmonic, which shows in more exaggerated form the intonation contour, since it is exactly twice the fundamental. But since the energy level of the first harmonic is lower than that of the fundamental, the trace tends to disappear at the low point of the word *"Oh."* Above the first can be seen parts of the second harmonic.

As noted above, we label this contour "heavy implication" and give it the label "There is more to this than meets the eye." The mode of expression is very indirect, since, as we will show in our expansion below, there is more interactional content in the intonation than in the text. As we will ultimately show, the intonation provides a connection between 1.8 and 1.9 which does not exist at the level of literal interpretation of the words.

Expansion

In the discussion of text and cues, we presented first steps in *analysis*, separating two forms of communication that are tightly interwoven in speech. Other forms of analysis will be required later, but our next step is a *synthesis*. We bring together all the information that we have that will help in understanding the production, interpretation, and sequencing of the utterance in question:

1. We expand the meaning conveyed by the cues into the nearest equivalent in textual terms, according to our best understanding of it.
2. We expand and make explicit the referents of pronouns to other utterances and events in other time frames.
3. We introduce factual material that is presented before and after this utterance, sometimes from widely separated parts of the interview.
4. We make explicit some of the shared knowledge between participants,

which we derive from a study of the therapeutic situation as a whole, other interviews, and the playback with the therapist.

Some of these expansions are quite mechanical, part of the automatic adjustment we must make in taking any utterance from context and placing it before a generalized audience. Even when we hear a text in context, though, we must bring together information from the immediately preceding and following material in order to understand the reference of pronouns, and we are only making this process explicit.

The task of developing a detailed interpretation of an utterance will also add components that are not immediately available in the context, but have great interactional significance. We can follow these operations in the expansion of 1.8:

1.8   TEXT

R.: ⟨_N*An-nd so—when—I called her t'day, I said,* ⟨_F *"Well, when do you plan t'come* **home?**⟩_F⟩_N

        EXPANSION

R.: ⟨_NWhen I called my mother today (Thursday), I actually said, ⟨_F"Well, in regard to the subject which we both know is important and is worrying me, when are you leaving my sister's house where {2} your obligations have already been fulfilled and {4} returning as I am asking you to a home where {3} your primary obligations are being neglected, since you should do this as {HEAD-Mo} head of our household?" ⟩_F ⟩_N

We first fill in the obvious referent of *her* and *today*. Ability to identify these "shifters" is a part of automatic linguistic competence. We provide a full expansion of the word *well* in this initial position of an utterance. The information on where mother is now and the status of her obligations to that household is derived from Episode 4. The particular complaint Rhoda has about her obligations being neglected is an interpretation of the previous utterance of 1.7, where Rhoda explains why she should tell her mother, "Look, you have been there long enough," supplemented with information on parent–child responsibilities discussed at many other points in the interview. The status of Rhoda's mother as head of her household is part of the general picture we reconstruct of the role obligations in several households, discussed at length in Chapters 4 and 8. The word *actually* is provided to underline the contrast between what Rhoda imagined that she would say in 1.7 and what she reports herself as actually saying in 1.8.

It should be clear that this expansion is open-ended. There is no limit to the number of explanatory facts we could bring from other parts of the interview, and the end result of such a procedure might be combining everything that was said in the session into one sentence.* For this reason, there is no fixed relation between text and expansion. Nevertheless, we can expand the notion of "mode of expression" to include the overall proportion of text to expansion. A brief text and a long expansion may be the result of heavy reliance on implicit information as well as heavily loaded intonation contours. The mode of expression can then be considered the overall proportion of the literal text to the expansion.

Clauses in the expansion that are preceded by symbols in curly braces are implicit *propositions,* which serve more than anything else to build the fabric of conversational interaction. One of the functions of the expansion in our analysis is to provide a context for these propositions.

As we will see, the expansion itself is often a help to our understanding and plays a crucial role in the analysis of *interaction*. But the expansion can also be somewhat deceptive, since there is an interactive component of over-explicitness, which throws many of the actions into a wrong light. This is a general property of microanalysis: ordinary behavior takes on a Machiavellian intricacy, and hostilities that are latent and unobtrusive become overpowering and oppressive. Expansions magnify the strains and tensions in the social fabric and will produce distorted interpretation unless we remember that the expansion loses the important dimension of backgrounding, which subordinates one form of social interaction to another.

Any microanalysis, therefore, will over-sensitize readers to the conflicts contained in ordinary interaction. Psychotherapists at the agency being studied expressed their appreciation for the insights gained, but remarked that this kind of analysis makes the therapeutic session seem like a type of "warfare," and makes the relationships with patients seem much more abrasive than they actually are. We have not fully solved the problem of how to restore the subjective effect of mitigating devices after analysis. We will only note here that mitigating devices do mitigate; they place in perspective behavior which would otherwise be intolerable for the participants.

Propositions. In the preceding section we located in the expansions a series of *propositions*. These may be defined as *recurrent communications*. Some are specific to the particular events being talked about; others are general and appear throughout family life or the therapeutic series. They may never have been stated in a concise, explicit form by the participants; but if we study various reports of interaction we usually find that the

---

*Garfinkel has dealt most explicitly and pointedly with the extraordinary amount of implicit material that must be restored to show how to understand utterances, and he has also pointed out that there is no limit to the process (1967, p. 38ff). The expansions of ordinary conversation that he reports from experiments with students are similar in many ways to the expansion of 1.8 provided above.

propositions implicit at one point are plainly stated at another. They represent the cognitive component of conversational transactions; in one sense, they may be defined as "what we are talking about," or what is "really being talked about." In our expansion of 1.8, we encounter three such propositions:

{2}: Mother has fulfilled her obligations at Household 2 (her married daughter's house)
{3}: Mother has neglected her primary obligations at Household 1 (Rhoda's house)
{4}: Mother should come home now

The first three propositions are specific to Episode 1. They are the "points" that she is making here, and which she uses to justify her position. The narrative that she tells is taken as an instance and example of these propositions: {2} is true because her mother has been long enough at her sister's household; {3} is true because she has left Rhoda to do the housework for 4 days, and {4} follows from {2} and {3}.

Propositions {2}, {3}, and {4} are recurrent themes, but basically are limited to individual episodes. As we go deeper into the interactional events of such reported conversation (see p. 131), there begin to appear other propositions based upon the underlying web of rights and obligations that have a more general character. In appealing to her mother for help and reminding her of her obligations, Rhoda is invoking her mother's role obligations as a competent head of the household {HEAD-MO}. Some propositions are even more general to the therapeutic situation and to Rhoda's problem. The most important appears in our expansion of 1.9:

1.9 R.: $\langle_N$ So my mother said to me, $\langle_F$ "Oh, I'm surprised; why are you asking me when I plan to come home, and do you have a right to ask that? There's more to this than meets the eye: Isn't it that {~AD-R} you can't take care of the household or yourself, as I've told you before, and I shouldn't have gone away in the first place?" $\rangle_F$ $\rangle_N$

The proposition referred to here is:

{AD-R}: R. is an adult member of the household.

and the ~ sign represents a negation of this proposition. The consequences of being an adult member of the household or not being one are quite important for Rhoda's daily life. Many of the disputes in her household concern whether or not she has the right to decide things for herself—to go to school, attend classes, engage in social life, and so on. Her illness is cited as evidence that she does not have these rights and must take the position of a dependent child. She argues that she has no disorder, and claims these rights. In Chapter 1, we indicated that some therapists feel that arguments over such rights and obligations—questions of relative power—are part of the etiology of anorexia nervosa.

It is evident that propositions may be part of the direct content of conversation, or may be referred to with varying degrees of indirectness. The way in which propositions are related to the text we call the *mode of argument*. We observe that participants in therapy and in conversation normally do not argue the propositions directly, but argue whether or not the events being talked about are instances of these general propositions. Parents tend to make certain longstanding propositions quite explicit: "You can't take care of yourself," "You don't help around the house," "You eat too much," and sometimes precede these explicit statements with remarks such as "I've told you a thousand times..." but adults refer to interactive propositions much less often.* If the mode of argument is very indirect, it may be difficult for one party to see what the other is "getting at"; or their intentions may be suddenly revealed in an unpleasant way. In any case, it is rarely possible to "say what you mean"; we will have many occasions to observe the consequences for conversational interaction of this fact. Remarks on the deceptive nature of expansions in the preceding section may apply equally well to propositions. There are many propositions that a person might endorse but that would be difficult for him to assert explicitly: for example, "I am better than you." One of the specific characteristics of therapy is that both patient and therapist are presumably working towards making certain propositions explicit.

Therapists are very much aware of the difficulty of extracting general propositions from ordinary conversation. In the following example from a family session studied by Fanshel, the therapist is trying to solve the problem of locating the underlying proposition:

Wife: *Why do I think he's talking this way?..... Well, listen to how many instances—we stopped at a fruit stand Saturday night—*
Therapist: [interruption] *I almost prefer not to hear this...*
Wife: *Oh? Not to hear it?*
Therapist: *Because the instance will be another instance.*
Wife: *Because whenever... all right, whenever I do something, whether it's right or wrong, it's always wrong in his eyes.*
Therapist: *Okay. So that's one reason.*

In our own therapeutic session, we will see the therapist making the same kind of strenuous effort to extract and make explicit the general propositions that are implicit in the anecdotes and examples given by the patient.

*It can also be shown that in most conversations both parties are arguing the propositions "I am a good person," and "We are in a right relationship to each other."

typical of a large number of propositions used in everyday life to criticize or support a person's activity in the roles that he plays. They are usually expressed as categorical judgments, but of the form "X never knows when to stop eating," or "X never raises his finger to help." They are seen most clearly as quantitative judgments that a certain person eats, helps, cleans, and so forth, more or less than he should: that is, his role performance is below a given threshold or above a given cut-off point. In actual interaction, though, they take the form of qualitative judgments that persons are above or below expected standards in that role performance. In our session, all references are to the claim that someone is below the standard:

{~EAT}   X does not eat enough
{~CLEAN}   X does not help clean the house

An expression such as Rhoda's "I do eat!" (5.9) must be seen as a denial of the claim that she doesn't eat enough: {~~EAT}. This is natural enough, since there is seldom any reason to claim that one does carry out normal obligations unless someone has denied or challenged this fact. There is also a generalized proposition about role performance, which is not uncommon in many conversations.

{STRN}   X's obligations are greater than his capacities.

Any one of these propositions can be connected with a cause, and a synthetic proposition created, "X is the cause of..." We have not formalized such statements except for one recurrent proposition that denies any personal responsibility: external circumstances are the cause of the problem. In this case, the problem is that of role strain:

{X:STRN}   External circumstances are responsible for role strain.

As the therapeutic session progresses, the therapist puts forward interpretations that require more complex combinations of the elementary propositions we are using here. Their significance will only be apparent when we reach Chapter 9, which deals with Episode 5.

We also encounter propositions with *constitutional predicates*. Certain people are said to have certain particular characteristics: they are lazy, overweight, thoughtless, and so on. The two which play a major role in our Episodes are:

{TIRE}   X tires (more) easily (than others).
{THIN}   X is thinner than he should be.

There are also general propositions that can stand alone without reference to individuals:

{S-CARE}   One should take care of oneself.

In addition to the fundamental predicates, there are a number of "operators" that modify or combine propositions into more complex forms in ways that parallel logical operations. As noted above, propositions are frequently negated, as indicated with the ~ sign. The negation of a proposition also can be negated, as when Rhoda says that it is not true that she can't get along without her mother, in 1.5[a]; she is in effect denying the accusation that she is not an adult, {~~AD-R}.

An operator which links two propositions is the assertion of a causal relation, which we symbolize with a colon; thus Rhoda frequently puts forward the proposition, {X:STRN}, 'external circumstances are the cause of her role strain.' A second such operator is the assertion of similarity, which we symbolize with an equals sign, =, as in the therapist's remark of 5.19[a], "maybe it's similar to the feeling that you had when...." This interpretation is abbreviated simply as $E_3 = E_3'$, a particular emotion (anger) felt by one person is similar to the emotion felt by another. Such operators can of course be formalized as higher-level predicates, with propositions as arguments, but the notation would then become quite unwieldy. As it is, we find many reapplications of operators to complex propositions, and there is of course no theoretical limit to the depth of complexity that can be achieved in conversational interaction.

It would be difficult to say whether there is a finite set of primitive propositions that could be used in conversation. Clearly, most of those cited here are specific to our general situation, though some may be found in all therapeutic encounters and some recur widely in social life. There is no reason why such propositions should form a closed set, though we might want a more elementary set of communicative devices, like paralinguistic cues, to form such a set. In each conversational type, we can imagine a general theory that would define the types of propositions that are possible, common, rewarding, and so forth. In therapy, we find a sharp division between meta-propositions, concerning the process of therapy, and the actual substance being discussed in therapeutic sessions. Therapist and patient accept the understanding that it is their job to isolate certain propositions. The patient must understand "who he is," what is the source of his difficulty, the role played by others, and so on. Therefore it becomes more important in therapy than in other conversations to isolate *propositions*, and they obviously may play a more important role in our analysis than they might in other situations.

The analysis of discourse therefore cannot begin with a fixed set of propositions. The analyst first must locate the recurrent messages in the conversation he is studying. The process of expansion, which we have sketched here and exemplified in later chapters, is the primary technique for this purpose. The need to isolate such propositions makes it even more evident that an atomic analysis of conversation, considering one sentence after another, is beside the point. A hasty glance at any given sentence will not reveal what the speaker is getting at. Only a detailed examination of the before and after, and all possible surrounding circumstances will make up for the fundamental difference between the outside analyst and the participant speaker. The analyst is not engaged in the interaction: he must make up for this limitation by reconstructing the event until he has knowledge almost equal to that of the participants.*

When we examine indirect modes of argument, we sometimes find that an underlying proposition is the main (cognitive) point that is being made; in other cases, it forms the connection between two such points. In either case, it is necessary to grasp these underlying propositions, at some level of awareness, in order to understand the point that the speaker is making. This leads us to the division between two major modes of argument: a point may be made by general statements or by giving an instance, normally in the form of a narrative. The narrative mode of argument is the most challenging for the task of isolating the underlying propositions, since the narrative as a whole can be seen as a single speech act whose interactive significance is determined by the evaluative message. The structure of narratives and the analysis of their evaluative organization will therefore play a major part in our analysis (see Chapter 3, pp. 104–105).

Interaction

The most critical step in our analysis is the determination of the *actions* that are being performed by speakers through their utterances. As we noted in Chapter 1, many linguists and philosophers have become increasingly concerned with what it means to do something with words. (Austin, 1962; Searle, 1969; Cole and Morgan, 1975; Sadock, 1974).

As we will see, the internal structure of speech actions is considerably more complex than this initial division between act and utterance suggests. The intuitive study of speech acts, which has been conducted concurrently with our own investigations of conversation over the past 10 years, has produced many rich and interesting insights: but a common characteristic of the more philosophical approach to speech acts is the absence of any treatment of the more abstract types of social interaction, which go beyond the linguistic structure. We find that the crucial actions in establishing coherence of sequencing in conversation are not such speech acts as requests and assertions, but rather challenges, defenses, and retreats, which have to do with the status of the participants, their rights and obligations,

---

*Many readers will feel that this process of analysis gives the analyst more information than the participants had and leads to over-interpretation of the situation. For the present, this issue must remain open. It does not seem likely that it will be settled by refusing to pursue an analysis beyond a certain point.

and their changing relationships in terms of social organization. We define *interaction* as action which affects (alters or maintains) the relations of the self and others in face-to-face communication. These relations move along several dimensions, which have been identified most usefully as *power* and *solidarity* (Brown and Gilman, 1960).*

Though the term *speech act* now has become commonplace for many linguists and philosophers, it still may have a novel or contradictory character for others. As we noted above, it is a common-sense assumption that words are one thing and actions are another. The term may be clarified by noting that a speech act is an action carried out by means of speech.

In any over-all view, it is obvious that actions are more important than utterances, since it is actions that have consequences and affect people's lives. In terms of meaning, the level of interaction can be defined as what is *really* meant in the deepest sense of 'really,' bearing in mind that there will be many hierarchical levels of actions, and it is not always clear where the action *really* is.† The action is what is *intended* in that it expresses how the speaker meant to affect the listener, to move him, to cause him to respond, and so forth. The interactional component of 1.8 will illustrate the depth of the hierarchical structures of speech acts:

1.8 R.: $\langle_N$ R. continues the narrative, $\langle_{IV}$ and gives information to support her assertion $\overline{1}\rangle$ that she carried out the suggestion {S}: $\langle_F$ R. requests information on the time that her mother intends to come home, and thereby requests indirectly $\overline{4}\rangle$ that her mother come home, thereby carrying out the suggestion {S}, thereby challenging her mother indirectly $\langle$?HEAD-Mo $\rangle$ for not performing her role as head of the household properly, simultaneously admitting $\langle$ STRN $\rangle$ her own limitations$\rangle_F$ simultaneously asserting again $\overline{1}\rangle$ that she carried out the suggestion {S}.$\rangle_{IV}\rangle_N$

The interactional statement is a compact summary that is the end result of an analysis.

---

*In the original article, which generated so many other sociolinguistic studies, Brown and Gilman analyze the semantics of pronouns such as *thou* and *you*, *tu* and *vous*, along the dimensions of *power* and *solidarity*. They do not derive these dimensions from their studies of pronouns but note that they are "fundamental to the analysis of all social life" (p. 253).

†There are two opposing senses of *really* in "What did he *really* mean?" and "Did he *really* mean it?" The first refers to some underlying speech action that is distinct from the most direct interpretation of the surface structure. The second use implies the existence of the same kind of hierarchy but focuses instead on the fact that the most direct or literal interpretation is not the one to be accepted in constructing a response.

It is interesting to observe that the English Language Research Group refers to "the 'real' meaning of what is being said" in their discussion of an underlying challenge in a union meeting (1973). This is the only other formal account we know of that explicitly recognizes the hierarchical organization of speech actions.

In presenting the structure of this statement, we first will deal with the main predicates which designate speech acts; then their relation to propositions and sequencing rules, which are shown by the embedded arrows; and finally to the hierarchical structure that relates the various speech acts within the utterance.

Interactional Terms. The terms we have chosen to describe speech events were influenced originally by the battery developed by Bales (1950). These form a closed set, divided first of all into the task area and the social–emotional area. The task area itself is divided into orientation, evaluation, and control; the social–emotional area into decision, tension management, and integration. Some of the same terms and dimensions appear in our own analysis, but there are two fundamental differences that lead to a completely different overall view of speech actions. Bales' observers categorize each speech event as it occurs with a single term, "act by act"; there is no room for ambiguity or overlap in the basic instructions. Our own analysis is quite the opposite in this respect; most utterances represent two or more speech actions. Secondly, all of Bales' actions are on the same level: the stream of speech is matched by a single plane of action. Our own view is that these relations are fundamentally hierarchical: the more abstract actions are identified and interpreted through the identification of others.

In this section we will lay out the battery of interactional terms, identifying each by its relation to the others and the basic dimensions of our analysis. We will not attempt to present a complex taxonomy of speech acts; our concern here is to give an organized view of the entire set of speech acts occurring in the five episodes of the therapeutic session. The index to interactional terms (pp. 382–383) shows the location of each occurrence of these acts in the interactional statements. In the next chapter, we will state the discourse rules that relate these speech actions more precisely to the surface utterances and to each other.

Meta-actions. Figure 5 shows an array of four groups of speech actions or "verbal interactions." The first set are "meta"-actions, which have to do with the regulation of speech itself. They describe the behavior of the speaker when he is doing something else besides "taking his turn." Someone must of course speak first in any conversation, and there are times when a completely new speech event is begun (like a narrative): we use the term *initiate* for this behavior. The speaker also displays initiative when he *redirects* the conversation into other channels or *interrupts* the other speaker.

In many conversations, speakers alternate short, sentence-length utterances, and typically *respond* to each other.* When one person speaks for

---

*We do not label each utterance with this speech action, since it is an obvious feature from the more detailed analysis of interaction that we provide.

SPEECH ACTIONS
(Verbal Interactions)

1. Meta-linguistic

initiate	continue	end
interrupt	respond	signal completion
redirect	repeat	withdraw
	reinforce	

2. Representations

   A-events (in A's biography)

A	B	
give information	reinforce	
express F	acknowledge	
demonstrate		
refer		

   D-events (disputable)

A	B	A
assert	deny	contradict
give evaluation	agree	support
give interpretation	support	
give orientation	give reinterpretation	

3. Requests

A	B	A
request X	give X	acknowledge
	[carry out] X	reinstate
	put off	redirect
		retreat
		mitigate
	refuse with account	renew
	refuse without account	accept
		reject
		withdraw in a huff

4. Challenges

A	B	A
challenge	defend	retreat
question	admit	mitigate
	huff	

X = action   F = belief
    information   uncertainty
    confirmation   exasperation
    agreement   deference
    evaluation
    interpretation
    sympathy

Figure 5. Speech actions referred to in the interactional statements.

any length of time, however, we will find it necessary to state that he *continues* a narrative or an argument. He may also *repeat* another speech act or a larger unit. Finally, he may encourage the other person to continue as he typically *reinforces* with *Mhm, Uh-huh,* and so on.

At the end of a larger unit, it may be appropriate for the speaker to *end* a discussion or narrative. The various means of doing so are not all known or recognized by any means; ending is a more complex act than beginning and, as we shall see, it often is done in a vague and confused way. In this particular session, the patient also signals *completion* of some speech event by repeating herself, in the exact words that she used at the beginning of that event. Finally, we will observe that the patient will sometimes *withdraw* from verbal interaction and produce long silences.

We thus identify three types of metalinguistic behavior, to be categorized roughly under the heading of the generic types, *initiate, continue* and *end*. But these all relate to the behavior of a single person. The more general types of speech behavior are those indicated by the other six terms, which deal with the alternation of speakers—turn-taking, or sequencing, the area of conversational structure that has been explored most successfully by Sacks, Schegloff, and Jefferson (1973).

Representations. A very large class of speech acts are representations of some state of affairs. One set is drawn from the biography of the speaker: these are A-events, that is, known to A and not necessarily to B. Normally A has privileged access to these events and can deal with them as an expert without fear of contradiction. The speaker may thus *give information* on these events or *express* various states of mind about them. The feelings F expressed in our episodes are listed at the bottom of Figure 5. As we have pointed out, the interactive style developed in the therapeutic interview tends to isolate these two kinds of behavior—reporting information and expressing emotion—in separate areas of discourse.

Occasionally the speaker introduces some specific piece of information that both therapist and patient know from some previous session or conversation. Here is will be appropriate to use the term *refer*. There are, of course, an enormous number of acts of reference in any conversation: almost every noun phrase refers to some event or proposition. We are interested, however, in designating only those acts of reference that are not given as new information but which do play an important part in the dynamics of the conversation to follow.

A larger set of representations deal with disputable events: D-events. In dealing with these events, both speaker and listener realize that the truth of the proposition cannot be assumed: the speaker acts in a way that shows he is aware that someone might disagree with him. The most characteristic way of presenting such information is to *assert* it. An assertion usually leads to a response.* There are two specialized kinds of assertions, which we label distinctly in this treatment. After presenting a series of events representing something that actually happened, the speaker will then *give an evaluation* of the significance of these events in emotional or socially evaluated terms. If the event is taken as symbolic of some other covert meaning, the speaker can be said to *give an interpretation,* which may be seen as a special kind of evaluation. The speaker may also provide a set of normative guidelines, which serve to orient the listener to a particular line of behavior; here she can be said to *give orientation.*

Assertions, evaluations, and *interpretations* are the actions of an initial speaker (A) in some sequence. In response to them, B may *agree with,* or *deny,* or *support* the assertion. B may also *give reinterpretation* after A has given an interpretation. Before or after B speaks, A may *support* his own statement with further evidence or argument. He may also *contradict* his own position by something that he says. Note that *agree, deny,* and *contradict* are discrete, cognitively oriented actions; to *give support* or *question* (see below) are actions of variable strength that are intrinsically affective.

Requests. A very large part of the analysis of discourse is concerned with *requests* of various kinds: requests for action, information, confirmation, attention, or approval. We include petitions, pleas, and suggestions in this category as *mitigated* requests, and orders, commands, and demands as *unmitigated* or *aggravated* requests. In general, there is a compelling character to requests, so the conditional relevance of what follows is much greater than that of some of the previous speech actions, and the various rules of requests given in the next chapter are correspondingly complex.

All requests are basically requests for an action of some kind from the other person, but we reserve "request for action" for some response broader than the individual speech act. Figure 5 lists at the bottom the various responses, X, that are requested in our materials: *action, information, confirmation, agreement, evaluation, interpretation, sympathy.* We use the term "suggestion" for a generalized request to follow a line of action whenever the certain conditions apply as in the basic suggestion of therapy to express relevant needs and emotions to others.

The complex sets of *requests* and *responses* to them are not categorized easily as A-events, or D-events, and so on, since they do not refer outside of the speech situation in the same way that assertions do. They may best be described as AB-events, since both speaker and listener are equally well aware of them.

In response to a request from A, B has three basic options: (1) he may *give*

*The term *remark* may be used to indicate an utterance that puts the least constraint on the next utterance: "Wow, I'm tired!" "It's a hot day." We do not find such utterances in this session, since the interaction is fairly intense and continuous.

X—the *information, confirmation,* or whatever is requested, or he may *carry out (perform)* the action or suggestion not necessarily by speech; (2) he may *put off* the request with an accounting; or (3) he may *refuse* it, with or without an accounting.

If the request is complied with, A may in turn *acknowledge* this action. If the request is put off, B may *reinstate* or *redirect* the request, in ways that various rules to follow will make evident. He may also *retreat** from his request or *mitigate* it.

An unaccounted refusal may lead to a break in social relations: A may *withdraw* from the interaction (in a "huff," in Goffman's terminology). For this reason, most refusals supply an accounting. But note that the division between the upper and lower half of this section of Figure 5 is usually difficult to maintain: most refusals appear as "putting off," and most examples of "putting off" are in reality refusals. Putting off naturally requires an account of some kind, and this account can be rejected in the same way as the accounting of a refusal. When A rejects B's account, B in turn may withdraw in a huff, and the example of this behavior in Episode 2 falls into this category.

Challenges. At a deeper level of interactive significance, requests often represent or are interpreted as more personal actions: challenges, criticisms, attacks, denigrations, insults; or praise, support, flattery, reinforcement. We will refer to the first set of negative terms as *challenges:* a challenge is any reference (by direct assertion or more indirect reference) to a situation, which if true, would lower the status of the other person. On the other hand, we will refer generally to *support* as that form of behavior which would reinforce or raise the status of the other person.

An intermediate step in making a challenge is to throw doubt upon a proposition that the other person endorses. We will use the term *question* for this action, in accordance with the normal use, "I question your opinion on that point."†

In response to a challenge from A, B may *defend* himself. This defense often includes a challenge or criticism of the person who initiated the first challenge. Family arguments typically take this form—the defense and challenge being delivered simultaneously.‡ B may also *admit* the challenge to be valid and suffer the consequence of accepting lower status; or he may

---

*In the interest of reducing our array of interactional terms, *retreat* includes 'abandon,' the limiting case.

†The term *question* is often used ambiguously to refer to interrogative utterances or requests for information, as well as to expressions of doubt. Since we use the term *interrogative* and *request* for the first two actions, we have reserved *question* for the third. In Chapter 3, it will appear that all of these actions can be reinterpreted more abstractly as requests (pp. 77–93).

‡This kind of oscillation or reverberation of challenges, defenses, and counter-challenges is sometimes called "malignant interaction" by the therapists.

break off verbal interaction in a *huff*. It is also possible for A to *retreat from, mitigate,* or *aggravate* his challenge, though this type of action does not play a major part in our material.

Finally, there are certain modifiers used in statements of interaction that indicate how an action is performed or how several actions are combined. Thus a speaker may *simultaneously* perform two actions, or perform one action which is *ambiguously* heard as one or the other of two actions. He may perform an action *hesitantly* or *confidently*. The structure of our interactional statement usually indicates that an action has been performed *indirectly*—connected with a surface utterance by a chain of several "therebys." Where it seems important to the course of the interaction, we sometimes indicate this indirection explicitly.

Mode of Interaction. There is a third assessment of indirection that can be found in conversation—the *mode of interaction*. The person can perform any speech action directly. In 1.8, Rhoda might have said, "Mother, please come home tomorrow and help me with the housework," or she could have made her request more indirectly than 1.8, asking, "Is my sister still going to work?" This mode of interaction is independent of the mode of expression, since a direct or indirect action could be performed with explicit verbal text or a heavy reliance on paralinguistic cues. The mode of argument is also independent of the mode of interaction. A direct action may include a direct expression of a proposition, such as, "Since you're my mother, please come home and help me as a mother should." Such a direct statement of a proposition could also be used to perform an action directly. Simply stating, "Well, you are my mother," or "Your main job is here" would be an indirect way of requesting her mother to come home.

The mode of interaction, therefore, reflects the extent to which the speaker uses the discourse rules of interpretation and production, which will be discussed in Chapter 3. The more indirect his mode of interaction, the more such rules of production and interpretation are required. The interactional analysis of 1.8 reproduced previously (p. 59) illustrates the way in which the propositions are embedded in the ongoing interaction. In this segment, we observe Rhoda performing the following actions: *continuing, giving information, requesting information, requesting action, challenging, admitting,* and *asserting*. Each of these actions is indicated in the paragraph by a propositional symbol contained in an arrow. An arrowhead pointing to the right indicates that the response is required; an arrowhead pointing to the left indicates that this action is a response to a previous action.*

---

*In one sense, every action is a response to something that has occurred before, but sequencing rules must indicate that some responses are more tightly constrained than others. Requests and responses, challenges and defenses, form pairs which Sacks has called "adjacency pairs" where such connections are tightest. The sense of our arrowheads is to establish conditional relevance: if the response has not been made, its absence would have been noted.

66 COMPREHENSIVE DISCOURSE ANALYSIS

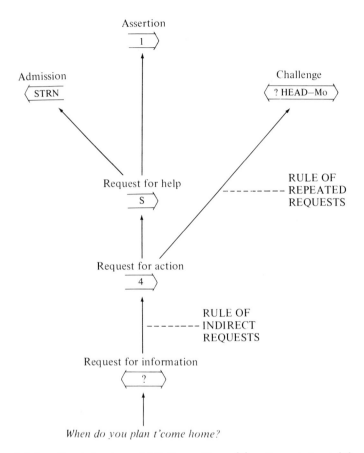

Figure 6. Interactional structure of 1.8. Propositions: {1} = R. carried out {S} correctly. {STRN} = R.'s obligations are greater than her capacity. {4} = R. requests her mother to come home. {?HEAD-Mo} = Mother is a competent head of the household [questioned].

The symbols inside the arrows are both general propositions and particular propositions limited to a given episode. The propositions within the arrow illustrate our initial characterization of conversation as a way of dealing with people by showing that particular events are examples of general propositions (p. 53). The arrows represent the "dealings," and the symbols inside them the propositions. A proposition may be simply asserted or referred to; in this case it appears inside the arrow without any qualification. A proposition may be questioned or challenged: in this case, it appears with a preceding question mark. A proposition may be denied or a request may be refused: it then appears with a preceding negation sign (~).

The interactional structure of 1.8 is displayed in Figure 6. This shows the results of the detailed investigations of Chapter 5; here we merely are illustrating the way in which the analysis is displayed, not arguing the analysis itself. Two actions in the interactional statement concern Rhoda's narrative—*continuing* and *giving information*. These are not shown in Figure 6, but only the six speech acts conveyed by the question, "When do you plan to come home?" This utterance is immediately and obviously seen to be a request for information, which through the Rule of Indirect Requests is interpreted as a request for action: {4}: Rhoda requests her mother to come home. At a higher level, this request for action is a way of carrying out the basic suggestion {S}: that one should express one's needs to relevant others. This implies proposition {1}: R.'s claim that in performing the request for action, she correctly carried out {S}. At the same time, Rhoda necessarily admits the proposition {STRN}: that her obligations are greater than her capacity. An outside listener might carry this analysis one step further, and say that {STRN} implies {~AD}: that Rhoda therefore is not able to function as an adult member of the household, but we will accept Rhoda's account in not following this reasoning (see Chapter 5). The branch from the request {4} shows that it also leads to a challenge to mother's performance of her role as head of the household, through the Rule of Repeated Requests. This rule states, among other things, that if the conditions for a valid request have been in effect for some time, then making such a request is heard as a criticism of the person addressed for not having performed that action before.

The Overall Structure of a Cross Section

The components of our cross-sectional analysis are the *text*, the *cues*, the *expansion*, and the *interaction*. These can be assembled into the three-dimensional structure of Figure 7. The forward plane of this cross section consists of three components making up "what is said." These are the *text*, the *cues*, and the *expansion:* the latter incorporates both local and general propositions. The background plane is the interaction component, "what is done." The relationships between these four components are characterized by three modes of directness or indirection. The relation of text and cues is the mode of expression, the way in which propositions are embedded in the expansion is the mode of argument, and the way in which "what is said" is related to "what is done" is the mode of interaction.

We already have referred to the fact that a hasty interpretation of such indirection may lead to the premature identification of "pathological" symptoms. We have no baseline for the total amount of indirection in ordinary interaction, but current studies of unmonitored conversation in-

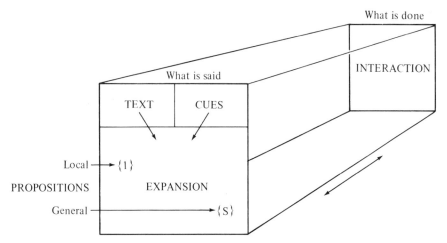

Figure 7. Discourse analysis: cross section.

dicate that it is very great. The dimensions of power and solidarity are important determinants of the degree of indirection. Requests to superiors are necessarily mitigated, and one way of mitigating is to use extremely indirect modes of argument and interaction. When the speaker and listener are closer to each other on the dimension of power, the degree of solidarity is reflected in a parallel degree of shared knowledge. Extremely indirect modes of expression are possible when a speaker and listener share a great deal of information, a point which has been noted very often. Since the underlying propositions are well known to people who share a common social background, the mode of argument also may be indirect. People who have been in close interaction for a long time, such as husband and wife, normally develop complex rituals of verbal exchange, and the modes of interaction may be even more indirect than between strangers.

It is tempting to see a parallel between this kind of conversational indirection and the behavior of hysteric patients, who will not state explicitly the propositions which seem to motivate their behavior. Anorexia nervosa itself is an indirect kind of communication. Many therapists are aware of the need for obtaining more direct modes of communication from the patients—to put them in touch with their own feelings and to get them to communicate to relevant others more directly. They often see indirection as the cause of emotional and cognitive confusion in family life.*

Encounter groups and marathon sessions are designed to break down the barriers that prevent direct communication, and to overcome the devices people use to hide their feelings from each other. However, it re-

---

*In Rhoda's words, "If I keep it in what's bothering me, then nobody else knows and everybody thinks everything is fine and good, and I end up—hurting my*self*."

mains to be seen how much more direct ordinary conversation might be, even in the healthiest of societies. There is certainly appropriate as well as inappropriate indirection. In many traditional societies, young members of the family do not speak freely with their older relatives, or do not speak to them at all. There is some reason to feel that some barriers to communication can be functional, allowing the development of relatively independent subgroups within a society. Therefore, we will trace the various types of indirection in the therapeutic session, including the quotations from family life, without assuming that it is all pathological. We recognize that some part of the psychological problems that Rhoda faces are expressed in her inability to communicate and recognize some facts and feelings, and a systematic examination of indirection will certainly help in tracing the mechanism involved. It would be self-defeating, however, to operate on the assumption that all indirection is pathological and should be eliminated.

SYNTHESIS: THE FLOW OF CONVERSATION

Our cross sections represent a static view of an utterance—a snapshot in which the social interaction is frozen for the time it takes to understand and analyze one sentence or utterance. We have compensated for the artificiality of such an analysis by bringing into the cross section the understandings, assumptions, and implications that precede and follow; but this is only an analytic expedient: Our primary interest must be in the coupling of one utterance with another, in the succession of cross sections, in the assembly of still frames into a moving picture. The individual actions that were analyzed in Figure 6 represent the open links or valences, which allow the coupling of another cross section. Our next step is to construct a flow chart in which a number of such cross sections are linked in a tight matrix of action and response, centering around a single topic or concern. We will also make observations about the overall structure of an episode and the overall direction of an interview. We will follow the patient and therapist through several fields of discourse and trace their varying preoccupations with the external world of social fact and the internal world of feeling. We will interpret where the therapist is going in the light of preliminary hypotheses about what the therapist is trying to do, illuminated and informed by our playback sessions. Yet our primary concern will be with the mechanism of discourse as it flows from minute to minute, seeing what makes it hang together or what makes it fall apart.

The central problem of discourse analysis is to discover the connections between utterances. We know that they are present when we participate in a conversation, and we can respond intuitively to coherence or lack of coherence in a tape-recorded conversation. In the conversation studied here, we will be concerned with the fairly rapid alternation of speakers, rather than with the long, connected discourse of one speaker. In each case, we can ask the question, in what way was B's utterance connected with the preceding utterance of A?

The ordinary, common-sense approach is that one sentence follows another, that a "question" or interrogative utterance is followed by an answer or a declarative sentence. It is simple enough to think of many cases where this is not so, but only a detailed microanalysis will show how abstract the connections are. As a result of our studies of therapeutic discourse, we can put forth a rather paradoxical proposition: *there are no connections between utterances*. Sometimes one surface expression will predict the form of the next as in "How are you?" "I'm fine." Yet obligatory sequencing is not found between utterances but between the actions which are being performed. It is not the linguistic form of interrogative which demands the linguistic form declarative, but rather requests for action which demand responses—to be complied with, put off, or refused. The following chapter will deal with the general rules of discourse that we have found necessary to account for the coherence of the conversation in this therapeutic session. Though these rules play an important part in our analysis of conversational interaction, they are basically ways of making explicit the intuitive analysis of speech acts that we all perform automatically. For readers who are interested primarily in the more substantive issues in therapeutic conversation, it will be possible to proceed directly to Chapter 4. Where specific rules of discourse play a crucial role in the therapeutic session, page references will be made to the most relevant sections of Chapter 3.

RULES OF DISCOURSE

In Chapter 2, "Comprehensive Discourse Analysis," we made a major distinction between two planes of conversational behavior. On the one hand there is the plane of "what is said," which includes the text, paralinguistic cues, and implicit reference to other texts and propositions; on the other hand, there is "what is done," the plane of interaction that is itself a multilayered complex of speech acts. The coherence of discourse was found to lie in the connections of these speech acts through a series of *sequencing rules,* the two planes being connected by a series of *rules of interpretation and production.* In this chapter, we will outline these rules of discourse, focusing primarily on the rules of production and interpretation.

This chapter presents an approach to discourse analysis that is motivated primarily by the needs of our study of therapeutic discourse. The rules as we have developed them over the past several years (Labov, 1970a,b) have been tested against the complex interaction reported in Rhoda's therapeutic session, but they have also been examined against a much wider range of material. They build upon earlier analyses of philosophers of ordinary language (Austin, 1962; Searle, 1969), and they have profited from the parallel investigations of those studying the conversational constraints on sentence grammar from an intuitive viewpoint (Gordon and Lakoff, 1971; Fraser, 1974; Sadock, 1974). The rules we will discuss are those that are required for understanding of the five episodes treated in this volume. In this chapter, we focus on those rules that bridge the gap between what is said and the most immediate interpretation of the actions performed by those words, as shown, for example, by the following utterances and actions.

1.8 *Well, when do you plan t'come* **home***?*
1.9 *Oh, Why-y?*

These discontinuities are greatest in the cluster of rules that center about requests, commands, questions, and so on—those speech acts that people use to influence the behavior of others most directly. They are therefore central elements in conversation as we conceive of it—a way of dealing with others in verbal interaction. This chapter may be of interest primarily to linguists and others concerned with the analysis of conversation as an ongoing technical field; readers who are concerned primarily with the substance of the therapeutic interaction may want to use this discussion primarily as a reference for elucidating the specific rules discussed in later chapters. The rules are formal in the sense that they use a controlled and limited vocabulary in their central terms—the speech actions and their preconditions. At the same time, they are written in ordinary language, and we have refrained from using formalizing symbols drawn from other fields. The connection with sentence grammar is made in some cases, but on the whole the rules governing the production of the speech actions are not specific enough to generate these utterances from the abstract description and the rules.*

Of the many approaches to analyzing conversation reviewed in Chapter 1, only a few are concerned with rules of discourse and the abstract constructions which operate at higher levels of organization. It may be helpful to place our approach to discourse rules in relation to these other approaches, particularly in regard to the kinds of evidence used and the knowledge of the situation required. Some of this work is entirely intuitive, and, like the philosophy of ordinary language, is based upon the knowledge that all members of the community are expected to carry with them at all times. The task of the intuitive linguist is then to formalize his intuitions; he does this by freely constructing examples of sentences and sequences of sentences, and then using his intuitions to decide if these are acceptable and/or how they would be interpreted. In the case of sentence grammar, the rules are formal enough to allow us to produce an unlimited number of other sentences, and the acceptability of these sentences allows us to check the validity of the rules. Linguists interested in extending their methods to conversation have not yet developed rules that are formal enough to produce systematically all possible conversations that might be controlled by the rules, and the validity of the rules must be checked by an informal search for counterexamples.†

The approach to conversational interaction developed by Sacks, Schegloff, and their associates (Sudnow, 1972) is strongly opposed to the use of intuitions to construct conversations. These authors work directly from observed texts, carefully transcribed down to the smallest details of sequencing and vocal gesture. To interpret these texts, they bring to bear their observations of repeated patterns in a large number of other texts that

---

*The nature and direction of the connection with problems of sentence grammar is indicated best in Gordon and Lakoff, 1971.

†Although the ideal of a generative grammar of sentences is to produce rules that could be checked in a systematic manner, the complexities uncovered in recent years have made it increasingly difficult to write rules that can be checked in this formal way.

have been studied in the same way. At the same time, they appeal directly to the reader to observe his own capacity to interpret these texts, with no more knowledge of the situation than is provided in the texts themselves (Sacks, 1972a,b). In most of these texts—telephone conversations, therapeutic sessions, candid recordings—the analysis is carried out without any knowledge of the speakers' background and situation other than what can be drawn from the particular section of text being analyzed. Some of these texts are gathered by participant–observers, but knowledge gained by these observers in the course of their work normally is not utilized.

There is no doubt that advances in our knowledge of conversation can be made by both the approaches outlined. Many general relationships between speech acts and sentence grammar can be uncovered by the use of intuitions alone. A number of very general mechanisms of conversational interaction have been discovered by Sacks, Schegloff, Jefferson, and others, without going too much beyond the limits of contextual inquiry outlined above. From our own observations of many of these ongoing studies, the advantages to be gained from limiting the amount of contextual information is questionable. Where we do not have specific knowledge of the context, we necessarily imagine it. The construction of such imagined contexts is an uncontrolled variable in the study, so rules that appear to be quite general are, in fact, limited by those conditions that we necessarily construct unconsciously as we imagine how we would interpret the utterances in general. Eventually we must construct discourse rules that are quite general and stand free of context; but with our present state of knowledge, the only way we can be sure that these rules are developing in a useful direction is to show that they apply over and over again in many different contexts. In any particular context, we will not know if a particular rule applies unless our knowledge of the contextual conditions is accurate. The problem of "correct interpretation" can never be solved completely, even if we are full participants in a situation; but as we will see, the application of basic rules of discourse depends upon particular knowledge shared among participants. This shared knowledge—of needs, abilities, rights, and obligations—forms the fundamental mechanism of the rules for making requests, putting off requests, etc.* In short, we all are searching for the most general rules that we can write; but to know they are the correct rules, we must have enough contextual information to be sure that they apply in any given case.

This chapter will present discourse rules that are organized around two central structures in conversation: requests and narratives. They are, in a sense, opposite structural types: requests are normally made, put off, chal-

---

*There are, of course, many standardized routines in which the general contextual conditions are seen to be constant, and here we can write rules that are relatively context-free. The discussions of "remedial interchanges" and "supportive interchanges" in Goffman (1971) are examples in point; see also the exploration of conversational openings in Schegloff (1968).

lenged, and so on, by a series of brief interchanges, often in the form of single sentences, between the parties in a conversation. Narratives are the central structures in many longer stretches of speech, where one person holds the floor for a much longer period of time. However, they are both interactive events, and as Sacks and Jefferson have repeatedly pointed out, narratives are accomplished by interaction between speaker and addressee just as much as requests and responses are.

Figure 5 of Chapter 2 (p. 61) displays 44 speech actions, organized under four headings: sequencings, representations, requests, and challenges. This diagram gives some indication of how these speech actions follow one another and the types of "adjacency pairs" that can occur, but it does not indicate how these actions are related to actual language: how the speaker knows what to do, and how the listener knows what has been done. Such rules of production and interpretation will form the main body of this chapter, and we will begin with the third group—requests— which plays a major role in therapeutic interaction. We will encounter kinds of requests that are inherently critical of the other person, and these will form a transition to our second major group of speech actions—*challenges*.

The third section will deal with the problem of establishing coherence between certain first and second parts of adjacency pairs that are not connected in any obvious way. We then discuss one major type of representation, the narrative, which plays an important part in four of the five episodes we are considering. We conclude with a brief consideration of sequencing rules.

Before we begin the exposition of the rules of discourse, it will be necessary to examine closely two central concepts that may be problematical in themselves: "rule" and "speech action."

Rules

Linguists use the term *rule* in ways that are distinctly different from the common, ordinary usage. To most people, "rule" means a prescriptive, explicit statement of what should or should not be done—a law, direction, command, moral, rule of thumb. It is a guide to action for a person faced with conscious choice. One such rule is that sentences should not end with prepositions; another is that the word "I" should not be used in dissertations. More serious rules about the use of language concern obscenity in print or directed toward authorities, laws of libel and slander, and so forth. The rules that are taught in English classes include both realistic norms for public speech and a series of less-realistic prescriptions that are largely ritual in character. Those who teach grammar to native speakers believe that these prescriptions are "rules of English," but those who teach speakers of another language have to confront the fact that the structure of a language is governed by a vast body of rules that are seldom perceived by native speakers.

The development of generative grammar in the past two decades has made linguists increasingly aware of the complexity of the syntactic rules needed to describe the most ordinary conversation. Though some of these involve conscious options, the great majority lie well below the level of consciousness and are quite obligatory. In psychology or sociology, such invariant rules are rare; it is difficult for those who have not studied linguistic details to appreciate the degree of invariance to be found in linguistic rules.

It is normal for people to concentrate upon the decisions that they must make. Speakers of English are aware of the existence of a rule governing "*Whom* did you visit?" as against "*Who* did you visit?"—whether or not they choose to obey it. However, they do not reflect upon the many rules they automatically obey in the formation of questions. One such invariant rule places a postverbal particle after pronoun objects. English speakers have a free choice in locating other noun phrases: *I picked the book* up or *I picked up the book*, but there is no choice at all about *I picked it up*. Native speakers do not have to reflect for a moment about the impossibility of *I picked up it*.

The rules of discourse that we present here are like the rules of syntax in their unconscious, invariant character. The rules of request that we will present are (as far as we know) compelling. A person can make a joke by refusing to apply them.

Would you mind taking the dust rag and just dust around?
No. [Does not move.]

The fact that such jokes are often played means that the rule operating here does not lie very far below ordinary consciousness. But the joke would not be funny if the rule did not exist and was not obligatory. By "obligatory," we mean that the speaker has no choice but to interpret a given action in the same way that all the members of society would.* His responses usually show us that he has so interpreted them. They do not always demonstrate this fact, and if we construct artificial violations his responses will not always demonstrate to us that the rules have been broken. The disturbances caused by such violations are often held below

---

*The obligatory nature of rules of interpretation in recognized by Sacks in the formulations he uses for a number of speech rules in "On the Analyzability of Children's Stories..." (1972b). The executive part of our Rules of Requests is in the format"... Then X will be heard as a valid Y..." Sacks' version of the same rule might read, "If a member originates a remark that can be interpreted as a request for action, and (here insert various beliefs and other conditions), then: hear it that way." The "sincerity conditions" of Gordon and Lakoff (1971) are obligatory rules of the same character.

the surface, and they may not emerge except under the most favorable circumstances.*

Some schizophrenic patients do respond consistently to such speech actions in an inappropriate way as in the example of incoherent discourse cited in Chapter 1:

A: *What is your name?*
B: *Well, let's say you might have though you had something from before, but you haven't got it anymore.*
A: *I'm going to call you Dean.* (From Laffal, 1965, p. 85.)

Whether they have lost their competence to interpret these questions correctly or do not do so for other reasons is not clear, but some of their behavior can be seen as a disturbance in the higher-level rules for the discourse rather than in the specifics of grammar.

Speech Actions

It will be very difficult to define an *action* by itself or set any boundaries to it. If a person is walking along, thinking about the weather, we could say of him that he was walking, strolling, going somewhere, thinking, reflecting, worrying, and so forth, and it would be difficult to say how many of these thoughts were individual actions, or when these actions began and ended. When people are interacting with each other, however, one person's actions set bounds to the actions of the other and, furthermore, help us to interpret what actions actually took place. If one speaker's action marks the boundary of the previous speaker's action, this assumes that the speakers have the competence to know when an action has been completed.†

Figure 5 lists interactional terms that include all of the speech actions that we will need in the five episodes. Though this is a long list, including many different kinds of requests, assertions, and metalinguistic actions, there is a much longer list that we have not mentioned. We have dealt with several rules that concern *challenges,* but there is no mention of *threats, promises,*

---

*The fact that the rule is compelling in some context does not mean that it is always to be applied. There are ambiguous situations where people incorrectly apply indirect rules of discourse instead of the more literal meaning. Ervin-Tripp (1976) has presented evidence of a number of cases where listeners have gone astray. For example, a caller on the telephone asks, "Is John there?" and is distressed to find himself suddenly speaking with John: he is preparing a surprise party and did not want to speak to John at all. Misunderstandings of this sort show that the rule exists in listeners' competence, just as children's over-generalizations show that they are capable of forming linguistic rules.

†A great deal of work has been done recently on *turntaking,* and the way in which speakers know when a turn of talk has been completed (Sacks, Schegloff, and Jefferson, 1974). This may or may not coincide with a speaker's ability to judge when a speech action has been completed and the response is demanded of him.

flattery, and so on. We deal with assertions, but not with *proclamations, boasts, apologies, excuses,* or many other actions that have been extremely important in discussion of rules of discourse (e.g., Searle, 1965).

I. REQUESTS

The Rule of Requests

The ordinary, common-sense understanding of commands is that they are executed with the use of the imperative in English. Thus the most straightforward way to order someone to come home is to say *Come home!* Conversely, the imperative *Come home!* normally is understood as an order, and this is contrasted with expressions such as *Will you please come home?* understood as a request, or *Isn't it about time for you to come home?* understood as a suggestion, or *It's getting late,* considered as a hint. The common characteristic of all of these speech events is that a speaker, A, is using verbal means to accomplish the end of getting the listener, B, to come home.* We subsume all these verbal techniques under a single abstract category, the *Request for Action.*†

Many general discussions of discourse problems have pointed out that the relationship between speech actions and utterances is much more complex than a one-to-one relation between imperatives and commands or requests. While this understanding is essential for progress in the field, there is an important sense in which the imperative is the unmarked‡ form of a request for action. Imperative constructions may be modified with the addition of forms like *please,* or *if you don't mind;* or they may be transformed by the addition of grammatical constructions like *would you mind . . .* so they are no longer recognizable as imperatives. Indirect forms of requests may not contain an imperative at all, but, for these forms to be

---

*Fraser points out (personal communication) that the speech act itself does not accomplish this action: its more limited function is to get the hearer to recognize that the speaker is trying to get him to act. Thus the speech act may succeed, but the listener may fail to act for reasons that may have nothing to do with the discourse. We still may assert that the speaker uses a verbal device to get certain acts accomplished, but this device is not necessarily sufficient in itself.

†The *Request for Action* includes a number of other subcategories of requests, which we will refer to in the following discussion: requests for information, for confirmation, for attention; these are all types of requests for action.

‡The "unmarked" character of the imperative does not relate to its social significance in this case, but rather to its structural position. In English, the imperative is a second person construction, with an underlying subject *you* (which appears most directly in the form "Drop that, won't you!"). It is thus connected closely with the directive function of language focused on the addressee. In most adult situations, the use of an unmodified imperative "Stop that!" is an aggravated form of command, and not a neutral expression.

recognized as requests for action, we need special mechanisms or additions to the basic rule of requests.

While the imperative is still the central element in the construction of requests, it is also true that many imperatives are not to be understood as requests for action at all. We must be able to distinguish jokes, insults, and proverbs from valid requests for action. This is the immediate function of the central Rule of Requests:*

RULE OF REQUESTS

If A addresses to B an imperative specifying an action X at a time T_1, and B believes that A believes that

    1a. X should be done (for a purpose Y) [*need for the action*]

      b. B would not do X in the absence of the request [*need for the request*]

    2. B has the *ability* to do X (with an instrument Z)

    3. B has the *obligation* to do X or is willing to do it.

    4. A has the *right* to tell B to do X,

then A is heard as making a valid request for action.

The rule is centrally involved in each episode, along with the many associated rules for making requests indirectly, putting off requests, requesting confirmation, and so on. Most of the discussion in the therapeutic session concerns events which involve the making or refusing of requests (see Chapter 5, p. 167).† The rule as it stands, in the form just given, will do a moderate amount of work for us in the episodes to follow. It will serve to distinguish a valid request from insults like *Drop dead*, from remarks like *Tell me another!*, or from jokes like *Give the President my regards!* The Rule of Requests does the essential work of letting us know when we are seriously

---

*This form of the rule is slightly more elaborate than earlier versions (Labov, 1970a, 1972a, Chapter 8): in particular, we have drawn the second part of precondition 3 and precondition 5 from Gordon and Lakoff's treatment. For a closer comparison with their "sincerity conditions," see below.

†As we have seen, Episode 1 is Rhoda's account of how she *requested* her mother to come home: *Well, when do you plan t'come home?* Episode 2 is Rhoda's response to the therapist's *request* that Rhoda *request* Aunt Editha for help; Rhoda shows how useless this would be by giving the account of Editha's response to her own *request, Would you mind taking the dust rag and just dust around?* In Episode 3, the therapist repeats her *request*, and Rhoda shows in even greater detail how she cannot depend upon Editha for help, with an account of what happened when Editha *requested* her to go out and eat in a restaurant instead of fixing dinner at home. She adds to this an account of how badly Editha behaves when she *requests* her to go to the store and get some milk or bread. Episode 4 is a response to the therapist's *request* for more information about Episode 1; it appears that mother is staying away from home because Rhoda's sister made repeated *requests* for her mother to stay at their house and babysit. Rhoda then gives a second version of her *request* to her mother to come home and help with the housework. Episode 5 is the therapist's major attempt to get Rhoda to recognize the existence of a number of underlying emotions; this takes the form of a number of *requests* for information, *Does it have anything to do with your weight? What are they feeling? What does that express?*

requested to perform an action, and when the imperative form has entirely different communicative value. But the simple imperative referred to in the rule is rarely used in actual conversational interaction; instead, requests are made through the Rule for Indirect Requests, which uses the preconditions 1–4 (see below), and through other even more indirect strategies.

We might consider a simpler account of conversational interaction in which the literal meaning of sentences is accepted and processed unless there is a specific reason to refer to the complex rule of requests (Fraser, personal communication), but the discussion of requests for information versus requests for action will indicate that this literal strategy would often lead to wrong results. It is very common for first interpretations of the surface meaning to yield requests for information, which are then interpreted as requests for action. If the Rule of Requests and its dependent rules for indirect requests were not available at all times, one would often accept such sentences as "Can you pass me the salt?" as requests for information. It appears that we must always be alert to the possibility that we are being requested to perform some type of action, and monitoring for this possibility takes precedence over other interpretations. This is another way of stating that the Rule of Requests and the Rule for Indirect Requests, considered subsequently, are always activated.

The four conditions for a valid request form a central mechanism that will be utilized by subsequent rules, and their operation will be made much more evident in the rules to follow. We will consider first three specific features of the rule formulation in the conditional *if* clauses and one in the executive *then* clause.

"An imperative." We argued that imperatives of the form *Do this!* or *Give me that!* are the basic forms in the Rule of Requests. It is also true that there are many mitigated forms that are obviously basic requests for action but do not contain imperatives:

Would you mind handing me that shirt?
Will you stop that?
You better not say that!

It is quite likely that the listener does not need any elaborate mechanism to recognize these as requests for action: the literal meaning of the additions *Would you mind* or *You better,* is rarely taken into account (see footnote on p. 83). Such mitigating expressions therefore function in the same way as *please.*

"At a time T_1." Many requests for action do not specify a time for the action to be performed:

Get milk.
Would you mind taking a dust rag and just dust around?

However, we enter *time* as an obligatory category because it is a necessary element in the interpretation of the action requested. If all the preconditions are present for a valid command, then the absence of any temporal expression is interpreted as meaning 'right now' or 'at the first available moment' or 'always' (as in *Be careful!*). Spatial expressions (locatives) do not have the same privileged status. *Get me a newspaper* is to be understood as 'right away' or 'as soon as you can', but there is nothing here to suggest where this action is to be done.

The obligatory character of the time category becomes apparent when we observe that this category can be utilized in making indirect requests as described later.

"B believes that A believes." The Rule of Requests does not refer to actual states of affairs, nor to what A believes to be the state of affairs, nor to what B believes. Our formulation refers to B's belief about A's beliefs. A may have made a very odd, insincere, or irrational request of B. What B does depends upon his belief about A's intention. It is clear that A, in making the request, must have some way of predicting what B will believe about when he himself believes. We are involved in a recursive set:

B believes that A believes...
A believes that B believes that A believes...
B believes that A believes that B believes that...

As an abbreviation for such an unlimited set of statements, we can say that A's beliefs are shared knowledge, social facts directly accessible to both A and B. We abbreviate the state of affairs by referring to the preconditions 1–4 as *AB-events*.*

"Valid request for action." The philosophical investigation of speech events frequently refers to *sincerity conditions*; the insightful discussion of requests by Gordon and Lakoff presents the request rule as a series of such sincerity conditions. Our term *valid request for action* is equivalent, but it emphasizes the objective nature of the social facts rather than implying something about the psychological state of the persons involved. There are cases in which the listener may condemn the speaker as entirely insincere but still feel obligated to carry out the request for action. Officers in the military services frequently give enlisted men commands that fail all of the precon-

---

*The notation "AB-event" is part of a set of terms that will be useful at many points in our exposition of the rules (see p. 62). These categorizations involve the knowledge that both participants have about the access each of them has to any given piece of factual information. Thus, AB-event means that both A and B know that both A and B have knowledge of this event. As for example, "Well, we're here together," or "it's still morning," and so on. See the Rule of Confirmation (p. 100) for the complete system.

ditions from a subjective viewpoint, but that are entirely valid according to the recognized social facts of what the speaker is expected to believe.

The Preconditions. The four conditions for a valid request rarely are stated explicitly when a request is made directly in imperative form. Their explicit use will be seen much more often in the rules for making requests indirectly, putting them off, or refusing them. The four refer successively to *needs, abilities, obligations* (or *desires*), and *rights.**

It is an interesting exercise to search for examples where one or more of the preconditions hold and the others do not hold. In the case of *Drop dead!* the utterance fails all four conditions: there is usually no real need for the person to drop dead, he cannot do so at will, he has no obligation to do so, and the speaker has no right to tell him to do so.

The full utility of the preconditions will be exemplified in the detailed discussions to follow. It is important to note that some of the preconditions actually may not exist until the moment the request is made. The words that form the request may also give information on the necessary beliefs. For example, *Give me a match* lets the hearer know that the speaker has a need for the match at the same time that he makes the request, even if there was no previous knowledge of his need. B may then infer that the condition existed at some previous time, and it therefore may be referred to as a precondition. These preconditions play an extremely important role in making requests indirectly, putting off requests, and refusing them. They also provide the major modes of mitigation and aggravation to be considered below.

The Rule of Requests is written in a form that applies equally to the speaker and the hearer. Operating under the conditions of this rule, the speaker constructs an utterance that will be recognized as a valid request; the hearer simultaneously is constrained to hear it as such. It is obvious that he may not fulfill the request, but within the common framework he cannot effectively deny that a request was made of him. Searle and Fraser approach the speech act from the speaker's perspective, and see it as successful if the speaker gets the hearer to recognize his intention (Fraser,

---

*Gordon and Lakoff utilize three of the five terms that appear in our rule: needs, abilities, and desires. Their equivalent of our *need* precondition is the predicate WANT; (and for 1b, simply the nonexistence of the action); their equivalent of *ability* is the predicate CAN; and of desire or willingness, their predicate WILLING. Obligations and rights do not appear in their discussion; this is understandable since they consider hypothetical conversations that are not located in any social context. As we will see, the importance of such social elements as rights and obligations are elicited and made obvious by the larger context of the social environment. The higher-level actions and the most important connections between utterances we will consider are necessarily involved with such social predicates, and these will play a crucial role in our examination of the actual episodes of the therapeutic interview.

personal communication). We have noted that the speaker's utterance does contribute something towards the state of shared knowledge that makes this recognition possible. However, this is only a small part of the structure of commonly recognized social facts that determines the interpretation of the utterance. In our study of the use of requests in the therapeutic session, it will become increasingly apparent that most of the information needed to interpret actions is already to be found in the structure of shared knowledge and not in the utterances themselves.

Rule for Indirect Requests

In our therapeutic session, and in many other conversations that we have reviewed, direct requests are in the minority. Demands of face-to-face social interaction require that mitigating devices be used between adults, or when a child is making a request of an adult. Many of the most complex examples of indirect relationships between surface structure and underlying speech acts involve the Rule for Indirect Requests. This rule is built on the basic Rule of Requests by referring to the preconditions for a valid request. It shows how such a valid request can be made without uttering the imperative expression "Do X!" There are many kinds of indirect reference to this desired action X; it is apparent that questions about X that exhibit an interest in X will be interpreted as requests for X to be performed—always bearing in mind that the basic preconditions prevail. Thus any question about the existential status of this action will be constructed as the request itself is. Some statements made about the existential status of the action do not make a request—usually negatives. On the other hand, some positive or probabilistic statements can be used as requests for confirmation, not requests for action (see below).

The Rule for Indirect Requests also makes use of the obligatory time slot, which plays a role in the central request for Episode 1: "When do you plan to come home?" The number of different ways of making indirect requests expands most rapidly, though, when we consider ways of referring to the underlying preconditions. The formal rule has four subsections,

RULE FOR INDIRECT REQUESTS

If A makes to B a Request for Information or an assertion to B about
   a. the existential status of an action X to be performed by B
   b. the consequences of performing an action X
   c. the time T_1 that an action X might be performed by B
   d. any of the preconditions for a valid request for X as given in the Rule of Requests

and all other preconditions are in effect, then A is heard as making a valid request of B for the action X.

To illustrate the operation of the Rule for Indirect Requests, we will consider possible variants of the requests made in Episode 2 of the therapeutic session (see Chapter 6).

2.6[b]   *"Wellyouknow, w'dy'mind takin' thedustrag an' just dustaround?"*

This was a request from the patient, Rhoda, to her Aunt Editha reported in a very rapid style as indicated above. Here Rhoda refers to the third precondition: Editha's willingness to carry out this action.*

Although our main discussion will deal with the text as it actually occurs, the discourse rules present a general view of speech actions and possible ways of executing them. We can illustrate various uses of the rule for the same underlying requests by constructing such alternative possibilities:

a.	Existential Status:†	*Have you dusted yet?*
		You don't seem to have dusted this room yet.
b.	Consequences:	*How would it look if you were to dust this room?*
		This room would look a lot better if you dusted it.
c.	Time Referents:	*When do you plan to dust?*
		How long will you let this go on?
		I imagine you will be dusting this evening.
d.	Other Preconditions:	
	Need for the Action:	*Don't you think the dust is pretty thick?*
		This place is really dusty.
	Need for the Request:	*Are you planning to dust this room?*
		I don't have to remind you to dust this room.
	Ability:	*Can you grab a dust rag and just dust around?*
		You have time enough to dust before you go.
	Willingness:	*Would you mind picking up a dust rag?*
		I'm sure you wouldn't mind picking up a dust rag and just dusting around.
	Obligation:	*Isn't it your turn to dust?*
		You ought to do your part in keeping this place clean.

---

*One mode of analysis is to consider *would you mind* as a frozen, mitigating form, without any content, comparable to *please*. As we note below, this is possible for a number of the indirect devices that are commonly used. In that case, this would be a mitigated form of a direct request under the basic rule; but since the Rule for Indirect Requests can account for these frozen forms, we include them in this analysis with the added note that there are varying degrees of "transparency" of the indirect constructions. We should add that it is also possible to use *would you mind* as an "opaque" reference to the other person's willingness to perform the action, so that an appropriate reponse might be *Yes, I would mind*. (For further discussion of this issue see Sadock, 1974.)

†The need to relate the assertions under a. and c. to the hearer B was brought to our attention by J. Sadock.

Rights: *Didn't you ask me to remind you to dust this place?*
                            I'm supposed to look after this place, but not do all the work.

In the fourth class of indirect requests, the number of possible variants appears to be multiplying rapidly. It is clear that there are an unlimited number of ways in which we can refer to the preconditions, and this poses a serious problem if we want to make firm connections between these discourse rules and actual sentence production. It is not at all obvious that a generative grammar* could be written that would carry us from the underlying speech action to the actual sentence forms. After the fact, we can identify a given remark or question as a reference to an underlying action X, but we cannot give the speaker a finite list of possible ways in which to refer to this action. The action of dusting a room can be referred to in very many ways, and a person's willingness to perform this action in very many ways; the end result is a very large, open set of possible indirect requests.

Mitigation and Aggravation. Throughout our discussion, we will be referring to the basic interactive dimension of mitigation and aggravation. In all discussions of discourse, analysts take into account the subject's desire to mitigate or modify his expression to avoid creating offense. Given the nature of most texts, we do not see the dimension of aggravation as often, but a consideration of all possibilities shows that this interactive dimension extends in both directions from the unmarked or neutral form of a request.†

In considering the possible realizations of the Rule for Indirect Requests, we encounter an immediate asymmetry in the use of certain subparts of the rule. It is very natural to ask *Can you dust this room?* as this is a conventional routine for mitigated requests. We do not so quickly see the context in which the corresponding assertion might be used: *You can dust this room,* or (to eliminate the ambiguity of *can*) *You have the time to dust this room.* At first glance, many people find such forms implausible because they sound impolite, but if we consider the very common types of discourse that take place between parents and their children, we may find that aggravating forms predominate in many households. There are several general princi-

---

   *That is, a set of rules that would produce all the well-formed utterances that could represent any given speech act, and no other utterances.

   †That is not to say that our possibilities are symmetrical in both directions. The number of mitigating possibilities seems to be elaborated far beyond those for aggravating. It should be noted also that there are other continuous dimensions along which speech acts vary that cannot be identified with mitigation and aggravation. For example, expressions of thanks and flattery may be minimized or intensified (Fraser, personal communication).

ples or tendencies that seem to determine whether a form is mitigating or aggravating. References to needs and abilities are generally mitigating, while references to rights and obligations are aggravating. The third precondition is split between *obligation* and *willingness*, which are in complementary distribution: if it is a social fact that an obligation does not exist, then the speaker may inquire into or assert the willingness of the other party to perform the action. The use of this half of the third precondition is therefore more polite than reference to an obligation.*

A second likely generalization is that requests for information are higher on the scale of mitigation than assertions, and that tag questions are intermediate. We then have three steps along the scale of mitigation:

You have enough time to dust the room.
You have enough time to dust the room, don't you?   MITIGATION
Do you have enough time to dust the room?

The three-way contrast yields even larger steps along the scale when we consider references to existential status:

This room is going to be dusted.
This room is going to be dusted, isn't it?   MITIGATION
Is this room going to be dusted?

The form *will you* is ambiguous within the rule because unstressed *will* still retains some of its original meaning of 'volition' as well as the existential meaning of 'future'.

You will dust this room.
You will dust the room, won't you?   MITIGATION
Will you dust the room?

Again, it will be possible to consider this use of *will* as "transparent," so that most listeners hear it immediately as a polite way of asking for the action; then *will* forms can be arranged with others along the scale of mitigation, here reversed towards aggravation:

Will you please dust the room?
Will you dust the room?
Please dust the room!   AGGRAVATION
Dust the room!
Dust the goddamn room!†

---

*There is a striking counterexample to this generalization noted by R. Lakoff (1969) showing that reference to obligation can be extremely polite, as in *You must have a cookie.*

†Note that the expletive *goddamn* is attached to the word *room*, though its force is directed to the listener. There are many other interesting grammatical aspects to aggravated forms of requests, but their investigation is not as relevant to our current study of therapeutic discourse as is the investigation of mitigation.

request may be refused with reasonable politeness is to give an accounting: an unaccounted refusal can lead to a break in social relations (a "huff" in Goffman's terms; see subsequent discussion). If an accounting is given, then it is always possible for the request to be renewed if the conditions governing the account can be shown to have changed. It is therefore quite rare to find an absolute refusal which does not permit the request to arise again. The great majority of reasonably polite refusals are forms of putting off a request, or what might be called indirect refusals. Once an accounting is given, one cannot say that the request has been refused in any permanent or absolute sense: it is only refused as long as the conditions mentioned in the accounting are found to prevail (or until the information requested is given). In that sense, any accounted refusal can be considered a form of "putting off" the request. This follows from a fundamental mechanism of discourse: in denying or questioning one of the preconditions for the request, B implicitly accepts all those preconditions that he has not denied or questioned. When his objections are met or his own requests for information are supplied, the original request is automatically reinstated (see p. 93).

Relayed Requests

A special mechanism for putting off requests comes into play when someone requests another person to make a request of a third person: if A requests B to make a request of C. In this case, all four preconditions may be in effect. Yet even if B has the *ability* to make the request of C, he may be able to assert that there would be no point in doing so, arguing from previous experience that he knows that C will not agree. Thus we have the special *Rule of Relayed Requests:*

If A requests B to make a request of C, and B asserts that C is not likely to comply with the request, B is heard as putting off the original request from A.

Requests for Information

We use the term *request* as a generic category, which includes many different kinds of actions. As noted above, we include commands, orders, pleas, petitions, and so forth, as various forms of requests in which the relative status of A and B differ, and, as a consequence, their mutual rights, duties, and obligations. There are also different kinds of actions requested: we can distinguish requests for *information, confirmation, attention,* and *permission*. There is a close relationship between requests for information and general requests for action; instead of saying, "Give me X," a speaker may say, "Give me information about X." All of the considerations that we brought to bear in discussing rules of requests also will apply, so we might dispense with a special rule for requests for information, but we can make the following observations about the differences in the preconditions between requests for action and requests for information. In requests for information:

1. The time T_1 is usually identical with the time of the utterance T_0, so much of the mechanism involving assertions and questions about time is set aside.
2. The *need* for the action to be performed is almost always signaled by the act of asking the question itself. However, there are many questions where it is obvious that A already has the information. When it is evident that A has the information, and there is no immediate need for the information, the utterance is then heard as one of a number of different speech acts, depending on the other conditions that prevail. One such speech act is the Request for Display, common in school situations, where the request is for B to display whether or not he has the information, and the information requested is actually the state of B's knowledge. There are also a variety of rhetorical questions, in which no information is being requested at all.
3. For many requests for information, we are dealing with "free goods" (a term originated by Erving Goffman), where the obligation to respond is constant and general for all B.
4. In the great majority of requests for information, A's right to ask for the information is general and constant.

We are therefore in a position to write a simpler rule, recognizing the fact that there will remain some cases where rights and obligations are an issue.*

REQUEST FOR INFORMATION

If A addresses to B an imperative requesting information I, or an interrogative focusing on I, and B does *not* believe that A believes that
   a. A has I
   b. B does not have I
then A is heard as making a valid request for information.

This rule does not specify what kind of response B will give, but only whether or not he will find it necessary to respond to the utterance as a

---

*Many of these cases involve a subtle difference between the right to request information and the right to have it. A classic case is the person who has a boil or lesion from a venereal disease. A friend may have a right to ask him what the matter is, but no right to have the answer. The problem is that in telling someone that he does not have the right to certain information, a great deal of information is released. This leads to many difficult problems of communication, which complicate the rules for requests for information, but these are not major problems in the sessions we are studying.

request for information. This rule excludes two special cases: where A plainly knows the answer and does not need the information, and where he knows that B does not have the information, and so could not get it from him. Both of these situations occur in a variety of forms, which can be termed variously "rhetorical questions," "test questions," "baiting questions," and so on (Labov, 1971).

This rule for requests for information is plainly much simpler than the basic rule of requests. It would obviously be advantageous if we could immediately recognize an utterance as a request for information, and use this rule without having to inspect all of the preconditions for the basic rule. But this does not seem to be possible in actual social interaction. It is necessary to inspect each request for information to see if it is governed by the Rule for Indirect Requests. The consequences of not responding to a request for action are serious and can lead to breaches of social relations. However, it may not be necessary for the listener to inspect *all* the preconditions of the basic Rule of Requests. As soon as it becomes evident that one of the preconditions for a valid request for action is not fulfilled, then the utterance can be treated as a request for information under the simpler rule.

We can see how this mechanism operates in one of the many requests for information directed to Rhoda by the therapist. In Episode 4, the therapist says:

4.4 Th.: *Now—tell me: Why is mother staying there so long—I don't understand. Is it something the matter there?*

Both interrogatives represents requests for information. In the first, the therapist addresses to Rhoda a request for information about her mother's staying at her sister's house. Rhoda has already shown that she does not have the ability to do anything about this; if this were not the case, this interrogative might very well be interpreted as an underlying request for Rhoda to do something about the situation. In the context of Episode 4, it is clearly a request for information: The therapist asserts that condition A prevails; she does not have the information I. Since the *ability* precondition of the Rule of Requests has been negated, we are sure that it is not a request for action. In the same way, it is clear that if there *is* something the matter at Rhoda's sister's house, Rhoda herself is not in a position to do something about it. The same utterance in other circumstances could very well be a request for action.

Putting off requests with requests for information. We have seen previously that many ways of putting off requests involve the use of interrogatives that are themselves requests for information. Many discussions of conversational forms refer to the phenomenon of "answering a question with a question." Two kinds of examples are often given:

A: *Do you want your raincoat?*
B: *Do you think it will rain?*

A: *How are you today?*
B: (with a shrug) *How should I be?*

We prefer not to use the term *question* for these responses, since this term ambiguously refers to either the interrogative form or the action itself, and this is a fundamental distinction of our analysis that we wish to maintain. In both of the examples given above, B answers with an interrogative form, but only in the second example could we say that he is "answering a question with a question." The utterance *How should I be?* actually is intended as an answer to A and is not expected to elicit an answer itself. However, *Do you think it will rain?* is not designed as an answer to the request for information *Do you want your raincoat?* It can be a sincere or valid request for information in a sense that *How should I be?* is not. It is a *response* to the preceding request for information, but a very particular type:

RULE OF EMBEDDED REQUESTS

If A makes a request for action of B, and B responds with a request for information, B is heard as asserting that he needs this information in order to respond to A's request.*

The Rule of Embedded Requests is very general and compelling, and never is violated in ordinary conversation as far as we know. When A hears B make his request for information, he automatically searches for a proposition of the form:

A person needs the information I in order to respond to the request for action X.

If A did not search for such a proposition, we would observe sequences like:

A: *Are you teaching tomorrow?*
B: *Did you say you have three children?*
A: *Yes.*
B: *No.*

In actual practice, the third line of such a dialogue might read, "What has that got to do with it?" since A would not find B's conduct coherent in the

---

*Note that the first request for action that A makes may be a request for information, which is a subcategory of request for action. The embedded request is usually in interrogative form, but of course it may also be a declarative or imperative form following the Rule for Indirect Requests.

light of the rule just given, and would then question the relevance of the response.

Because requests for information are subcategories of requests for action, the Rule of Embedded Requests is recursive: it sets up the conditions for its further application, and we can get one series inserted within another. The parallel to self-embedded structures within a sentence is clear, and in both cases the rules produce very complicated sequences that in actual practice are difficult to realize.*

The Rule of Embedded Requests is used very often in our therapeutic session as well as in other conversations that we have examined.

1.8 ... *"Well, when do you plan t'come* **home***?"*
1.9 *"Oh, why-y?"*

1.9 does not fit the rules for requests for information given above in respect to the important condition that the listener must believe that the speaker believes that he does not have the information. In this case, Rhoda's mother indicates by her intonation contour that she already knows the answer to her question. This is therefore a "rhetorical request for information." It may be answered by giving the information requested, but other options that are not open to a valid request for information are possible too.

The fact that 1.9 is a rhetorical request for information has important consequences for Rhoda's interpretation of what her mother is doing. We have included all such responses under the general heading of "putting off" a request, but there are obviously different degrees of sincerity in the mechanism used, which indicate the different intentions of the speaker. We can say that 1.9 does more than put off the request: it is a refusal in an important sense. We can therefore invoke a *Sub-Rule of Redundant Responses:*

If A makes a request for action of B, and B responds with a request for information which A and B know that B does not need, then B is heard as provisionally refusing the request.

*Schegloff notes the parallel between embedded sentence structures and embedded requests (1972), but there may be special conditions on such double insertions that are needed in order to make the series intelligible. We do not have any evidence of such unmodified sequences as

    A: *Are you going to teach tomorrow?*
    B: *Is it going to rain tomorrow?*
    A: *Are you asking me?*
    B: *Yes.*
    A: *No.*
    B: *Yes.*

In such cases, it may be necessary to insert phrases that identify the correct bracketing, for example, *"Are you asking me?" "Yes." "Well I don't think so." "Well in that case, I am gonna teach."*

Reinstating Requests

An important consequence of all that has preceded is that the normal way of refusing requests offers an opportunity for the request to be made again. Since most refusals involve an accounting in some form, such as a request for further information, they can be defined by the requester as only temporary refusals. It is possible for him to maintain his position and continue to make his request by complying literally with any request for information which has been made of him. It will not be necessary for him to repeat his request if he gives the information without delay. Thus there is a further *Rule for Reinstating Requests:*

If B has responded to a request for action from A by making a request for information, and A gives that information, then A is heard as making the original request for action again.

Such a situation sets up the possibility of a long chain of repeated requests.

II. CHALLENGES

Requests Heard as Critical

So far, we have been considering requests for action and information as relatively neutral events from an interactive point of view. These speech actions have been discussed in the linguistic literature as communicative techniques that are basically extensions of sentence grammars that are used to facilitate the exchange of referential information. But our examination of requests for action and information in actual discourse shows that their interactive significance goes far beyond the communicative functions we have discussed so far. We find that most of these requests are employed to accomplish other purposes, which strongly affect the social and emotional relations of the persons involved.

An appropriate use of requests involves more than the form: the timing of the request is also important. A person who is competent at performing the roles assigned to him in relation to others will make his requests in ways that are consistent with his role as a competent person. Before he makes a request, it first must become evident to him that he cannot help himself and therefore has to impose on others for their assistance. At the same time, there are circumstances when he expects the other person to see his need first and help him without being asked. If he is disappointed in this expectation and is forced to make an explicit request, he frequently will demonstrate his displeasure. If a request is not responded to when it is first made, both speaker and listener know that a repetition of the request is loaded with social consequences. In all these matters, we see that requests can affect the relative social status of the two persons involved; a failure to make requests appropriately or respond to them appropriately often is cited as evidence that the other party cannot fill the social role he has been claiming.

We first will consider the general rule of etiquette that one should be attentive to other persons' needs so they do not have to make explicit requests for ordinary routines of social interaction. The operation of this rule may be seen in the crowded aisles of supermarkets. When people are asked to move so that another person can pass, they frequently apologize to the stranger for having been in the way. In these situations, the person who receives the request frequently shows a startled reaction, as if he has realized for the first time that a condition prevails that should have been corrected without his being asked. A general consideration here is that there are many obligations that a person must fulfill in order to be seen as performing his normal role in society with full competence. Mothers are expected to look out for their children before they get into trouble, teachers are expected to foresee their students' needs, hosts to anticipate their guests' desires, and pedestrians to anticipate the path of other pedestrians so that they will not come into collision (Goffman, 1971).

When a person takes an action implying that another person did not perform some of these role obligations, he is necessarily heard as criticizing that other person's competence in that role. This applies to problems of initiating role performance, performing the role correctly, or terminating it appropriately.

All these considerations underlie an important rule of discourse which operates in many points in our text:

RULE OF DELAYED REQUESTS
If A makes a request for B to perform an action X in role R, based on needs, abilities, obligations, and rights which have been valid for some time, then A is heard as challenging B's competence in role R.

This rule shows that the basic Rule of Requests refers to and is based on a large part of the social structure that is relevant to any given context; an understanding of the rights, needs, and obligations that are invoked is needed if we are to understand the force with which requests are made.

Most people become conscious of the mechanism reflected in the Rule of Delayed Requests only in the most overt cases, especially when the request is repeated. The rule just given includes the case where a request for action has already been made, and not complied with. In this case, the four preconditions obviously have been in effect, and the criticism is felt even more forcibly than if the request had not been made. We can state this corollary as:

RULE OF REPEATED REQUESTS
If A makes a request for action X of B in role R, and A repeats the request before B has responded, then A is heard as emphatically challenging B's performance in role R.

Because repeated requests are an aggravated form of criticism, challenging the other's competence quite sharply, it is a common practice for speakers to mitigate their repetitions by varying their form. Though a challenge to competence is always present when a request is repeated, the more the surface structure is varied, the less strongly is this challenge felt. This principle applies to requests repeated after B has responded to the first request by refusing it or putting it off, as well as to the case where B has not responded at all.

When Rhoda asks her mother in Episode 1, 1.8, *When do you plan to come home?* we do not immediately feel the force of the Rule of Delayed Requests. However, if we refer backward to her imagined question of 1.7: *Look—uh—I mean y'been there long enough* we can see the Rule of Delayed Requests operating more clearly. The fact that Rhoda begins her projected utterance with *Look* indicates that she feels that it will be necessary to call her mother's attention to something her mother has been overlooking. It seems that any use of *look* in initiating a request would imply that the other person has not been giving full attention to the needs of the person speaking.

As an example of the Rule of Repeated Requests, let us consider three requests put to Rhoda by the therapist:

2.2[f]   Th.: *Now **what** about Aunt Editha, she doesn't help you in the house?*

2.4[a]   Th.: *Well, what would happen if you **said** something to her—to—since we're in the, in the business of **talking**, yes.*

3.1[a]   Th.: *But what would happen if you—um—you know—tried to arrive at some working relationship with her—* . . .

There are many other ways of criticizing and challenging in conjunction with requests. One specific form that recurs in our text is the use of the "Yiddish rise–fall intonation," which appears in such expression as:

2.8[b]   R.: ***That** looks **clean** to you?*

3.22   R.: *I s'd, "That's **enough**?"*

The rise–fall intonation is documented in texts (see pp. 201, 246), and its significance has been discussed in linguistic analysis (Weinreich, 1956). It may be translated roughly as 'If you think this is the case, you are crazy.' There are many more obvious ways of aggravating criticisms by showing impatience, abruptness, and anger in the prosodic features used with the request. In general, the making of requests is a delicate business and requires a great deal of supporting ritual to avoid damaging personal relations surrounding it.

General Challenges to Competence

The Rule of Delayed Requests and the Rule of Repeated Requests can be seen as special cases of a more general principle that governs challenges to other persons' competence. We can state the most general rule as follows:

RULE OF OVERDUE OBLIGATIONS
If A asserts that B has not performed obligations in a role R, then A is heard as challenging B's competence in R.

This rule applies so often in the course of ordinary conversation that we will be specifying its occurrence only in those special cases where it is not obvious. Most of the general propositions we find in conversation will include some challenge to another person's competence as a result of his failure to perform some role in a way that satisfies the speaker. At this point, it may be appropriate to define the term *challenge* again. First we must define a *status* as a position of a person in the social structure, which includes a set of rights and obligations. To maintain a status, a person must behave in a competent or appropriate manner according to the prevailing social norms.

Many statuses are relatively permanent, and even when a person's competence in that status is severely criticized, he continues to hold it. His *esteem* in that status may be lowered. Thus a parent may be criticized as careless or irresponsible, but only under the most extreme circumstances will society deprive a person of the rights of a natural parent.*

Though challenges to a person's competence in a status may not result in an immediate loss of that status, the challenge must always be heard in light of the fact that some persons have been deprived of a status that is normally ascribed to them, or at least deprived of some of the rights that go with that status. A father can be deprived of his rights over his children, or even the right to live with them. A prince can be dethroned, so even if he maintains that he is the true and rightful prince, he will have lost the rights that accompany that status.

The status of *adult* is a crucial one in our material and in many other therapeutic sessions that we have studied: it is marked by its instability and is the subject of many challenges. The importance of maintaining adult

---

*The distinction between loss of status and loss of esteem in that status has been pointed out to us by E. Goffman (personal communication).

status cannot be overestimated: it includes the right to make a wide range of decisions that affect a person's own future. In one meaning, *adult* is an ascribed status: anyone over 18 is technically an adult in certain legal senses. There are many social mechanisms that deprive grown persons of full adult status and place them in the position of dependent persons without the rights of an adult. This loss of adult rights affects people who are seen as sick, unemployed, aged, or criminal. The struggle for these rights is a crucial matter in family interaction, and challenges to a person's adult status is a serious matter within the family.

A *challenge* is *a speech act that asserts or implies a state of affairs that, if true, would weaken a person's claim to be competent in filling the role associated with a valued status.* It therefore follows that a challenge, if successful, may result in a person's losing his claim to hold the status involved.

Challenging Propositions

Instead of challenging the behavior of a person in a certain role, we often find a challenge directed to a proposition he has uttered. A challenge to a proposition is often termed a *question,* and we will use the term "question" in this sense (as distinct from 'interrogative' and/or 'request for action'). It is possible to raise a question about a statement or proposition that has no immediate consequences for personal interaction.

A: *It's only 3:00.*
B: *Your watch must be a little fast.*

The crucial case for our purposes arises when a statement is made that is fully supported by the status of the speaker, so a question or challenge directed to that statement is necessarily a challenge to the competence of the person to hold that status. Thus we have the *Rule for Challenging Propositions:*

If A asserts a proposition that is supported by A's status, and B questions the proposition, then B is heard as challenging the competence of A in that status.

The operation of this rule is seen most closely in interactions with authorities. If a policeman makes a remark about the time of the day, as above, there is no challenge to his status in questioning it. If, however, the question is directed at some proposition supported by his authority, his reaction can be very sharp. It is impossible to question a policeman's assertion that a car is blocking the way or that someone has been driving too fast, etc., without questioning his status and authority.

In our therapeutic session, we observe a distinct reaction from the therapist to behavior by the patient that seems to question the basic suggestion of therapy: that one should express one's needs and emotions to relevant others. In questioning this suggestion, Rhoda is necessarily questioning the therapist's fundamental competence; it is not surprising that she is able to evoke such a reaction (see Episode 3).

One obvious characteristic of challenges and questions is that they demand a response as immediately as requests for action or information. In our interactional statements, this characteristic will be indicated by arrows that point forward (to the right), indicating an expectation of something to follow. What is expected? Because these actions have even sharper consequences for personal relations than do requests for action, the options are more sharply outlined. The reply to a challenge or question is either a *defense* or an *admission*. One might then characterize challenges more generally as "requests for admission or defense."

III. COHERENCE

We have considered in some detail a wide range of requests along with some modes of negative response. We can turn now to some forms of positive response to requests for information, where the information requested is being supplied. In most cases, there is no problem in recognizing the discourse rules operating because the grammatical form of the response is connected closely to the grammatical form of the request for information; but there are many cases where this is not so, and a formal examination of the sequences involved would not show any obvious coherence even when our intuitive responses plainly register this as coherent discourse. We will consider next several such cases and the discourse rules that apply.

Rule for Indirect Responses

The Rule of Embedded Requests (p. 91) shows that there may be many implicit propositions that must be located if we are to demonstrate the coherence of discourse. This becomes even more evident when we consider certain responses to requests that take the form of declarative sentences. In general, we know that a response is tied coherently to a request if it takes a syntactic form that is easily reconstructed as parallel to the request. In the case of responses to a simple yes–no question, the answers usually can be expanded to supply the existential qualifier that is missing in the request. Thus we would expand:

A: *Are you going home?*
B: *Yes.* → Yes, I am going home, or Yes, it is true that I am going home.

In many cases, there is partial ellipsis, which may be filled in by regular rules. The substitute form *so* stands for a complete proposition:

5.11[b]   Th.: *Does it have anything to do with ... your ... weight?*
5.12[c]   R.: *No, I don't think so!* → No. I don't think it has anything to do with my weight!

However, in many cases there is no simple rule of ellipsis that allows us to see the connection between the response and the preceding request. Typically we have such sequences as:

> A: *Are you going to class today?*
> B: *It's such a beautiful day.*

If A is satisfied with B's response, it is because he sees it as the coherent reply to his request. Without any rules of ellipsis to relate this overt syntactic form of the response to his question, he must locate it in an underlying proposition by the following:

RULE OF IMPLICIT RESPONSES
If A makes a request of B of the form Q (S_1), and B responds with a statement S_2, and there exists no rule of ellipsis that would expand S_2 to include S_1, then B is heard as asserting that there exists a proposition, known to both A and B, of the form *if* S_2, *then* $(E)S_1$.

Here E is an "existential" of the form *likely, usually, probably, certainly*, etc. Thus in the example given above, A should be able to locate a proposition of the form, If it is a beautiful day, then persons (including B) (are less likely to, are certain not to, somewhat less inclined to) go to class. If A does not locate such a proposition, he is entitled to return to B and say, "What has that got to do with the price of eggs?" or some other idiomatic responses to possible irrelevance. This is an invariant rule, in the sense that B's statement forces A to examine his own knowledge for the possibility of such a proposition. The search for the underlying proposition is parallel to the search involved in the Rule of Embedded Requests above (see p. 91).

In our text, we find that Rhoda typically answers the therapist's requests by giving a narrative illustrating her point, without any overt statement of its relevance. For example:

3.1[a]   Th.: *But what would happen if you—um—you know—tried to arrive at some working relationship with her ...*
3.2[a]   R.: *Sso-like-las'night—like, on Wednesday night is my late—one of my late nights—*

Here the therapist must supply the connection herself. But it is not a simple application of the Rule of Implicit Responses given above. She is expected to evaluate the narrative as a whole, see the evaluative point, and conclude, 'If this is so, then persons, including R, would be less apt to arrive at some working relationship with this person.'

Rule of Confirmation

So far, we have been considering cases that are initiated by requests in interrogative form. There are many cases where the responses of listeners indicate that they heard a request, though no interrogative precedes.

3.15[a]   Th.: *And it never occurred to her to prepare dinner.*
   [b]   R.: *No.*
   [c]   Th.: *She was home all afternoon.*
   [d]   R.: *No, she doesn't know how.*
3.17[a]   Th.: *But she does go to the store...*
   [b]   R.: *Yes.*

These yes–no responses indicate that a yes–no question was perceived; yet the first sentence is in the form of a declarative statement. This is the result of one of the simplest and most consistent rules of discourse that operate in ordinary conversation, the Rule of Confirmation. It depends upon the classification of statements according to the shared knowledge involved. We can set up the following fundamental classification, which will be useful for other rules of discourse as well:

   A-events: Known to A, but not to B.
   B-events: Known to B, but not to A.
   AB-events: Known to both A and B.
   O-events: Known to everyone present.
   D-events: Known to be disputable.

These classifications refer to social facts—that is, generally agreed upon categorizations shared by all those present. If there is any doubt about the status of a particular event, it automatically falls into the class of D-events. A-events are those that typically concern A's emotions, his daily experience in other contexts, elements in his past biography, and so on. We can thus state the following:

RULE OF CONFIRMATION
If A makes a statement about B-events, then it is heard as a request for confirmation.

This rule explains the behavior of Rhoda in the examples given above. The therapist makes a statement about events they both agree are known only to Rhoda. 3.15[a] is heard as equivalent to "And isn't it true that it never occurred to her to prepare dinner?" The fact that this is a request for confirmation and not a simple request for information is shown in what happens when B has to contradict A's expectation. A recent series of interviews considering life in New York City included a question designed to

Here the indefinite time reference *once* serves the function of introducing the narrative in accordance with the rule. Episode 3 shows a parallel placement of a narrative:

3.1[a] Th.: *But what would happen if you—um—you know—tried to arrive at some working relationship with her—* . . .

3.2[a] R.: *Sso-like-las' night—like, on Wednesday night is one of my late—one of my late nights—*

Here the only reference to the general proposition that might have answered the request is the word *like*, which is immediately followed by the time reference *last night*, which orients the listener to the narrative to follow. Note that in all the cases cited, the orienting sentence is not a reportable event in itself and does not function as a speech action that would respond in itself to the request of the therapist.

Narrative Sequencing. Once the listener knows that a narrative is being delivered, he will automatically apply the basic narrative rule. The fundamental structure of narrative depends upon the use of "narrative clauses," which have as their main verbs preterit or present forms: that is, verbs referring to the actual occurrence of actions that might be separated in time from other actions.* The structure of the narrative is established by the presence of *temporal junctures* between these narrative clauses. If the order of the clauses was reversed, then the interpretation of the sequence of the original events also would be changed. This fact not only defines the narrative structure itself, but rests upon the fundamental rule of interpretation:

RULE OF NARRATIVE SEQUENCING

In a narrative, if A refers to an event with a sentence S_1 that has a nonstative main verb in the preterit or present tense, and then refers to another event with a sentence S_2 of the same structure, then B will hear A as asserting that the event referred to by S_1 took place before the event referred to by S_2.

Such sequencing appears in the conversational exchange Rhoda reports between herself and other members of the family:

---

*The basic form for a narrative involves nonstative preterit past tense forms, such as *went*, *thought*, and so on. Present tense forms frequently used to indicate "past more vivid" in the traditional sense. The rules for the use of historical present" are not well known; in current American English, the use of past and present forms. In this people are not aware of their own use, and only observation of narratives in actual conversation will reveal this fundamental rule. 3.9[a], *She s'd* . . . versus 3.11[a] *Sh' says* . . .).

4.12   So I says t'her, "Are you coming home **tomorrow** *morning?*"
4.13   So she s'd, "Why-y?"
4.14   A-and–I said, "–well, it's getting a little too **much.**"
4.15   So she s'd, "See, *I told you so.*"

Here the rule of narrative sequencing leads us to infer that the utterances were ordered in exactly this way: 4.12, 4.13, 4.14, 4.15. A similar inference is made about actions:

> 3.14[b]   So she rested in the afternoon,
> an' she got on the subway,
> an' met me in a restaurant.

In many other languages, the sequencing of these actions would be unambiguously signalled by grammatical particles, for example, Swahili -ka-, but in English, this information is entirely derived from the rule of narrative sequencing.

Evaluation.   One of the characteristic aspects of adult narrative is that the events forming the central and reportable part of the narrative itself are signals as such to the listener. A variety of devices serving this purpose have been described in previous studies: the use of intensifying modifiers, complex syntactic devices that bring together several events, the use of negatives and modals to refer to other events, which did not occur but which might have occurred, and so on. Perhaps the most important rhetorical device is to delay the forward movement of the narrative at a certain point by the use of many non-narrative clauses, which hold the listener suspended at that point in time. This is the device used by Rhoda in the narrative of her first episode to signal that the main point of the narrative was her action in telephoning her mother (see Chapter 4). Although the movement of the narrative was quite swift through the first several events (delivered in the first 4 sentences), the action is suspended for a very long period of time (12 sentences) before the central event. It is then followed by four narrative clauses without any further interruption.

However, the insertion of evaluative devices does not follow from any obligatory rule of narrative. It is possible to tell a story in which the point is not clear, in which the evaluation is not marked, where the listener has himself to do the work of locating the central or reportable event. If he cannot do so, and fails to get "the point" of the narrative, he may signal this by saying, *I don't get it*, or *So what?* or a number of other unpleasant remarks.

The ability to recognize the evaluative point of a narrative is a crucial matter for participants in conversation. Many speakers use narratives to put forward general propositions and begin directly without stating explicitly that the story they want to tell is designed to make a specific point. The listener is prepared to recognize the beginning of the narrative by the Rule of Narrative Orientation. He then must be able to interpret the over-all point of the narrative correctly if he is to understand it as a coherent part of the stream of conversation. The clearest cases involve narratives used as responses to requests for information.

RULE OF NARRATIVE RESPONSE

If A makes a request for information to B, and B immediately begins a narrative, then B is heard as asserting that the evaluative point of the narrative will supply the information requested.

Coda. One of the most important problems to solve in delivering a narrative is how to finish it. Each narrative clause contains with it the implicit question for the listener, *And then what happened?* Even if the evaluation clearly has marked the main point of the narrative, the listener may not know when the account is over and when it is appropriate for him to respond or speak next. Some storytellers have difficulty in carrying out this task, since an unlimited number of other events may have followed the one they were reporting. Most adult narrators are in command of a number of devices to accomplish the task: to bring the listener back to the present time and so let him know that the narrative is completed.

... *And I see that man now and again...*
... *When they see me now, they say, "What's happening?" and I say, "Nothing."*
... *And ever since that time, I feel paranoid about riding in a car...*

One also can make general observations that are timeless in character, which have the same effect, or even can state that the narrative is finished: *And that's what happened.* In our therapeutic session, the patient uses a rather special device: she returns to the present time by restating her proposition in exactly the same words that she used at the beginning,

1.14   R.: *Now . . . . . I think I did the right thing, I think that—*

Listener's evaluation.   If we understand that a narrative plays a role in a discourse similar to that of a single speech action, then it is expected that the listener will respond to that action appropriately. Our most general characterization of the place of narrative in discourse is that it is given as an instance of a general proposition. It is not required that the listener agree to the proposition, or even that he disagree. He must, however, indicate to the narrator that he has understood how this narrative is to be interpreted, that it is intended as evidence for a specific proposition. This can be done by agreeing or disagreeing with the proposition, or by employing many other types of less specific acknowledgment. In response to the narrative of Episode 1, the therapist agrees with the basic proposition:

2.2[a]   Th.: *Yes, I think you did too.*

In the second episode, the therapist responds to the first narrative with a simple reinforcing response: *Mmm*. The patient follows this with another short narrative, to show that her aunt basically is helpless, and the therapist responds:

    2.11[a]   Th.: *She **presents** herself as **very** helpless and needing to be waited on hand and foot.*

This kind of response is governed by fundamental rules of sequencing that we have not considered to this point. Such responses are important in the understanding of narrative structure because they demonstrate that the listener has used the appropriate rules of interpretation and evaluation, which we have discussed above.

V. SEQUENCING

The first group of speech actions in Figure 5 of Chapter 2 concerns the sequencing of conversational terms. These are governed by very general rules of conversational interaction that have been explored by Sacks, Schegloff, and Jefferson. Their synthesis (1974) of the rules governing sequencing or turntaking is a set of optional rules; at this level of organization, these sequencing rules will generate all possible conversational sequences. Schegloff has explored further the timing of interruptions, and many of his principles can be exemplified in the data from our therapeutic session (Schegloff, 1974).

At another level of organization, it is possible to point to some very general rules of sequencing that concern requests. Figure 5 of Chapter 2, (p. 61), illustrates the basic options open to the listener in responding to requests and challenges. These are, of course, crucial choice points, and a detailed study of any conversation would have to explore any constraints upon the choices that are the products of the conversational structures.*

The rules of production and interpretation that we have been discussing in this chapter are quite complex; the sequencing rules are relatively simple. The most important sequencing rule concerns the area of requests and may be stated quite simply. Requests must be acknowledged and responded to. The three basic modes of response are shown under B of section 3 of Figure 5. One can give the response requested—that is, perform the action or give the information. One can put off the request.

---

*In her unpublished studies of an Israeli kibbutz, Malcah Yaeger has reported a rule of discourse that puts unusually strong constraints upon responses to requests: In general, all responses to requests must be positive. A refusal, no matter how it is accounted for, is considered unreasonable and aberrant behavior. The action of refusing a request must be carried out in a later interaction, sometime after the original request was made.

Thirdly, one can refuse, with or without an accounting. (However, it was shown above that an accounted refusal and a put-off are not distinguished easily.)

In response to B's response, A can do the following:

1. If B has complied with the request, A can acknowledge this, with thanks. In this straightforward routine, the next possible action is a *minimization* by B:

    Please pass the salt.
    Here it is.
    Thanks.
    Don't mention it. (Goffman, 1971)

2. If B puts off the request, A can reinstate it, redirect it to others, or retreat (withdraw). He can at the same time mitigate or aggravate the request.
3. If B refuses the request, with an accounting, A can renew the request or accept the refusal. He can equally well accept the refusal if it is given without an account, but in this case, he may also respond with a *huff*. (Goffman, 1971)

In our discussion of assertions and challenges, it appeared that many of these speech acts can be further analyzed as requests of various kinds, and the sequencing rules that govern them then follow naturally from the sequencing rules for requests. In this chapter as a whole, the rules for interpretation and production have absorbed much of the complexity that has appeared elsewhere in discussions of sequencing.

Goffman's studies of remedial and supportive interchanges (1971) show how the rituals of face-to-face personal management will constrain the possible responses to greetings, requests, etc., yet our understanding of the main body of conversational interaction cannot possibly lead us to general statements about when parties will respond positively, negatively, or neutrally to a request.

In this book, we are very much concerned with the nature of resistance in the therapeutic session, and the work that the therapist is trying to do is designed to illuminate the answer to this question in relation to a particular therapeutic session. If the therapist knew just what prevented the patient from following the suggestions that are generally agreed to, then the problem of therapy would be solved. Our understanding of this higher-level sequencing can follow only a detailed examination of the conversational interaction itself. In the subsequent chapters, we will apply our discourse rules in the comprehensive analysis of the therapeutic session.

EPISODE ONE
I think I did the right thing.

The interview we will examine is the 25th in the series of therapeutic sessions with Rhoda, age 19, whose background is discussed in Chapter 1. This interview took place in New York City in the 1960s. The tape recording and the text begin with the very first words spoken in the session; there is no exchange of small talk or preliminary settling down, which often takes place. Instead, the patient herself immediately begins the discussion that provides the substance and substantive issues of this session.

1.1[a] R.: *I don't.. know, whether... I–I **think** I did–the right thing, jistalittle.. situation came up... an' I tried to uhm...... well, try to........ use what I—what I've learned here, see if it worked.*
[b] Th.: *Mhm.*
[c] R.: *Now, I don't know if I did the right thing.*

We will consider Episode 1 in this chapter and the one that follows. It is the initial presentation of the patient, and it is terminated by the therapist when the patient has finished presenting the new material. The interview then moves in other directions, but eventually returns in Episodes 4 and 5 to the issues raised in Episode 1. These issues are connected directly with the main problem of the patient as the therapist sees it.

The text of Episode 1 is presented as a whole on pp. 363–364 in Appendix A; it can be read verbatim before any analysis and consulted independently throughout the discussion. Whether the reader is a clinician, a linguist, a psychologist, or a student in training, he may want to raise the general question, "What is going on here?" He may have a theoretical framework of his own, approaching this problem from an abstract point of view, but as a first step he certainly will want to answer some common-sense questions about the behavior he is observing. We see that the patient takes the initiative: What is she trying to do? She begins with the statement that she thinks she *did the right thing.* What is this *thing?* She gives an account of

113

something that happened in her everyday life; how much confidence can we place in her version? Does it give us any insight into what actually happens in Rhoda's life?

There are other questions raised by the form in which the patient makes her presentation. The reader will observe a great deal of hesitation, even lack of conviction, in the patient's style. This is strongly impressed upon the therapist; in fact, she reacts overtly by saying, (2.2b) *What's your question?* (see the beginning of Episode 2). What *is* the patient's question? The reader may ask himself, "If I were the therapist, how would I react?" What role does the therapist play in this first episode, if any? What determines when and where she responds to the patient, and why does she finally decide to intervene more actively? From the therapist's point of view, the most important questions are: Is the patient making any progress? Is she becoming more independent? Does she have a clearer view of her own emotions, and is she better able to manage her relations with others? Since our analysis will eventually explore answers to these questions, the reader may be able to evaluate them better if he has confronted the problems himself first. He may prefer to study the entire text of five episodes in advance, but also to consider Episode 1 as a separate unit. This confrontation with the raw data is an essential element of our approach, which requires more contact with the details of actual speech than the summaries and narrative accounts that are frequent in psychiatry, social work, and theoretical writings in psychoanalysis (see Chapter 1, p. 3).

We will now begin the systematic study of Episode 1, utilizing step by step, the analytic and integrative methods we have described as "comprehensive discourse analysis." In Chapter 2 (pp. 38–40), we discussed the segmentation and numbering system we have adopted, with the caution that only the major divisions into episodes play a significant role in our final analysis. The numbering that is convenient for Episode 1 follows the structure of Rhoda's narrative as she presents her account of how she called upon her mother to come home.

Before we can begin to expand and elaborate what is communicated, we first must obtain an exact representation of the text, separating the words spoken from the prosodic features that we will also have to expand in the light of the surrounding context.

Separating and Identifying Paralinguistic Cues

As we attempt to transcribe the first words of Episode 1, the most striking fact is Rhoda's hesitation—the difficulty she seems to have in getting her words out.

1.1 [a] R.: *I don't.. know, whether.... I—I **think** I did—the right thing, jistalittle.. situation came up... an' I tried to uhm...... well, try to........ use what I—what I've learned here, see if it worked.*

In our representation of the text, we indicate some of the prosodic features by the devices of literary dialect. Each period in the hesitations represents a half-second, so that the pause before *use* is actually 4 seconds—a very long pause indeed. We show in type the difference between a "comma" intonation and a sudden break or self-interruption, indicated by the dash. We also indicate that some words are said very quickly without normal pause, such as *jistalittle,* to give the reader a sense of extra-rapid, condensed delivery. A few of the differences in vowels and consonants that mark casual versus formal style also are indicated, such as *an'* versus *and, usu'lly* versus *usually,* and so forth. A close phonetic transcription of the text would provide a massive amount of information that is largely irrelevant.*

The most important stylistic cues in Rhoda's speech are prosodic: variations in pitch, length, and loudness, which we refer to as *paralinguistic cues.*† Some of these can be shown quite easily in the ordinary spelling of our text: hesitations, self-interruptions, and spurts of rapid, condensed speech; but the intonation contours involving pitch changes cannot be shown in this way, nor can the special voice qualifiers such as "glottalization." We will present the most important of such cues, including those shown in the text, in a separate section to the right of the original text.

We have used the general heading of *tension* to summarize the interactive effect of a variety of linguistic cues, all of which disrupt the even flow of

1.1	TEXT	CUES
[a]	R: *I don't .. know, whether ... I—I think I did–the right thing, jistalittle .. situation came up ... an' I tried to uhm ...... well, try to .... use what I—what I've learned here, see if it worked.*	Tension: hesitation, self-interruption, uneven tempo; condensation and long silences, 3 and 4 sec [Figure 8].

*As we mentioned in Chapter 1 (p. 5), we hoped originally to use some of the characteristic sociolinguistic variables of New York City speech as indicators of stylistic shifting in the interview (Labov, 1966). But the interaction between Rhoda and the therapist has continued for such a long time that a fairly regular style has been achieved. We do notice a variation in the (ing) variable, which is easily expressed in ordinary typography: *nothin'* versus *nothing.* Rhoda also shows the typical variability in the pronunciation of final and preconsonantal *r,* and she uses this variable to express degrees of formality, but not often enough to play an important role here. Essentially, her verbal style is that of a lower middle class female, of Jewish background, with a minimum of correction: the vowel in *bad, man, ask* is very high, even higher than the vowel of *where;* the vowel of *off, lost,* and so forth is also very high, similar to the vowel of *sure.* Rhoda seems to have the sociolinguistic style characteristic of many younger, urban, lower middle class females who tend to maintain a fairly regular, uncorrected style in rapid speech, even when they are being a bit nervous and careful.

†These subjective variables correspond roughly to the physical dimensions of frequency, duration, and amplitude, but the correlations are complex and not fully understood (Fry, 1955).

speech. This is the traditional view, which has evolved from studies of face-to-face interaction, incorporated into Bales analysis (1950); Mahl's work has demonstrated a close correlation between such "nonfluencies" and emotionally charged material in the content of speech (Mahl and Schulze, 1964).

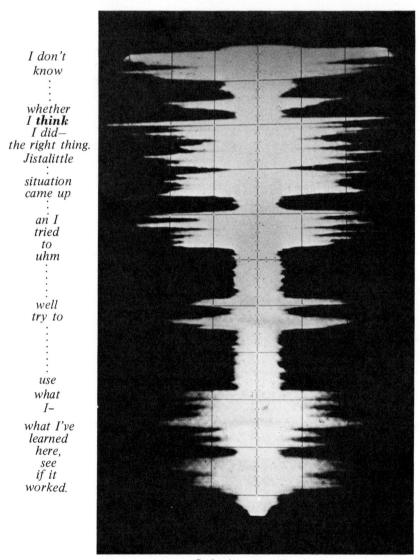

Scale: 1 square = 2 seconds

Figure 8 (= Figure 2). Spectographic display of Rhoda's initial hesitation in 1.1. (1 square = 2 seconds.)

Where intonation contours play an important role, we will expand this "cues" section with displays from spectrographic analysis, showing the actual rise and fall of pitch. Where there are striking patterns of silence and rapid speech, the overall tempo will be illustrated best by an oscilloscopic display such as Figure 8 (= Fig. 2) for 1.1. This display shows the overall amplitude against time, so that the reader is afforded a direct visual impression of this prosodic cue.

Expanding the Text

Given such an analysis, we can now take the individual parts and relate them directly to the initial questions posed above. We not only inquire: "What is being said?" but also "What is being conveyed?" or, as we noted above (Chapter 2, p. 59), "What is *really* being meant?" and, ultimately, "What is being done?" as the speakers interact. To answer these questions, we must put the material back together again, into an *expanded* text. In this expansion, we will rewrite the paralinguistic cues in their explicit verbal equivalents, recognizing that there will inevitably be disagreement on the exact form of the wording.

All of the paralinguistic cues that we have isolated in 1.1[a] seem to provide the general message of "uncertainty," which we may render explicitly as 'I am not sure.' The text itself reads *I don't. . know* which also is conventionally understood as uncertainty and not a negative assertion, but then we find that the word *think* is given contrastive stress. Contrastive stress forces us to locate the implicit proposition that is being used as a point of contrast. The stressed expression, *I **think**,* can be contrasted with the more confident *I **know*** in 1.5[a] and the more hesitant *it seems that* in 1.5[d]. We express this intermediate position as *I am not sure of some things, but I claim that. . .*

Once we translate these self-interruptions and hesitations into explicit form, the rest of the text might actually be condensed rather than expanded since there is quite a bit of repetition. *I am not sure of some things, but I claim that I did the right thing, when just a little situation came up, and I tried to use what I've learned here to see if it worked.* Yet a careful examination of this text shows that there are many expressions that cannot be assigned any direct meaning without further expansion. First of all, there are pro-forms: anaphoric elements that refer to unstated objects, facts, or propositions.

*the right **thing**
just a little **situation**
use **what** I've learned
learned **here**
see if **it** worked.*

What is the *thing* that was done? What is the *little situation*? What is the *what* Rhoda has learned? Two of these pronouns are easily related; the

The expansion "E" represents our best representation of "what is being said" so far.

The four arrows leading to E indicate that there are many sources for the expanded text. The relationship of Text to Expansion is an important characteristic of verbal interaction, which varies widely from person to person and situation to situation. If the verbal text is explicit, and can be understood by someone who shares a minimum of common experience with the speaker, then the T/E mode will be relatively direct. Without calculating any quantitative measure, we can say that the ratio T/E is high. However, in much of family interaction and conversation between close associates, we find that there is a great deal of shared knowledge, which may be drawn from a very wide range of events, and the conversation will appear quite cryptic to outsiders. In some families, and in some ethnic groups, the load carried by C, the paralinguistic cues, is very large, so that again there is no close match between T and E. We will call this characteristic the *mode of expression:* the T/E relation of the explicit text to the expanded text.

The arrow coming from the left indicates information drawn from expanded texts previous to this one. The right hand arrow is information drawn from texts to follow. One might question whether or not we are entitled to look at future texts in order to interpret the current one. It might be argued that the speaker or listener knows only what has occurred in the past and has no way of sharing our overview. Furthermore, one could argue that the unfolding events changed the speaker's mind, changed his own view of his original meaning.

It is true that we always must be on the alert for any sudden change in a speaker's meanings and understanding; but this caution should not be allowed to stand in the way of our understanding the text. Throughout these five episodes, we will examine many cases where a speaker's brief utterance must be analyzed by juxtaposing it with the more detailed expressions he uses later. On the other hand, we have no cases where we could reasonably say that the speaker's later remarks or elaborations would lead to incorrect interpretation of his original statement if the two were placed side by side. The reasons for this may be that we are dealing with an extended therapeutic series, where the behavior of therapist and patient is relatively constant, and the changes in understanding that do occur evolve slowly.* In general, we must admit that we are not inside the patient's mind, and we need all the help that we can muster in order to see what he understands by his expressions and what he intends others to understand.

---

*It is true that we have a clearer view of what followed than the participants at the moment of speaking, but it is also true that speaker and listener have a much richer knowledge of the things that have been said in the past and that might be said in the future. The third principle which we cite from *The First Five Minutes* (p. 7) is that of recurrence: "The diagnostically crucial patterns of communication will not be manifested just once."

Propositions

When episodes were analyzed, and we returned again to the material of Episode 1, we found a number of themes that were general to the therapeutic session and others that recurred throughout Episode 1 or one or two others. We will identify both types of recurrent material as explicitly as possible, as a help to reconstructing the meanings that are referred to only briefly by pronouns, hinted at indirectly, or buried deeply in the interaction. A superficially recurrent theme of Episode 1 is:

{1} I think I did the right thing.

Our expansion indicates that {1} is linked ultimately to a more general proposition that recurs throughout the therapeutic series:

{S} One should express one's needs and emotions to relevant others.

The generality of {S} extends beyond this therapeutic series: it seems to be a recurrent proposition in all therapeutic work and the theories which govern it. No matter how nondirective the orientation of a therapist may be, we find that this general suggestion is present in the communication.*

Once we have identified {S}, it is possible to restate the local proposition {1} more abstractly:

{1} Rhoda carried out {S} correctly.

We will use the term *proposition* for recurrent communications (Chapter 2, p. 51). These are predications of some degree of generality—important enough to the interactants to be referred to more than once in the course of an interview or therapeutic session.† In this respect, our use of the term is not radically different from that of Skinner (1957, p. 8) or Searle (1969, p. 29), who uses the term to indicate something more abstract than any given sentence or "illocutionary act." Searle notes that "A proposition is to be sharply distinguished from an assertion or statement of it," and that will

---

*If one were to say simply, "express one's needs and emotions," the suggestion would be far more limited, because most therapists recognize that there are people to whom one should be reticent. The relevant others here will turn out to be Rhoda's mother, sister, and aunt.

†We note that the term *proposition* is used by Lennard and Bernstein (1960, p. 40) as a unit of surface structure: "a verbalization containing a subject and predicate either expressed or implied." Lennard and Bernstein paraphrase this as "the verbal expression of a single idea"; they are dealing with the simpler process of segmenting the words actually spoken. By introducing expansions drawn from other utterances, we make it possible to isolate more abstract references, which are stated fully in other points in the interview. The important characteristic is their use as reference points for the interactive process, which implies the general and abstract character noted above.

be obvious in our use of the term. Sometimes, a proposition is asserted fully, and sometimes merely referred to.*

Such underlying propositions also play an important part in ordinary conversation. The more that the speakers share as common knowledge, the more they are likely to refer to such propositions rather than assert them.† A great deal of the actual interaction between speakers consists of arguments about whether an event just observed or reported is an instance of general propositions known to both of them though not necessarily believed by both of them. Propositions such as "You're always late," or "You never clean up after yourself," or "You're not very considerate of other people" are essential elements of family interaction, and it will prove impossible to demonstrate the coherence of such interaction without the recognition of such abstract propositions. They are sometimes asserted fully, often with the tag "I've told you over and over" or "I've told you that before."

We can now insert the propositions we have recognized in the expansion.

EXPANSION

I am not sure, but I claim that {1} I did what you say is right, or what may actually be right, when I asked my mother to help me by coming home after she had been away from home longer than she usually is, creating some small problems for me, and I tried to use the principle that I've learned from you here, {S} that I should express my needs and emotions to relevant others, and {?S} see if this principle worked.

We have already embodied the proposition {S} in our expansion above, but now we will recognize it as a formal element in the analysis by identifying it with a symbol in curly brackets preceding the statement itself.

Our expansion also shows that this suggestion {S} is questioned by the speaker, who not only wants to *use what I've learned here* but also *see if it worked*. We recognize the ambiguity contained in this message by placing {?S} before this second element of the expansion. We thus preserve the full ambiguity of the message in our expansion.

The relation between the propositions and the text gives us another

---

*It is plain that the text is full of "propositions" in the sense of predications and arguments, but we use the term as shorthand for "underlying propositions," which are conceived of as persistent potential reference points in the interaction between speakers. Within the context of the therapeutic session, this emphasis on recurring or underlying propositions is important. The therapeutic session is designed to produce a great deal of talk; the therapist expects that this talk will contain many of the same statements, reiterated in slightly different forms, over and over again. We follow the therapist herself in focusing on these recurrent propositions, with the justification that we draw them directly from the text by the method of expansion outlined above.

†These are *AB-events* in the terminology of Chapter 3, the shared social knowledge of speaker and listener.

mode of analyzing verbal interaction that allows us to indicate how direct or indirect communication may be. Propositions can be stated explicitly, but more often they are placed well in the background, or referred to indirectly as in 1.1[a]. As positions are defended, it often happens that they are made more explicit; this is indeed what happens in Episode 1. Some arguments are never made explicit, particularly those that challenge propositions and are heard as challenges to status, as in {?S}. We will refer to the relationship of proposition and text as the *mode of argument*.

Interaction

So far, we have concentrated upon "what is said" in 1.1[a]. We have also implied that something is "being done" by the combination of text, cues, and propositions. In our presentation of comprehensive discourse analysis in Chapter 2, we argued for the existence of a second plane, which runs parallel to the entire construction we have presented so far—the plane of *interaction*. We also indicated the complex nature of the relations between what is said and what is done, indicating that any attempt to get at the "real meaning" of conversation must inevitably deal with this plane of actions. Finally, we argued that the fundamental connections between one utterance and another do not lie on the plane of what is said, but rather exist as sequencing rules between actions. This point is dramatically demonstrated by some of the sharp breaks in surface structure that occur later in Episode 1. In the same way, we see that 1.1[a] cannot be understood as simply a verbal expression: the therapist's reactions and Rhoda's further behavior are intelligible only if we ask what actions are being performed by this utterance.

First, we can see that some metalinguistic action is being performed. Rhoda *initiates* the session and presents material on which the therapy can proceed. She does this by two acts of reference: she *refers* to some action she performed the week before and also to something she has learned in previous sessions.

It is not accidental that Rhoda initiates the session by providing material for discussion. As we noted at the outset, there is no small talk or other business. Fanshel was struck by this at the *Playback* session, and the therapist made it plain that this procedure had become institutionalized in the course of the first 24 sessions.

FANSHEL: I NOTICE SHE STARTS OUT ON HER OWN STEAM...
THERAPIST: OH, I WAIT FOR HER TO...
FANSHEL: DID SHE HAVE TROUBLE IN THE BEGINNING...?
THERAPIST: BUT SHE KNOWS WHAT HER RESPONSIBILITIES ARE.

In this procedure, it is not enough simply to report something. Rhoda is expected to show some awareness of the significance of these events, and this is not a simple thing for her to do.

When we examine the text explicitly, we see that Rhoda begins with the verb *think*. But the speech action Rhoda performed is obviously not "thinking." She asserts a proposition {1}, and *expresses* a certain degree of belief in it.* This expression seems to demand a response, and as we will see, it is repeated in the exact same form as a signal for the therapist to respond at the beginning of Episode 2.

If all that Rhoda did was to assert {1}, the interpretation of 1.1[a] would be quite straightforward. But the expression of doubt is more than a slight modification or mitigation of her assertion. It can be seen as a contradictory form of behavior, a questioning of the very proposition that she has been asserting. Such an interpretation is supported by the behavior of the therapist herself: At the beginning of Episode 2, after Rhoda has repreated 1.1[a], the therapist says:

2.2[b]   "Well, what's your **question** . . ."

The therapist's question is stimulated by an ambiguity which we can perceive ourselves. The proposition {1} *Rhoda did the right thing* can be interpreted straightforwardly with the verb *did* as its major predication. In that case, the question is directed at whether or not Rhoda succeeded in doing it—that is, carrying out {S}. But {1} can also be interpreted as having *right* as its highest predication, equivalent to 'The thing that I did was right.' In that case, the question is directed at whether or not the {S} that Rhoda attempted to carry out was correct.

We thus see that 1.1[a] must minimally include an act of initiation, two acts of reference, and possibly two types of questioning; but the actions performed cannot stop there. One of these questionings cannot be done without implying another action—a challenge. A challenge is any (speech) action that makes problematical the status of the listener. (Chapter 3, p. 93)

The therapist's irritable reaction at the beginning of Episode 2 seems to show that she, too, sensed a challenge in Rhoda's overall position. Yet there is no explicit reference to the therapist's status. Rather, we find that the item being questioned is related implicitly to an essential aspect of the therapist's role. Although her field of expertise is not defined formally, it must include the field of interpersonal transactions. When one doubts the basic proposition of the therapist that one should "express one's needs to relevant others," the action then can also be seen as questioning the competence of the therapist. This action is much more abstract than any of those we have mentioned so far, and it is connected with the others by the Rule for Challenging Propositions discussed in Chapter 3 (p. 97).

To see how this rules applies, we must consider the relationship of the

---

*We distinguish an *assertion* from a *remark* in that the former seems to require a specific response.

suggestion {S} to the therapist's status. A competent therapist is qualified to deal with the field of interpersonal transactions and their intrapsychic consequences, and to provide that guidance which the patient seeks for dealing with social and emotional problems.* The suggestion {S} is not incidental to the therapy, but is supported by the full weight of the therapist's status as a person qualified to deal with social and emotional problems. The Rule for Challenging Propositions then applies:

If A asserts a proposition that is supported by A's status, and B questions the proposition, then B is heard as challenging the competence of A in that status.

The actions carried out in 1.1[a] are performed on the three separate propositions:

{S}	One should express one's needs and emotions to relevant others.
{1}	Rhoda carried out {S} correctly.
{INT-TH}	The therapist interprets the emotions of others.

The surface expression, *I don't know,* is thus seen as an action of ambiguously questioning two separate propositions: there are no immediate interpersonal consequences if R. questions her own competence as expressed in {?1}. However, if she is questioning {S}, this immediately leads to a further action: a challenge to the competence of the therapist by the rule just given. The second half of this initial sentence asserts the proposition {1} and thereby asserts {S}, since (as indicated in the following phrases), R. argues that {1} was an instance of {S} and in carrying out {1} she thereby carried out {S} and thereby endorses or asserts {S}.

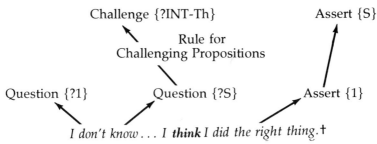

I don't know . . . I think I did the right thing.†

---

*This is indeed the basis of the contractual arrangement between Rhoda and the therapist, or rather between Rhoda's brother, who is paying for the therapy, and the therapist. Rhoda was referred to the agency by an internist who recognized the existence of social and emotional problems that went beyond the physical problems he was prepared to deal with.

†We might ask whether or not the same ambiguity is to be seen in the assertion as in the question. An assertion of {1} necessarily implies an assertion of its embedded propositions {S}; but the question reverses the relationships. If {1} is questioned, {S} is not necessarily questioned; if {S} is questioned, then it necessarily follows that {1} is invalid.

In all of our analyses of speech actions we will see such vertical arrangements, which indicate that two or more actions are being performed simultaneously. There is usually no irresolvable conflict between these actions. One may be implemented by another; asserting {1} "thereby" asserts {S}. However, there are also conflicting actions which are not easily accepted as taking place simultaneously, so the entire performance may be heard as ambiguous. In 1.1, we have two examples of such ambiguity: R. asserts that she did the right thing, but by her hesitation actually questions whether or not she did the right thing. By the general principle asserted in Chapter 2 (p. 48), the paralinguistic cues predominate in the interpretation, and the therapist perceives Rhoda's presentation as a question. Yet this question is also ambiguous (which leads the therapist to ask, *What's your question?*), and this is not resolved by any general rule.

Like the therapist, the analyst can react to ambiguous cues from the speaker; but he also is in no position to say how much of this ambiguity was intended consciously or even could be perceived by the speaker if she were to study her own words. The question of speakers' conscious *intentions* (or the presence of "unintended effects") does not play a significant

---

1.1 TEXT	CUES
R.: *I don't .. know whether ... I—I **think** I did—the right thing, jistalittle .. situation came up .... an' I tried to uhm ...... well, try to .... use what I—what I've learned here, see if it worked.*	Tension: hesitation, self-interruption; uneven tempo; condensation and long silences, 3 and 4 sec. [Figure 8].

EXPANSION

I am not sure, but I claim that {1} I did what you say is right, or {?1} what may actually be right, when {4} I asked my mother to help me by coming home after she had been away from home longer than she usually is, creating some small problems for me, and I tried to use the principle that I've learned from you here, {S} that I should express my needs and emotions to relevant others, and see {?S} if this principle worked.

INTERACTION

R. initiates the session in Interview Style [IVS] by referring ⟨ S ⟩ to the previous suggestion of the therapist and an incident from everyday life and asserting ⟨ 1 ⟩ that she did right in carrying out {S} thereby asserting ⟨ S ⟩. She simultaneously expresses uncertainty about her assertion, ambiguously questioning ⟨ ?1 ⟩ that she carried out {S} correctly and questioning ⟨ ?S ⟩ that {S} is appropriate,
    thereby challenging ⟨ ?INT-TH ⟩ the competence of the therapist.

role in our analysis. This issue seems to us to revolve around how conscious the speakers are of their own verbal processing; by analogy with grammatical studies, we can infer that such awareness of intervening mechanisms is quite limited and does not play an important part in personal interactions.

We are now ready to present a complete cross section of 1.1[a] that includes the plane of interaction.

The symbols for interaction are inserted in arrows pointing left, right, or in both directions. These arrows indicate the relations of the actions performed here to the sequencing rules that may be operating, connecting one cross section with another. Thus *reference* is characteristically a leftward- or backward-operating action, which does not contain in itself immediate consequences for the next action to be performed. Assertions, as mentioned above, are forward-looking in just the opposite sense. Questions characteristically include both the act of reference to some previous event or statement and a demand for a reply. Challenges are double-faced in the same way.

The arrows embedded in the interactional statement are also graphic expressions of the overlapping character of speech actions. Chapter 2 showed how our expansion of the semantic interpretation includes past as well as present events, differentiating our approach from those modes of analyses that define speech actions by isolating individual utterances. In this therapeutic session it is abundantly clear that speakers locate themselves and others at remote points in time, and the speech actions themselves bind past and future conversations into a continuous web of temporal linkages.

This spread of reference over time is compounded by the fact that many questions or challenges may be mitigated and performed so indirectly that no explicit reference to particular events is made at the time. Later reference may be made to these implicit questions or challenges by acts that are themselves very indirect. We will have ample opportunity to study this degree of indirection as we develop even more complex diagrams of the actions being performed by any one utterance. We will see that the abstract nature of speech acts forms a necessary protection against direct confrontation between speakers of unequal status and competing views.

Our cross section deals only with 1.1[a]; there remains 1.1[b], a reinforcing *Mhm* from the therapist, and 1.1[c], where Rhoda repeats the initial message of 1.1[a]. If we construct a separate cross section for the *Mhm* it will necessarily be an abbreviated one. Instead of developing "what is said" in the Expansion section, we will want to look primarily at the interactional significance of the therapist's contribution. This requires first a good look at the timing of the signal and the intonational contour that accompanies it.

It is apparent that Rhoda is looking for some kind of acknowledgment of

128   EPISODE ONE

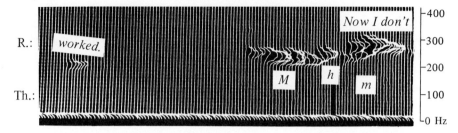

Figure 9. Pitch contour of reinforcement *Mhm* in 1.1[b].

her assertion {1} from the therapist. There is a definite pause [30 msec] after Rhoda's last words of 1.1[a], *see if it worked*. The therapist can hardly respond to Rhoda's assertion or her implicit challenge until she has some notion of what actually happened yesterday. She therefore produces a simple reinforcing signal. Figure 9 shows the pitch contour of the therapist's voice as she says *Mhm:* it rises slightly in the middle and then falls. This is typical of what we may call a "neutral" or noncommittal reinforcement; as we will see, it contrasts with stronger reinforcements which show sharper rises and different terminal points of inflection. The "unmarked" or neutral sentence contour of American English generally is recognized to be 2 3 1: beginning in the mid-range, a slight rise near the end, and a final falling contour with fading volume. Encouraged, Rhoda then proceeds immediately with *Now,* and repeats the beginning of 1.1[a], with much more confidence, this time without the many prosodic cues of uncertainty. The cross section of 1.1[c] follows in a straightforward manner from what has already been said; it reasserts {1}. Rhoda then begins a narrative from everday life and moves into another field of discourse.

Fields of Discourse

As Rhoda begins her narrative, we note immediately a change of style in both her vocabulary and her prosodic features. In Chapter 2, we outlined the structural basis for the radical shifts of such fields marked by the simultaneous change of many stylistic features; 1.1[a] is a good example of Rhoda's interview style, IV, with its hesitations, glottalizations, and vague reference to therapeutic discussions. In the narrative that begins with 1.2, we see the rapid, straightforward account typical of Rhoda's everyday style, EV, with very little affect and very little introspection. Embedded in the everyday style, we will see concentrated bursts of emotional, highly idiomatic language which we identify as family style, F.

We will mark the fields of discourse by angled brackets around portions of the text and the expansion. As Figure 1 indicated (p. 37) the interview style must be considered as the largest frame of the therapeutic session. Just as the excerpts from family style are conditioned by the fact that they

FIELDS OF DISCOURSE   129

1.1	TEXT	CUES
[b]	Th.:⟨_{IV}Mhm.⟩_{IV}	Reinforcement Level 1:2 ↑. [See Figure 9.]

INTERACTION

Th.: Gives support.

	TEXT	CUES
[c]	R.: ⟨_{IV}Now, I don't know if I did the right thing.⟩_{IV}	Tension release: fast tempo, falling contour

EXPANSION

R.:⟨_{IV} I am not sure, but I claim that {1} I did what you say is right, or what actually may be right, when I asked my mother to help me by coming home after she had been away from home longer than usual.⟩_{IV}

INTERACTION

R.: R. repeats the assertion of 1.1[a] with more confidence.

---

are contained within Rhoda's narrative in everyday style, so the everyday style must be understood as contained within the frame of the therapeutic session, and the surrounding interview style. We usually will not mark the interview style with angled brackets, but it will be understood that these outer brackets are omnipresent.

For every speaker and every therapeutic session, there might be different sets of co-occurrent features that define fields of discourse. For Rhoda, we can point to two sets of indicators, in her paralinguistic cues and her lexical choices.

1. Paralinguistic Cues
    IV: hesitation, long silences, false starts, glottalization (creaky voice); falsetto and whine.
    EV: Continuous speech without pause, rapid, level intonation.
    F: Special intonation contours carrying strong implication and affective meaning, some of Yiddish origin.
2. Lexical Choice
    IV: Vague reference (*situation, thing*...);* euphemisms: *bother, just a little*...).

---

*In many therapeutic sessions, the interview style of the patient is marked by the frequent use of formal terms drawn from the vocabulary of psychotherapy: *relationship, hostility, aggression, compulsion,* and so on. Rhoda does not use these terms freely; see 3.6[b] for an outstanding exception with dramatic consequences.

130 EPISODE ONE

> EV: Unmarked vocabulary with few affective or evaluative expressions.
> F: Idiomatic, affective expressions (*a little nuts*).

The characteristic features of everyday style are accentuated when Rhoda's account takes the form of a narrative. Narrative syntax is simpler and more straightforward than ordinary conversation, and in narrative Rhoda's flow of language is especially free of the typical complications of her interview style. Many of the sections of EV are, in fact, narratives and fall under the discourse rules for narrative discussed in Chapter 3. To bracket these narrative sections, we will use the abbreviation N instead of EV: It is to be understood that N is a subtype of the EV field of discourse.

Rhoda's Narrative

In 1.2, Rhoda begins a narrative from everyday life. This is a common pattern in many therapeutic sessions, for good reason. Many interviews begin with such "grist for therapy"; in the course of this particular study of the therapeutic interview, about half of the sessions take this form. In other interviews, there may be a continuation of discussions in the interview situation, and at some later point anecdotes from everyday life are introduced for further analysis. Sometimes there is vacillation in the choice of which incident will be explored; it is part of the skill of the therapist to see the therapeutic potential in a given incident. In the *Playback* sessions, therapists frequently criticize themselves as they re-listen to a session for not having picked up and explored a particular incident because they did not see this potential immediately.

What makes one incident more useful for analysis than another? It is the extent to which this incident reveals the fundamental themes of the therapeutic work—the patient's success or failure in grasping the basic propositions already put forward for consideration and the mechanism of resistance to recognizing these propositions. In this particular case, the therapist encourages the patient to develop the incident in full; but, as we will see, she will decide not to explore its significance immediately and turn in another direction for Episodes 2 and 3.

We have developed one view of comprehensive discourse analysis through an examination of the very first unit in the therapeutic session. Now we are presented with a very different kind of material, as Rhoda presents the main body of substance for therapeutic analysis.

> 1.2[a] R.: *Sunday .. um—my mother went to my sister's again.*
> [b] Th.: *Mm-hm.*
> [c] R.: *And she usu'lly goes for about a day or so, like if she leaves on Sunday, she'll come back Tuesday morning.* [*Hm.*] *So—it's nothing.*

We will first examine the text and the paralinguistic cues, and then will develop as much information as we need to expand the text and embed the underlying propositions.

We recognize 1.2 as the beginning of a narrative not only by the shift of style to EV but by the basic rule of narrative orientation (Chapter 3, p. 106). Rhoda begins with a time reference to the past, followed by an event that is not reportable in itself and clearly is not in itself an exemplification of the general propositions of 1.1. We then retrospectively recognize that 1.1 is a story preface, and is an abstract of the narrative about to follow. 1.2 is the orientation section of the narrative, which establishes the time (*Sunday*), the place (*Rhoda's household and her sister's*), the persons (*her sister and her mother*) and the behavioral setting (*her mother's going away*). 1.2 is also the first narrative event. The account seems quite straightforward. There is no confusion, lack of coherence, or break in the surface structure that would demand further analysis. One vague reference to be expanded would be the pronoun *it*, in *it's nothing*, but that can readily be seen to refer to the whole situation Rhoda has just described. Before concluding that we have obtained all the information we need to understand the situation, we must turn to the paralinguistic cue which shows the therapist's *Mm-hm* in 1.2[b].

Our regular procedure in approaching any section of the interview is first to consider the literal text and then to turn to a separate view of the prosodic cues. In many cases we find in these cues surprising elements that indicate we have not understood the text fully.

In 1.2[b], the therapist provides reinforcement of a special kind. Figure 10 shows the pitch contour. The *Mm-hm* has a level falling contour, quite distinct from the neutral rise and fall of 1.1[b]. We assign 1.2[b] the general meaning 'expected sympathy', and our expansion of the reinforcement will then be: "Not again! That's too bad."

This interpretation of the therapist's reaction is confirmed by Rhoda's response. Her next comment, in 1.2[c], shows that she has picked up the signal of sympathy and rejected it. Figure 10 shows that she begins speak-

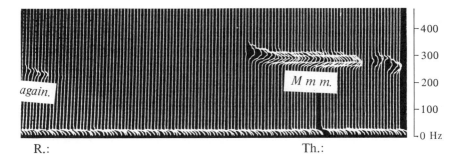

Figure 10. Pitch contour of sympathetic reinforcement *Mm-hm* in 1.2[b].

ing even before the therapist's *Mm-hm* is finished. The further information on the situation that she provides in 1.2[c] implies that she has not yet stated the problem that is bothering her, and she concludes, *So—it's nothing*. What prompted the therapist's sympathetic reinforcement? The answer is not at all evident from the text of 1.2[a]. The whole sequence of 1.2[a], [b], [c] is incoherent unless we supply more contextual information in our process of expansion.

To understand the significance of this material for therapy, and to see what use Rhoda makes of it, we must know more about the structure of Rhoda's family life and the network of obligations in which she finds herself. Fortunately, it is not necessary to do an independent research project to obtain this information. At many other points in this session and other sessions, Rhoda gives us all the information we need about the organization of the households and the push and pull of social obligations that form the problem.

The problem Rhoda is beginning to expound concerns the interlocking obligations of two households displayed in Figure 11; this is only a part of the complex network that is to be introduced in the Episodes to follow. Each column or row in Figure 11 represents a role set—two or more individuals who share a set of role obligations. The upper horizontal row is Rhoda's household, labeled here Household 1; it consists of Rhoda, her mother, and her maiden aunt, Editha (who will figure in Episodes 2 and 3). Among these three adults, there is an apportionment of the responsibilities of cooking, cleaning, and generally maintaining the household. Each block represents the status of an adult member of the household who may be said to have the following rights and duties on the basis of the data presented to us by Rhoda:

1. The obligation to perform certain household duties when there is a socially recognized need. In the Episodes considered here, the particular duties mentioned are cleaning the house, buying food, and preparing meals.
2. Since each member has obligation in other role sets, he has the right to call on others to fill in for him in this role set when his other duties exert a claim upon him. Conversely, he has the obligation to respond to others' needs in the same way. That is, these obligations are not rigidly partitioned, but are fluid and must be adjusted to fit the immediate situation.
3. An adult member of the household has the right to join in making decisions that affect the household (as well as decisions about her personal life). A typical decision discussed in Episode 3 is whether to go out to eat in a restaurant, or to prepare dinner at home.

Rhoda's mother is the *head* of Household 1, as shown by a number of assumptions made throughout the five episodes. She sets the tone of interaction, provides a model for the others, and reserves the right of final

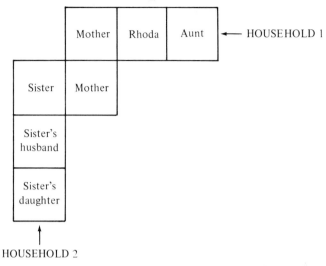

Figure 11. Role sets and households in Rhoda's family.

decision on a number of important matters. A generally shared assumption is that a home maintained by a parent for a young adult remains the home of that parent—if there is any movement, usually the young adult moves out to set up an independent household.

Many of the issues discussed in the therapeutic interviews concern Rhoda's status in Household 1: is she an independent, adult member of the household or is she not? Children, or dependent members of the household, have different sets of rights and obligations. For example, they often perform fewer duties and do not share the final responsibility to see that jobs are completed; they do not share in the decision making in the way that adults do, and are seldom completely free to determine their own personal futures. These will be important issues in the discussion to follow; to deal with Rhoda's everyday life situation, the therapist must be aware of these normal conventions of our society.

Figure 11 shows a second role set for Rhoda's mother. She is also the mother of a married daughter—a set of role obligations which run across two households; this is a structural situation having its own inherent problems.* The other member of this role set, Rhoda's sister, is shown as a member of a third role set—Household 2, consisting of Rhoda's sister, her husband and two children. If Rhoda's sister stayed at home, and took care of her own children, there would be no strong claim on her mother's time. However, Rhoda's sister occasionally works, and when she does so, she usually asks her mother to take care of her children. She then draws her mother away from Household 1. As a result, Rhoda and her aunt have to

---

*For evidence on such extended family ties in our society, see Litwak, 1960a,b.

do the cleaning and cooking that Rhoda's mother usually does. This is usually for only a day or so, as Rhoda points out in 1.2[c]; it does not create role strain for her—*it's nothing*.

With this background, we are in a better position to expand 1.2. The mode of expression is quite direct, and the paralinguistic cues contribute very little to the message beyond the text. The expansion is based on the structure of role relations just set forth.*

> 1.2[a] On Sunday, my mother, whose help I need at home, went away again to the home of my sister, who doesn't need my mother's help as much as I do, and doesn't have as much of a claim on her time, the kind of thing which has caused me trouble in the past.

The expansion of 1.2[b], as noted above, is simply and roughly, "Not again! That's too bad." We then expand R.'s response as:

> 1.2[c] My mother has often gone away before for two days, and I haven't had any trouble dealing with that situation; so it's nothing to be worried about, and I'm not asking for sympathy because my mother went away for only two days.

Just after Rhoda completes her exposition of the circumstances in 1.2[c], she pauses. On close listening, one can hear the therapist add another reinforcement as acknowledgment just a moment before Rhoda continues with, *So—it's nothing*. Figure 12 illustrates the location of the therapist's *Hm*, which is almost completely overridden on first listening, so that we have inserted it in the text of 1.2[c]. We might condense the expansion of 1.2[c] into a proposition in role terminology:

> 1.2[c] Absence of role partner from Household 1 for two days does not create role strain for R.

This proposition certainly can be argued. Other sections of the interview show that this particular opinion has been disputed by Rhoda's mother. It is claimed that Rhoda cannot take care of herself when her mother is away. The dispute revolves about an underlying proposition which plays a major role in the therapeutic session:

---

*We might abbreviate Rhoda's description of the situation in formal terms of the role relations of Figure 6:

1.2[a] Rhoda's role partner in Household 1 has taken up role obligations in Household 2.

We could thus condense the expansion to give a parsimonious statement of what has occurred in role terminology. However, this is not yet a social proposition of the sort we have shown to be inserted in the expansion; this information is actually an A-event (p. 62), and propositions are necessarily D-events, which can be disputed, with implications for the succeeding interactional events.

RHODA'S NARRATIVE   135

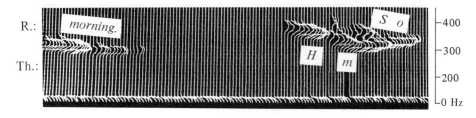

Figure 12. Pitch contour of therapist's acknowledging *Hm* in 1.2[c].

{AD-R}   Rhoda is an adult member of the household.

We will see that this is a serious and important proposition, because admitting or denying adult status is equivalent to admitting or denying a great many rights and obligations that adults have, but dependents do not. As noted above, it includes the right to decide how to dispose of one's time, to choose one's friends, one's own clothes, to decide how much rest one needs. In family terms, this proposition usually rests on whether or not Rhoda can "get along without her mother." The argument is not only about the substance of this question, but also about who can make such a judgment. We will therefore add to the expansion of 1.2[c] the embedded proposition: "Because {AD-R} I am an adult member of the household."

We are now in a position to consider the interactive character of 1.2 and complete the discourse analysis for this section. The complete cross sections for 1.2 are shown on page 136.

The interactional component of 1.2 deals with the initiation of the narrative structure and the response to the therapist's reaction to it. Rhoda initiates the narrative in 1.2[a], beginning with an orientation section in the normal manner, and efficiently tells the therapist the time, the place, the actors involved, and the behavioral setting for the events she is concerned with. However, she runs into some difficulty, since this setting is an event that produces a sympathetic response from the therapist in 1.2[b]. This was *not* designed as the evaluative point of the narrative. Rhoda seems to realize that she would be put in a weak position if she were seen as expecting sympathy just because her mother went away. Her next remark in 1.2[c] is necessary for her to establish her own basic proposition: that she can take care of herself, and is an adult member of the household.* Therefore she cannot continue with the narrative without providing some evaluation of the event that is actually no more than the orientation section of her narrative. She adds a directly evaluative remark, *So—it's nothing,* which is directed to the therapist. She steps outside of the narrative framework to

---

*The proposition {~STRN} is inserted here to indicate a denial of the existence of "role strain," to be developed in 1.3.

1.2

[a] **TEXT**
R.: ⟨_N*Sunday .. um—my mother went to my sister's again.*⟩_N

CUES
Narrative style: fast tempo, falling contour.

EXPANSION
R.: ⟨_N On Sunday, my mother, whose help I need at home, went away again to the home of my sister, who doesn't need my mother's help as much as I do and doesn't have as much of a claim on it, the kind of thing which has caused me trouble in the past.⟩_N

INTERACTION
R. initiates a narrative from everyday life ⟵⎯ by providing orientation on time, persons, place, and behavioral setting.

[b] **TEXT**
Th.: ⟨_{IV} *Mm-hm.*⟩_{IV}

CUES
'expected sympathy' [See Figure 10.]

EXPANSION
⟨_{IV} Not again! That's too bad.⟩_{IV}

INTERACTION
Th. responds by giving sympathetic support.

[c] **TEXT**
R.: ⟨_{IV} ⟨_N *And she usu'lly goes for about a day or so, like if she leaves on Sunday, she'll come back Tuesday morning.*⟩_N (*Hm.*) *So—it's nothing.*⟩_{IV}

CUES
Formality: *nothing* with -ing variant.

Reinforcement: *Hm.* [See Figure 12.]

EXPANSION
⟨_{IV} ⟨_N My mother has often gone away before for only two days, and {~STRN} I haven't had any trouble because I am an adult {AD-R} ⟩_N so it's nothing for me to be worried about when my mother goes away for only two days, and sympathy isn't necessary.⟩_{IV}

INTERACTION
R. gives evaluation of narrative thus far as not requiring sympathy thereby asserting AD-R ⟶ her adult status and thereby refusing support.

inform the therapist directly that 1.2[a] was not a serious problem worth remarking.

This rapid interaction between patient and therapist indicates how active "listenership" is, and how alert the speaker can be to the responses of the listener. Analysts are sensitive to the existence of reinforcement, as used by themselves or others; but it should be noted also that the speaker has to understand, evaluate, and accept the kind of support being offered by the reinforcing cues of the listener. If it is the wrong cue, the speaker knows that he has set the listener on a false trail and must correct before proceeding.

1.3. Rhoda now proceeds with the second event* of her narrative, which has created the problem that has been troubling her in the past week.

1.3[a] R.: *But—she lef' Sunday, and she's still not home.*

In light of the discussions of the social relations diagrammed in Figure 11, it is clear that certain expected role obligations are not being fulfilled by Rhoda's mother. This is the situation that was temporarily denied in 1.2[c] but now is developed. Her mother's absence has created a strain on Rhoda's capacities, since she cannot fulfill all of the responsibilities that are imposed on her. We symbolize this recurring proposition as {STRN},† which was denied in 1.2[c] as {~STRN} but is to be asserted in 1.3.

{STRN} R.'s obligations are greater than her capacity.

Rhoda does not state this explicitly, but relies upon the therapist's knowledge of her household situation; the therapist responds appropriately in 1.3[b]. She reinforces with a much stronger expression of sympathy than she used in 1.2[b]: *O-oh*. This reinforcement rises to a higher pitch level: the *O-oh* expresses surprise as well as sympathy. Figure 13 shows the pitch contour of this expression, which contrasts with the more restrained reinforcement of 1.2[b] in Figure 7.

1.3[b] Th.: *O-oh.*
　[c]　R.: *And . . . I'm gettin' a little nuts a'ready.*

Armed with this sympathy, Rhoda now gives further external evaluation to emphasize just how difficult the situation is for her: *And . . . I'm getting a little nuts a'ready.* She uses family language to express an important propo-

---

*1.3[a] is not a narrative clause in the sense that was developed and discussed in Chapter 3. As a negative statement with a copula verb form, it describes a condition that was true as soon as her mother left, and is still true. It is therefore an evaluative clause not separated by temporal boundaries from the other events, and 1.3[a] actually can be considered a further characterization of 1.2.

†This might be shown more fully as {STRN-R} but since this predicate is always applied to Rhoda, we will use the shorter notation {STRN}.

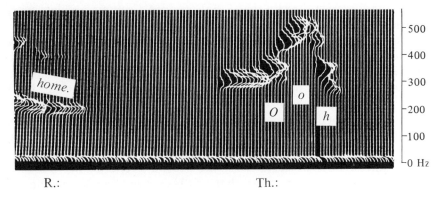

Figure 13. Pitch contour of sympathetic *O-oh* in 1.3[b].

sition from the standpoint of therapy. Patients are encouraged to be in touch with their emotions and be aware of what they are feeling. Rhoda here expresses the proposition that she feels the emotion of frustration and confusion, which we will symbolize as $\{E_1\}$. She expresses this in family style, with at least three features that differentiate this style from the more neutral narrative in EV. First, there is the *-in'* variant, contrasting with the *-ing* of 1.2[c]; second, the expression, *a little nuts,* and third, the use of the postposed adverb *already*. This use of *already* is an element of Yiddish-influenced syntax in New York City speech, a direct translation of Yiddish *sheyn*, with the meaning of 'intensification'.

We then see that the structure of 1.3 parallels that of 1.2: an element of the narrative, a response by the therapist, and an evaluation of this response by Rhoda. The cross section of 1.3 on page 139, with text, cues, expansion, and interaction shows a parallel structure that can be compared with the cross section of 1.2 on page 136.

The patient and therapist are now in harmony in that they both understand what the issue is—at least as far as the external social situation is concerned. The therapist is aware of the role strain produced by the situation diagramed in Figure 11, and she is competent to judge the consequences of the social situation outlined above. In fact, she will be called upon to do more than understand this passively. In Episode 5, she will feel it necessary to express social judgments about the problems of this complex network and the role strain it creates. It is extraordinary to see how much social competence is required of the therapist and how she is called upon to act as an arbiter of social norms—as an informal sociologist. This understanding and this work is a necessary prerequisite to the psychological work that she wishes to carry out in this interview.

The role strain produced by this situation would be considered normal—a problem of daily life, which most people could handle. But the emotions produced in Rhoda are much stronger, felt more profoundly,

RHODA'S NARRATIVE   139

than one might expect. Eventually the therapist will try to make Rhoda aware of her disproportionate response and help her search for the reason.

1.3	TEXT	CUES
[a]	R.: ⟨$_N$But—she lef' Sunday, and she's still not home.⟩$_N$	

EXPANSION
⟨$_N$ But my mother, my role partner in our household, left Sunday, and this is Thursday, four days later, and she's still at my sister's and not home to help me with our obligations, which are beyond normal and {STRN} have created role strain for me as a member of the household.⟩$_N$

INTERACTION
R. continues the narrative and gives information to reorient the therapist on the point of the narrative.

	TEXT	CUES
[b]	Th.: ⟨$_{IV}$ O-oh.⟩$_{IV}$	Reinforcement: 2 4 2, 'surprised sympathy; "That bad!"' [See Figure 13.]

EXPANSION
⟨$_{IV}$ Oh! It's *that* bad!⟩$_{IV}$

INTERACTION
Th. responds ⟵ by giving stronger sympathetic support.

	TEXT	CUES
[c]	R.: ⟨$_F$ And ... I'm gettin' a little nuts a'ready.⟩$_F$	Tension: expressive family style: -in' casual; *nuts,* slang; *a'ready,* Jewish syntax. Tension: hesitation.

EXPANSION
⟨$_F$ And I am now feeling {E_1} the emotion of frustration and confusion.⟩$_F$

INTERACTION
R. gives further evaluation of narrative ⟵$_{E_1}$ by giving information on her emotional state in family style.

1.4 and 1.5. Though Rhoda and the therapist are in harmony about the problem, Rhoda still feels that there is much to be said in evaluating the situation. Instead of proceeding with the narrative, she begins a long exposition of her understanding of the psychological issues involved. In this statement, she includes the claim that she understands what she thinks the therapist has been trying to get her to see. She is quite verbose here, and we can help the exposition by condensing rather than expanding.

The evaluation of the narrative that Rhoda provides in 1.4 is still largely within the framework of everyday life.

1.4[a] R.: *I's . . . I haven' been doin' too much school work*
   [b] *because—here this has to be done, here that has to be done,*
   [c] *and . . . . . I really—I'm getting tired. It-It's—I have too much to do, an' I can' con'trate on any one thing.*
   [d] Th.: *Mhm.*
1.5[a] R.: *So . . . . . it's in—it's **not** that I—. . . I mean I—I—I've proved, I **know** that I can get along without my mother, it isn't that—I—I can't get along **without** her, but it—*
   [b] *I know that—I don't have any **school**, an' she's gone away–she went away for a week, an' a **half** an'—i' didn' bother me in the leas'.*
   [c] Th.: *Mhm.*
   [d] R.: *But it seems that—I have jist—a little too much t' do.*

She is dealing with external circumstances, and the underlying proposition, made more explicit in 1.5, is that these external circumstances are the cause of the strain that she feels. Although she still speaks with some fluency, her speech pattern symbolizes the strain with repetitions and a long pause in 1.4[c]. The most striking indication of the emotional stress she is expressing is the morphological condensation of *concentrate* to *con'trate*. Most such condensation is in function words: auxiliaries, conjunctions, and so forth—and it is unusual to find content words like *concentrate* being condensed.

We have expanded Rhoda's reference to her "getting tired" by referring to other discussions of her family's claim that she should not go to school because she should "never get tired" (see Episode 5).

The basic proposition {STRN} that Rhoda argues in 1.4 is again that there are too many claims upon her capacity, a situation that is resulting in role strain. To understand the implications of this theme, we have to know that there are two other propositions in the background. According to Rhoda's family, Rhoda tires easily (that is, more easily than normal); we will symbolize this proposition as:

{TIRE} Rhoda gets tired (more easily than normal).

Her family attributes this condition to a further alleged fact that will play a major role in Episode 5:

{~EAT} Rhoda doesn't eat enough to stay healthy.

1.4

TEXT	CUES
[a] R.: ⟨_N *I's . . . I haven' been doin' too much school work*	Tension: self-interruption, hesitation, glottalization.
[b] *because—here this has to be done, here that has to be done,*	Suppressed laughter on *been doin'*. Sharp intake of breath before
[c] *and . . . . . I really—I'm getting tired. It-It's—I have too much to do, an' I can' con'trate on any one thing.* ⟩_N	*because*. Morphological condensation: *con'trate*.

EXPANSION

R.: ⟨_N [a] I haven't been doing as much school work as I should do to satisfy my obligations as a student, [b] because there are many different jobs in the house that I have to do in addition to my school work, since mother is not at home to help and [c] {TIRE} I am therefore getting tired, which my mother and my sister say I should never do. {STRN} It's because my obligations are greater than my capacity. ⟩_N

INTERACTION

R. gives further evaluation of 1.3 of the narrative by giving information about the circumstances of everyday life, asserting that STRN ⟩ her obligations are greater than her capacity.

TEXT	CUES
[d] Th.: *Mhm.*	2 2 ↑, 'neutral reinforcement [see Figure 14.]

INTERACTION

Th. reinforces.

Neither of these two propositions are argued overtly here; but the force of Rhoda's expression and the tension she shows cannot be understood unless we recognize the existence of these underlying propositions.

The therapist acknowledges Rhoda's claim in 1.4[d], again a neutral reinforcement with a level, rising contour though somewhat longer than 1.1[b] (Figure 14). This occurs just where Rhoda is beginning to slow down and show signs of uncertainty. The therapist's reinforcement seems to give her the reassurance to continue, and she does so with a rush in 1.5. We might expect her to continue the narrative after such a lengthy evaluation; but she steps even further out of the situation that she is reporting, back in the interview situation, and begins a long exposition of the issues involved

142   EPISODE ONE

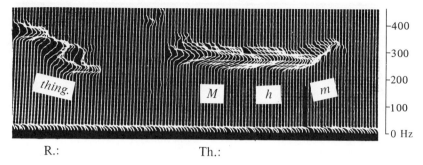

Figure 14. Pitch contour of reinforcement *Mhm* in 1.4[d].

between her and her family. In 1.5, we find more evidence of tension as Rhoda hesitates, interrupts herself, and then pours out her argument with greater speed. We have a number of indefinite *it's* to reconstruct, and our expansion shows that they refer to "the reason for my getting tired..." and other signs of emotion {E_1} and strain {STRN}. She recapitulates the argument that she has been having with her mother, and vigorously denies the proposition that she "can't get along without her." She does not give us a direct quote from her mother saying "you can't get along without me," but it is evident that her mother has been the source of this accusation, which is ultimately equivalent to claiming that {~AD-R} Rhoda is not an adult member of the household. It is now evident that this is the argument underlying the more superficial problem stated in 1.4. When Rhoda denies {~AD-R}, she does so with extraordinary emphasis. Figure 15 shows that her voice jumps over an octave.

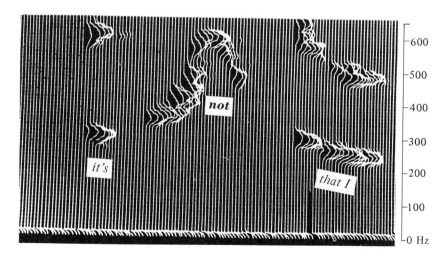

Figure 15. Pitch contour of Rhoda's emphatic negation in 1.5[a].

She breaks off at this point, but the rest of 1.5 allows us to reconstruct the missing half: "it's not that I [can't get along without my mother]."

The therapist's reinforcement of 1.5[c] (Figure 16) is more than simple encouragement. It is an acknowledgment of the complex argument that Rhoda is making, which we may sketch graphically as:

The vectors are claims of causal relationships; Rhoda denies the causal link on the left, and posits the link on the right. The complex proposition inserted in the expansion presents this causal argument in a linear form:

$$\sim(\sim\text{AD-R: TIRE})$$

Thus Rhoda denies the proposition that her being tired is the result of her not being an adult (since she is an adult). The therapist's acknowledgment is the beginning of a series of responses that encourage Rhoda as she recapitulates some of the basic ideas of therapy in 1.6. Although Rhoda is doing much of the talking, there is considerable interaction between therapist and patient in 1.5 and 1.6. The argument Rhoda is summarizing seems to be only between herself and her mother, but we cannot forget that she is also defending herself before the therapist. If the goal of therapy is for Rhoda to establish her independence, Rhoda must demonstrate here that she is indeed an independent person. After the therapist's reinforcement, Rhoda restates her basic argument:

1.5[d]   R.: *But it seems that—I have jist—a little too much t'do.*

Here we see a compilation of three forms which serve to mitigate the situation: *it seems, just,* and *a little.* Rhoda asserts that her fatigue is not caused by any deep problem, but it is simply that external circumstances have given her more work than she can perform. In contrasting the present problem with the ones that occurred previously, Rhoda does not blame her mother: an impersonal situation is responsible for the role strain that she

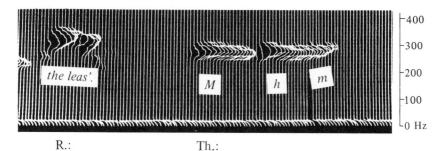

Figure 16. Pitch contour of reinforcement *Mhm* (Level ∅) in 1.5[c].

1.5

TEXT	CUES
[a] R.: ⟨$_{IV}$So..... it's in—it's **not** that I—... I mean I—I—I've proved, I **know** that I can get along without my mother, it isn't that—I—I can't get along with**out** her, but it—	Exasperation: falsetto and heavy stress on **not**. Tension: hesitation, self-interruption. [See Figure 15.]
[b] I know that—when I don't have any **school**, an' she's gone away—she went away for a week, an' a **half** an'—i' didn' bother me in the leas'.⟩$_{IV}$	Tension release: speed and relative fluency.

EXPANSION

R.: ⟨$_{IV}$ [a] The reason for {TIRE} my getting tired, and my hesitation, is not that I can't get along without my mother as she has said {~~AD-R}. I've proved that I can get along without her and *I am an adult member of the household*. [b] As proof of this, my mother went away for a week and a half once before when I didn't have any school, and this didn't bother me in the least.⟩$_{IV}$

INTERACTION

R. gives further evaluation of the narrative by denying her mother's assertion that ⟨ ~(~AD-R: TIRE) ⟩ the strain that she feels is caused by the fact that she is not adult and asserts ⟨ AD-R ⟩ that she is an adult member of the household by other evidence.

TEXT	CUES
[c] Th.: *Mhm*.	2 2 ↑ 'neutral reinforcement' [See Figure 16.]

INTERACTION

Therapist acknowledges the argument.

TEXT	CUES
[d] R.: ⟨$_{IV}$ *But it seems that—I have jist—a little too much t'do.*⟩$_{IV}$	

EXPANSION

R.: ⟨$_{IV}$But the problem is different now: I have too many things to actually do, with my school work and housework combined.⟩$_{IV}$

INTERACTION

R. asserts that ⟨ X:STRN ⟩ external circumstances are responsible for the strain that she feels.

feels. Our interactional statement here registers the absence of interaction with her mother, since it is clear that she is not explicitly blaming her mother for this situation. This attribution of the blame to impersonal forces is a proposition that we symbolize as {X:STRN}: external circumstances are responsible for the strain felt by Rhoda. Graphically:

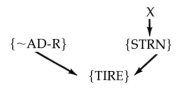

1.6. Rhoda's next remark sounds as if she were returning to the narrative events; but these are "pseudo-events." She reconstructs her argument by claiming to remember what she was thinking about just before the critical action that she took. She has fully expounded the emotional and social situation; now she relates this to the basic proposition {S} that one should express needs and emotions to relevant others, to justify her initial claim that she "did the right thing."

1.6[a] R.: *So at first, I wasn' gonna* **say** *anything. Then I remembered— that—if I keep it* **in** *what's bothering me*
   [b] Th.: *Mhm.*
   [c] R.: *then nobody else knows an' everybody thinks everything is fine, and good*
   [d] Th.: *Mhm.*
   [e] R.: *and I end up—hurting myself.*
   [f] Th.: *Right!*

The argument which Rhoda pictures as passing through her mind is a fairly clear statement of the basic suggestion of therapy. The mode of expression is much more direct than usual, and the mode of argument is also unusually direct:

{S} if you keep in what is bothering you, then everyone else will think that you are fine, no one will try to help you, and so you will end up hurting yourself

The therapist responds to Rhoda's restatement by an increase in the level of her reinforcement beginning with 1.6[b] until she reaches the explicit utterance of 1.6[f]: *Right!* So far, *right* is the only word which the therapist has uttered in the whole episode, except for the reinforcing signals fitted into Rhoda's monologue. As they do not interrupt the flow of the other person's speech, we may consider these as "suprasegmental" cues like the intonation contours that are superimposed upon the person's own sentence.

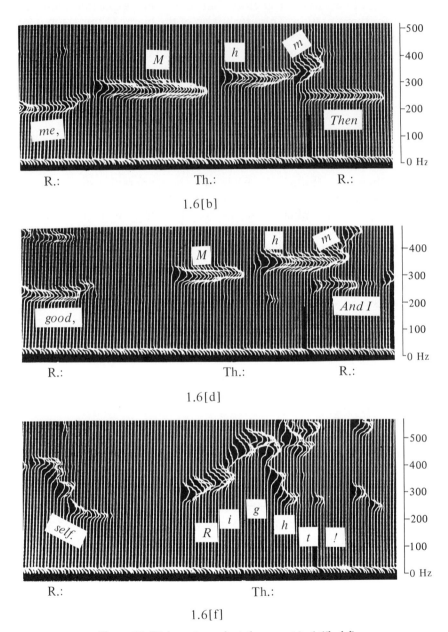

Figure 17. Pitch contour of reinforcement in 1.6[b,d,f].

Since the therapist has uttered only one word, it may seem to many observers that she has not been active, but a closer look at the series of reinforcements in 1.5[c], 1.6[b], 1.6[d], and 1.6[f] indicates that she is being very active indeed, following closely the patient's efforts to prove her point. Figure 17 shows the successive increase in pitch levels of 1.6[b] and [d], which register the increasing level of intensive participation of the therapist, culminating in 1.6[f]. This strong support of the basic suggestion shows the therapist's feeling that the point being made by Rhoda is a crucial one for the course of therapy, that the patient has grasped a central theme of the interview situation.

In terms of the narrative structure, Rhoda's statement of 1.6 is "external evaluation," recast in the frame of a narrative event—her thought at the time. This evaluation is an explicit restatement of what was said in 1.1—

1.6 TEXT	CUES
[a] R.: ⟨N *So at first, I wasn' gonna say anything. Then I remembered—that—if I keep it in what's bothering me*⟩N	Reinforcement: 2 3 ↑, 'good', [see Figure 17.]
[b] Th.: ⟨IV*Mhm.*⟩IV	Reinforcement: 3 4 ↑, 'very good', [see Figure 17].
[c] R.: ⟨N *then nobody else knows an' everbody thinks everything is fine, and good*⟩N	Reinforcement: 2 4 2, 'excellent', [see Figure 17].
[d] Th.: ⟨IV *Mhm.* ⟩IV	
[e] R.: ⟨N *and I end up—hurting myself.*⟩N	
[f] Th.: ⟨IV *Right!* ⟩IV	

EXPANSION

R.: ⟨IV [a] So when I first called my mother, I wasn't going to say anything to her about my needs and her obligations, which as you know is my usual way of behaving, but I know now, as you have shown me that {S: *if I don't express my anger and frustration to others in the household* [b] (Th.: Yes, you're on the right track.) [c] R.: *then they won't know that I'm angry and frustrated* [d] (Th.: Yes, you're certainly on the right track.) [e] *and I would by this failure to express my emotions hurt myself*} and I see that my own behavior has been a source of my difficulties. [f] (Th.: Right! This is what I've been suggesting!)⟩IV

INTERACTION

R. continues the narrative with reconstructions of her thoughts as events, giving external evaluation in interview style within the narrative of everyday life, thereby asserting ⎯1⎯⟩ her behavior was governed by the suggestion {S} learned in therapy, thereby requesting approval ⟨⎯⎯ from the therapist. Th. gives progressively stronger support.

that Rhoda did carry out the therapist's suggestion. It evaluates the central action of the narrative to follow in 1.8.

In the *Playback* session, Fanshel was struck by the fact that Rhoda's evaluation seemed to illuminate the first vague intentions that she expressed in 1.1.

FANSHEL: SHE STARTED OUT THE DISCUSSION SAYING THAT SHE WANTED TO TEST OUT... SOMETHING.
THERAPIST: SOMETHING... YES.
FANSHEL: ... AS TO WHETHER SHE REALLY—
THERAPIST: THAT'S SOMETHING SHE LEARNED, IN TREATMENT.

As we examined Fanshel's comment in light of our long reexamination of the text, it seems that he sensed even then the ambiguity of Rhoda's expression. But as he was hesitating, trying to express what it was that she really was trying to say, the therapist made explicit the message of her comment, *Right!*, which they had just heard on tape—that Rhoda was restating one of the most important lessons she had learned in treatment.

1.7. Though Rhoda has now stated her evaluation quite abstractly, she still is not ready to continue the narrative. Instead, she restates the theme in a more concrete form by roleplaying: she rehearses for the therapist the kind of remark she normally would say to herself before calling up her mother.

1.7[a] R.: *Which would be that if I kept letting her **stay** there and didn' say, "Look—uh—I mean y'been there long enough," I'd just' get tired an-nd I-I'm not doing my school work right.*
[b] Th.: *Mhm.*

This bit of role playing is cast in family language, clearly different from the deliberative style which preceded. It is marked stylistically by two features: the demand for attention *look* and the elliptical comparative *long enough*.

For linguists, such unstated references in the comparative construction have always been among the most difficult syntactic constructions to resolve. An extraordinary amount of meaning can be concentrated in a single morpheme such as *enough, too,* or *that:*

> He is not *too* strong.
> It's not *that* big.
> I've worked *so* hard.
> It's not *enough*.
> He's stron*ger* now.

Linguists search for a formal, underlying structure that will provide the material needed for the semantic interpretation of such concise utterances. These comparatives are puzzling because so much of the structure as well as the content seems to have been deleted; it is one of the fundamental principles of linguistic analysis that any abstract structures that are posited should be equally available to the native speaker. In traditional linguistic arguments, the effort is made to reconstruct the material from the isolated sentence itself; but in recent years, more and more linguists have realized that the recovery must be made from nearby sentences as well. In our analysis, we have expanded the scope of this research to a much wider range than linguists have been willing to do before; the expansion of the utterance must draw upon the whole body of shared knowledge that we can recover from an examination of this interview, other interviews, and even conversations with the therapist herself.

You've been there long enough.
↑
You have been at my sister's house long enough to take care of any obligation to her household that you may have had...

In our analysis of Rhoda's narrative so far, we have not had to call upon many complex rules of discourse. The actions that Rhoda has been performing have been classed mainly as "giving information," "giving evaluation," and "asserting." We have developed these actions explicitly on the basis of our knowledge of her family situation. This relatively simple set of speech actions is related to the fact that Rhoda developed the argument on an impersonal basis, and the other figures in the family interaction have been kept well in the background. As Rhoda nears the confrontation with her mother, though, we will see reflected a more complex type of interaction.

We will analyze the interaction in Rhoda's roleplaying in some detail, but the full explication of the discourse rules involved would best be postponed to our analysis of what Rhoda actually says, which is reported in the next chapter. Since 1.7 is an *imagined* roleplaying of the critical event that is the central action of Episode 1, we would expect it to show all of the implications of the request that Rhoda reports herself making. But as we will see, it contrasts sharply with her actual report in that it is more aggressive—much further along the *aggravation* side of the aggravation–mitigation polarity. It is plain that Rhoda is assuming the right to criticize her mother in 1.7.

Behind this criticism lies the general status of her mother's competence as head of the household, a social proposition comparable to {AD-R}, the issue of Rhoda's competence.

{HEAD-Mo}   Mother is (a competent) head of the household.*

---

*If we begin with the fact that mother is the head of Rhoda's household, it follows automatically by a very general proposition that mother's primary responsibility is to this household. This is so general that it need not be coded in relation to this particular analysis, but we can say that *heads of households as have their primary obligations maintaining the normal functioning of their households.*

This formulation refers to the structural outline in Figure 11, where we see mother participating in Household 1 with Rhoda and Aunt Editha. Since she is the head of that household, her primary obligations are now urgent, since she has fulfilled her secondary obligations in Household 2. However 1.7 does more than assert this. It carries out two actions: a criticism and a request, as shown in Figure 18. Figure 18 shows that the structure of 1.7 includes three assertions, a request, a challenge, and an admission. The assertions are localized in Episode 1, and are therefore marked with arabic numerals; but the challenge, the admission, and the request are themes that recur throughout the therapeutic session and therefore have more general labels. The branching of Figure 18 is typical of the face-to-face interaction we are studying.

Figure 18 begins with the surface statement of 1.7: *Look, you been there long enough.* Our study of the social relations developed in Figure 11 allows us to see this as the assertion of a local proposition:

{2} Mother has fulfilled her secondary obligations to Household 2.

From this it follows immediately that

{3} Mother has neglected her primary obligations to Household 1.

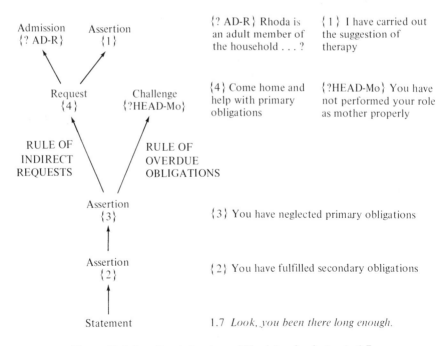

Figure 18. Interactional structure of Rhoda's role playing in 1.7.

To this point, there are no strong interactive consequences: Rhoda can be heard as simply analyzing the situation as it stands.

The interactional complexity of 1.7 becomes more evident as we see that assertion of {3} is an indirect means of making a request for action. This follows the Rule for Indirect Requests (Chapter 3, p. 79). Assertion {3} is a statement about a need for an action, which is the subject of the local proposition:

{4} Rhoda requests her mother to come home immediately.

Since all the other preconditions are in effect (as we will see in detail in the following chapter), it follows that 1.7 would be heard as a valid request for the action {4}. Since {4} would be an instance of Rhoda expressing her needs to relevant others, carrying out {4} would also be equivalent to carrying out the basic suggestion {S}, and if Rhoda had said 1.7, she would then be supporting her initial assertion {1} that she had done the right thing. But at the same time, it will become increasingly apparent that expressing such needs would also be heard as an admission that Rhoda cannot take care of herself, an admission {?AD-R} that brings into question her own adult status.

Returning to assertion {3} in Figure 18, we observe another branch, leading to a questioning of the proposition {HEAD-Mo}. This follows from the Rule of Overdue Obligations (Chapter 3, p. 96). Since Rhoda would be asserting that her mother had not performed her obligations as head of Household 1, she would be heard as challenging her mother's competence in that role. Such a challenge or criticism would not of course result in her mother's losing such a status (as Rhoda might lose her adult status), but it would result in her mother's having lower esteem as head of the household.

This brief statement is only an outline of the analysis; we will present a more detailed exposition in Rhoda's report of the actual conversation in 1.8.

Figure 18 shows graphically how speakers are forced to mitigate their actions by indirect means, masking them by other speech actions. The mode of mitigation selected by the speaker is a kind of action in itself. This action has to take into account the power relationships of the persons involved. In Rhoda's roleplaying of 1.7, she takes a relatively strong position in regard to her mother, reversing the normal situation in which a mother would tell her daughter, "You've been there long enough."* She does use some indirection; the power relationships between mother and daughter control the verbal output of 1.7 even in imagination and are responsible for the fact that the basic request {4} and challenge {?HEAD-

---

*This observation was made originally by Harvey Sacks in relation to 1.8, but it is even more pointed in the formulation of 1.7.

152   EPISODE ONE

1.7   TEXT   CUES
[a] R.: ⟨_IV_ Which would be that ⟨_N_ if I   Tension release: intake of breath after
kept letting her **stay** there and didn' say,   enough.
⟨_F_ "Look—uh—I mean y'been there long
enough," ⟩_F_ I'd jus' get tired ⟩_N_ an-nd
I-I'm not doing my school work right. ⟩_IV_

EXPANSION

R.: ⟨_IV_ And it would follow from this suggestion {S} that if I kept letting my mother stay at my sister's house and didn't say to her something like ⟨_N_ "Look at what you know but are avoiding: {2} You have been at my sister's house long enough to take care of any obligation to her household, and {3} you are neglecting your primary obligation to me and our household, and {4} so I am asking you to come home right away," ⟩_N_ and {S} if I didn't express my needs and feelings in that way, then {TIRE} I would get tired, which everyone says I am not supposed to do, and since this is already beginning to happen to me, since {STRN} I'm not performing my obligations at school well enough, ⟩_IV_

INTERACTION

R.: R. gives further evaluation of the narrative, by role playing her forthcoming request to her mother, asserting 2⟩ that her mother's secondary obligations have been fulfilled, thereby asserting 3⟩ that her mother's primary obligations are being neglected, thereby challenging ?HEAD-Mo ⟩ her mother's role performance, and thereby requesting 4⟩ that her mother come home thereby asserting again ⟨1 that she was about to carry out the suggestion {S} of therapy.

           TEXT   CUES
[b] Th.: _Mhm._   Reinforcement: 2 3 4, Level 3, 'very
                                                good'.

INTERACTION

Therapist reinforces at a high level.

Mo} do not appear on the surface. But the masking and mitigating operations that are diagrammed in Figure 18 are less indirect than those found in the actual report of the verbal interaction given by Rhoda.

Though there are many steps needed to reconstruct Rhoda's actions and propositions in 1.5–1.7, these are not very remote from what she is saying on the surface. She is "thinking out loud," as she evaluates the action that she contemplates taking. From our studies of narrative structure, we know that such suspension of the action frequently precedes the most important event, so the listener is aware that what follows is really the "point" of the narrative as a whole. This is certainly the case here: Rhoda's very next utterance is a report of the crucial action that is the focal point of this entire therapeutic session. She has taken an action she believes to be "the right thing," and this action is now reported in a conversation that seems to reflect the actual relations between Rhoda and her mother better than anything that has preceded. The kinds of discourse relations involved are much more abstract; much less is said on the surface, and much more seems to be done below the surface. Breaks between the surface and the deep structure are more dramatic, and the discourse rules needed to elucidate them are more complex. Our next chapter will shift the locus of interaction from the therapeutic session to the transaction between Rhoda and her mother.

5

EPISODE ONE (CONTINUED)
When do you plan t'come home?

After her long evaluation of her relations with her mother, and her discussion of what she might say and do about her immediate problem, Rhoda plunges back into the narrative proper. From this point on to the end of the episode, the therapist does not intervene or comment in any way. Nor does Rhoda evaluate again the events that she describes. Her long suspension of the action in 1.4, 1.5, 1.6, and 1.7 suggests that the very next narrative event is to be the main point of her account. In that long digression, she has created the backdrop against which the main action will be seen.

Rhoda has laid the groundwork for us to evaluate her action: she has shown us that what might be ordinary action for some people is a crucial one for her. In asking her mother for help, she has laid herself open to the criticism that {~AD-R} "She can't get along without her mother," a proposition which she has been trying to disprove for some time. Yet if she does not ask for help, she will not be responding to {S} the basic suggestion of the therapy, and will be placing herself under an even greater strain than she has known before.

Rhoda takes up her narrative by reporting the crucial conversation with her mother. After a moment's hesitation, she gives us a straightforward quotation of what she actually said:

1.8 R.: *An-nd so—when—I called her t'day, I said, "Well, when do you plan t'come home?"*

Rhoda's question is in family style, but the mode of expression relies less on paralinguistic cues than do many other examples to follow. Certain lexical items show the interactive technique of family style. A simpler form of the request would have been: "When are you going to come home?" but Rhoda inserts *plan to* as a main verb: impressionistically we react to this as an expression of exasperation. For concrete justification of this impression, we can compare the request with the imagined one of 1.7, *Look, y'been there*

155

long enough. Rhoda underlines the fact that it is a major undertaking to get her mother out of her sister's house. There is a sarcastic undertone in making such a simple action the subject of a plan. At the same time, *plan to* places the responsibility of the decision on Rhoda's mother: as we will see, she ultimately evades that responsibility. The contrastive stress on *home* adds to the urgency of the request by highlighting the fact that her mother is still at Household 2, instead of at Household 1, where Rhoda thinks she should be.

The *well* that begins Rhoda's question has been expanded considerably in our cross section. As a discourse marker, *well* refers backwards to some topic that is already shared knowledge among participants. When *well* is the first element in a discourse or a topic, this reference is necessarily to an unstated topic of joint concern. Although Rhoda's remark is certainly not the first element in the actual conversation she had with her mother, it has the force here of referring to such an unstated topic, known to both Rhoda and her mother, and clearly the "reason" for the call.*

We expand the actual request for information to include two local propositions peculiar to this episode, which were cited in Figure 18, and which show the underlying structure of "Look, you've been there long enough." These themes refer to social propositions but are tied to the particular events that we have been discussing here.

{2} Mother's immediate obligation to Household 2 has been fulfilled.
{3} Mother's primary obligation to Household 1 is being neglected.

These two propositions are the major elements that we add to the text in our expansion. They combine to a further implication:

{4} Mother should come home now.

There is a further presupposition we might identify here, a general proposition that is necessary to connect {2} and {3} with {4}. Competent heads of households do not neglect their responsibilities when there is no competing obligation, and the claim on mother is based on the fact that she holds this status.

{HEAD-Mo} Mother is (a competent) head of Household 1.

We combine these elements into the following expansion:

EXPANSION

R.: ⟨_N When I called my mother today (Thursday), I actually said, ⟨_F "Well, in regard to the subject which we both know is important and is worrying me,

---

*Harvey Sacks pointed out to us the referential force of *well* in this case. For relevant observations on the perceived "reason for call," see Sacks and Schegloff, "Opening Up Closings" (1974).

when are you leaving my sister's house where {2}: any obligation you have has already been fulfilled and returning home where {3}: your primary obligations are being neglected as {4} you should do as {HEAD-Mo} head of our household? $)_F$ $)_N$

Though the expansion interprets more fully the significant implications of what Rhoda has said from a cognitive viewpoint, it does not tell us what she is doing with the utterance of 1.8. On the surface, it is a request for information about a time: the time that her mother is planning to come home. But the contrastive stress on *home* suggests that location is the important element: that her mother is somewhere else and not home, where she should be. The intuitive response of everyone who reads or hears 1.8 is to read through the manifest content of a request for information about time and hear a request for action. We symbolize such a request by embedding the imperative {4} in an interactive arrow:

$\boxed{4}$)Rhoda → mother: Come home now!

In a very real sense, the request for action $\boxed{4}$) is the main point of the narrative, the central focus of Episode 1 and the therapeutic session as a whole. It is the "right thing" that Rhoda claims to have done in Chapter 4. But our expansion does not yet justify formally the connection between Rhoda's request for information and her request for her mother to come home. This is a mitigated request, as requests often are. In this situation, the degree of mitigation must be very high.

It would be quite difficult for us to imagine Rhoda saying to her mother, "Mother, you come home right now or else!" As noted in Chapter 4, this is the type of remark which mothers make to daughters, and such forms are obviously unacceptable in the daughter-to-mother direction. The indirect and mitigated character of the request does not disguise its challenging nature, since (as Sacks has pointed out) it is not just the form, but the very nature of the request, which is most appropriate for parents to ask children rather than the reverse. Parents are not usually considered accountable to their children as to the time that they plan to come home. Given this challenge, it will be necessary for Rhoda to be able to deny formally that she was rude to her mother. If, for example, her mother should say, "What do you mean, saying that to me?" Rhoda could answer, "All I did was ask you when you were planning to come home." In other words, the obvious challenge of the underlying request can be explicitly denied, and the work done to mitigate the request is an important factor in interpersonal relations.

We must now explicate in more detail the formal connections between the surface question and the underlying request, and then we will pursue the deeper challenges and criticisms that follow from the request. In our general discussion of discourse analysis (Chapter 3) we developed the following Rule of Requests:

If A directs to B an imperative specifying an action X at a time T_1, and B believes that A believes that
- 1a. X should be done for a purpose Y [*need for the action*]
- b. B would not do X in the absence of the request [*need for the request*]
- 2. B had the *ability* to do X (with an instrument Z)
- 3. B has the *obligation* to do X or is willing to do it.
- 4. A has the *right* to tell B to do X,

then A is heard as making a valid request for action.

Even in the most direct requests, these unstated beliefs must be present if we are to distinguish a true request for action (or command) from jokes, insults, threats, and other utterances that take an imperative form on the surface. But this is only one of many uses of this rule, which is employed more often than any other in the study of face-to-face conversational interaction. It is an essential apparatus for understanding how requests are made, put off, and so on. Since therapy is concerned with the way in which people deal with one another, negotiate their needs, and make their desires known, it is understandable that this rule would be operating in one form or another in every important topic considered by the therapist and patient together.

The Rule of Requests states the basic conditions for interpreting explicit imperatives. Other rules are needed to explicate the ways in which the many and varied surface forms that we interpret as requests are connected with the underlying action. The further extensions of this rule also show how mitigation and aggravation are done, utilizing the very conditions that insure the validity of the command. The Rule for Indirect Requests (Chapter 3, page 82) brings together three different ways of using the basic rule without stating the request explicitly:

If A makes to B a request for information or an assertion to B about
- a. the existential status of an action X to be performed by B
- b. the consequences of performing an action X
- c. the time T_1 that an action X might be performed by B
- d. any of the preconditions for a valid request for X as given in the Rule of Requests

and all other preconditions are in effect, then A is heard as making a valid request of B for the action X.

In Chapter 3, we illustrated some of the many ways in which this rule can be used; in this case, Rhoda makes a request for information of her mother about the *time* when the action is going to be performed. The four preconditions are all in effect: Rhoda's mother believe that Rhoda believes that

1. Her mother should come home to help do the housework and does not seem to be doing so without being asked.
2. Her mother has the ability to come home.
3. Her mother has an obligation to come home, because she is the head of the household.
4. Rhoda has the right to tell her mother to come home.

Again, we emphasize the point that it is not necessarily true that Rhoda's mother believes all this; but since she believes that Rhoda believes this, she will hear 1.8 as a valid request for action. As we will see, further interaction between Rhoda and her mother center about preconditions 1 and 2; 3 and 4 are not discussed, but they are at the center of the therapist's later discussion with Rhoda, and Rhoda's decision to call her mother up and ask her to come home is the result of preconditions 3 and 4 being supported in therapy.

To understand fully the Rule for Indirect Requests, we must see how it is employed to do the work of mitigation and aggravation, disguising or sharpening the challenges to power relationships involved. Among the most mitigating forms are those that refer to the time of an action or whether or not it has been performed—cases 1 and 2 in the Rule for Indirect Requests. Questions or statements about the first two preconditions are also usually mitigating, as we pointed out in Chapter 3. It is a much more challenging affair to use preconditions 3 and 4 for making indirect requests; reference to rights and obligations often leads to the aggravating of requests, and this is much more characteristic of family conflict that has reached the point of overt breach. The power relationships in Rhoda's household are at issue, but the issue is below the surface. Rhoda never challenges her mother directly; in a symmetrical way, her mother's way of handling decisions and conflicts of authority is to talk about Rhoda's needs and abilities as well as her own. The same preconditions are used for putting off requests. We will see some evidence that Rhoda's mother also makes use of preconditions 3 and 4 when she responds.

The identification of 1.8 as a request for action is a fairly easy case: it fits in with the general rule of requests, and it corresponds to our intuitions. However, our intuitive responses do not provide the kind of convincing evidence that is needed to advance the study of conversation: the rule must be supported by demonstrations that it has indeed applied in a number of particular cases. The main evidence for this is in the behavior of the participants themselves. Rhoda's mother responds to 1.8 in a way that plainly shows she interpreted it as a request, as we will see in our discussion of 1.9 below.

1.8	TEXT	CUES
R.: ⟨_N An-nd so—when—I called her t'day, I said, ⟨_F "Well, when do you plan t'come **home?**"⟩_F ⟩_N		Exasperation: *plan to,* 'implication of deliberation'; contrastive stress on **home.**

EXPANSION

R.:⟨_N When I called my mother today (Thursday), I actually said, ⟨_F "Well, in regard to the subject which we both know is important and is worrying me, when are you leaving my sister's house where {2}: any obligations you have already have been fulfilled and returning home where {3}: your primary obligations are being neglected as {4} you should do as {HEAD-Mo} head of our household? ⟩_F ⟩_N

INTERACTION

R.: R. continues the narrative, and gives information to support her assertion ⟨1⟩ that she carried out the suggestion {S}. R. requests information on the time that her mother intends to come home and thereby requests indirectly ⟨4⟩ that her mother come home, thereby carrying out the suggestion {S}, and thereby challenging her mother indirectly ⟨?HEAD-Mo⟩ for not performing her role as head of the household properly, simultaneously admitting ⟨STRN⟩ her own limitations and simultaneously asserting again ⟨1⟩ that she carried out the suggestion {S}.

Granted that 1.8 is a request for the action {4}, it is not difficult to see that it is also an action of a more abstract kind. In asking for her mother to come home, Rhoda is asking for help: she is expressing her needs to the most relevant other and carrying out the suggestion {S}. We will symbolize this general request by placing {S} in an interactive arrow:

⟨S⟩ Rhoda asks relevant others for help.

We must now consider a more difficult question, the identification of an action that lies even further beneath the surface. As in the case of 1.7, *Look, y'been there long enough,* we observe a challenge to mother's competence as head of the household. In the overt utterance of 1.8, this challenge is more carefully masked than in 1.7. Let us then compare the surface structure of the imagined formulation with the reported one. Instead of a question about the time condition for the action as in 1.8, 1.7 is a statement about precondition 1—her mother's need to be away from home. Though 1.7 was an indirect request, it was less indirect than 1.8 in several respects: 1.7 is a declarative statement, and 1.8 is an interrogative; statements are in general less mitigating than interrogatives; 1.7 also implies a judgment about the proper performance of role relations, and therefore activates a personal challenge—Rhoda's mother has not performed her role as head of Household 1 properly {?HEAD-Mo}.

In the interactive statement of 1.8, the request for action $\boxed{4}$ is represented as two different kinds of action, as shown by the full cross-section on p. 160. On the one hand, 1.8 is seen as a request for help; on the other, it is a challenge to mother's competence. The challenge of 1.7 was made by stating that the appropriate cut-off point for her mother's role performance at her sister's house had been passed. Given the interlocking structure of the households, it automatically followed that {3} her mother's primary obligations are being neglected, and she has passed the threshold point for initiating her role performance as head of the household. This invoked the most common rule for criticizing someone's competence, the Rule of Overdue Obligations.

If A asserts that B has not performed obligations in a role R, then A is heard as challenging B's competence in R.

The principle connecting 1.8 with the challenge is much less obvious. It depends upon the fact that Rhoda is making requests that might have been invoked for some time. There are no new circumstances that Rhoda is bringing to her mother's attention. It follows that her mother should have known enough to take this action on her own. The challenge follows by the Rule of Delayed Requests:

If A makes a request for B to take an action in role R, based on needs, abilities, obligations, and rights which have been valid for some time, then A is heard as criticizing B's competence in role R.

It is not accidental that Rhoda imagines herself as using a less mitigating form with her mother than she actually does. This seems to be quite typical of adult interaction, especially when a person is dealing with someone in a superior status. We tend to follow the reverse pattern in interaction with children. It seems to be common for adults to imagine themselves using polite and mitigating forms to children, but then to make the request in a sharply aggravated form in actuality.

Figure 6 of Chapter 2 diagramed the abstract relations of 1.8, (p. 66) which may be consulted at this point. We see that the request is realized as two even more abstract actions. On the one hand, it is clearly an *assertion* that Rhoda "did the right thing" $\boxed{1}$. On the other hand, it is necessarily an *admission* that Rhoda feels strain: her obligations are greater than her capacity $\boxed{\text{STRN}}$. She has already admitted as much to the therapist in 1.4[c], and she admits this strain again to her mother in 1.10.

1.4[c]   ... I really—I'm getting tired. It-it's —I have too much to do ...

1.10   ... *Things are getting just a little too* **much**!... *i's jis' getting too hard*...

Though we have said that this proposition {STRN} is a necessary precondition for a valid request, it is also true that making the request is tantamount to making the admission. The fact that the request for help $\overline{S}$ can be seen simultaneously as an admission of incapacity and an assertion of independence is the fundamental contradiction of Rhoda's position.

We can now compare the more abstract structures of 1.7 (p. 150) and 1.8. The interaction for 1.7 shows the same underlying challenge to Rhoda's mother and the same admission of role strain on Rhoda's part. It also implies the assertion that the suggestion was carried out, which applies to 1.7 only hypothetically, but to 1.8 in actuality. The only differences between the two utterances are at the lower levels, which connect the utterance with the request for action. Here 1.7 involves directly the two local propositions {2} and {3}, in order to relate the statement *Y'been there long enough* to a request. 1.8 uses a different route, where these propositions are only implicit preconditions of the Rule of Requests and need not be shown as such.

The difference between 1.7 and 1.8 may be only a matter of surface etiquette. Even in challenging her mother and seeking to direct her behavior, Rhoda shows a surface deference that is appropriate to her situation. It is an open question as to how effective such mitigation is in reducing the challenge implicit in the request.

We have erected a complex structure for 1.8; we must now see what Rhoda's mother made of it. Which of these speech actions did she recognize, and which did she respond to?

1.9. Mother's response to Rhoda is very short:

So she said, "Oh, why?"

At first glance, it would seem that her mother failed to recognize all the complexities we found in 1.8. She was able to deal with the request in two simple words; but the relationship between 1.8 and 1.9 suggests that 1.9 is not simple at all.

1.9 shows us the most dramatic example of a break in surface structure. Though we know intuitively that this is coherent discourse, and a competent response to 1.8, the question *Why?* does not follow by any regular rule of ellipsis from what Rhoda has just said. Normal syntactic rules of ellipsis operate as follows:

A: *I'm going downtown.*
B: *Why?* ← *'Why are you going downtown?'*

Such rules of ellipsis locate in preceding utterances the information needed to reconstruct the elliptical form as a full sentence with its full semantic

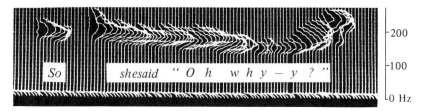

Figure 19. Pitch contour of 1.9, "Oh why—y?"

interpretation. If we try to apply this procedure to 1.9, we get nonsense:

R.: *When do you plan to come home?*
Mo.: *Why?* ↚'Why when do you plan to come home?'
↚'Why do you plan to come home?'

The only way that we can account for 1.9 as coherent discourse is to say that it is a response at some deeper level than the superficial expression Rhoda used.*

As we begin our systematic analysis of 1.9, we note immediately that it is accompanied by a very special paralinguistic cue: a low, falling–rising contour (2 1 2), which we have given the general gloss of 'heavy implication'. Figure 19 shows the movement of the fundamental frequency. The great variety of interpretations that can be imposed on this signal are caused by the generality of its fundamental meaning. If this is superimposed on a short response to any request or assertion, it conveys to the other party that the speaker has found it necessary to reflect carefully on what has just been said—in other words, that there is a strong implication of something implicit beneath the surface in the preceding utterance. We use the more expanded gloss, 'There is more to this than meets the eye'. If this expression of heavy implication concerns something that has been discussed before and both speakers know what the issues are, the signal of heavy implication can convey the additional information that 'This proves again that I was right' or, more commonly, 'I told you so'. Both of these meanings find a place in our contextual expansion.

The contextual expansion of 1.9 is quite long compared to the text, indicating that the mode of expression is very indirect. It takes into account much other information besides the immediate context and the paralinguistic cues. We will need all the sophistication we can bring to bear to interpret this utterance: paralinguistic cues, rules of discourse, and the juxtaposition of many different elements from other parts of the interview.

---

*A sequence such as this is often characterized as "answering a question with a question," but this adds no greater insight into the meanings conveyed here, especially since *question* is an ambiguous term as normally used. See Chapter 3, p. 64.

EXPANSION

R.: So my mother said to me, "Oh, I'm surprised; why are you asking me when I plan to come home, and do you have a right to ask that? There's more to this than meets the eye: isn't it that {~AD-R} you can't take care of the household by yourself and I shouldn't have gone away in the first place, as I've told you before?"

Evidence for the expansion of 1.9 is provided at two other points in the session, where Rhoda repeats her account, and plainly indicates her realization of what the 2 1 2 intonation contour means. In Episode 4, she gives the account of the same event:

4.12 So I says t'her, "Are you coming home tomorrow morning?"
4.13 So she said, "Why—why?"
4.14 A-and—I said—uh—"Well, it's getting a little too much."
4.15 So she said, "See, I *told* you so."

4.15 is an explicit statement of the meaning of the intonation contour. Which is closer to the actual event: the account of Episode 1 or the expansion in Episode 4? We believe that Episode 1 comes closer to the actual exchange and Episode 4 is an elaboration of what was implicit. We argue this for three reasons: (1) Indirect evidence shows that the typical mode of verbal exchange in this family relies heavily on condensed, implicit meanings in heavily loaded intonation contours, as will appear in Episodes 2 and 3 as well; (2) In other cases, Rhoda elaborates when she goes over something for the second time, bringing out her underlying intention or understanding in response to probes from the interviewer (see Episode 3); (3) A third retelling of the incident occurs outside of the episodes we analyze. Here Rhoda concentrates her attention on the intonation contour itself: she actually suppresses the lexical item *why* and quotes instead the expression of "surprise," *oh*.

> So why—so I'll say to her, like, y'know if you don't wanna go, say you don't wanna go, but don't use me as an excuse. (Right!) But that's different—now I—so—but—*now*—when I see—that she says "Oh!", so I said, "What do you mean 'Oh'?" "The situation," I said, " is a little different from when I said the last time."

This third account gives us much more explicit cues to the underlying propositions that are being referred to by Rhoda's mother. Our expansion locates the issue in the central proposition: whether or not Rhoda is an adult member of the household (Chapter 4, p. 135). The symbol {~AD-R} indicates a denial that Rhoda can hold that status.

We might have expanded further to show that behind this challenge to Rhoda's adult status is a challenge to another status: that Rhoda is not a healthy, normal person. Her history of sickness is frequently raised by her family in such forms as "Rhoda should never get tired." This is a repeated proposition of the form:

{SICK-R}   Rhoda is sick.

Besides being deprived of some of the rights of healthy, normal adults, sick people have additional obligations. They are required to take care of themselves in such a way that they will not be additional burdens to those who are responsible for them. This kind of behavior is governed by an even more general proposition:

{S-CARE}   A person should take care of himself.

The amount of responsibility which {S-CARE} imposes upon a person depends upon his age and adult status. Yet we hear many people being criticized because "they do not take care of themselves," heads of households as well as children. If we combine the two propositions that Rhoda is sick, and that she does not take care of herself, we have a strong criticism that she has failed to live up to her moral obligations. In not performing properly the role of a sick person, she is offending other members of the household, burdening them with anxiety, and being morally delinquent. No matter how weak or sick a person is, social norms expect them to perform properly the role of a sick person: take advice from mothers and doctors, follow through a regimen of health care, and so forth. One characteristic of children is that they don't always take care of themselves; they need adult supervision to be sure they do. If it is established that Rhoda doesn't take care of herself, there is a strong implication that she is not an adult {~AD-R}; it follows that she cannot properly make decisions about going to school, going out on dates, and other prerogatives of an adult. These are serious issues for her.

The interaction of 1.9 is analyzed here as if it actually took place as it was reported. Mother's essential task as an interactant is to respond to the primary action performed by Rhoda in 1.8. The fundamental sequencing rule applies to any valid request; a failure to respond would be a severe violation of normal social obligations. It is clear that 1.9 is a *response* to the request, but it is also clear that Rhoda's mother has not *complied* with the request: She has not given the information requested, nor has she refused the request; she has "put it off." Our expansion shows that she does this by asking about two of the underlying preconditions of a valid request: Rhoda's need (which her mother knows about) and Rhoda's right to ask (which her mother challenges). Superficially, this is a request for information, and we must look to general rules that explain the significance of using a request for information after a request for action. This is the very general Rule of Embedded Requests discussed in Chapter 3 (p. 91):

166 EPISODE ONE (CONTINUED)

If A makes a request for action of B, and B responds with a request for information, B is heard as asserting that he needs this information in order to respond to A's request.

At the more superficial level, the request for information on why Rhoda must ask her mother to come home, the answer is already known. We can therefore invoke the additional Rule of Redundant Responses (Chapter 3, p. 92):

If A makes a request for action of B, and B responds with a request for information which A and B know B does not need, then B is heard as provisionally refusing the request.

In Figure 6, we showed that 1.8 can be represented as a structure of six actions. One of these, the assertion ⟨ 1 ⟩, lies outside of the family conversation. The request for information, the request for action ⟨ 4 ⟩, and the request for help ⟨ 5 ⟩ are jointly put off by the request for information "Why?" How does Rhoda's mother respond to the challenge ⟨ ?HEAD-Mo ⟩ and the admission ⟨ STRN ⟩? Figure 20 shows how this is done.

1.9	TEXT	CUES
R.: ⟨_N So she said, ⟨_F "Oh, why?" ⟩_F ⟩_N		Surprise: *Oh,* 'contrary to expectation', Heavy implication: 2 1 2, 'There's more to this than meets the eye'. [See Figure 19.]

EXPANSION

R.: ⟨_N So my mother said to me, ⟨_F "Oh, I'm surprised; why are you asking me when I plan to come home, and do you have a right to ask that? There's more to this than meets the eye: Isn't it that {~AD-R} you can't take care of the household by yourself and I shouldn't have gone away in the first place, as I've told you before?" ⟩_F ⟩_N

INTERACTION

Mother asks R. for ⟨ ? ⟩ further information which she already has, thereby putting off R.'s requests for action and for help ⟨ ~4,~5 ⟩ and asserts indirectly that she knows that the answer to her own question is that R. is asking for help because she cannot perform the obligations of household, thereby ⟨ ?AD-R ⟩ challenging R.'s status as an adult member of the household.

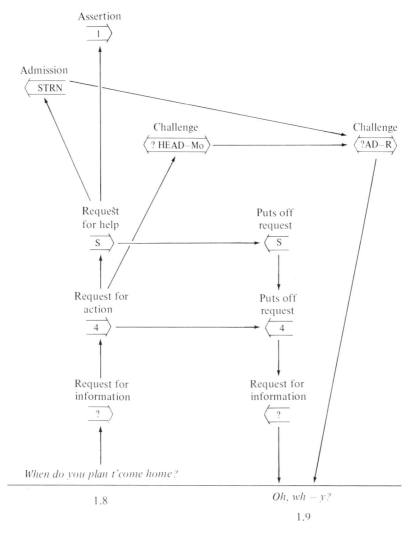

Figure 20. Sequencing of 1.8 and 1.9.

Here for the first time we begin to assemble several cross sections into a sequence, indicating the intricate ways in which a complex verbal action is answered at several levels of abstraction. The horizontal arrows connect ⟨ 4 ⟩ and ⟨ S ⟩ in 1.8 to the two actions of 1.9, which simultaneously put off both. The admission ⟨ STRN ⟩ and challenge ⟨ ?HEAD-Mo ⟩ are answered jointly by the challenge ⟨ ?AD-R ⟩. This challenge is connected directly with the intonation contour 2 1 2,* while the putting off is connected with

---

*And perhaps the expression of surprise *Oh*.

the word *Why?* In one sense, 1.9 is simpler than 1.8, since there are fundamentally only two actions being performed. But her mother's *Oh, why?* is more intricate in another sense: it uses discourse rules to accomplish a great deal with very little effort.

1.10. Rhoda is now faced with two messages as a result of her mother's complex action, 1.9. She has more than one possible response; she could

1. Ignore the intonation and respond to the request for information;
2. Denounce her mother's request for information as irrelevant—since her mother already knows the answer—and insist on a response to her request;
3. Ignore her mother's request for information and respond instead to the implication of the intonation contour.

Rhoda's actual response is marked by the reappearances of the suprasegmental features of tension.

1.10   R.: *An-nd I said, "Well, things are getting just a little too* **much!** [laugh] *This is—i's jis' getting too hard, and . . . . . . I—"*

This is quite different from the fluent interaction of 1.8, 1.9, and 1.11 to follow. The many indicators of tension resemble those we have seen in the interview style of 1.1: hesitation, glottalization, and silence. In addition, there is nervous laughter. Figure 21 displays these disturbances in timing, giving us an overall view of the defensive posture adopted by Rhoda. Her lexical choice also shows a great deal of indirection. Instead of saying, "I have too much to do" she uses the vague pronouns *things* and *it*. These impersonal terms shift the focus away from herself. In addition, she uses such mitigating forms as *just* and *a little too much*. All of these cues demonstrate the tension Rhoda feels in the contradictory position where she must demonstrate her lack of independence by the very action which asserts her independence.*

In our expansion of 1.10, we attempt to capture the hesitant and apologetic tone explicitly:

R.: And then I said to my mother, "Maybe I shouldn't have asked you to come but {X-STRN} all the jobs I have are too much for me to carry out with the strength that I have."

Our expansion shows that Rhoda has chosen the first option listed above as her response to 1.9: she responds to the request for information. But as

---

*Knowing that 1.9 can be seen as a challenge to Rhoda's right to ask for help, her hesitancy can also be seen as an apology for having violated the rules governing the relationships between mother and daughter.

Figure 21. Hesitation and pause in the timing of Rhoda's response in 1.10. (1 square = 2 seconds.)

our quotation from later in the interview showed (p. 164), she really is not sure that she did the best thing in 1.10; in fact, she says that next time she will choose the third option and challenge her mother's expressive intonation contour. There is no challenge in 1.10, but rather an apology. It is a defensive posture, which argues that external circumstances are the cause of her immediate problem—and certainly not the behavior of her family. This is perhaps the weakest of the possible responses that Rhoda might have made, but it avoids family conflict. We symbolize this proposition as: {X: STRN}.

170   EPISODE ONE (CONTINUED)

{X: STRN}   External circumstances are the cause of Rhoda's role strain.

On the surface, Rhoda is simply asserting {STRN} again. But if we compare 1.10 with the other expressions of this proposition, we could see they differ significantly:

{STRN}   *I'm not doing too much school work.* (1.4)
I'm getting tired. (1.4)
I can' con'trate on any one thing. (1.4)
What's .. what's bothering me .. (1.6)
I just get tired. (1.6)
I'm not doing my school work right. (1.7)
Things are getting just a little too much. (1.10)
I's jus' getting too hard. (1.10)

The difference between 1.10 and the other expressions is clear: in the other six cases, the first person pronoun is involved as subject or object. In 1.10, Rhoda does not appear as directly involved, but impersonal circumstances and situations are invoked. Though it is clear that Rhoda is the one who is affected, 1.10 asserts indirectly that the problem lies outside.

Though 1.10 may be weak, it is efficient in that it does simultaneously respond to the two actions of 1.9. In response to the challenge {~AD-R},

---

1.10	TEXT	CUES
	R.: ⟨_N *An-nd I said,* ⟨_F *"Well, things are getting just a little too* **much***!* [laugh] *This is—i's jis' getting too hard, and . . . . . . I—"* ⟩_F ⟩_N	Tension: choked laughter, hesitation, glottalization, long silence. [See Figure 21.]

EXPANSION

R.: ⟨_N And then I said to my mother, ⟨_F "Maybe I shouldn't have asked {4} you to come home, but {STRN} all the jobs I have are too much for me to carry out with the strength that I have." ⟩_F ⟩_N

INTERACTION

R. gives the information requested by her mother by asserting ⟨ 2 ⟩ that her obligations are greater than her capacity, thereby reinstating her request ⟨ 4 ⟩ that her mother should come home and thereby asserting indirectly ⟨ X:STRN ⟩ that external circumstances are the cause of this, thereby responding hesitantly to her mother's challenge ⟨ ?~AD-R ⟩

RHODA'S DEFENSE   171

Rhoda submits the defense {X:STRN}; she cannot be responsible for circumstances, and therefore her status as an adult should not be questioned. In response to the more superficial request for information "Why are you asking...?" Rhoda gives the information requested—the simple fact that things are too much for her {STRN}. In so doing, she performs a third action, by the Rule for Reinstating Requests (Chapter 3, p. 93):

If B has responded to a request for action from A by making a request for information, and A gives the information requested, then A is heard as making the original request again.

She has therefore successfully returned the problem to her mother, who must answer her request again. Yet in the course of so doing, Rhoda has made herself vulnerable. She has been forced to state explicitly that she cannot cope, and her defense to the underlying challenge, "You can't take care of yourself" is a very weak and indirect one. In her imaginary roleplaying of what she would do next time, we can see how she could actually have been in a stronger position. If she had replied, "You've been there long enough," as she had planned to do, she would have replied to her mother's challenge effectively by putting the blame on her mother's lack of competence. This tactic, the second route outlined above, is not available to Rhoda, as we will see: it is much more typical of her mother's mode of interaction. If she had followed the third route and challenged her mother's expression of heavy implication ("What do you mean, 'Oh'?"), then her mother would be faced with a different kind of challenge. But Rhoda has followed the first route, and these other routes are closed to her.

1.11.   Rhoda's mother responds to her reinstated request by shifting the responsibility for the decision away from herself, using the complex network of role obligations we have displayed in part in Figure 11 (p. 133). Her answer shows none of the hesitation and embarrassment that Rhoda shows:

1.11   *She s'd t'me: "Why don't you tell **Phyllis** that?"*

The contrastive stress on *Phyllis* implies that someone else has been told instead: we know in fact that this other person is Rhoda's mother. The question cannot of course be understood unless we supply more data, drawn from other parts of the interview. Phyllis is the name of Rhoda's married sister, who lives with her husband in Household 2. In Episode 4, we will learn that it was Phyllis who made the original request that led to Rhoda's mother's leaving home. Since she is the one who made the request, it might follow that Rhoda should ask her if she still needed the mother's help. Our expansion brings these social facts to bear:

EXPANSION

R.: ⟨_N So mother said to me, "Well, since Phyllis is the one that asked me to stay here at her house and take care of her children, why don't you tell Phyllis that you need help and that she should let me go instead of telling me, since I can't help you unless she lets me go?" ⟩_N

This expansion is still at a relatively superficial level; there are no general or local propositions inserted in it, and how this is a response to Rhoda's request is not made explicit. To see how this is so, it will be helpful to work out the subtle chain of presuppositions and implications that proceed from 1.11.

First, we should observe that any WH-question presupposes the rest of the statement that is not questioned. This leads us to reconstruct for 1.11 the presupposition *You haven't told Phyllis that, for some reason.* But every negative assertion poses another problem: under what conditions would it be relevant to assert that something did not happen.* If we assert that something did not happen for some reason, then it follows that this negation is relevant because of the violation of some expectation. Someone must have expected it to happen or believed that it should have happened. This leads us to the implication that *one would expect that Phyllis would be told that,* or, in simpler form, *Phyllis should be told that.*

We are now in a position to utilize the information provided by the contrastive stress on *Phyllis*. Two propositions are contrasted. If Phyllis should have been told that, it follows that this other person should not have been told that, thus completing the contrast. We therefore can construct the following chain:

1.11 Why don't you tell *Phyllis* that?
      ↓
1.11′ You haven't told Phyllis that for some reason.
      ↓
1.11″ One would expect that you would have told Phyllis = You should have told Phyllis.
      ↓
1.11‴ You should have told Phyllis, and you should not have told the person that you did tell, that is, me.

We must now add the information contained in Episode 4 and in the social obligations indicated in Figure 11. Rhoda's mother has a potential obliga-

---

*This general property of some discourse elements is known as *conditional relevance* (Schegloff, 1972; Sacks, 1972a). In discussions of adjacency pairs such as requests and responses, we say that the occurrence of the second member of the pair is relevant upon the occurrence of the first—so that if it does *not* occur, its absence will be noted. Negative statements are responses to some such failure of an event to occur: not a speech event alone (*He didn't say hello*) but any kind of unfulfilled expectation (*He pushed, but the door didn't open*).

1.11	TEXT	CUES
R.: $\langle_N$ She s'd t'me, $\langle_F$ "Well, why don't you tell **Phyllis** that?" $\rangle_F \rangle_N$		Contrastive stress: **Phyllis**, 4 4 3 contour.

EXPANSION

R.: $\langle_N$ So mother said to me, $\langle_F$ "Well, since Phyllis is the one that asked me to stay here at her house and take care of her children, why don't you tell Phyllis that you need help and that she should let me go instead of telling me, since I can't help you unless she lets me go?" $\rangle_F \rangle_N$

INTERACTION

Mo. requests information from R. as to the reason that R. did not make her request $\overline{\langle\ 4\ }$ of her sister, thereby asserting indirectly that R. should have asked her sister, thereby asserting indirectly that she herself is not able to respond to request thereby $\overline{\langle\ \sim 4\ }$ refusing R.'s request to come home and $\overline{\langle\ \sim 5\ }$ refusing her request for help.

---

tion to Rhoda's sister, which was activated under appropriate conditions. If their mother has incurred this obligation, she cannot be discharged from it except by the person to whom she was obligated. It follows then that Rhoda's mother does not have the ability to comply with Rhoda's request—that is, she is using the Rule for Putting Off Requests to refuse Rhoda's request, citing that precondition 2 does not hold—she does not have the ability to do what is asked. She therefore refuses the request to come home, and the request for help fails.*

1.12. Most readers will have no difficulty in understanding what Rhoda's mother is up to in 1.11. They will interpret this complex action swiftly and accurately, and Rhoda certainly has the ability to do so too. The problem is: How should Rhoda respond? She is faced with a bewildering hierarchy of statements, implications, and assertions, all superimposed on the request for information 1.11. On reflection, we can see that the fundamental action of Rhoda's mother was the refusal; Rhoda might have responded to this at the highest level by saying "Because you're the right person to ask—you can come home if you want to!" This would have replied to all of her mother's presuppositions and implications, as well as to the simple request for information, and once more would have reinstated Rhoda's request. What Rhoda actually says is:

1.12 *So I said, "Well, I haven't talked to her lately."*

---

*She also indirectly refuses the request to supply information on when she plans to come home, since apparently she is not formulating any such plans.

174   EPISODE ONE (CONTINUED)

We might expand this simply by making the connection, "I haven't talked to Phyllis lately so I couldn't ask her." Our actual expansion in the cross section brings in more details and data, but basically the response is still at the most superficial level of 1.11: Rhoda gives the information that was requested.

It is evident that Rhoda has been outmaneuvered. The consequence of her answer 1.12 is that her request is tabled. She has fallen into a verbal trap of a classical type: her mother has begged the question and Rhoda has accepted the fact. The general rule of discourse operating here was cited in Chapter 3 (p. 103) as the Rule for Admitting Presuppositions:

If A responds to a request for information from B by giving that information, without specifically mentioning the presuppositions of the request, then B admits those presuppositions.

If Rhoda has been adept at verbal maneuvering, she might have responded at any one of the three higher levels. For example,

(to 1.11')   There is no reason for me to tell Phyllis that! (or) Why would I tell Phyllis that?
(to 1.11")   What makes you think that I should have told Phyllis that?
(to 1.11''') Because you're the right person for me to tell! (or) You're no child, Ma! You can come home if you want to.

1.12   TEXT   CUES
R.: ⟨_N So I said, ⟨_F "Well, I haven't
talked to her lately," ⟩_F ⟩_N

EXPANSION

R.: ⟨_N And I said to mother, ⟨_F "Well, you may be right; I should tell Phyllis and not you. The only reason I haven't done so is not that I shouldn't speak to her, but only that I haven't had the chance to talk to her since Tuesday when your absence became longer than usual, and so I have not been able to tell her." ⟩_F ⟩_N

INTERACTION

R. gives information requested by her mother, thereby agreeing with her mother's assertion that the request should have been made to R.'s sister, thereby agreeing that her mother's assertion that her original request for action and help ⟨ ~4,5 were inappropriate, thereby retreating from these requests, thereby ⟨ ~1 contradicting her original assertion that she had carried out the therapist's suggestion.

Rhoda adopts none of these tactics. She replies instead at the literal level of 1.11, and she therefore admits implicitly that she should have told Phyllis instead of her mother, and that her mother does not have the ability to answer her request.

Rhoda performs a fairly simple action in 1.12; she simply gives the information requested. Yet our statement of the interaction is still quite complex, since this simple action has many consequences. She gives the information, and thereby agrees with her mother that the original request for action and help were not appropriate; in so doing, she retreats from and in fact abandons these requests. This then reflects on her original assertion that she had carried out the therapist's suggestion. It might seem that this was a half-hearted attempt to obtain help since it was so easily abandoned. Yet we must take into account the fact that Rhoda's mother is, first, very adept at verbal maneuvering in family situations, and, second, in a position of authority over Rhoda. Rhoda does not find it easy to deal with her mother, and her mother is not easy to deal with.

Figure 22 assembles five cross sections for this crucial conversation. It adds the interaction of 1.10–1.12 to the moves of 1.8–1.9 as pictured in Figure 20. In 1.10, we see Rhoda responding to her mother's actions of 1.9 in two ways: she *gives* the information requested and *defends* herself against the challenge. She indirectly *reinstates the request* for action and the *request for help*; both of these requests are *refused* by Rhoda's mother in 1.11. The figure shows that this refusal is done by very indirect means, with three speech actions intervening between the surface request for information and the refusals. The solid arrow that connects 1.11 with 1.12 shows Rhoda responding at the lowest level of action. The dotted lines show her implicit agreement to the presuppositions and implications of her mother's move. At the top of the diagram, we see the connection between the overlying assertion {1} made in 1.8 and the upshot of the narrative in 1.12. The entire sequence of 1.8 to 1.12 shows that the action that Rhoda took did not lead to a good result for her and does not support fully her original assertion. It is true that she carried out the basic suggestion by calling up her mother; but if she did it "to see if it worked," she gives no evidence that it did.

Each of the solid horizontal lines show the application of a sequencing rule that is realized in the actual behavior of the speakers: it is something that they did. The horizontal dotted lines represent the consequences of their actions which follow by regular rules of discourse, but are not so immediately actions in themselves. Thus the reinstatement of the request and the acceptance of the presuppositions are shown by dotted lines. The first three actions then appear as the most complex, because they each perform at least two distinct actions. The last two are simpler in their sequential structure but involve more intricate rules of production and interpretation.

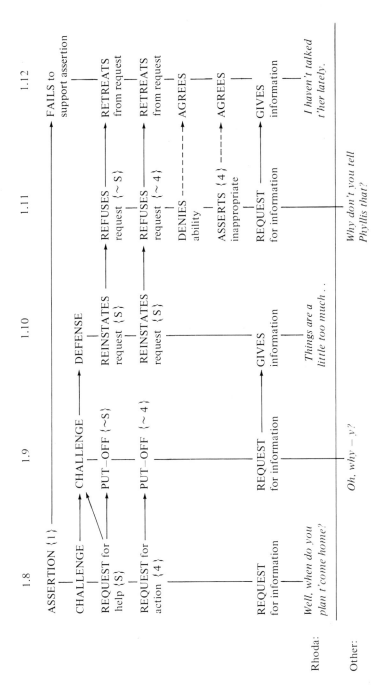

Figure 22. Sequencing of Rhoda's narratives in 1.8–1.12.

1.13. Since Rhoda has made the fundamental concession to her mother's point of view, her narrative is in fact concluded. She shows some consciousness of having been outmaneuvered, since her next remark is confused and uncertain. She is now faced with the problem of ending her narrative, confronting the fact that its implications are quite ambiguous. What she says is equally ambiguous:

1.13 R.: *And—uh . . . I'm just gonna* **tell** *her.*

Here again, we see hesitation, ambiguity, and vagueness as symbols of tension in Rhoda's delivery. It is not even clear whether 1.13 is inside the narrative or a comment about the narrative within the interview situation. Is she telling her mother that she's going to tell her sister that her mother must come home? Or is she planning to tell her mother next time she talks to her that she simply must come home? Our expansion explicitly shows these two ambiguous possibilities, and the interactional statement reflects the two possibilities as well. This ambiguity permits Rhoda to blur the actual outcome of the narrative, asserting implicitly that it did not make any difference.

We might think at first that Rhoda is a very poor storyteller, since her account trails off in an extremely confused and indeterminate way. However, if we think in terms of the point Rhoda was trying to make—that she had carried out the suggestion of the therapist—it is apparent that she has rearranged the difficult material in a way that is most favorable for her. She

---

1.13	TEXT	CUES
R.: $\langle_{IV/N}$ *And—uh . . . I'm just gonna* **tell** *her.* $\rangle_{IV/N}$		Tension: hesitation, ambiguity and vagueness.

EXPANSION

R.: $\langle_{IV}$ I'm telling you that I'm positively going to tell my mother next time I come home that I think—it's up to her to decide to come home, in spite of what she might think or say. $\rangle_{IV}$

or

R.: $\langle_N$ I said to my mother, $\langle_F$ I certainly will tell Phyllis that {4} I want you to come home when I get a chance to talk to her next as you suggest. $\rangle_F$ $\rangle_N$

INTERACTION

R. ambiguously asserts that she will make her original request $\langle\underline{4}$ to her mother again and carry out again $\langle\underline{5}$ the suggestion of the therapist or gives more information on her narrative that she agreed with her mother that she will redirect her original request $\langle\underline{4}$ to her sister.

178   EPISODE ONE (CONTINUED)

has elaborated the thinking that led up to the decision to speak to her mother, which reinforces her claim. The fact that all this had no practical result, obvious to us from examining the last few utterances, is played down in Rhoda's manner of presentation. There might be an even more skillful way to do this, but if we understand her task, we can see that her manner of presentation is far more irrational.

We may note that the ambiguity here is systematic. In one sense, it means that it is not clear whether Rhoda succeeded or not in carrying out the suggestion of the therapist; in the other sense, it is not exactly clear that the suggestion did not work. On careful analysis, we can see that it did not, but the narrative manages successfully to obscure this point.

1.14. Rhoda had originally established the evaluative point of her narrative by the long insertion of 1.7, which suspended the action just before the crucial step of calling her mother. She now underlines this point with a restatement of her initial assertion:

1.14   R.: Now..... *I think I did the right thing, I think that—*

She ignores the manifest outcome of the situation and repeats her initial assertion in exactly the same words. In terms of our technical analysis of narrative, this is a *coda*, and brings us back to the present through this repetition (Chapter 3, p. 109). Her coda shows that any further question ("And then what happened?") is no longer appropriate. It is at this point that the therapist intervenes, for the first time since her reinforcing remark of 1.6. This raises the question: what is the competence of the therapist that determines that this is the point for her to enter more actively into the

---

1.14	TEXT	CUES
R.: ⟨$_{IV}$ *Now.....I think I did the right thing, I think that—* ⟩$_{IV}$		Tension release: fast tempo and strong articulation.

EXPANSION

R.: ⟨$_{IV}$ I am not sure, but I claim that {1} I did what you say is right, or {?1} what actually may be right, when {4} I asked my mother to help me by coming home after she had been away longer than usual. ⟩$_{IV}$

INTERACTION

R.: R. signals completion of her narrative by repeating the assertion ⟨ 1 ⟩ in the same words as 1.1 [c], thereby giving information that she has completed her justification of this assertion, thereby requesting indirectly the therapist to give evaluation.

exchange? Rhoda does not stop speaking: it is necessary for the therapist to interrupt her. But the interruption was actually called for by Rhoda; she indicates that she is ready for the other person to speak by repeating what she said at the beginning of the episode in the exact words that she used before. As we will see, this is a common pattern in Rhoda's conversational style.

Our cross section of 1.14 shows the parallels to 1.1. The exact repetition of 1.1[c] is a signal that gives information about the termination of the narrative and the turn at talk. Chapters 4 and 5 as a whole show that the evaluative point of this narrative includes both {1} and {?1}. It therefore appears that the assertion {1} (that Rhoda did the right thing in {4} asking her mother to come home) is a disputable, or D-event. The Rule of Disputable Assertions then applies: (Chapter 3, p. 101)

If A makes an assertion about a D-event, it is heard as a request for B to give an evaluation of that assertion.

The fundamental action being performed in 1.14 is therefore a request for the therapist to evaluate Rhoda's assertion {1}.

What "Happens" in Episode 1?

An overall view of the interaction in Episode 1 must be divided into two parts: what happens between the patient and the therapist, and the reported interaction in the patient's family. As far as patient and therapist are concerned, we can say this:

1. The session opens, as often happens, with the patient putting forward material that will serve as grist for therapy—an event from everyday life that has occurred in the last few days before the session.
2. The particular material put forward here is central to the course of therapy since it is related explicitly to the major suggestion of the therapeutic series—that the patient express her needs and emotions to others in her immediate family. The patient's claim that she carried out the suggestion is crucial since her specific problem is that she internalizes the needs she has and expresses them in terms of her own bodily suffering.
3. The therapist receives this material with appropriate feedback and is most active when the patient is explaining the underlying logic of the suggestion as brought forward in the earlier interviews.
4. The exposition of the patient is allowed to run its course until she herself signals that she is ready to be interrupted.

Episode 1 also gives us a clear view of the kind of verbal interaction that takes place in Rhoda's family. If this were the only account of the phone call with her mother, we would be more hesitant in interpreting it as a good representation of what took place. Since there are three separate accounts of the same incident in this interview, we are on reasonably safe ground in inferring that this is the normal type of verbal interaction in Rhoda's family. Whenever distortions are present, Rhoda's account represents the social reality in which she lives, a reality that has been conveyed to her by verbal interaction in the family.

Our exposition of the underlying assumptions and mechanisms of this family interaction may make it seem extraordinarily complex. But there is nothing unusual in this behavior or the rules that are operating here. The same discourse rules and the same indirection seem to be typical of conversational behavior in general. The extent of the indirection and the asymmetry between Rhoda and her mother may be in part responsible for her difficulties, and it may be helpful for her to learn to cope with this kind of interaction; but it does not seem to be different *in kind* from the verbal interaction that takes place in other interviews and in everyday life. This indirection has four aspects:

1. Although the patient shows herself making a request for help of her mother, the actual forms she uses are not as direct as those she originally plans to use—they are more indirect, more mitigated.
2. The basic interactional problem is one of assigning blame for a difficult situation. The patient is struggling to assign this to external circumstances, while the mother continually presses the point that it is the patient's personal inadequacy. No matter what the patient feels, she does not counteract this by explicitly placing any blame on her mother (in fact, as we shall see, she even makes excuses for her mother and helps absolve her from any blame). The inner anger which she feels towards her mother is confined to paralinguistic cues of hesitation and frustration, rather than expressed as a statement that her mother is at fault in not giving her the help she needs. This use of paralinguistic cues is parallel to her use of bodily symptoms in expressing her emotions.
3. Rhoda makes her initial request in a mitigated form, but with some implications which are critical of her mother. Her mother picks up these implications and counters them with even sharper criticism in return. In the course of the interaction we have just studied, Rhoda is led down a path which effectively cancels her efforts at independence.
4. The end result of Rhoda's attempt to express her needs and emotions to her mother is that her mother does not come home. Rhoda's manner of presenting this event focuses on her actual decision to speak to her mother and minimize the events that led to an unsatisfactory outcome.

6

EPISODE TWO
That looks clean t'you?

We now will apply the technique of comprehensive discourse analysis developed in the last two chapters to the second episode in our interview, with special attention to the more active role played by the therapist. Though the numbering of the individual utterances is primarily for convenient reference, divisions into episodes are based on properties of the interview material itself. There is no physical break in the conversation, but there is a marked shift from Episode 1 to Episode 2 in both topic and pattern of verbal interaction between patient and therapist. Episode 2 enters an entirely different area under the active direction of the therapist, and the theme of Episode 1 will not be encountered again until we reach Episode 4.

At the end of Episode 1, Rhoda marked the logical end of her exposition by repeating the words that she used at the outset, and this becomes the point of departure for Episode 2. It is apparent that Rhoda expects some reaction from the therapist—approval or recognition of her action, and possibly some interpretation.

    2.1   R.: *Now . . . . . I **think** I did the right **thing**, I think that—*
    2.2[a] Th.: *Yes, I think you did, too.*
    [b]   *Well, **what's** your **question**?*
    [c]   *You know, you have a lot of **guilt** about it,*
    [d]   *You have a **very full** schedule at school . .*
    [e]   R.: *Yes, at school—*
    [f]   Th.: *Now **what** about Aunt Editha, she doesn't help you in the house?*

2.2. The text quoted above represents only the words that were spoken, and, here especially, we must examine the paralinguistic cues for a full understanding of the therapist's actions. We will follow our usual practice of considering the paralinguistic cues separately before expanding the text with its embedded propositions, and analyzing the interactional impact of these elements; the cross sections organize this information systematically.

The over-all style of the therapist leaves no doubt that she is entering the conversation in a very active way. There is a short silence between Rhoda's last words and the therapist's first entrance, which suggests that the therapist may have indicated to Rhoda that she was ready to speak through a facial gesture. The stream of speech that flows from her is so forceful that it is not until 2.2[d] that she takes a breath.

In contrast to Rhoda's hesitant style, the therapist begins with a forceful double stress and extra high pitch on her initial *yes;* but what she actually says is marked by a succession of sharp breaks in the surface structure. It is not immediately obvious what the connections are between her phrases, and why she shifts so rapidly. We will therefore consider separately the six different subsections of 2.2.

Both the literal meaning of 2.2[a] and the emphatic stress on *yes* show *agreement* with Rhoda's position. We have no difficulty in expanding the elliptical form *you did* to indicate that the therapist was referring to whatever Rhoda was talking about. Presumably then, the therapist is endorsing whatever assertions and propositions were contained in 1.14 (repeated here as 2.1). In the light of the analysis of Chapter 4 and 5, it would seem difficult for the therapist to agree with all of the ambiguities in Rhoda's presentation. It would therefore be premature to state that the action performed by 2.2[a] is one of agreement. Like many *yes* responses, it is clearly intended to be supportive in an interactive sense, and this is reflected in the interactional statement: 2.2 accomplishes agreement.*

In the next phrase, the therapist indicates that she is indeed moving in a slightly different direction. The discourse marker *well* shows that what will follow is relevant to what preceded, but also marks a distinct shift of topic. The intonation contour that follows is strikingly different, and far from supportive. It contains a repeated high stress, which plainly signals annoyance or exasperation, as displayed in Figure 23 on page 184.

2.2[b]   *Well, what's your question?*

To expand this utterance, we have to understand what the word *question* refers to. It seems to be in response to those elements in Episode 1 that we also identified as questions or challenges. The ambiguities of 1.1 and 1.14 could be read as questioning or challenging the therapist's competence,

---

*There appears to be a general mechanism of conversational interaction operating here. One way of redirecting the topic of a conversation is to acknowledge the last speaker's point by saying "Yes, the....." inserting into this blank any noun phrase that appears in the last speaker's utterance, and then continuing with another topic not directly related. Though we have examples of speakers using this device operating in other conversations, it is not clear how generally it can be applied.

2.2

	TEXT	CUES
[a]	Th.: ⟨_IV_ Yes, I think you did, too.	Tension: Yes, extra high pitch.
[b]	Well, **what's your question?**	Exasperation: 2 3́ 2 3 2, high, falling contour with heavy stress. [Figure 23]
[c]	You know, you have a lot of **guilt** about it, ⟩_IV_	
[d]	⟨_EV_ You have a **very full** schedule at school.. ⟩_EV_	(Th. takes a breath.)
[e]	R.: ⟨_EV_ Yes, it's a little—⟩_EV_	
[f]	Th.: ⟨_EV_ Now **what about** Aunt Editha, she doesn't help you in the house? ⟩_EV_	Mitigation: 3 3 ↑ high, rising contour without heavy stress and weakening of volume.

EXPANSION

[a] Th.: ⟨_IV_ Since you obviously expect comment and approval from me, yes, I also believe that you did the right thing in carrying out the suggestion {S}....
[b] And conceding this, what is the question implied in the hesitation of your narrative, and why are you questioning something we agree about—
[c] You have demonstrated that {E_2: You feel guilt} about expressing your needs to your mother or carrying out the suggestion or failing to carry it out properly.
[d] But you don't feel guilt for any good reason ⟩_IV_ ⟨_EV_ because {X} you have a very full schedule in your primary obligation at school, and were therefore justified in {4} asking for mother to come home and were not giving up your claim {AD-R} to be an adult member of the household. ⟩_EV_
[e] R.: ⟨_EV_ Yes, it's a little too much for me to do. ⟩_EV_
[f] Th.: ⟨_EV_ Now turning away from mother to a different aspect of your problem, does Aunt Editha help with the obligations of your household, and if not, shouldn't you ask her to do so since she is an adult member and has the obligation? ⟩_EV_

INTERACTION

[a] Th. interrupts, agreeing with the patient about her claim of Episode 1 ⟨_1_
   Th. re-directs, agreeing with the patient, thereby giving support ⟨_1_ to her claim of Episode 1.
[b] Th. re-directs, requesting information on the patient's unexpressed attitudes, and simultaneously expressing exasperation, thereby challenging the patient to examine her emotions. ⟨_?E_⟩
[c] Th. re-directs, asserting ⟨_E_2_⟩ that the patient feels an emotion of guilt, thereby continuing her challenge.
[d] Th. re-directs, asserting that R.'s primary obligations are at school, thereby giving support ⟨_X:STRN_ to R.'s claim that external circumstances are the cause of her problem, thereby asserting indirectly ⟨_?E_2_⟩ that R.'s emotion is

184 EPISODE TWO

inappropriate, thereby challenging ⟨ ?(?1) ⟩ R's questioning of her original assertion that she did the right thing.
[e] R. begins to agree with the therapist's assertion.
[f] Th. interrupts, re-directing, and requests confirmation that other role partner does not carry out her obligations, thereby requesting ⟨ 5 ⟩ that R. ask E. for help, thereby requesting again that R. carry out the basic suggestion of therapy {S}.

---

and our reading of the intonation contour in 2.2[b] gives additional evidence for this view. Rhoda's question can certainly be questioned: If she really understood the basic suggestion of the therapy and was ready to apply it, then why does she display such uncertainty? The therapist's question notes the ambiguity: Is Rhoda's question directed to the ideas, to the therapist's competence, or to her own? Obviously 2.2[b] is a request for information, as our interactional section shows. Yet the intonational cue plainly expresses a critical reaction directed at Rhoda's performance as a patient; it puts into question her status as a patient who understands the basic suggestion of therapy.

2.2[c]. The most basic sequencing rule of discourse is that one must respond to a request: but the therapist does not allow Rhoda to respond to her request for information, or to any other speech act implicit in 2.2[b]. Instead, she continues with 2.2[c]; in focusing on *guilt*, she provides one possible answer to her own inquiry.

2.2[c] *You know, you have a lot of **guilt** about it.*

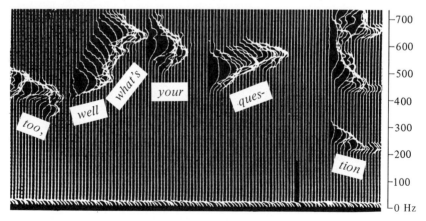

Figure 23. Pitch contour of therapist's intervention *what's your question* in 2.2[b].

The therapist begins this new tack with a discourse marker, *you know*,* which generally represents an appeal for solidarity or support; here she recognizes the fact that she is entering an area of disputable statements. She then introduces a lexical marker of interview style: the term *guilt* is drawn from the therapeutic vocabulary of meta-terms used for talking about talk. It refers to one of the underlying feelings that Rhoda might be encouraged to realize.

{E_2} Rhoda feels guilt.

The notion of 'guilt' carries a strong demand upon the patient to examine her deepest feelings about what she has just said. Our contextual expansion must deal with the focus of this guilt: what is the referent of *it* in *guilt about it?* It is not immediately clear what Rhoda may expect to feel guilty about—telephoning her mother, asking for help, carrying out the therapist's suggestion, or failing to be effective. We cannot complete the interpretation of 2.2[c] since the therapist immediately redirects the discussion along slightly different lines. This next move serves to clarify the challenge of 2.2[b] by suggesting that the emotion displayed by Rhoda was not entirely appropriate.

2.2[d] *You have a very full schedule at school . .*

2.2[d] follows immediately upon 2.2[c] without any discourse marker or conjunction to show its relationship to the preceding. We must therefore reconstruct the connection from our knowledge of the social relations involved. Figure 11' expands the structural relations in Household 1, which we presented first in Figure 11. Rhoda appears at the intersection of two role sets—Household 1 and school. Like her mother, Rhoda has two major obligations. These are the circumstances {X} that Rhoda referred to in 1.5 and 1.10, which are responsible for the strain {STRN} and for her feeling frustrated and confused {E_1} (see Chapter 4, p. 145). Our expansion must draw upon this situation to provide a rich enlargement of the text of 2.2[d]. The therapist is not relying too heavily here on paralinguistic cues, and the mode of expression is relatively straightforward: but the basic propositions are put forward elliptically in this rapid shifting and the mode of argument is quite compact. Our expansion supplies "but you don't feel guilt for any good reason..." and the interactional statement is correspondingly complex. On the surface, the therapist is stating one of Rhoda's justifications for feeling strain; conversely, this suggests that any guilt Rhoda may feel for calling up her mother is quite unjustified, and she therefore showed an inappropriate emotion. Any guilt that Rhoda would have felt for carrying

---

*This characterization of *you know* is primarily from T. Labov, supported by her ongoing research on moral language.

186 EPISODE TWO

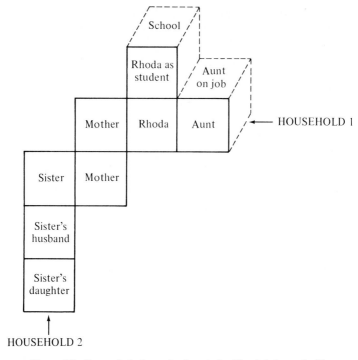

Figure 11'. Expanded view of role sets for Rhoda's household.

out the therapist's suggestion is also inappropriate, and the suggestion was therefore appropriate. We thus see that this intricate chain connects the therapist's support of Rhoda with her own defense of her suggestion and rejection of Rhoda's implicit challenge.*

The therapist now takes a breath, and Rhoda begins to answer by agreeing with the last supportive statement 2.2[d].

2.2[e] R.: *Yes, it's a little—*

Presumably, Rhoda is about to elaborate on the theme of 1.10, "things are getting a little too much." Before she can do so, the therapist interrupts her for a second time and redirects the topic once again to an even more

---

*The therapist's tactic here shows that she finds it necessary to act as an arbiter of social norms. Implicit in the therapist's judgment is the notion that Rhoda's obligations as a full-time student are primary, just as Rhoda implies indirectly that her mother's primary obligation is to Household 1. The concept of primary and secondary obligations is therefore essential to this argument: it allows Rhoda to maintain her claim to adult status and yet ask her mother to come home to take up her primary obligations as head of Household 1. Since Rhoda's mother has challenged this status in Episode 1, it seems clear that the therapist is taking sides with Rhoda against her mother.

distantly related subject. The discourse marker *now* introduces this shift to the major focus of Episode 2: Aunt Editha.*

> 2.2[f]   Th.: *Now **what** about Aunt Editha, she doesn't help you in the house?*

The shift is not without any connection to 2.2[d]: Figure 11' shows that Aunt Editha's situation is quite parallel to Rhoda's. She is an adult member of Household 1 and a secretary in a commercial firm downtown. She represents another resource that Rhoda might use to solve the problem of {X: STRN}. On the surface, the therapist constructs a simple request for confirmation about Aunt Editha's activity. The paralinguistic cues, however, are those associated with a highly mitigated request: a high rising contour without heavy stress and fading volume at the end. The fact that 2.2[f] is not even a request for information, but rather a request for confirmation, shows it as one of the most mitigated forms of requesting action. The therapist assumes that Aunt Editha does not help in the house, allowing for the possibility that Rhoda has explored this source of help already. Her rising and fading intonation may be read as a further assurance, "This is only a possibility, not an assertion, so don't feel that I am attacking you or Editha by saying this." The result is that of tentative suggestion to which the answer is probably "No."

Our expansion of 2.2[f] draws upon the social relations illustrated in 11'. The interactional statement indicates that it is a request for action, and we may consider for a moment how the Rule of Requests is employed here. The request for confirmation is about whether or not Aunt Editha has been carrying out her obligations without being prompted. If not, there is a *need* for Rhoda to request her to do so. Rhoda certainly knows that the therapist believes that she has the *ability* to do so, and the basic suggestion of therapy is that she has the *right* to do so. Aunt Editha's position in the household is such that she has an *obligation* to help. Rhoda should therefore have no difficulty in understanding that this is a repetition of the basic suggestion of the therapy, in a new form. The fact that it occurs in such an extremely mitigated form indicates that the therapist is being extremely cautious in making any such suggestion to Rhoda.

The Therapist's Intervention as a Whole

The fluctuating pattern of the therapist's intervention introduces several basic propositions. Our understanding of the mode of argument of therapy would lead us to expect that the therapist would evaluate Rhoda's narra-

---

*As compared to *well*, *now* represents a greater change in the direction of the topic of the conversation.

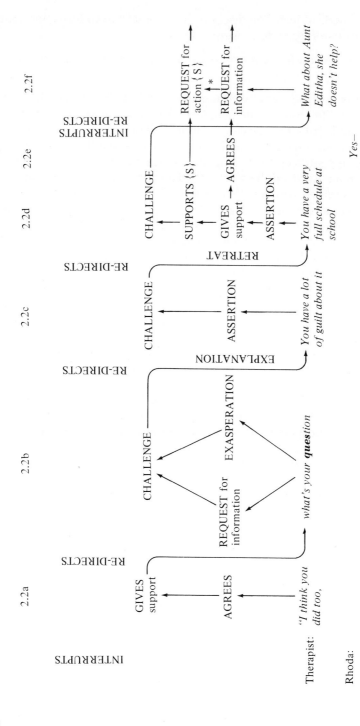

Figure 24. Sequencing within therapist's intervention of 2.2 (*Rule of Requests).

tive as an instance of some general proposition. She does not do so, but introduces a new proposition about Rhoda's feelings, and then begins to introduce a new set of ideas about Rhoda's other obligations and Aunt Editha. The rapid alternations implicit in the therapist's utterance suggest the presence of a self-correcting process that is made explicit in this remarkable example.

The therapist's intervention is presented graphically in Figure 24. At the top of the diagram, the speaker-sequencing indicates that the therapist interrupts twice and redirects the interview four times. At the bottom, the most specific linguistic level, we see a declarative sentence followed by an interrogative, two declaratives, and another interrogative. We also see a number of lexical signs that the therapist has not made up her mind on what to do after Rhoda has finished the presentation of Episode 1. Discourse markers such as *well, now,* and *you know* have a temporizing and delaying function as well as an organizational one. We hear the therapist thinking out loud when she asks about Rhoda's "question," and then quickly decides not to let Rhoda answer her own *request* for information.

At the next more abstract level of speech actions, we see that the therapist first *agrees* with the patient, *requests* information from her (and *expresses* exasperation), makes several *assertions, gives support,* and then makes a *request* for information.

Several deep-seated propositions are referred to in this rapid alternation, and these lead in turn to the recognition of higher-level speech acts. In 2.2[c], the therapist *asserts* {E_2} an emotion of guilt, which she detects beneath the surface of Rhoda's account. Within the context of therapy, any reference to an unexpressed emotion may be heard as a *request* of the patient to examine her emotions—and a *challenge* to prove that she is capable of doing so. One of the general propositions of therapy, as important as the suggestions {S} we have discussed above, is the principle that the patient should be "in touch with her own feelings." We refer to this proposition as:

{INSIGHT} The patient should gain insight into her own emotions.

We have only a brief reference to this important principle here; in Episode 5 (Chapter 9) the therapist returns to this area for extensive exploration. At this point, however, she has apparently decided that Rhoda is not ready for a direct confrontation with feelings of this sort, and therefore cannot pursue the challenge of 2.2[c] to the appropriateness of this emotion associated with Episode 1. Instead, she redirects with an argument on the level of everday behavior, *supporting* Rhoda's argument that external circumstances are responsible for her difficulties. This argument also *supports* the therapist's original suggestion that Rhoda do something about it, and therefore represents an implicit *challenge* to Rhoda's expression of an inappropriate emotion about her action. We symbolize this challenge as {?(?1)}:

the questioning of a question. Here the therapist is bringing to bear her sociological competence rather than dealing with the fundamental emotions that are from her point of view the basic causes of the difficulty (Chapter 9).

Figure 24 also shows a fifth turn in the argument, as the therapist redirects towards another topic that at first glance seems to be unrelated. The logic of her move is apparent from Figure 11', since she is working out all the implications of Rhoda's social situation. This reference to the involvement of Aunt Editha must inevitably be seen as a request for action, and the therapist is careful to mitigate this suggestion as much as possible. As always, she is aware of the fact that Rhoda's response to direct suggestions may be disastrous.

As we have seen, the request itself is made in a very indirect form, which does not even mention Rhoda on the surface. In the light of the shared knowledge of the preconditions in effect here, Rhoda certainly sees 2.2[f] as another suggestion that she must face. Since she is not immediately involved, she can begin her defense by turning the attention entirely to Aunt Editha.

We can sum up the decisions that the therapist made in this way: Reacting to Rhoda's narrative, she saw how she might make some progress by turning Rhoda's attention to the emotions evident in her mode of expression; but she decided that this would be premature, and retreated to a more external, less threatening domain. Aware of the difficulty of any direct suggestion to Rhoda, she proposed another way of implementing the basic suggestion of therapy in an extremely mitigated form.

The sequential structure shown in Figure 24 is unusual. We have said before that sequencing rules operate between actions at a relatively abstract level; but here the therapist does not permit the normal sequencing to take place. She redirects the conversation by new utterances that are then seen to be actions that repeat her earlier versions in a somewhat mitigated, reoriented form. The logic connecting her successive challenges and requests for action is not dictated by discourse rules, but rather by the strategy that she is following in the therapeutic situation.

Rhoda's Response: 2.3

Rhoda's long speech of 2.3 begins with the confirmation finally requested by the therapist; the form of 2.2[f] presupposes Rhoda's immediate answer: *No.*

2.3[a] R.: *No like*
  [b] *she'll go.... sh-I dunno, like the **house** could—like my mother wasn't home for a week, and the house gets **dusty** ...*
  [c] *Now **she** could **sit** there an' the dust could be **that thick** and doesn't **bother** her*

[d] *But yet it bothers me, I mean if I.... I—n-not—not that I-I run around the house **cleaning** ev'ry-ev'ry time,*
[e] *But it's jis' that I know that if I see the house getting dirty, it sorts of **bothers** me, I 'on't like to live in a dirty house but*
[f] *—she could sit, the dust could be that—*

Since the therapist seems to agree with her, it is not immediately clear why Rhoda continues to talk and enlarge on this subject. If we assume that this speech is also a response to the more abstract suggestion {S} of the therapist—that Rhoda ask Editha to help—we can see it as a coherent sequential move.

In 2.3, Rhoda uses many modes of expression characteristic of her family style. There are prosodic cues, which we group as an expression of *tension:* hesitation, self-interruption, whine. The message conveyed is that she is so choked with emotion at the unreasonableness of Editha's behavior that she cannot begin to describe it accurately.

Our interpretation of the message conveyed by these signals of tension may appear to be subjective, our own intuitive reactions to the prosodic cues. However, our interpretation is not based upon this isolated instance. At many points throughout this episode, and throughout this session, we find similar cues: choking, hesitation, glottalization, and whine. Rhoda regularly uses these signals to indicate helpless anger: she finds herself unable to cope with behavior of others that injures her and seems to her unreasonable. This does not mean that the same signals of tension will be used by other speakers in the same way. We find that each speaker has his own repertoire of speech devices to signal emotions that reflect his own history. There is not yet available a general grammar of prosodic cues that shows us the whole range of meanings and signals associated with them: it is only the fact of our common experience that allows us to interpret their meaning. These social conventions are idiosyncratic selections from a general domain.

Rhoda uses other devices to indicate her helpless exasperation at this situation. Indexical quantifiers like *that thick* imply that the violation of normal standards is gross to the point of straining our verbal resources. Other cues of stress and intonation express sarcastic exasperation at Editha's unreasonable behavior. All of these expressions of emotion are counterbalanced with mitigating expressions indicating that Rhoda's anger is not extreme and that she is actually taking a moderate, adult position on the question of cleanliness. Thus she is not angered by the situation, it only "bothers" her. Even this is too strong: Rhoda further mitigates the expression to "sort of bothers me." The suppressed laughter of 2.3[e] is opposed to the tense whine of 2.3[b]. Our expansion attempts to elucidate the significance of these many indirect modes of expression.

As we compare the text and the expansion for 2.3, the argument emerges quite plainly: Editha *doesn't* help and there's no use in asking her for help since she shows no adult sense of responsibility in cleaning the house. This argument revolves about two basic propositions embedded in our expansion:

{~AD-E}   Editha is not an adult member of the household.
{AD-R}   Rhoda is an adult member of the household.

The argument is carried out by categorical statements in an aggravated form about Editha and in a mitigated form about Rhoda. It concerns the standards of cleanliness that would lead one person to start cleaning and another person to sit still. The mode of argument is characteristically categorical.* Rhoda does not say that Editha's threshold for initiating performance is a *little* lower than her own, but rather asserts that there is no point at all at which Editha would start cleaning. On the other hand, Rhoda's standards are normal—she has an appropriate threshold and an appropriate cut-off point for behavior.

Rhoda's mode of expression does more than assert her status as an adult, a person who knows the appropriate limits of behavior. She is also portrayed as a *reasonable* person, one who does not become overemotional at someone else's limitations: She simply accepts the fact that the other person is hopelessly unreasonable and is not disturbed by it:

{RSNBL-R}   Rhoda is a reasonable person.

In conversational interaction the usual meaning of "reasonable" is that a person obeys conversational norms. A reasonable person is someone that you can talk to: You cannot talk to an unreasonable person, and there is no purpose in trying.

The mode of interaction in 2.3 is quite different from the rapid fluctuations we observed in 2.2. Whereas the therapist began to do a great many things briefly in rapid succession, Rhoda is doing two things at great length, using many more words than are necessary. Rhoda attacks Editha's competence; in technical terms, she challenges her status as an adult and defends her own. Since Editha is not one of the parties to the immediate situation, we must interpret this attack in relation to what the therapist and Rhoda have been doing. It seems evident that Rhoda is responding to the unstated request for action in the therapist's question about Aunt Editha. She is building up a case to show how hopeless it would be to make such a direct suggestion. The overkill in her mode of argument is then to be understood as a reaction to this suggestion that she might have done something else to carry out the basic suggestion in therapy.

Thus Rhoda rejects an indirect request indirectly. The therapist's proposal of 2.2[f] is a special case of a request to make a request, and here Rhoda's rejection is directed to the embedded request. It is true that Rhoda

---

*Such categorical behavior is not only characteristic of Rhoda; it appears to be the normal mode of argument for disputes about performance of everyday role obligations.

| 2.3 | TEXT | CUES |

[a] R.: ⟨_EV_No like
[b] she'll go.... sh-I dunno, like the house could—like my mother wasn't home for a week, and the house gets **dusty**...

Tension: Hesitation, self-interruption; **Dusty** (4 2) with whine: 'helpless exasperation'

[c] Now *she could sit there* ⟨_F_ *an' the dust could be* **that thick** *and doesn't bother her*⟩_F_

Derogation: *she could sit* there: 'sarcastic exasperation and childish behavior'

[d] But yet it bothers me, I mean if I.... I—n-not—not that I-I run around the house **cleaning** *ev'ry-ev'ry time,*

Tension: hesitation, constriction and glottalization.
Mitigation: **bother** for 'makes me

[e] But it's jis' that I know that if I see the house getting dirty, it sort of **bothers** me, I 'on't like to live in a dirty house but

angry, *it's jis' that* and *sort of* **bothers** *me;* lax, rapid intonation; suppressed laughter on *I don't like.*

[f] —*she could sit, the dust could be that*— ⟩_EV_

Tension: self-interruption. Repetition of 2.3[c]

EXPANSION

[a] R.: ⟨_EV_ No, Editha doesn't help with the housework (and therefore your suggestion {5} won't work).
[b] This is the way she usually behaves: No matter how dirty the house gets, she will not do anything. For example, one time when my mother went away for a week, as she has just done now, the house got very dusty and Editha didn't do anything.
[c] Editha could sit still, unlike any normal person {~AD-E}, even when the dust is very thick, and she does not see any need to clean.
[d] But in contrast to Editha, the dirty house makes me uneasy just as Editha's ignoring the dirt makes me angry. Don't misunderstand me—I'm not so extreme as to clean all the time and do nothing else {RSNBL-R}.
[e] The situation is no more or less than this: I know that I'll become uneasy or even angry when the house gets dirtier every day and no one does anything to clean it because {AD-R} I am a normal, responsible adult.
[f] But {~AD-E} Editha, unlike any normal person, could sit still when the dust is very thick... ⟩_EV_

INTERACTION

[a] R. gives the confirmation requested.
[b] R. gives information and evaluation by characterizing E.'s standards of role performance as deficient, thereby challenging E. ⟨~AD-E⟩ as not being an adult member of the household, thereby denying that she has the ability to get Editha to help, thereby refusing indirectly the request of the therapist ⟨~5⟩ that she request Editha to help, thereby refusing the basic suggestion ⟨~S⟩ as unworkable.

194   EPISODE TWO

[d] R. gives further information that her own standards of role performance are normal, thereby asserting again $\overline{\text{AD-R}}\rangle$ that she is an adult member of the household.

[e] R. signals by repetition her readiness to be interrupted and thereby requests evaluation.

---

has the ability to make this demand of Editha, but the action would be a fruitless one since she would not be able to make Editha comply. It is a common situation for someone to ask a second person to make a request of a third. This request can be refused without saying "yes" or "no," as indicated by the Rule of Relayed Requests (Chapter 3, p. 88). The second person can simply note that his action would be fruitless since there is no way that he can get the third person to carry out the request. He can imply that he would be willing, but put off the request effectively.

2.4. The therapist seems to recognize that Rhoda's response was a refusal of her request, no matter how indirect, because her response to this overlaps and cuts off Rhoda's long speech.

2.4[a]   Th.: *Well, what would happen if you **said** something to her—*

The discourse marker *well* indicates that the therapist is going to take a slightly different turn along the same route, and the contrastive stress on *said* indicates that she is now going to suggest a specific action rather than inquire about the general circumstances in 2.2. The intonation contour is again the high falling pattern that the therapist uses for mitigated requests.

It is not hard to see embedded in this request of 2.4[a] the fundamental propositions that were developed in Episode 1: the motivating problem {STRN} and the fundamental suggestion {S}. In our expansion, we have indicated what the therapist had in mind by utilizing her more explicit suggestion to follow in Episode 3 (3.1[c]). It should be apparent that the action performed in 2.4[a] is still somewhat indirect, since she does not make this explicit. The contrastive emphasis on *said* is a step forward from the very indirect request of 2.2. It plainly indicates that Rhoda should say something instead of just thinking about it; but 2.4 is still superficially a request for information about the consequences of some action. By the option *b* in the Rule for Indirect Requests (Chapter 3, p. 82) this is heard as a request for action.

The structure of 2.4[a] is plainly disguised to mitigate the pointed character of the basic suggestion; but strangely enough, the therapist does not let Rhoda respond to this suggestion. Instead, she interrupts Rhoda with a comment that seems cryptic on first encounter:

2.4[b]   Th.: *Too—since* (R.: *Well, you know, sh—*) *We're in the, in the business* (R.: *Yes.*) *of **talking**, yes.*

THERAPIST'S SUGGESTION

2.4 TEXT CUES
[a]Th.: ⟨$_{EV}$ *Well, what would happen if you said something to her*— Contention: overlapping interruption,
Mitigation: 3 3 →
[b] *Too*—since (R.: Well, you know, sh—) ⟩$_{EV}$ ⟨$_{IV}$ *We're in the, in the business* (R.: Yes.) *of talking, yes.* ⟩$_{IV}$ Tension: self-interruption, hesitation.

EXPANSION
[a] Th.: ⟨$_{EV}$ I understand; but looking at it further, would it help to solve your problem {STRN} that your obligations are greater than your capacity if you {S} expressed your needs to Editha and actually said something like, "You work all day, and I go to school all day... Let's figure out what *you* should do and what I should do about cleaning." ⟩$_{EV}$
[b] ⟨$_{IV}$ Don't answer before I remind you {AUT}: that the therapist does not direct the patient's life and that we are allowed to talk about anything here; I'm asking a question but it is not a directive for action, and you can answer it without committing yourself to take such action. ⟩$_{IV}$

INTERACTION
[a] Therapist requests information about the consequences of requesting help from E., thereby requesting indirectly that ⟨ 5, S ⟩ R. carry out the basic suggestion by asking Editha for help.
[b] Th. further mitigates her request by denying the connection between the request for information ⟨ AUT and any possible request for action.

In the final analysis, this addition serves to blunt or mitigate the directive character of the suggestion. Behind it there lies a fundamental proposition of therapy, the *principle of the patient's autonomy:*

{AUT} The therapist does not direct the patient's life.

In 2.4[a], the therapist was engaged in discussion of Rhoda's everyday life situation, but in 2.4[b] the therapist herself shows tension, interrupting herself and hesitating before she inserts a meta-comment about what they are doing. She explicitly denies that she is making a suggestion for action. The fact that she makes such disclaimer does not mean that it is effective, but it is another sign of her recognition that direct suggestions to Rhoda are dangerous. The therapist continues to show the oscillation that she displayed in 2.2; she already has decided that this is not the appropriate moment to touch on the most emotionally charged question, and she is not yet ready to make a direct suggestion on the matter of Aunt Editha.

2.5. Rhoda's response to the therapist's request amounts to a refusal. It is not made directly, but follows her normal pattern of replying with a

2.5 TEXT CUES

[a] R.: ⟨_EV_ *She—looks, well—w—once I said sumpin' to her, and she... looked sort of funny, like then—she—r-realizes it,* (breath) *and then....*

Tension: self-interruption, glottalization, hesitation, silence.

[b] *It's like I **hurt** her, in some way... It's like—I-I dunno, I can't explain it, but I—*⟩_EV_

Tension: glottalization.

EXPANSION

[a] R.: ⟨_EV_ In such situations, Editha looks hurt. One time I did ask her to help clean, as you suggested, and she looked at me with an odd expression, as if she realized only then that the place needed cleaning, and then—

[b] the expression on her face was *hurt*, though nothing I did would account for it, since I did not say anything that would hurt a normal person. {~AD-E} It is very hard to explain her conduct but I will simply tell you what happened and you can judge. ⟩_EV_

INTERACTION

R. responds to the request for information by asserting that E. responded to an earlier request ⟨_6_ with an inappropriate emotion {7} thereby asserting indirectly that ⟨~AD-E⟩ E. is not an adult member of the household thereby refusing the requests ⟨_~5_ that she ask E. for help and put S into effect.

---

narrative from everyday life instead of a general statement. She introduces this anecdote with an abstract of the narrative to follow (Chapter 3, p. 105), which foreshadows her interpretation of the *funny look* that Editha gave her when she asked her to help.

> 2.5[a] R.: *She—looks, well—w—once I said sumpin' to her, and she... looked sort of funny, like then—she—r-realizes it,* (breath) *and then....*
>
> [b] *It's like I **hurt** her, in some way... It's like—I-I dunno, I can't explain it, but I—*

The paralinguistic cues Rhoda uses in this abstract are the familiar ones of self-interruption, glottalization, hesitation, and silence. The tension that she displays indicates that she is "choked up" by the irrational character of Editha's behavior. Behind this emotional display is the basic proposition that Editha is not adult and accountable, which the narrative itself will make more evident. The narrative also introduces the general theme characteristic of Episode 2:

{6} R. has requested Editha to help.

There is further foreshadowing of the third theme of the Episode:

{7} Editha showed an inappropriate emotion.

The significance of 2.5 will of course become clearer when the actual narrative is presented.

2.6. In the narrative proper, Rhoda changes to a different field of discourse, repeating the style shift that we saw in Episode 1. She now gives a rapid and fluent account of what happened with some direct quotations in family language. This vivid account of family life will enable us to set aside for a moment the consideration of interaction between therapist and patient and focus again on the kind of interaction that occurs in Rhoda's family, this time between her and Aunt Editha.

At all times, we must bear in mind that this information is filtered through Rhoda's reports and that the frame of the interview situation influences what she says. Yet the striking change in style and the vivid quotations from the family interaction suggest that we are getting a direct view rather different from the style of 2.5. Since Rhoda's narratives do not make the point that she claims for them, it is not unreasonable to take them as evidence as to what in fact happened. If a narrative confirmed Rhoda's claim that she is independent and understands the nature of her problem, we might be skeptical that the events actually occurred. When we see that the narrative of events make the reverse point, and see a consistent style of interaction reported for the family from one episode to the other, we can take it as a more credible view of family interaction.

The beginning of Rhoda's narrative shows many false starts, continuing the tension of her abstract, and indicating that this was not an easy task for her to perform.

2.6[a] R.: *I said t'her* (breath) *w-one time—I asked her—I said t'her,*

But Rhoda's following report of her actual behavior with Editha shows that she was quite aggressive and used many of the verbal devices that seemed to be common to her family interaction. The request itself is reported with a burst of fluency; it is so fast that most people cannot understand it when it is first played to them. Rhoda accelerates her tempo to the point that word boundaries disappear and function words are contracted and collapsed:

2.6[b] R.: *"Wellyouknow, wdy'mind takin' thedustrag an'justdustaround?"*

This burst of speed is part of a more general pattern that masks the aggressive nature of Rhoda's interaction with Editha. Rhoda also uses more conventional mitigating devices to make the request: *would you mind* can be read as 'please' and the word *just* serves to mitigate the action that is being requested. Embedded in these standard mitigating forms, we have 'Please take the dust rag and dust around', a fairly direct mode of expression.

2.6   TEXT   CUES
[a] R.: ⟨_N _I said t'her_ (breath) _w—one_   Tension: rapid reiteration,
time—I asked her—I said t'her,   condensation
[b]   ⟨_F_ _"Wellyouknow, wdy'mind takin'_   Tension: rapid condensation;
thedustrag an'justdustaround?" ⟩_F_ ⟩_N_   Mitigation: _would you mind_ for 'please';
                                                    justdustaround for 'dust'; low-pitched
                                                    level.

EXPANSION

R.: ⟨_N_ There was one time that I {6} asked Editha to carry out her obligation to help in the household by saying ⟨_F_ "Since you and I know that the house needs cleaning, and you are a member of our household with normal obligations, would you mind taking the dust rag and do a little dusting?" ⟩_F_⟩_N_

INTERACTION

[a] R. initiates a narrative about ⟨_6_⟩ a previous request to request help from Editha, thereby giving more information in response to therapist's request for information and suggestion ⟨_5_⟩.

[b] R. makes a request for action ⟨_6_⟩ in slightly mitigated form for E. to help carry out household obligations, and thereby carries out the suggestion ⟨_5_⟩ in regard to E.

All of the standard preconditions of the Rule of Requests are present here (Chapter 3, p. 78). It is reasonable to assume that Editha would have taken the request seriously; she must believe that Rhoda believes that (1) the house needs dusting, (2) Editha has the ability, and (3) the obligation to do it, and (4) Rhoda has the right to ask for this action.* If all of the conditions of this request have been true for some time, then 2.6[b] is actually a criticism of Editha by the Rule of Overdue Obligations (Chapter 3, p. 96). In this situation, it certainly would have been less aggressive for Rhoda to use some of the indirect means of making requests that have been illustrated above. She may have actually mitigated her request by hurrying over it in the way that she reports it; or this condensed form may be a way of mitigating her behavior for the therapist. More direct evidence of Rhoda's aggressive attitude appears in what follows.

*Since Editha is older than Rhoda, it may seem at first that the fourth precondition might not hold: _Does_ Rhoda have the right to ask her to help around the house? However, Editha's status in the household is quite low. In the _Playback_ session with Fanshel, the therapist makes this revealing analysis of Editha's social and psychological status:

... SHE IS CERTAINLY HELPLESS IN THE HOUSE... AND SHE HAS NO EGO. NO LIFE OF HER OWN. SHE DOESN'T INITIATE ANYTHING. SHE'S A FOLLOWER. SHE ASKS FOR NOTHING AND SHE'S A TOTALLY MASOCHISTIC PERSON...

2.7. Within Rhoda's narrative, we see a normal sequence of request and response. Editha is now reported as refusing the request, using the Rule for Putting Off Requests (Chapter 3, p. 90). She takes issue with the precondition that the house *needs* dusting. The paralinguistic cues add additional information showing that Rhoda detected an aggressive implication in Editha's response. There is the falling-rising contour on *me*, which we have identified as 'heavy implication,' and in addition an expression of surprise, *Oh*.

2.7 R.: *Sh's's, "Oh-I—it looks clean to me,"* . . .

The note of surprise that Editha adds to her refusal can best be read as a surprise that Rhoda would have made such an inappropriate judgment on the cleanliness of the house. Editha may not have used this particular device: Rhoda uses *Oh* to indicate surprise and heavy implication quite regularly in her reports of family interaction, and this may be her translation of other cues.* There is no absolute way of proving that a criticism or challenge was present in Editha's reported response; as always, the demonstration that a challenge was understood lies in the response to the participants themselves, and Rhoda's response of 2.8 demonstrates this fact fully. We can also support the interpretation of *Oh* by the parallels between Editha's challenge and Rhoda's mother's challenge in 1.9. It was pointed out there that Rhoda is quite sensitive to the *Oh*, and when she

---

2.7	TEXT	CUES
R.: ⟨_N_ *Sh's's,* ⟨_F_ *"Oh-I-I—it looks clean to me,"* . . . ⟩_F_ ⟩_N_		Heavy implication: 2 1 2, [1 2 on *me*]. Surprise: *"Oh"* Contrastive stress on *clean*: 'clean, not dirty'.

EXPANSION

R.: ⟨_N_ And Editha said to me, ⟨_F_ "Oh, I'm surprised that you made such a request; the house looks clean enough to me, and {~AD-R} you must not know anything about keeping up a house to make such an inappropriate request. ⟩_F_ ⟩_N_

INTERACTION

E. denies the need for the request that she help clean the house, thereby refusing this request ⟨~6⟩, simultaneously challenging R.'s standards of role performance, and thereby challenging ⟨~AD-R⟩ R.'s competence as an adult member of the household.

---

*See 5.16 [c], *Oh, Rhoda should never get tired;* 5.24 [a], *Oh, you're thin.* For Rhoda, *Oh* is the most common means of expressing the feeling of implicit rebuke in the speech of others.

retells Episode 1 she says that the *next time* she will respond, "What do you mean, 'Oh'?"

Our abstract analysis of the interaction of 2.7 makes a strong case for the aggressive implications of Editha's response. By challenging Rhoda's standards of role performance, she thereby challenges Rhoda's competence as an adult member of the household. If Rhoda has assumed the position of second head of the household, in the absence of her mother, then such an implication cannot be allowed to go unchallenged in turn—given the general character of interaction in this household.

2.8 Editha has refused Rhoda's request; this refusal was coupled with an accounting: that the furniture was clean. Rhoda's response to this tactic is to reject the account.

2.8[a] R.: *An' then I went like **this**,*
[b] *an' I said to her, "**That** looks **clean** t'you?"*

Here we see a good display of the characteristic style of verbal interaction of Rhoda's family: an indirect mode of expression that relies on gesture and intonation to convey challenges and criticisms. We also observe the "rise–fall" intonation, originally a Yiddish feature, and now widely used in communities influenced by large groups of Jewish-Americans. Figure 25 shows this intonation contour as it appears in 2.8[b]: In this sentence, the contour produces a heavy stress on *clean* and an extra-high rise on *you*, without the optional falling contour at the very end.*

Rhoda's intonation is accompanied by an even more aggressive physical gesture. The movement she refers to as *like **this*** is clearly that of wiping a finger across a surface and holding it up for inspection.

Rhoda's response of 2.8 must be understood in the light of the more general fact that the adult status of both parties has already been put in question. There is an underlying argument concerning the relative positions of Rhoda and Editha in Household 1: Are they both entitled to make requests of each other, sharing equally in the obligations of the household, and deciding the appropriate time to carry out these obligations? In our expansion of 2.8 we have no difficulty in locating the challenge to Editha's status, which is the first interpretation of the intonation contour that Rhoda uses: "You are incompetent to judge." The analysis of interaction in 2.8 must be more elaborate. In 2.8[a], Rhoda demonstrates the *need* to dust,

---

*For a full account of this intonation pattern, see Weinreich (1956). This intonation pattern is now heard quite widely throughout American English, and has spread well outside of the original Yiddish-influenced pattern. One can now say in American English, "*This* is a *cigarette?*" meaning 'you're crazy if you think this is a cigarette' as a satirical but extreme criticism of the object in question. It also puts in question, in a semiserious way, the competence of anyone who would take the other point of view. See also 3.22 for another example from Rhoda.

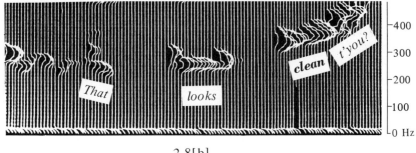

2.8[b]

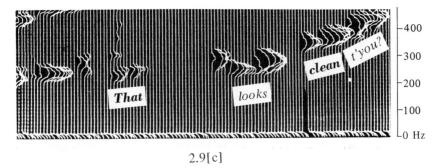

2.9[c]

Figure 25. Intonation contours of Rhoda's self-reports, *That looks **clean** t'you?* in 2.8 and 2.9.

and thereby contradicts Editha's denial of the precondition that the furniture needs dusting. According to the Rule for Reinstating Requests in Chapter 3 (p. 93) this request will be reinstated only if Editha refutes Rhoda's position. In 2.8[b], the surface expression is a request for confirmation (the normal interpretation of the rising contour). With the special intonation added, there is a simultaneous assertion that Editha's statement was inappropriate, and Rhoda thereby challenges Editha's standards of role performance and responds to Editha's challenge to her own competence: {~~AD-R} "It is not true that I am not a (competent) adult member of the household." Rhoda's response shows aggressive behavior that is appropriately symmetrical to Editha's behavior.

2.9. Since there are two basic actions performed in 2.8, Editha had two main choices in her response. She could have continued to contest the need for dusting, responding to 2.8[a]; or she could have responded to the personal challenge of 2.8[b]. She chooses the second option and gives the behavioral display that is referred to as a "huff" in Figure 5 on page 61.

2.8 TEXT	CUES
[a] R.: ⟨_N_ *An' then I went like this,*	Aggravation: gesture, 'Look at the
[b] *an' I said to her,* ⟨_F_ "*That looks clean t'you?*" ⟩_F_ ⟩_N_	dirt'. Aggravation: 2 2 3 ↑ Yiddish rise–fall intonation, 'If you think this is clean, you are crazy' [Figure 25].

EXPANSION

[a] R.: ⟨_N_ And then I made the gesture of wiping dust off the furniture with a finger,

[b] And I said to Editha, ⟨_F_ "Does a table with that amount of dust look clean to you? If so {~AD-E} you are incompetent to judge and do not know what 'clean' means." ⟩_F_ ⟩_N_

INTERACTION

[a] R. gives information on the need to dust, thereby contradicting E.'s denial of the *need* precondition for the request, thereby reinstating the request. ⟨‾6‾⟩
[b] R. requests confirmation ⟨‾?‾⟩ that E. made the statement she was just heard to make, thereby ⟨‾~‾⟩ asserting that the statement was inappropriate, thereby ⟨‾~AD-E‾⟩ challenging E.'s standards of role performance, thereby ⟨‾~~AD-R‾⟩ defending herself against E.'s challenge to her.

    2.9[a] R.: *And she sort of . . . I d'no—sh'sort of gave me a funny look as if I—hurt her in some way.*

The sequence of narrative events is displayed in Figure 26; here the pattern of requests and the pattern of challenges are seen operating at separate levels. On the level of intermediate speech actions, the initial request for action {6} is immediately blocked by Editha's assertion, through the Rule for Putting Off Requests. Rhoda's next move controverts the assertion that was utilized in that put-off, and simultaneously reinstates her original request by the automatic rule. The huff which follows serves to terminate the exchange: Editha does not carry out the request. However, this huff cannot be seen as a response to the intermediate speech actions. The coherence of Figure 26 can be understood only at the highest level of abstraction, where Editha is seen as challenging Rhoda's competence, Rhoda defends herself and simultaneously challenges Editha's competence, and Editha retreats in a huff.

    Rhoda's evaluation of the narrative follows the final event:

    2.9[b] R.: *and I mean I didn' mean to, I didn't **yell** and **cream.***
          [c] *All I did to her was that "**That looks clean to you?**" . . . .*

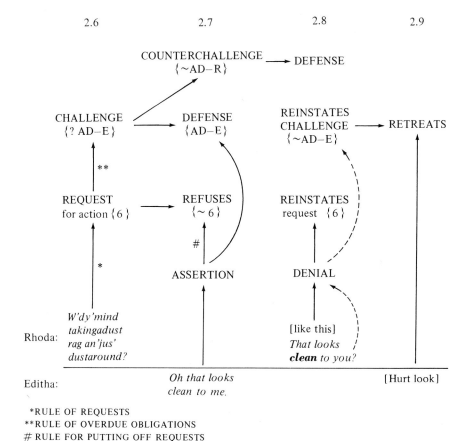

Figure 26. Sequencing of narrative, *That looks clean t'you?* of 2.6–2.9.

Rhoda makes this explicit evaluation in a way that continues the point of her initial abstract: Editha's behavior was incomprehensible and incoherent. The evaluation of 2.9[b], [c] focuses on an alleged lack of connection between the fourth and fifth events of the narrative. According to Rhoda, there was no basis in the interaction for the funny look that Editha gave her; in other words, she denies entirely the highest level of interaction that is sketched in Figure 26, and shows Editha's behavior as completely unreasonable. The paralinguistic cues Rhoda uses here recapitulate and repeat those which she used in the narrative. In 2.9[a], she returns to the tense, choked-up approach that registers bewilderment at Editha's behavior (as forecast in 2.5). In 2.9[b], she uses the rapid and condensed form of family

204 EPISODE TWO

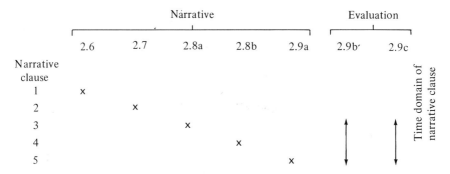

Figure 27. Narrative sequence and evaluation in Episode 2.

style, and in 2.9[c], she repeats the aggravating intonation contour of 2.8[b], simultaneously denying the meaning of that intonation.

The comments of 2.9[b] and [c] form an evaluative coda to the narrative, external to the events themselves. Rhoda addresses them to the therapist, arguing explicitly for her interpretation of these events. Figure 27 sketches the structure of the narrative as a sequence of five distinct actions, each separated in time, followed by an evaluation which covers times 3–5 and focuses upon the lack of connection of 2.8[b] and 2.9[a].

The cross section of 2.9 shows that Rhoda is conveying two distinct but related ideas in her evaluation of the narrative. According to Rhoda, Editha's hurt look shows that {~RSNBL-E} she is not a reasonable person that can be talked to; Editha's failure to respond to Rhoda's rejection of her accounting shows {~AD-E} that she is not competent to evalute such situations and therefore not an appropriate person to deal with. Both of these messages challenge the validity of the therapist's suggestion that Rhoda ask Editha for help.

In terms of ordinary interaction, Rhoda seems to be entitled to deny the meaning of her intonation patterns. We have made the general point that such indirect modes of expression have an important function: they are *deniable,* and the interactants can maintain normal relations by overlooking challenges to each other's status. Anyone who is at all familiar with the gesture and intonation used in 2.8 will realize that Rhoda was aggressive and challenging towards Editha; but it is equally true that it is "normal" for Rhoda to deny this and claim that all she did was make a request for confirmation.

Although Rhoda may be entitled to deny this aggression in ordinary social circumstances, it is clear that she is not looking at the situation from the same analytic perspective that the therapist uses. The anger Rhoda is expressing here is quite transparent to the therapist.

The therapist does not immediately comment on this episode in the *Playback* session, but a later point in the *Playback* she reflects:

THERE IS A SIDE TO RHODA THAT IS CRYING TO COME OUT... AS SELF-EFFACING AND HELPLESS AS SHE IS PRESENTING HERSELF, THERE IS ANOTHER ASPECT TO HER... WHICH IS REALLY QUITE DOMINEERING, HOSTILE, VERY AUTHORITATIVE.

The therapist realizes that Rhoda's efforts to carry out the suggestion and express her needs to others are hampered when she expresses aggression and her needs at the same time, so producing a defensive reaction from others. In her later reassessment, she recalls this very episode as perhaps the most revealing of Rhoda's "other side":

2.9   TEXT   CUES

[a] R.: ⟨ₙ And she sort of.... I   Tension: self-interruption, stammering,
d'no—sh'sort of gave me a funny look as if   'bewilderment'.
I—hurt her in some way,
[b] and I mean I didn't mean to, ⟨ғ I   Tension: rapid and condensed.
didn' **yell and scream.** ⟩ғ
[c] All I did to her was that ⟨ғ "That   Aggravation: (Same intonation as
looks **clean** to you?" ⟩ғ.... ⟩ₙ   2.8[b]) [Figure 25].
[d] Th.: Mmm.   Reinforcement: 2 2 → 'Expected,
                                              thoughtful sympathy'.

EXPANSION

[a] R.: ⟨ₙ And Editha gave me a kind of strange look that I can't account for, as if I had insulted her in some way, even though nothing I did would explain {7} the emotion she showed.
[b] And the reason I'm bewildered is that I didn't intend to insult Editha and produce that emotion, I didn't raise my voice or show anger to Editha when I showed her the dirt,
[c] the only words I said to Editha were, ⟨ғ "That looks *clean* to you?" ⟩ғ ⟩ₙ

INTERACTION

[a] E. retreats from the verbal interaction and responds to R.'s challenge by a huff. R. gives evaluation of E.'s response as ⟨ 7 an unjustified reaction to an imaginary insult, thereby asserting that ⟨ ~RSNBL-E E. did not behave in a normal way.
[b] and [c] R. denies that she attacked E. by raising her voice or expressing anger, thereby ⟨ 7 asserting that E.'s emotion was not appropriate, thereby asserting again that ⟨ ~AD-E E. is not a competent adult thereby refusing the therapist's suggestion ⟨ 5,S that she ask E. for help.

WHAT YOU CAN'T SEE IS THE GESTURE. WHEN SHE SAID TO EDITHA, "DON'T YOU THINK YOU OUGHT TO DUST?" AND EDITHA SAYS, "WHY—IT LOOKS CLEAN TO ME" AND SO SHE DOES THIS... SHE WENT [TAPPING SOUND] "... THIS IS CLEAN?"

It must be remembered that the therapist is recalling Rhoda's words some 10 minutes after this particular part of the tape was played, and she is recalling Rhoda's gesture 2 weeks later. We see that she has transformed one part of the reported conversation to a more aggressive form: Rhoda's request for action of 2.6[b] loses its mitigated character and shows instead a request for information directed at Editha's *obligation*. As we noted above (Chapter 3, pp. 84–86), indirect requests made by references to obligations are aggravating rather than mitigating. In addition, the therapist adds an intonation contour that rises more sharply and is more insistent than the one Rhoda actually used. All these changes reflect her final evaluation of Rhoda's behavior as aggressive.

This overall interpretation is based upon an accurate evaluation of Editha's response of 2.7, and her aggressive counter in 2.8 (and 2.9). The therapist accurately remembers Rhoda's response as a request for confirmation with the rising intonation contour. It is interesting to compare the therapist's intonation contour (Figure 25') with the intonation contour that Rhoda actually used in 2.8 (Figure 25): the therapist matches the high rising contour at the end. She also adds a high contour at the beginning, stressing the incredulous reaction to *this*. The direct observation of Rhoda's

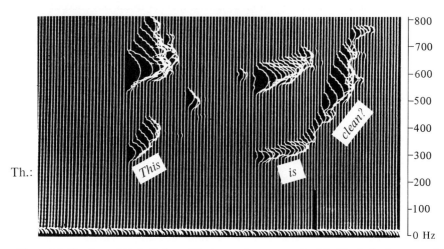

Figure 25'. The therapist's imitation of the intonation contour for 2.8, *That looks clean to you?* in the *Playback* session.

behavior by the therapist confirms the analysis we derived from our monitoring of the audio tape alone.

Repression of emotion is a central problem for the therapeutic session as a whole. As we will see, the therapist believes that her main task is to overcome Rhoda's tendency to deny the underlying significance of her behavior and to recognize her own emotions. When the therapist takes note of the anger that is passing back and forth in family life, she also notes the way in which this anger is concealed. We have observed above that the patient develops in the therapeutic session a style of reporting that is pseudo-rational, as if she could examine her own behavior without feeling any emotions; but in her accounts of everyday life, the full range of emotion becomes evident in the quotations from family style. Part of the therapist's difficulty is that the very machinery used by normal, competent interactants can be used to obscure a person's own view of his behavior. If a person cannot use indirection and mitigation, he is incompetent, but if he cannot recognize the emotions behind this behavior, he is disabled in another way. Resistance to therapy may take the form of a refusal to read these emotions.

Rhoda has now finished her short narrative of 2.6–2.8, which she intended to illustrate the point made in the abstract of 2.5—that Editha is incompetent and abnormal because she reacted as if she was hurt for no reason at all. The same story might have been told to illustrate how clever Rhoda was in repartee—how she put Editha in her place. It might also have been told to show that Editha simply does not do the work that would be expected of her. A fourth possibility would be for Rhoda to use the story to illustrate her ability to assert herself. The actual interpretation that Rhoda hoped to make is provided for us in her addendum of 2.9[b] and [c]. This is an "external evaluation," outside of the narrative structure. The narrative events themselves seem to be unaffected by Rhoda's interpretation, yet it is not uncommon for storytellers to transform radically the events they are reporting to fit in with their own evaluation and project a flawless image of themselves. If Rhoda had that competence, transforming the act and the actors to fit her interpretation, it would be much more difficult for the therapist to use these narratives as a window into the pattern of family interaction.

What the therapist sees is that Rhoda has again failed to get help from other members of the family. She did not get help from her mother and she did not get help from her aunt. The mechanism is not quite the same in the two cases; the end result is the same. It is an open question whether this mode of family interaction is a symptom or a cause of the family's difficulties, but the overall pattern is quite clear. The therapist responds by simple reinforcement, postponing her evaluation of the situation to a later time. Rhoda is encouraged to continue her attack on Editha.

208 EPISODE TWO

2.10 TEXT	CUES
[a] R.: ⟨_EV_ *An' like—if I—y'like, she'll go t'th'* **store** *and get little* **things** *but . . . . um . . .*	Derogation: *little* **things**, 'nothing important, just the least a person could do'.
[b] *Uh—she . . . like iflaskhertobuyonething . . she'll always come back w'something else. If I ask her t'get—this—a* **small** *one, she'll come back with a* **large** *one—or . . .* (breath)	Tension: condensation, hesitation.
[c] *She . . .* **I** *d'no, she jist doesn't do it* **right**. *It's just she—*⟩_EV_	Exasperation: 3 3 3 whine, 'It's frustrating, there is nothing one can do about it'.

EXPANSION

[a] R.: ⟨_EV_ And as another example of why one can't turn to Editha for help, she will go to the store and buy a few things for the house if someone asks her,
[b] but if you ask her to buy one particular thing such as a small size, she will always come back with something else such as a large size. In every case, she doesn't do the job you asked her to do as it should be done. ⟩_EV_

INTERACTION

R. gives further information and evaluation ⟨ ~AD-E of E.'s incompetence as an adul⁺ member of the household, thereby giving support to her indirect refusal ⟨ ~S,S to the request that she ask E. for help and put {S} into effect.

2.10. Rhoda now goes on to give further instances of Editha's incompetence. 2.10 is a pseudo-narrative: it gives a sequence of the *kinds* of things which occur, implying that there was at least one such actual series of events. Rhoda points out that Editha is incompetent even in the most ordinary exchanges of everyday life.

At this point, the amount that is said begins to outrun what is being done, and the verbal material bulks much larger than the interactional content. It seems as if Rhoda's complaints about Editha can continue without end. She expresses exasperation by whining and repeating herself until the therapist intervenes with an interruption.

2.11. The therapist's intervention begins with an interruption. We see again that Rhoda's way of signaling the end of her contribution is to enlarge continuously upon a certain theme, until the therapist has picked up the signal. This interruption is therefore not a sign of impatience, but simply an appropriate moment to respond. The therapist now faces the problem of coping with Rhoda's resistance to the suggestion that was put forward, which carries, as we have noted, implicit challenge to the therapist's own competence.

2.11[a] Th.: *She presents herself as very helpless and needing to be waited on hand an' foot.*
[b] R.: *Yes.*
[c] Th.: *An' she's really used to this in her relationship with **mother**.*
[d] R.: *Yes.* (breath)

The kind of interpretation that the therapist here interposes is different in nature from anything we have seen so far. It is clearly in interview style, which gives full support to the therapist's claim to competence as the interpreter of emotions. Note that Rhoda's response to this kind of interpretation is in a very different style from that which immediately preceded. She uses the formal *yes* instead of the more informal *yeh* (3.9, 4.18) and shifts into a kind of repressed and minimally expressive behavior, which we will see becomes extremely marked in Episode 5. Rhoda makes a strong claim to competence in the everyday life situation, and feels quite free to interpret the behavior of others within this context, but she retreats before the therapist's claim to be able to interpret emotions in the interview context.

The second remark of the therapist, 2.11[c], we label as an *identification*. It is more complex than other assertions or interpretations, and sets up a relation between relations. The therapist agrees with Rhoda that Editha is behaving like a child and suggests that the relationship between mother and Editha sets the pattern for the relationship between Rhoda and Editha. She makes this interpretation much more explicit in the *Playback* session with Fanshel:

... SHE WAS BEHAVING WITH AUNT EDITHA THE WAY HER MOTHER BEHAVES WITH HER. SHE WAS TREATING HER AUNT LIKE A HELPLESS CHILD.

The therapist hopes that Rhoda can achieve some insight into this parallel and expresses the belief that Episode 2 already reflects this process. The therapist does more than put forward a parallel, however: she also posits a causal relationship that would explain Rhoda's own problem. As head of the household and the most dominant person in the household, Rhoda's mother has apparently caused Editha to behave in a helpless way by treating her as dependent, and the inference is that she has done the same with Rhoda. At a later point in the *Playback* session, the therapist refers to Rhoda's behavior in the same words that she has just used to refer to Editha:

WHAT SHE DOES IS SIMILAR TO A REACTION FORMATION—SHE DOES THE OPPOSITE... SHE BECOMES VERY HELPLESS.

2.11 TEXT   CUES
[a] Th.: ⟨_IV_ *She presents herself as very helpless and needing to be waited on hand an' foot.*
[b] R.: *Yes.*   Formality: 3 2, yes, breathy, 'acquiescence'.
[c] Th.: *An' she's really used to this in her relationship with* **mother**.
[d] R.: *Yes.* (breath) ⟩_IV_

EXPANSION
[a] Th.: ⟨_IV_ Editha presents herself as {~AD-E} *not* an adult member of the household and as *very* helpless and needing to be waited on, hand and foot.
[b] R.: I understand your point and accept it.
[c] Th.: Editha is very much accustomed to being treated as helpless and needing to be waited on hand and foot by your mother.
[d] R.: I understand. ⟩_IV_

INTERACTION
Th. interrupts in IVS and ⟵~AD-E gives interpretation of E.'s behavior as not that of an adult, thereby gives support to R.'s assertion and ⟵~5 implicitly supporting R.'s refusal of her request thereby retreating from her suggestion.

In giving this elaborate interpretation, the therapist agrees with Rhoda, and necessarily accepts her grounds for refusing the initial suggestion of Episode 2. As we will see, the overall structure of this interview is marked by a succession of such advances and retreats.

Though the therapist has taken one step backward, it appears that her excursion into the relationship between Rhoda and her Aunt Editha has been a fruitful one. The parallel between Rhoda's behavior to her aunt and her mother's behavior to Rhoda will become more marked in what follows. It is also clear that Rhoda does not feel threatened when she discusses her relationships with her aunt in the same way that she does in giving accounts of her exchanges with her mother.

In studying the verbal interaction between therapist and patient, we find considerable significance in the asymmetry between interview style and the narratives of everyday life. The therapist emits abstract statements, which carry much more power and interpretive force than Rhoda's remarks. Rhoda typically uses narratives that do not make explicit the nature of her response. In this way, Rhoda invites the therapist to sum up or label her contributions in a more parsimonious manner. The therapist provides for Rhoda a repertoire of concepts and terms that she can use to view her

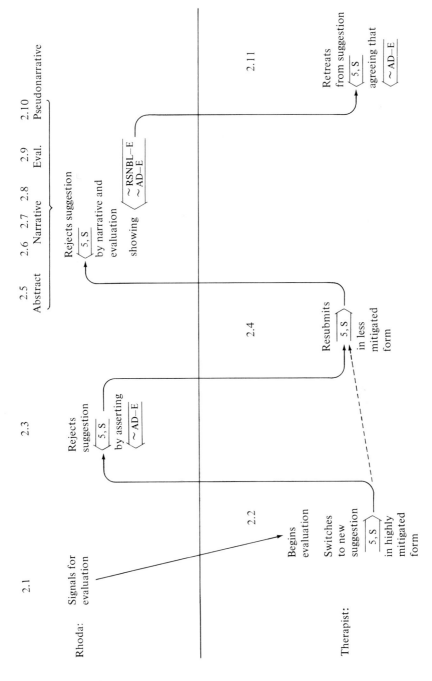

Figure 28. Strategic interaction of Episode 2.

own behavior. At the same time, it is inevitable that this new battery of terms and ways of looking at human relations will change the patient's view of herself.

We can now take an overview of what has happened in Episode 2. The structure of Episode 1 was relatively simple—a narrative by Rhoda with Rhoda's evaluation. Episode 2 shows rapid interaction between Rhoda and the therapist, with a number of advances and retreats.

Figure 28 shows the strategic interaction of Episode 2: The initiative is with the therapist, and we can observe here the larger pattern in which she employs particular tactics to reach her overall goal. In 2.1, Rhoda signals that she is ready for an evaluation of the proposition she put forward in Episode 1. In 2.2, the therapist begins to give such an evaluation but switches instead to a new form of the basic suggestion, which she puts forward in a very indirect form. Rhoda rejects this indirect suggestion by a diatribe against Editha. The therapist then puts this suggestion forward again in 2.4, in a form that is still mitigated but more direct than before. Rhoda's response is basically the same—an attack on Editha, but this time in the form of a narrative with a preliminary abstract, a basic action, and an external evaluation at the end. She pursues this with a pseudo-narrative on the same theme until the therapist finally intervenes in 2.11 with an evaluation. This takes the form of a retreat from the basic suggestion, acknowledging the force of what Rhoda has to say.*

Though the therapist does introduce in her evaluation some new ideas that may be the basis for further exploration, the basic pattern of Episode 2 is that the therapist has made a few tentative explorations in a certain direction and has been rebuffed. Episode 3 continues her effort to get Rhoda to explore the possibilities of solving her problems without her mother's help.

---

*Note that Rhoda's argument is based upon the fact that she is herself the expert on what takes place in everyday life. This is the basis that she uses for her resistance to the therapist's suggestion, but it must not be considered a purely negative factor. If Rhoda did not have an area that she could talk about without fear of contradiction, her participation in the interview would be confined to the type of formal acquiescence we see in 2.11, and the therapist would have nothing to work with.

EPISODE THREE

I know you don't like to eat alone.

Episode 2 seemed to be terminated conclusively when Rhoda rejected the therapist's suggestion that she turn to Aunt Editha for help. It is somewhat surprising, then, to find that Episode 3 is a replaying of Episode 2. The same theme is reintroduced, and both actors persist in their orientations. We see, again, through Rhoda's reports, the pattern of family interaction that prevents cooperation between members of the household. We also see a good deal more interaction between therapist and patient. The therapist plays the role of the patient for a moment, modeling a possible pattern of interaction for her to follow. The patient begins to play the role of a therapist, beginning to interpret the emotional dynamics of others, and there is considerable jostling between therapist and patient before their normal distribution of roles is restored.

3.1. At the end of Episode 2, we saw that the therapist had agreed with Rhoda's general contention that her aunt would not be of very much assistance; the therapist's analysis of Editha's helpless and dependent character might seem to make any further appeal to her beside the point. Yet, the first word of the therapist in Episode 3 is *But:* conceding all that Rhoda has said, the therapist puts the suggestion to her again, in a less direct form.

> 3.1[a]   Th.: *But what would happen if you—um—you know—tried to arrive at some working relationship with her—*

Like the request of Episode 2, it is framed as a request for information: "What would happen if you..." However, the request now includes a model for Rhoda's behavior. Instead of being a request about what Editha does, it is a request for information about what Rhoda might do.

The therapist shows considerable hesitancy in making her suggestion and uses her regular mitigating intonation on the key phrase *what would*

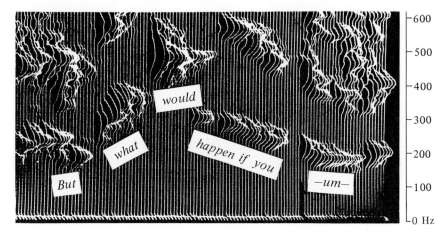

Figure 29. Mitigating contour on therapist's suggestion of 3.1.

happen, a high rising contour with fading volume. (See Figure 29.) When she turns to spelling out her suggestion, in the field of everyday style, her delivery is much more straightforward. Our expansion adds to this statement the understandings that we draw from what has immediately preceded: the therapist has conceded the major argument about Editha, yet puts the request again as if the argument had not been made. When we examine the form of this request, we find that it fits into our general rule without any difficulty. Of the four preconditions, 1, 3, and 4 are in force, since Rhoda believes that the therapist believes that there is a *need* for the suggestion to be made, that she herself has an *obligation* to make it, and that the therapist has a *right* to make the suggestion. (For documentation, see 1.5 and 1.6 in Episode 1, p. 145.) The only issue, then, revolves around the second precondition—is it believable that Rhoda has the *ability* to get Editha to help? If Editha is as incompetent as Rhoda claims she was in Episode 2, then Rhoda would have to be a miracle worker to get any help from her. The therapist's new request is only slightly mitigated, since she has simply added the fixed form, *What would happen if you* . . . If we removed this phrase, we would simply have the direct command, "Try to arrive at some working relationship with her!" Note that all the therapist's mitigating intonation pattern is concentrated on this single phrase. In the rest of her intervention, she lays out a very specific model for Rhoda to follow.

Repeated requests are difficult matters to handle in face-to-face interaction. If a request is repeated in exactly the same words, the action is normally heard as a sharp criticism of the role performance of the other. This

THE THERAPIST'S INTERVENTION   215

point is formulated expressly as the Rule of Repeated Requests (Chapter 3, p. 95):

If A makes a request for action X of B in role R, and A repeats the request before B has responded, then A is heard as emphatically challenging B's performance in role R.

3.1	TEXT	CUES
[a]	Th: ⟨$_{IV}$But what would happen if you—um—you know—tried to arrive at some working relationship with her—	Mitigation: high rising intonation, whát woùld happĕn (Figure 29).
[b]	To say ⟨$_{EV}$—you work all day an' I go to school all day—	
[c]	Maybe when we... uhm.. get to the point where we have t'have some—uh—effort made about dinner and so on that it could be joint, you know, let's figure out what **you** should do an' what I should do. ⟩$_{EV}$ ⟩$_{IV}$	Mitigation: euphemism, *get to the point where we*, 'when we have to cope with being left alone'.

EXPANSION

[a]   Th.: ⟨$_{IV}$ But even though {~AD-E} Editha lacks the adult standards of social responsibility and role performance, let me ask you hypothetically {S} What would happen if you tried to arrive at a working arrangement with her, since you haven't in fact tried to do so yet.
[b]   If you say to Editha, ⟨$_{EV}$ "You work at your job eight hours a day and I work at school eight hours a day.
[c]   Maybe when mother, who usually makes dinner, is away and we have to make dinner, we could do it together rather than each fixing it separately. Let's {COOP-R,E} figure out what *you* should do and what I should do to get it done." ⟩$_{EV}$ ⟩$_{IV}$

INTERACTION

[a]   Th. requests information on the consequences of asking E. for help, thereby requesting again ⟨S⟩ that R. should express her needs to E., thereby challenging ⟨?~AD-E⟩ Rhoda's argument for rejecting the suggestion already made.
[b] and [c]   Th. performs the role of R. making the suggestion ⟨COOP-R,E⟩ to E., thereby suggesting that E. do so and simultaneously challenging ⟨?AD-R⟩ R.'s competence to perform the role of adult without instruction.

Therefore second requests normally are made in a somewhat different form, but even in this case they must be interpreted as rejecting the accounted denial or put-off of the other party. We have indicated the nature of this challenge in our interactional statement for 3.1.

There is a second problem in the personal relations of therapist and patient, which develops from the therapist's action in 3.1: she *performs* the patient's role.

> 3.1[b] *To say—you work all day an' I go to school all day—*
> [c] *Maybe when we . . . uhm . . get to the point where we have t'have some—uh—effort made about dinner and so on it could be joint, you know, let's figure out what* **you** *should do an' what I should do.*

As the therapist models behavior for Rhoda, she goes into detail in a way that contrasts sharply with her brief comment at the beginning of Episode 2. She makes full use of her informal sociological competence in explaining how role partners should deal with each other—how a rational person might go about relieving role strain. In specifying the actual words that Rhoda might use, she recognizes the fact that Rhoda has not been competent at this kind of interpersonal relations in the past.

The concluding clause of 3.1[c] embodies a very important theme of therapy, which necessarily appears whenever the therapist enters into the complicated network of interpersonal relations that govern the patient's encounters in everyday life.

{COOP} Role partners should cooperate to solve mutual problems.

Although it may seem helpful and cooperative to model behavior in such detail, it can also be heard as "talking down" to or even being maternal towards Rhoda at this point. We have already seen that it is challenging for the therapist to reiterate the suggestion after it has been rejected. This challenge to Rhoda's competence as an adult member of the household is reinforced by the therapist's taking Rhoda's role and showing her how to play it. The frustration and bewilderment that Rhoda shows in her response seems to show that she is reacting to this challenge. She is being encouraged and chided at the same time.

3.2. The normal response to a request for information is to give that information; the response to a request for action is to indicate compliance or give an accounted denial. Rhoda does none of these: instead, she begins a narrative of her latest encounter with Editha.

> 3.2[a] R.: *Sso-like-las' night—like, on Wednesday night is my late—one o' my late nights—*
> [b] Th.: *Mm.*
> [c] R.: *—I have two late nights, Tuesday and Wednesday.*
> [d] Th.: *Mm.*

This is not an account of what *would* happen, but an account of what did happen. Rhoda does not state explicitly the relevance of her narrative to the therapist's request, though we may infer something from her long drawn out *Sso-like-*. We spell out a logical connection in our expansion, but it is important to note that Rhoda's normal style of response is to argue directly with anecdotes. She begins with a rush, changing her syntax several times in the middle of the sentence. Normal editing rules will not restore this to well-formed structure but would yield instead an ungrammatical "On Wednesday night is one of my late nights." It is clear that 3.2 is not in itself responsive to 3.1. By the Rule of Narrative Orientation (Chapter 3, p. 106), it can be recognized as the beginning of a narrative that promises to be responsive in its over-all evaluative point. 3.2 provides orientation to time and one main character of the narrative to follow.

Our interactional statement recognizes that Rhoda responds to the therapist by giving the information requested in 3.1. It does not indicate a more important fact—that she has not yet responded to the therapist's indirect request for action; but the emotion that is signaled by her vehemence and confusion shows us that she does recognize the presence of this request.

The therapist recognizes that something responsive will be forthcoming, and supports the direction in which Rhoda is moving with two noncommittal reinforcements: *Mm*.

3.2   TEXT   CUES

[a]   R.: ⟨_N_ *Sso-like-las' night—like, on Wednesday night is my late—one o' my late nights—*   Tension: fast tempo, ungrammatical editing.

[b]   Th: *Mm*.   Reinforcement: 2 2, tentative acceptance.

[c]   R.: *—I have two late nights, Tuesday and Wednesday.* ⟩_N_   Reinforcement: 2 2, tentative acceptance

[d]   Th: *Mm*.

EXPANSION

R: ⟨_N_ But { COOP} I have tried to make arrangements with Editha and it doesn't work. Let me give you an example. Last night, Wednesday, is one of the two nights, Tuesday and Wednesday, when I stay late at school. ⟩_N_

INTERACTION

R. initiates narrative, giving orientation to time and situation, and thereby giving information requested by Th.

[b] and [d]   Th. reinforces.

218   EPISODE THREE

3.3. After this short beginning, Rhoda seems to change her mind about telling the story of what happened in her encounter with Editha; she tries to abbreviate the narrative to a single-sentence abstract (Chapter 3, p. 105). Simply by stating that "the whole story came out to be..." she does not succeed in communicating her point to the therapist.

> 3.3[a] R.: *So—I said t'her—well, uh... well—the whole story came out to be—that she doesn't—she doesn't like to eat alone.*
> [b] Th.: *Mhm.*

Rhoda adds to her abstract the paralinguistic cues that imply shared confidence in her phrase *the whole story came out to be.* Her breathy quality might imply that she caught Editha trying to get away with something, but that she was found out. Yet it is still not clear what this shared confidence is about. Our expansion is an attempt to overcome some of this confusion and make plain to the reader what seems to have happened, but there still will be some complications that will not be cleared up until the entire episode is finished. In this expansion, we have drawn from the rest of the episode to show the kind of rational statement Rhoda might have made if she had been able to sum up the point in a single sentence.

Rhoda's narrative revolves, then, around propositions concerning an emotion—loneliness. The argument she is presenting concerns who actually feels that emotion. We present these propositions in a general form:

3.3	TEXT	CUES
[a]	⟨$_N$ So—I said t'her—well, uh... well—the whole story came out to be—that she doesn't—she doesn't like to eat alone. ⟩$_N$	Implication: she doesn't like to eat alone; breathiness, 'shared confidence'.
[b]	Th.: *Mhm.*	Reinforcement, 2→, neutral

EXPANSION

R.: ⟨$_N$ When I said something to Editha about dinner, she misinterpreted what I said as meaning that {E_4} I was lonesome and {8} I didn't want to eat alone, and so Editha suggested that we go out to eat, but it turned out that in fact {E_{4a}} Editha was lonesome and {8_a} she didn't want to eat alone. ⟩$_N$

INTERACTION

[a] R. interrupts her own narrative by giving an abstract: $\overrightarrow{8a}$ E. feels the emotion of loneliness.
[b] Th. reinforces.

{E₄}   Rhoda feels loneliness.
{E₄ₐ} Editha feels loneliness.

and in the particular form of the issue raised in this Episode:

{8}   Rhoda doesn't like to eat alone.
{8ₐ} Editha doesn't like to eat alone.

In therapeutic terminology, Rhoda is saying that Editha tried to project her own feeling of loneliness onto Rhoda. Without presenting any details or arguments, Rhoda tries to enlist the therapist's support at the outset by assuming that she would share this interpretation.

3.4. As Rhoda moves into the justification for her interpretation, she picks up speed and condenses her words, passing over her own interpretation as quickly as possible. She adds a component of moral indignation with a nasal whine and a high pitch on *how does she know*, with a sense of exasperation parallel to the bewilderment she expresses at Editha's incomprehensible behavior in Episode 2.

3.4[a]   R.: *But she doesn' say—that she doesn't like to eat alone, sh'say, "I know that you don't like to eat alone."*

[b]   *An' now how does she know—I never said anything about not eating alone.*

The nasal whine in 3.4[b] appears in our expansion as {~RSNBL-E}, a sharp criticism of Editha as a person who says ridiculous things. There is also a note of moral indignation, since Editha has violated one of Rhoda's prerogatives—to speak for herself. An emotion of loneliness, which she might feel can be classed as an "R-event," something that is known to Rhoda, on which she is the sole authority.

Interpreting the emotions of others is considered to be the prerogative of a therapist, and not within the competence of laymen; in the interactional statement, we symbolize Rhoda's indignant challenge to Editha's attempt by ⟨?INT-E⟩. This contains the status predicate {INT}, which we first encountered in Rhoda's dubious reaction to the therapist's suggestion of Episode 1.

{INT-X}   X is able to interpret the emotions of others.

Through this Episode, Rhoda alternates between direct quotations in family style and very rapid statements of her own point of view as in 3.4[b].

| 3.4 | TEXT | CUES |

[a] R.: ⟨_IV_ ⟨_N_ *But she doesn' say—that she doesn't like to eat alone, sh'say, "I know that you don't like to eat alone."* ⟩_N_ Tension: condensation

[b] *An' now how does she know—I never said anything about not eating alone.* ⟩_IV_ Exasperation: *Hŏw dŏes shĕ knŏw*, with nasal whine, tension: condensation.

EXPANSION

[a] R.: ⟨_IV_ But even though {8a} Editha is the one who doesn't like to eat alone, she doesn't say that she doesn't like to eat alone, ⟨_N_ she said to me, {8} "I know that you don't like to eat alone." ⟩_N_

[b] And let's look at {~RSNBL-E} the ridiculous thing she said: How does Editha know {8} that I don't like to eat alone, since I've never said anything about not eating alone. ⟩_IV_

INTERACTION

R. gives information that E. made an assertion ⟨ 8 ⟩ about an R-event, without any evidence from R., thereby ⟨ ?8 ⟩ challenging E.'s proposition, and thereby ⟨ ?INT-E ⟩ challenging E.'s competence as an interpreter of emotion.

3.5. It is not clear whether Rhoda would have continued with her original narrative at this point, but the therapist intervenes actively, focusing her attention on Rhoda's interpretation of Editha's unreasonable behavior.

3.5[a] Th.: *Mhm—she couldn't possibly know—*
    [b] R.: *But—but—*
    [c] *... sh's'z, "You don't like to eat alone."*

The therapist's intervention is quite firm, since it deals with a problem which lies squarely within her own area of expertise—the interpretation of emotions. To make this point, she must override Rhoda's attempts to continue (*But—but—*). As soon as she can, Rhoda continues her denunciation of Editha's position, repeating her own reasonable statement and beginning a longer exposition {~RSNBL-E} of how irrational Editha's statement was.

3.6. Rhoda's extended denunciation of Editha in 3.6 may be termed informally a "diatribe"; technically it is an external evaluation of a narrative (Chapter 3, p. 109) which appears in 1.6. Her speech is very rapid and condensed, drawing on the indirect and ironic verbal style characteristic of her family. An editorial comment is superimposed on *I can't eat in a restaurant* by an intonation contour signaling that this is an absurd state-

| 3.5 | TEXT | CUES |

[a] Th.: ⟨$_{IV}$ *Mhm—she couldn't possibly know—* ⟩$_N$ Reinforcement: 2 2 3 ↑, strong support
Emphasis: *couldn't pŏssibly know*

[b] R.: *But—but—*

[c] ⟨$_N$ ... *sh's'z, "You don't like to eat alone."* ⟩$_N$

EXPANSION

[a] Th.: ⟨$_{IV}$ That makes sense: {?INT-E} she couldn't possibly know {8} that you felt like not eating alone if you didn't say anything about it. ⟩$_{IV}$

[c] R.: ⟨$_N$ But Editha said to me, {?8} "You don't like to eat alone." ⟩$_N$

INTERACTION

[a] Th. interrupts giving support, and gives further support of the proposition ⟨ ?INT-E that E. could not know a R-event, and simultaneously prevents R. from continuing.

[b] R. attempts to continue.

[c] R. repeats E.'s proposition ⟨ 8 , and in the light of 3.4 [b], ⟨ ?INT-E challenges again E.'s credibility.

---

ment. It is unlikely that the therapist or anyone else could understand every detail of the point that Rhoda is making in 3.6[a], because she talks very fast, interrupting herself very often: The effect is one of great emotional turmoil.*

The Therapist's Interventions

3.7. The therapist now intervenes in the first of a series of remarks that have a notably insistent and almost strident quality. We have indicated some interruptions and some strident overlap in the text of 3.6–3.11, but even when this is not the case, we have "pseudo-interruptions" where the therapist begins speaking almost immediately after the patient stops talking. Some listeners are puzzled that the therapist is pursuing Rhoda so closely, but the issue involved here is an important one for the course of therapy in general: what are the proper roles of therapist and patient in dealing with interpretation of emotions? In our general presentation of the interview situation, we argued that both therapist and patient must have

---

*Throughout this part of the Episode, there is an insistence on the phrase, *eat alone*, which has a somewhat irritating effect. So far in this Episode we have *she doesn't like to eat alone, you don't like to eat alone, said anything about not eating alone, you don't like to eat alone, you're eating alone, she doesn't like to eat alone.*

| 3.6 | TEXT | CUES |

[a] R.: ⟨$_{EV}$ *I can't eat in a restaurant—if you sit in a counter—I mean—if you goin' to a restaurant for a san'wich—you're eating alone, but—so you sit at the counter—it doesn't bother me—* ⟩$_{EV}$

Tension: extreme condensation, self-interruption, high whine, cou̇nter, 'exasperation'; Implication: I cȧn't eȧt; Mitigation: *bother* for 'become emotionally upset'. Tension: self-interruption.

[b] *So she doesn't—so—anyway, I—the way I interpreted that was that she doesn't like to eat alone.* ⟩$_{IV}$

EXPANSION

[a] R.: ⟨$_{IV}$ ⟨$_{EV}$ If she meant to say that I can't eat in a restaurant without feeling lonesome—that's absurd! {~8} If you go into a restaurant and sit at a counter, as I do for lunch everyday, you are eating alone. But what difference does it make if you sit at a counter—it doesn't make an emotional problem for me. ⟩$_{EV}$
[b] So Editha doesn't have any reason to say that. In any case, I, myself, interpret her statement that {8} I don't like to eat alone as meaning {8a} that she, Editha, doesn't like to eat alone. ⟩$_{IV}$

INTERACTION

[a] R. challenges E.'s statement ⟨ ~8 ⟩ that R. doesn't like to eat alone by showing that it does not fit the facts of everyday life.
[b] R. gives evaluation of E.'s statement ⟨ 8 ⟩ as meaning the opposite ⟨ 8a ⟩ and thereby indirectly asserts INT-R ⟩ that she is competent to interpret the emotions of others.

| 3.7 | TEXT | CUES |

Th.: ⟨$_{IV}$ *Well, but she didn't say that.* ⟩$_{IV}$

Doubt: weİl → "wait a minute.' Contrastive stress: sȧy thȧt, 'may have *meant* that but did not *say* that.

EXPANSION

Th.: ⟨$_{IV}$ Well, you may be right but Editha didn't say explicitly what you say she meant {?INT-R} and are you really justified in making an interpretation that she meant that {8a} she doesn't like to eat alone and {E4$_a$} feels lonesome. ⟩$_{IV}$

INTERACTION

Th. interrupts, acknowledging R.'s interpretation, but makes an assertion about an R-event, that E. said 8a ⟩ that she does not like to eat alone, thereby requesting confirmation of that event, thereby asserting that R. needs overt evidence to report E.'s emotions, thereby challenging ?INT-R ⟩ R.'s competence to interpret the emotions of others.

their mutually exclusive areas of personal competence (Chapter 2, p. 35). The patient knows intimately the events of her everyday life (A-events) and can report what happened without fear of contradiction. The therapist is an expert at interpreting the emotions of others: The normal claim that an individual might make—"I know what I feel"—is open to question in the therapeutic situation. It would follow that the patient's interpretation of the emotions of others also can be challenged by the therapist.

In this episode, Rhoda reports her own emotions as she normally is encouraged to do. It is natural enough for a patient to model her own interpretive style on that of the therapist, and here Rhoda begins to interpret the emotions of others. In the same way, the patient might begin to diagnose her own symptoms with her physician, who could show an amused tolerance or object sharply. Whether or not the therapist does object in this case, the social situation is so defined that she has the right to say to the patient, "You are not competent to do *this* kind of work."

What is the therapist's view of her own intervention? At a later *Playback* session, she discussed this tactic in connection with the problem that Rhoda doesn't express herself freely in school.

> ... YOU SEE THEY ARE SO SYMBIOTIC IN THE FAMILY, THEY ARE CONSTANTLY SAYING WHEN SHE TELLS ME, "MY MOTHER AND MY SISTER THINKS THIS OR FEELS THIS," I SAY, "WHAT DID THEY SAY?" ... "DID *SHE* SAY IT?" ... "IS THIS WHAT *YOU* THINK?" ... MAKING THE DIFFERENTIATION ...

The therapist feels that Rhoda is not always clear about what she has said and what others have said. In the light of this kind of confusion, she is very reluctant to allow Rhoda to impose her interpretation upon reports of what others have said. The first step, in her view, is for Rhoda to be clear on what actually was said.

Here we see the therapist struggling to obtain a clear view of what actually happens in family interaction. Rhoda's accounts are her main access to this situation; she plainly feels that some of Rhoda's accounts are more reliable than others. As our analysis indicates, the brief excerpts in family style are more reliable indicators of this reality than passages like 3.6, where Rhoda steps outside of the narrative situation and begins to use the evaluative language of the therapeutic situation. The therapist's intervention shows that she also follows this line of reasoning.

3.8–3.9. Rhoda now begins to answer the therapist's challenge, but it quickly becomes apparent that she is not clarifying the situation or giving a coherent report of the conversation. The therapist then intervenes again, using the clarifying tactic that she described in the quotation just given:

3.8[a]   R.: *So sh's't'me, I know you don' like t'eat alone, and she says—*
[b]   Th.: *So what did you say?*
[c]   R.: *So I said, "Well, I don't mind."*

3.8	TEXT	CUES

[a] R.: ⟨$_N$ *So sh's't'me, I know you don' like t'eat alone, and she says—* ⟩$_N$

[b] Th.: *So what did you say?*   Exasperation: did you say, sudden interruption.

[c] R.: ⟨$_N$ *So I said,* ⟨$_F$ *"Well, I don't mind."* ⟩$_F$ ⟩$_N$ Derogation: I don't mind, "that's nothing to me."

EXPANSION

[a] R.: ⟨$_N$Editha said to me, {8} "I know you don't like to eat alone," and Editha said— ⟩$_N$

[b] Th.: But you must have said something when she said something {8} untrue about you, so what did you say to Editha then?

[c] R.: ⟨$_N$Then I said to Editha ⟨$_F$"Well even though you say I don't like to eat alone, {~E$_4$} eating alone doesn't bother me."⟩ $_F$⟩ $_N$

INTERACTION

[a] R. repeats 3.5[c], thereby *not* responding to Th.'s request for confirmation and challenge.

[b] Th. interrupts, requesting more information on the events, and expresses exasperation at R.'s not answering her request and challenge.

[c] R. denies information requested by therapist. ⟨$_N$ R. denies E.'s assertion ⟨~E$_4$ that R. feels lonely.⟩ $_N$

In the rapid interchanges of 3.7–3.11, there are no new propositions introduced: The therapy does not move forward in any substantial way, but the interactional depth is considerable. Our cross sections show how the same themes are worked over back and forth until some account is given that satisfies the therapist's demand for cognitive clarification.

    3.9[a] R.: *She s'd, "Yeah, but it sorta gets lonesome in the house when you don't come home."*
       [b] *like if I were to eat out—*
       [c] Th.: *She didn't say, "for* ***you.****"*
       [d] R.: *She—*
       [e] Th.: *She gets lonesome for you—f'****her.***
       [f] R.: *No—I said t'her:*
    3.10 R.: *I said t'her, "D'you get lonesome?"*

The paralinguistic cues for these sections are outlined in some detail in the cross section. We observe repeated signs of tension through interruption, overlap, and speech errors. We also observe a number of derogatory intonation contours superimposed on Editha's reported comments. Rhoda reports herself as using a phrase in family style with a heavy derogatory intonation: *I don't mind*, one of many signs that Rhoda is still preoccupied with the outrageous assertions of Editha, rather than responding to the insistent request of the therapist; but in 3.9, our view of the events that actually took place begins to be transformed. In response to the intervention of the therapist, Rhoda pictures herself as forcing the truth from her aunt, and now quotes her aunt as asserting in so many words the very interpretation which she, Rhoda, had made in 3.6[b].

3.9	TEXT	CUES
[a]	R.: ⟨_N_ *She s'd, "Yeah, but it sorta gets lonesome in the house when you don't come home."*	Derogation: same intonation as in 3.8[a]. Mitigation: *it sorta gets* for 'I get'.
[b]	*like if I were to eat out—*	Tension: strident overlap; over-careful articulation of *for*.
[c]	Th.: *She didn't say "for you."*	
[d]	R.: *She—*	Tension: repressed interruption.
[e]	Th.: *She gets lonesome for you—f'her.*	Tension: mistake in pronoun assignment.
[f]	R.: *No—I said t'her:* ⟩_N_	Tension: strident overlap; intake of breath before *no*.

EXPANSION

[a] R.: ⟨_N_ Editha said, "Yes {~8} you may not mind but {E_{4a}} I get lonesome in the house when you don't come home on one of your late nights like tonight.
[b] And like if I were to eat out in a restaurant she would get lonesome.
[c] Th.: Haven't you noticed that Editha didn't say that {E_4} it gets lonesome for *you*, meaning Rhoda?
[e] Th.: She implied that it gets lonesome for *her*, Editha.
[f] R.: No, Editha didn't say it gets lonesome for me, and so I then said to her, ⟩_N_

INTERACTION

[a] R. gives information that E. did say ⟨ E_{4a} overtly that she felt lonesome, thereby responding to Th.'s request for confirmation ⟨ ?8a and thereby defending herself against ⟨ ?INT-R Th.'s challenge to her competence to interpret the emotions of others.
[c-e] Th. interrupts stridently and asserts an R-event that E. did not attribute loneliness to R., thereby requesting confirmation, thereby giving an interpretation of R.'s narrative, thereby ⟨ ?INT-R ⟩ challenging R.'s status as interpreter of other's emotions, thereby asserting INT-Th ⟩ her status as the interpreter of emotions.
[f] R. gives confirmation requested ⟨ 8 thereby agreeing with Th.'s reinterpretation, and continues the narrative.

The effect of the therapist's insistent interventions on the progress of the conversation can be seen most clearly in Figure 30. This displays Rhoda's entire account in the framework of narrative analysis (Chapter 3, p. 104 ff.). The vertical axis is time, and each utterance is shown with a vertical extension corresponding to its extension in time. The abstracts, which sum up the whole narrative, and the orientation clauses, which place us in time and space, are usually in the form of general statements that are true throughout: this is true of Rhoda's orientation in 3.2. Narrative clauses that correspond to actual events are separated from each other in time (with "temporal junctures") and are represented on these diagrams by a single x. However, Rhoda has hardly begun her first narrative event in 3.3 before she interrupts herself with a long series of evaluative remarks referring to the entire narrative. The last of these, 3.6[b], is the interpretation that is challenged by the therapist in 3.7.

Rhoda's response to this challenge is to begin the narrative with an event which is not clearly located in regard to anything that she has said so far: a remark of Editha's. As the therapist repeatedly presses for a clarification, Rhoda develops a whole series of narrative events that consist of interchanges between her and Editha. This account is plainly in response to the therapist's intervention, and is naturally suspect because it is a defense against the therapist's challenge. Rhoda finally satisfies the therapist by transforming her interpretation into a literal report of what Editha had said.

We have seen before that Rhoda's basic mode of argumentation is to use narratives to answer requests for information, suggestions, and challenges. Here one can observe again that Rhoda uses narratives to argue abstract issues. This particular narrative must be seen as strongly determined by its use as a response to the therapist's challenge to Rhoda's competence as an interpreter. Whereas we have given arguments to support the narrative of Episode 1 as a reasonable account of what happened in Rhoda's family, this narrative might be looked at as a less reliable account because it is a response to the therapist's challenge.

The mechanism that the therapist uses to accomplish the reorientation of roles is of some interest to discourse analysis. Rhoda's narrative report in 3.9[a] shows Editha using a very impersonal expression in which the local topic of "not wanting to eat alone" is transformed, for the first time, into the emotional predicate of "feeling lonesome." This is done in a very impersonal way, which does not attribute the emotion of loneliness to any one person: *It sorta gets lonesome*... Rhoda does not comment on this statement but prepares to go on with the factual account which we expand as 3.9[b]: "Like if I were to eat out in a restaurant." This sentence must be reconstructed from 3.14 since the therapist intervenes with the request for confirmation in 3.9[c]: *She didn't say, 'for you.'*

This request follows the Rule of Confirmation discussed in Chapter 3 (p.

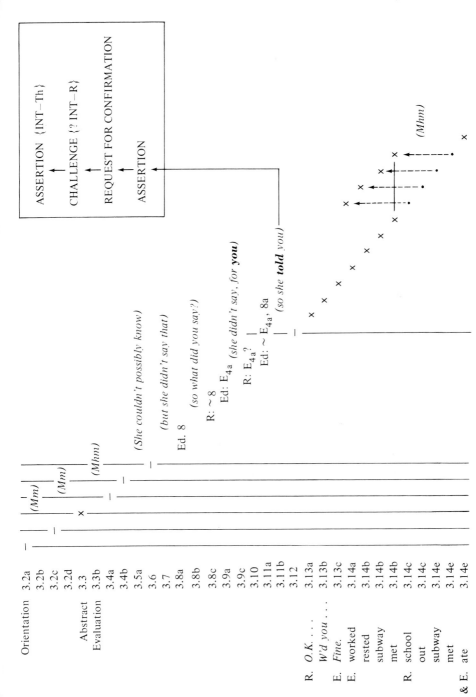

Figure 30. Narrative structure of Episode 3 with therapist's interventions.

100), which is simply that: *If A makes a statement about a B-event, then it is heard as a request for confirmation.* The therapist makes this request in the same way several times, and our interactional analysis of 3.9[e] shows that she "thereby" gives an interpretation of R.'s narrative, and "thereby" asserts her status as the interpreter of other's emotions. She has, in fact, performed the interpretation upon Rhoda's narrative. This follows the Rule of Reinterpretation:

If A makes a statement to B, and B requests confirmation of some element which was not in focus in that statement, then B is heard as asserting that that element should have been in focus.

In this case, Rhoda's report of Editha's statement did not mention any person as feeling lonesome. It is obvious that Editha did not say, "It gets lonesome for you," (meaning Rhoda); when the therapist requests confirmation of this, she performs an act of interpretation.

We therefore have a typical hierarchical arrangement of (1) declarative sentence, (2) request for confirmation and (3) reinterpretation. The interactive effect of these rules is not independent of their relations to each other. Whatever work is done by a declarative statement usually is done more forcefully than the same work done by an interrogative (see Chapter 3, pp. 78–79). The act of reinterpretation has further consequences, and these consequences are stronger because the reinterpretation was done this way.

Reinterpretations necessarily carry with them the implication that the first interpretation was not adequate or correct, and are therefore a challenge to the competence of the first interpreter. The further consequence of this request for confirmation is that the therapist is correcting a faulty interpretation of Rhoda's. By failing to focus on the persons involved in Editha's statement, Rhoda has not stressed the elements in the situation that the therapist feels important. We thus see that the speech action requesting confirmation is at a higher level a challenge to Rhoda's status as an interpreter, and it is also thereby an assertion of the therapist's status. This hierarchical structure is shown in Figure 30, expanding the structure of this intervention of the therapist.

3.10. Figure 30 shows that the therapist's intervention has prompted Rhoda to begin the narrative proper, as a response to the repeated suggestion that she enlist Editha's help. Her first response effort was {~RSNBLE} to show how unreasonable Editha was, and the rest of the narrative accomplishes the same purpose in other ways.

We saw in 3.9[b] that Rhoda was going to continue with the factual part of the narrative. Under the therapist's stimulus, she takes a different tack, and reports herself in 3.10[a] as interrogating Editha in an expert way, making it perfectly clear by Editha's own confession that she had projected her emotion on to Rhoda.

THE THERAPIST'S INTERVENTION   229

| **3.10** | TEXT | CUES |

R.: ⟨_N_ *I said t'her,* ⟨_F_ *"D'you get lonesome?"* ⟩_F_ ⟩_N_   Derogation: *Do you,* heavy implication: 'So that's it after all'.

EXPANSION

R.: ⟨_N_ I then said to Editha, ⟨_F_ "Are you now admitting that it is you {8a} who doesn't like to eat alone and not me {~8} because it is you and not me who feels lonesome {E_{4a}, ~E_4}." ⟩_F_ ⟩_N_

INTERACTION

R. requests from E. ⟨ ?8a ⟩ a confirmation of E.'s statement 3.9[a], in regard to the persons involved, thereby asserting the significance of the persons rather than the circumstances, thereby challenging ⟨ ?E_4_ ⟩ E.'s earlier assignment of the emotion to R.

3.10   R.: ⟨_N_ *I said to'her,* ⟨_F_ *"D'you get lonesome?"* ⟩_F_ ⟩_N_

The heavy stress on *you* has a derogatory implication: 'So that's it after all". We expand this as "Are you now admitting that it is you and not me who feels lonesome?" To the extent that we accept Rhoda's version of this incident, with all our reservations, it shows us one important aspect of the family pattern. Members mask their emotional needs by indirect appeals. It is Editha who has appealed for help, and Rhoda, who hears the request, recognizes what was being asked for. She then exacts a heavy price in return for help: Editha must admit that she is the one who feels lonesome. The confession of dependency lowers Editha's status; Rhoda now will show herself as independent and Editha as helpless.

3.11. Rhoda's report of the family interaction shows the extreme intonation patterns of family style. She reports Editha responding with a falsetto squeal which is quite similar to her own defensive *It's **not** that I can't get along without my mother* (Figure 15).

3.11[a]   R.: ⟨_N_ *Sh'says,* ⟨_F_ *"Well, not that I get lonesome, but I don't like to eat alone.* ⟩_F_ ⟩_N_

The use of mitigating tactics by Editha is quite evident here. Editha denies the main proposition that {E4a} she feels the emotion of loneliness, but admits the local proposition {8a} that she doesn't like to eat alone. We will see Rhoda using the parallel defense in Episode 5, where she denies that she was angry, but admits that something "just bothers her." The interactional interpretation of 3.11[a] is on two levels: what Rhoda is doing (supporting her interpretation of Editha's original statement) and what she shows Editha to be doing (denying that she feels lonesome, but admitting

230   EPISODE THREE

3.11
TEXT	CUES
[a] R.: ⟨_N_ Sh'says, ⟨_F_ "Well, not that I get lonesome, but I don't like to eat alone." ⟩_F_ ⟩_N_	Tension: Wéll, nót thát, [falsetto].

EXPANSION

R. ⟨_N_ Editha says, ⟨_F_ "What you said is not exactly true: I don't get lonesome {~E$_{4a}$} it's only the feeling {8a} that I don't like to eat alone." ⟩_F_ ⟩_N_

INTERACTION

R. continues the narrative giving information to support her interpretation of E.'s statement: ⟨_N_ E. denies ⟨ ~E$_{4a}$ that she feels lonesome, thereby responding negatively to R.'s request for confirmation, and then admits the emotion in a mitigated form {8a}.

TEXT	CUES
[b] Th.: ⟨_IV_ Oh, so she **told** you. ⟩_IV_	Tension release: extended, declining contour.

EXPANSION

Th.: ⟨_IV_ So that is what I expected, and different from what you told me before—Editha told you that {8a} she didn't like to eat alone and you did not infer it. ⟩_IV_

INTERACTION

Th. repeats a part of R.'s narrative statement of 3.11[a]—requesting confirmation that R. has retreated from her claim to have interpreted underlying emotions, thereby defending her challenge ⟨ ?INT-R to R.'s competence to interpret the emotions of others.

---

it too). We could suspend the description of what Rhoda is doing until the narrative is completed, but we have already seen that the narrative takes a specific turn here in response to the therapist's challenge.

The final act in this series of interventions is the therapist's pointed comment of 3.11[b]:

  3.11[b] Th.: *Oh, so she **told** you.*

Our contextual expansion of the therapist's *Oh* draws its significance from the entire series of interventions: 'So that is what I expected, and different from what you told me before'. The understanding that now emerges between patient and therapist resolves more than cognitive confusion:

3.11[b] removes the conflict between therapist and patient in the proper allocation of their roles, and reestablishes the original solidarity of the two actors looking at the situation from the same point of view.

The reader may be struck with a parallel of the interaction between therapist and patient in the interview situation and the interaction between Rhoda and her aunt within the narrative. Just as it is important for Rhoda to make it plain who is asking who for help, so it is important for the therapist to make it plain what kind of statements Rhoda can introduce as *givens* for the therapeutic work. Yet, while Editha has suffered a decline in her standing as an adult member of the household, Rhoda is in a more favorable position. It is now accepted that she uncovered her aunt's subterfuge and "smoked her out."

3.12. This resolution is confirmed and solidified in 3.12, where both parties to the dispute come to a harmonious understanding.

3.12   TEXT   CUES
[a]   R.: ⟨$_{IV}$ Yes
[b]   ⟨$_N$ after—after I ast her, 'cause to me
that sounded like **she** didn't like to eat
alone. ⟩$_N$ ⟩$_{IV}$
[c]   Th.: Ye-es.   Tension release: 2 2 ↓ 'confidential
                                     understanding'.

EXPANSION
[a]   R.: ⟨$_{IV}$ Yes, Editha did tell me {8a} that she didn't like to eat alone
[b]   ⟨$_N$ but only after I asked her {E$_{4a}$} if she was the person who was lonesome, because her statement that it sort of gets lonesome in the house or that {8} I didn't like to eat alone gave me the impression that {8a} she didn't like to eat alone. ⟩$_N$ ⟩$_{IV}$
[c]   Th.: Yes, we both see through her behavior.

INTERACTION
[a]   R. agrees with reinterpretation, thereby acknowledging the redefinition of her role as interpreter
[b]   R. gives evaluation of her success in obtaining the information from E. that she had interpreted E.'s earlier statements ⟨$\underline{\ 8\ }$ as inappropriate, thereby defending herself against ⟨$\underline{\ ?INT\text{-}R\ }$ the challenge to her competence as interpreter by showing her competence as an interviewer.
[c]   Th. gives support to R.'s interpretation, thereby mitigating her challenge ⟨$\underline{\ ?INT\text{-}R\ }$.

---

232   EPISODE THREE

3.12[a]   R.: *Yes*
   [b]   *after—after I ast her, 'cause to me that sounded like **she** didn't like to eat alone.*
   [c]   Th.: *Ye-es.*

Rhoda no longer lays claim to a deeper interpretation of her aunt's remarks, but she does claim that she had the insight to detect her aunt's peculiar behavior and challenge it on the spot. She thus demonstrates a skill as an *interviewer*, which depends upon the ability to react suspiciously when things "don't sound right." The therapist gives her support in a drawn out *Ye-es*, which shows a shift from challenge to mutual understanding. Thus the therapist suggests that she and Rhoda both understand the peculiar behavior of her aunt; the paralinguistic quality of this response is a clear example of "tension release."

The Helplessness of Editha

3.13. Free to finish her narrative, Rhoda continues with her main objective: to show that Editha cannot help herself, and cannot be relied on to help others. The confession that Rhoda has extracted from Editha is not forgotten; we see it reflected in Rhoda's next remarks.

3.13[a]   R.: *"Oh," I said, "Okay, we'll meet an' we'll go out to eat."*
   [b]   *I said, "Would you like that?"*
   [c]   *So she said, "Fine."*

The significance of *Okay* is expanded as 'I'll agree to help you since $\{E_{4a}\}$ you feel lonesome.' An even stronger reference to Editha's dependent position is the heavy implication of *would you like that*. The heavy, even stress pattern of this intonation contour is shown in Figure 31. It can be identified impressionistically as the intonation that is used in placating a child who is asking for something unreasonable. Just as Rhoda's mother uses the intonation contour of *Oh, why-y?* (Figure 4), so Rhoda challenges the adult status of Editha through the implication that Editha is behaving

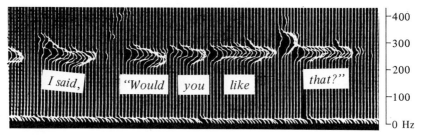

Figure 31. Pitch contour of Rhoda's derogatory *"Would you like that?"* in 3.13[b].

3.13

	TEXT	CUES
[a]	R.: ⟨_N "Oh," I said, "Okay, we'll meet an' we'll go out to eat."	Derogation (heavy implication): $\overset{2}{would}$ $\overset{2}{you}$ $\overset{2}{like}$ $\overset{2}{that}$, "I don't like it, but I'll do
[b]	I said, ⟨_F "Would you like that?" ⟩_F	it to please you since you're just a
[c]	She said, "Fine." ⟩_N	child (Figure 31).'

EXPANSION

[a] R.: ⟨_N So I said to Editha, "I'll agree to help you since {E_{4a}} you are lonesome. I suggest that we meet after work and go out to eat together, since {8a} you don't like to eat alone."
[b] I said, ⟨_F"Since {~AD-E} you can't behave as an adult, I'll have to go out of my way to please you, and I hope that satisfies you." ⟩_F
[c] Editha said to me, "Going out to eat together will be fine as far as I can see." ⟩_N

INTERACTION

[a] R. acknowledges E.'s admission of her need for help, and suggests that they go out to eat together, thereby ⟨ COOP carrying out joint action with E. to solve family problems.
[b] R. requests agreement for this joint plan, and simultaneously expresses exasperation as being forced to make this suggestion, and asserts indirectly that E. has to be treated as a child and ⟨ ~AD-E is not an adult member of the household.
[c] E. agrees as requested.

---

like a child. A speaker uses this intonation contour to agree with a request and yet make it plain that he is conceding to the other person's desires only because he is more mature. Rhoda organizes this narrative to show that she tried to arrive at a working arrangement with Editha and carry out the therapist's suggestion {COOP} that she work out a joint plan with Editha.*
Here again she shows herself using an aggressive style of verbal interaction that undercuts the surface proposal for mutual understanding.

3.14. Rhoda now proceeds to state her case against Editha in a fluent narrative that we have come to recognize as her everyday style.

---

*The focus here is on action and not on the basic suggestion {S}, which concerns the expression of needs that precede joint action. In Episode 3, the person who is expressing needs and emotions to relevant others is Editha; if we accept Rhoda's account, it appears that Editha is no better than she is in doing this. Rhoda's aggressive style of response shows why this might be so. The parallel between her response to Editha and her mother's response to her is quite striking.

234   EPISODE THREE

3.14[a] R.: *So it ended up that she only worked half a day yesterday.*
   [b] *So she rested in the afternoon, an' she got on the subway an' met me in a restaurant.*
   [c] *But meanwhile I had gone t's-s—t'school since eight o'clock in the morning, and here it was six I came out.*
   [d] Th.: *Mm.*
   [e] R.: *And then I had to go on the train an' we met, an' we ate.*

Here there are none of the hesitations, condensations, and interruptions that we observed before the harmonious resolution of the conflict between

---

3.14 TEXT	CUES
[a] R.: ⟨N So it ended up that she only worked half a day yesterday.	
[b] So she rested in the afternoon, an' she got on the subway an' met me in a restaurant.	
[c] But meanwhile I had gone t's-s—t'school since eight o'clock in the morning, and here it was six I came out.	Tension: breath before *and*, tightly suppressed laughter on *came*. Reinforcement: 2 2 ↓, reinforcement, first level.
[d] Th.: *Mm.*	
[e] R.: And then I had to go on the train an' we met, an' we ate. ⟩N	Tension release: 2 2 1, deep breath: 'finality—that was that'.

EXPANSION

[a] R.: ⟨N And independently, it turned out that Editha worked only in the morning, yesterday.
[b] And then she rested at home yesterday afternoon, got on the subway, and met me in a restaurant.
[c] But while Editha was resting, I had been going to school all day, since eight o'clock in the morning, and so I was tired—and I didn't come out of school until six o'clock, so it would have been a lot easier to go home.
[e] And then I had to travel from school to the restaurant on the subway, and Editha and I met and we ate together, which was really tiring for me. ⟩N

INTERACTION

[a] R. continues narrative, and gives further evidence that E. did not carry out an equal share of her obligations as an adult member of the household, thereby asserting again ~AD-E that E. is not an adult member of the household, thereby challenging the suggestion ?COOP-R,E that she should cooperate with E to solve problems, thereby challenging again the suggestion that ?S she express her needs to E.

Rhoda and the therapist. The mode of expression is quite direct, and our expansion differs from the text only in a few points, which bring out the significance of paralinguistic signals. In the phrasing of 3.14[c], there is a sharp intake of breath after *morning* and tightly suppressed laughter on *I came out*. The listener is given to understand that it was a tense and somewhat ridiculous situation for Rhoda to be in. She does not explicitly say that it was ridiculous for her aunt not to prepare dinner in the afternoon, but the inference is there. Rhoda defines her own situation as "going to school all day." We know that college students do not attend classes for eight hours continuously, and Rhoda's aunt might therefore have said that Rhoda had as much time to rest and relax between classes as she had at home; but Rhoda can take advantage of the social definition of the student as being "at work" from eight in the morning until six at night.*

Returning to Figure 30, we see that 3.14 contains eight narrative clauses, which conclude Rhoda's narrative. One unusual feature of this sequence is that it contains a flashback, which is quite common in literature but rather uncommon in narratives of personal experience. 3.14[a] and [b] follow Editha through the course of the day to the point that she meets Rhoda; 3.14[c] and [e] take Rhoda back to early morning and follow her through the day to the meeting point in the restaurant. Though we have expanded the text a bit to show the implications of these actions, the statement of interaction is quite brief. It is clear that Rhoda feels that she was imposed on, and that Editha was being irresponsible. It is factually true that Rhoda and Editha carried out joint action by having dinner together. Nevertheless, Rhoda implies in her narrative account that this was not a help to her but an additional burden: she implicitly denies that the joint action solved any mutual problem. The therapist's suggestion of {COOP-R,E} of 3.1 [c] is thereby rejected, and with it the original idea that the suggestion {S} be applied to Editha.

This negative conclusion is not heavily stressed. In terms of narrative analysis, we would say that the main evaluative point of Rhoda's account is the exchange in 3.9 between her and Editha, which forced Editha to admit that she was lonesome.

3.15. The therapist now provides this evaluation herself. Rhoda had signaled that she was through by taking a deep breath before her final utterance *an' we ate*, and concluding with a final intonation contour. The expectation is for the therapist to comment on Rhoda's account and evaluate Rhoda's point that her aunt could not be asked to help.

3.15[a]   Th.: *And it never occurred to her to prepare dinner.*

---

*At another point in the interview, it appears that Rhoda gets up at five o'clock in the morning so that she can appear at school at eight. She is capable of making fairly simple activities appear very difficult.

[b] R.: *No.*
[c] Th.: *She was home all afternoon.*
[d] R.: *No, she doesn't know how.*

The therapist's mode of expression shows no marked intonation contours, but the expression *never occurred to her* is highly marked. This is a form of derogation which revolves about a very particular use of *occur:* if B has failed to do an action X, which A is known to have desired and expected, then an assertion that it did not *occur* to B to do X implies that B is below the expected norms of adult competence and is not a reasonable or reliable person. Our expansion introduces again the proposition {~AD-E}, that Editha is not an adult member of the household.

The therapist uses a familiar rule of discourse in bringing out the implicit evaluation of Rhoda's narrative. By the Rule of Confirmation, she makes a direct statement about a B-event that only Rhoda would know, and Rhoda gives the confirmation as expected. She does this a second time in 3.15[c],

---

3.15   TEXT   CUES
[a] Th.: ⟨$_{IV}$ *And it never occurred to her*   Derogation. It never *occurred* to her.
to prepare dinner.
[b] R.: *No.*
[c] Th.: *She was home all afternoon.*
[d] R.: *No, she doesn't know how.* ⟩$_{IV}$

EXPANSION
[a] Th.: ⟨$_{IV}$ And is it true that Editha did not think of preparing dinner for both of you as {~AD-E} an adult member of the house should do, even though she should have and you did think of it?
[b] R.: No, Editha did not think of that.
[c] Th.: And she did not do this even though she was home all afternoon, and had the time to do so.
[d] R.: No, she doesn't know how to prepare dinner. ⟩$_{IV}$

INTERACTION
[a] Th. asserts that E. showed no signs of normal performance as an adult member of the household, thereby ⟨ ?AD-E requesting confirmation of this fact, and thereby supporting R.'s challenge to her suggestion ⟨ ?COOP .
[b] R. gives confirmation requested.
[c] Th. repeats action in 3.15[a].
[d] R. gives confirmation requested and gives additional information to show ⟨ ?AD-E that E. is not an adult member of the household.

adding a circumstance that makes it plain that Editha's behavior was all the more unreasonable.

It is noted above that the central point of 3.15[a] revolves about the interpretation of *never occurred*, and this depends upon the fact that it would be expected that Editha would prepare dinner. The conditional relevance of the negative statement is itself evidence for this expectation: that is, the only reason the absence of this event would be noted is that its presence was expected. But again, the use of the Rule of Confirmation underscores the nature of Editha's violation, since such a request implies that the therapist would not have believed it unless it was confirmed. This indirect way of proceeding can therefore be seen as a forceful way of agreeing with Rhoda's condemnation of Editha, and it is now apparent that the therapist has reversed her position. She brings to bear her own social expertise—her ability to recognize the normal pattern of social obligations in such a situation—to support Rhoda's analysis of Editha's incompetence.

At this point we may ask, why has the therapist reversed herself? She has made two efforts to get Rhoda to communicate her needs to her Aunt Editha, and in each case she has met with total resistance from Rhoda. Rhoda's own evidence shows that the suggestion {S} has not been carried out in a way that it could succeed. The therapist might point this out and continue to press for her original suggestion, but Rhoda has a wealth of anecdotal detail drawn from everyday life to prove that the suggestion will not work. The therapist is in no position to contradict all of this evidence, whether or not she believes that it represents the whole situation. In order to work with Rhoda, she has to take Rhoda's data at its face value and work with the information that Rhoda has provided.

This is a necessary consequence for the partition of the domains of competence in the therapeutic situation; if the therapist were to challenge Rhoda's competence as a reporter, there would be very little basis for a continued conversation. Such a tactic would seriously weaken the kind of support that the therapist wants to give Rhoda; when Rhoda perceives a conflict, the therapist will want to align herself with her rather than with the other side. On the other hand, there is no reason to think that the therapist believes that such conflicts are inevitable or based on social reality, or that she actually has abandoned her original suggestion. In future sessions, she will continue to explore ways of putting her fundamental suggestion into effect.

* * *

The next few minutes of the session repeat the content we have analyzed already. Rhoda continues to expand at some length on the general theme {X:STRN} that "things are a little too much for her": she cannot handle her school work and do the cooking and housecleaning at the same time. In the course of this exposition, she reveals that she had gotten up that

238   EPISODE THREE

morning at five o'clock in order to get to school at eight o'clock. The therapist picks this up as a point worth remarking, but receives Rhoda's explanation without comment. Rhoda then expands further on how tired she was as a consequence of the arrangement she made with Editha about going out to eat, and the therapist expands on her view of Editha's dependent position—that Editha behaves like a "completely dependent boarder." We present this text without analysis as 3.16.

3.16 R.: *Like the only thing is that—like let's say, a steak. Now steak—I don't—you can't prepare that—I don'—sometimes I don' know exactly* [breath] *what time I get in the house,*
Th.: *Mm.*
R.: *and sometimes see when my mother's home, so she has something that could be made, so I can eat, but—when I come home*
Th.: *uh huh*
R.: *and we-i-it's easier 'cause*
Th.: *Of course.*
R.: *because like sometimes if I get held up so I'll come in 20, 25 minutes later.*
Th.: *Yeah.*
R.: *Sometimes I'll come in earlier, so if there's steak that really can't be made until I come in the house, so it doesn't get overdone or underdone, but when my mother's home she makes something—that could be eaten when I come in—so naturally it's easier and—saves me less time, an' I can go do my homework because I can't stay up that late, because I get up extremely early,*
Th.: *Mm.*
R.: *I know—like this morning I got up at 5—in order to get to school on time.*
Th.: **Why** *did you do it?*
R.: *I get up at 5.*
Th.: **Why?**
R.: *Because it's—I have to leave the house after 6—to get t'my sch-school 8:00.*
Th.: *It takes so long to travel?*
R.: *When I leave my house at a quarter after six, I get to school at about—25 to 8, 20 to 8—and—I have to be at school between 10 to and 8. An I don't like to come in the las' minute.*
Th.: *Well—how—what time do you get there?*
R.: *'Bout 25 to, 20 to—about 25 to, roughly.*
Th.: *Uh uh. Mhm.*
R.: *So it isn't that I can sit up till 12:00 and study 'n' get up 11:00 the next morning. So—uh—so. We went and we—let me—we went*

out t'eat. Now we came home 8:00, and really, when I came home 8:00, I didn' exactly feel like doing homework, but I did as much as I-I could, an' then I ended up falling asleep anyway. So—uh—jis' what I'm trying to say is that when my mother isn't home—I don't—when I look at it, it looks like I—that I—can't get along without her but I don't—

Th.: *Well I think there's a great deal of reality as you discuss this, and that—in—it you might be able to take care of yourself—at home—but actually what you have is also a **boarder**—a completely dependent **boarder** to take care of, in the form of Aunt Editha, who for the 20 years that she's been living with mother has never done anything in the house at all*

R.: *Mm.*

Th.: *and it really is not possible for you to do both, with such a heavy load*

R.: *No—even without her um—i-it just seems to be anyhow—because even if she wasn't home, let's say she wasn't there, it's going out to eat two nights a week—I mean—it's just that it gets tiring, run from school and go into the restaurant an' then come home,*

Th.: *Mm hm.*

R.: *an then I have to wash my clothes for the next day* [laugh] *uh—y'know—and—*

We pick up the analysis again as Rhoda returns to the theme that "things are a little too much" for her by showing that it is actually easier when her aunt is not home. This develops into a renewed attack on Editha's competence.

*   *   *

Going to the Store

3.17. Rhoda's final word on the story of going to the restaurant is that Editha couldn't prepare dinner because she didn't know how. In the second narrative, we see Editha doesn't even know how to buy food.

3.17[a] R.: *If my aunt wasn't home, then I'd be.. It even makes it—just a **drop** easier because then she would go to the store, or I would have to come home and run to the store.*
   [b] Th.: *Mhm.*
   [c] R.: *But—*

Our first task is to reconstruct the missing sentence after Rhoda interrupted herself. Our expansion is based on the consequences of the narra-

240 EPISODE THREE

3.17	TEXT	CUES

[a] R.: ⟨_EV_ *If my aunt wasn't home, then*   Tension: self-interruption.
I'd be—⟨_F_ . . *It even makes it—just a **drop**
easier because then she would go to the
store, or I would have to come home and*
⟨_F_ *run to the store,* ⟩_F_
[b] Th.: *Mhm.*
[c] R.: *But*— ⟩_EV_

EXPANSION

[a] R.: ⟨_EV_ If my Aunt Editha wasn't staying at home, then I'd be better off because I could go straight home myself and not worry about her. It is even a little easier for me when Editha doesn't stay home because then Editha goes to the store on her way home or else I would have to go home myself and then go the store for food for dinner. ⟩_EV_

INTERACTION

[a] R. gives further information ⟨ X:STRN ⟩ on the circumstances which are responsible for her obligations being greater than her capacity, and inadvertently gives information on role obligations which Editha has performed.
[b] Th. acknowledges R.'s information.

---

tive: "If my Aunt Editha wasn't staying at home, then I'd be better off because I could go straight home myself and not worry about her." The connection to the next sentence is not immediately clear until we realize that Editha would be going to the store on her way home from work, a possibility that is left unstated in Rhoda's 3.17[a]. (We also have to understand *or* as 'or else'.) There are several indirect expressions in 3.17 which heighten the emotional force of Rhoda's message. No great help can be expected from anything that Editha does, but it would be *a drop* easier if she could go to the store. On the other hand, we see that frantic haste would be involved in the other alternative, where Editha would be home and Rhoda would have to *run to the store.*

The interactional statement shows that 3.17 is not focused on the incompetence of Editha but upon the general proposition {X:STRN}: that external circumstances are responsible for her obligations being greater than her capacity. The therapist acknowledges this message in 3.17[b], but on a moment's reflection she realizes that Rhoda has volunteered information that contradicts, or at least counters, the claim that Editha is of no help to her. We introduce the term *inadvertently* in our interactional statement to indicate information that is revealed but not asserted, not intended to be a

GOING TO THE STORE   241

| 3.18 | TEXT | CUES |

[a] Th.: ⟨_{EV} *But she does go to the store..*
[b] R.: *Yes,* ⟩_{EV}

Doubt: 2 2 →, 'not asserting this, and can be corrected'.

EXPANSION

[a] Th.: ⟨_{EV} But even though you have shown that Editha is a deficient role partner in so many ways {~AD-E}, haven't you just said that Editha does go to the store and therefore can be of some help to you and isn't it possible that you have exaggerated?
[b] R.: Yes, Editha does go to the store, and so she does seem to help in some ways. ⟩_{EV}

INTERACTION

[a] Th. interrupts, and asserts a proposition implicit in 3.16 but not asserted by R., that—Editha does perform an adult obligation, thereby requesting confirmation of this proposition, thereby giving the evaluation that this information is relevant to the suggestion ⟨ 5 that Rhoda ask Editha for help thereby supporting ⟨ 5, thereby challenging ⟨ ?~S ⟩ Rhoda's rejection of the original suggestion.
[b] Rhoda gives confirmation requested thereby admitting some support for the suggestion ⟨ 5 that she could turn to Editha for help.

---

speech act but rather something that is seen as relevant to an earlier action.*

3.18. The therapist cuts off Rhoda's *but*— with a *but* of her own, which indicates the contradictory nature of Rhoda's information.

3.18[a]   Th.: *But she does go to the store..*
   [b]   R.: *Yes,*

In addition to the *but,* the therapist uses an emphatic *does,* which is the most overt way of establishing the importance of an event that has been down-focused. This is a more overt realization of the Rule of Reinterpretation, which challenges a speaker's original interpretation and makes an

---

*We use the term *simultaneously* to indicate two parallel speech actions, sometimes at different levels of abstraction, both part of the strategy that seems to be intended by the speaker. *Inadvertently* implies that the speaker would not have wanted to use this information in connection with this or some other speech event, and it is therefore relevant for someone else to call attention to it. It implies that the speaker is not in complete control of all the information that she is displaying; it is an abstract analogue of the *slip,* which is a major concern of psychoanalysts.

242   EPISODE THREE

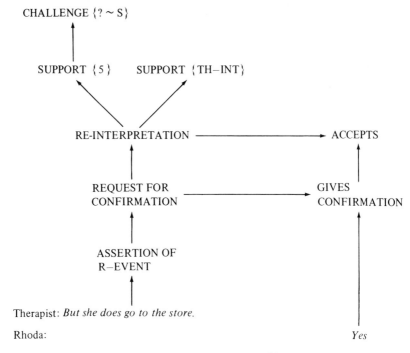

Figure 32. Interactional structure of 3.18.

emphatic main prediction out of some element that was subordinated or only implied. At the same time, the therapist uses a nonfinal intonation that is neither interrogative nor declarative, thus inviting Rhoda to disagree if she can.

Rhoda's reply of 3.18[b], *yes*, alerts us to the fact that the therapist has again used the Rule of Confirmation, asserting a B-event which only Rhoda knows. The hierarchical structure of this simple intervention of the therapist is shown in Figure 32. When Rhoda says *yes*, she is doing more than giving the confirmation that was requested: she is also committed to the reinterpretation and the challenge to her own rejection of the basic suggestion in regard to Editha.*

---

*One could construct responses to the therapist's intervention that would reply directly to these higher-level actions. Instead of admitting "yes," Rhoda might have countered {5} directly by saying "She isn't that much help when she *does*," or if Rhoda was practiced at this type of higher-level maneuvering, she might have answered the deeper challenge by a remark such as "Well, I can appreciate help when it's real help."

3.19–20. Rhoda seems to have been forced into an admission in 3.18[b] that undercuts her own argument. She counters in her usual style by giving more anecdotes to show that Editha is not a reliable or reasonable person who could help her. Rhoda begins with a pseudo-narrative referring to things that are usually done, rather than telling of something in particular that happened. As we examine the mode of expression of the orientation of the pseudo-narrative in 3.19, we see repeated self-interruption used again to signal her sense of uncomprehending exasperation at Editha's incompetent and unreasonable behavior.

The pseudo-narrative embodies a new local proposition,

{9} Rhoda requests Editha to go to the store.

This proposition must be seen as a response to the initial proposition of Episode 2:

{5} The therapist requests Rhoda to request Editha to help.

This is, of course, an instance of the general suggestion {S}.

The hypothetical statement of 3.19 is recognized as an introduction to a pseudo-narrative under the Rule of Narrative Orientation (Chapter 3, p. 106); then it must follow that the pseudo-narrative itself is a response to the therapist's intervention of 3.18[b] under the Rule of Implicit Responses (Chapter 3, p. 99).

Even though this is a pseudo-narrative, we can use it to examine once again the typical pattern of family interaction, which we indicate by bracketing the family interaction in the cross sections.

3.19 R.: *If I w't'say, "Get **milk**, or **bread**,"* . . . *At fir—*
3.20 R.: *"**Why** do you need it?"*

Rhoda quotes Editha as responding in the characteristic family style, where ellipsis and intonation play a major role. We cannot simply expand 3.20 to "Why do you need milk and bread?" The uses of milk and bread are quite apparent. The extra stress and length on *why* signals the fact that two questions are condensed into one, which we approximate in our expansion as "Why do you ask me to get that? Do you really need it?"*

Our interactional statement of 3.20 makes it clear that Editha's response is a challenge to Rhoda's competence: it raises the possibility that Rhoda has not actually looked to see if she has bread or milk. The mode of argument is also quite indirect, since this criticism of Rhoda's competence is not stated

---

*We can readily see the parallel between 3.20 and Rhoda's quotation of her mother's crucial response in 1.9, *Oh, why-y?* The indirect mode of expression relies heavily on the challenges implicit in requests for information about reasons for doing things. A more common prosodic cue that does the same work is to use a comma intonation after *why*.

3.19	TEXT	CUES

R.: ⟨$_{EV}$ *If I w't'say, "Get* **milk,** *or* **bread,"** . . . *At fir—* ⟩$_{EV}$ Tension: self-interruption.

EXPANSION
R.: ⟨$_{EV}$ But {~AD-E} Editha really isn't any help in going to the store. What usually happens is that if {9} I ask E. to get **milk** or **bread**, the first thing she'll say to me will be . . . ⟩$_{EV}$

INTERACTION
R. initiates a pseudo-narrative on Editha's behavior, and gives orientation to situations when {9} Rhoda asked Editha to help.

3.20	TEXT	CUES

R.: ⟨$_{EV}$ ⟨$_F$ *"Why do you need it?"* ⟩$_F$ ⟩$_{EV}$ Stress and extra length on *why*.

EXPANSION
R.: ⟨$_{EV}$ Editha will say to me, ⟨$_F$ "Why do you ask me to get that? Do you really need it?" ⟩$_F$ ⟩$_{EV}$

INTERACTION
E. requests information from R. on the reason for ⟨ ?9 ⟩ the request of 3.19 and whether or not a need exists, thereby putting off the request ⟨ ~9 ⟩ thereby challenging ⟨ ~AD-R ⟩ R.'s competence as an adult member of the household.

---

in so many words. The mode of interaction is equally indirect. The Rule for Putting Off Requests (Chapter 3, p. 86) shows us the mechanism used here: Editha makes a request for information about the need for the request, thus effectively putting it off. We might note that there are less-challenging ways of mitigating this refusal, and even though Editha does not make a direct refusal, she is shown as refusing the most elementary forms of cooperative behavior. The use of the pronoun *you* emphasizes this point. By questioning the need for bread and milk, Editha challenges the competence of Rhoda, which is implied in her request. The kind of joint thinking {COOP-R,E} the therapist suggested in 3.1[c] places heavy emphasis on the use of *we*, and Rhoda's report of Editha's language shows Editha as unwilling to take a joint view.

GOING TO THE STORE   245

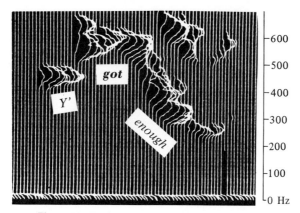

Figure 33. Pitch contour of 3.22, *You got enough.*

3.21–22. The pseudo-narrative of 3.19–20 implies that one such event actually occurred. As if to support this implication, Rhoda now begins a narrative of such a case (see Rule of Narrative Orientation, Chapter 3, p. 106). The narrative begins after Rhoda has asked Editha to go to the store:

3.21   R.: *I-I mean I looked at her one day,*
3.22   R.: *She s'd t'me, "Why—w'you got enough."*

Rhoda begins with the same glottalization and hesitation that she regularly uses to convey her sense of bewilderment at the irrational behavior of Editha. The word *look* refers to a paralinguistic response that Rhoda made to Editha, and it is itself an elliptical reference to a particular kind of look, for example, "I looked in amazement..." As we attempt to expand 3.21, we discover that the time references are implicitly reversed, and here Rhoda's narrative mode of expression can be quite confusing unless we are used to it. Our expansion of 3.21 shows that this is an abstract of the evaluative point of the narrative: "As an example of what I mean, I had to look* at her one day in amazement after she said..."

In quoting Editha's response, Rhoda again uses a condensed family style with a heavy reliance on intonation patterns and the condensation of two sentences into one. Figure 33 shows the pitch contour of *You got enough.* The extra high pitch on *got* drops suddenly to the low pitch of *enough*. An obvious interpretation of this contrastive stress is, "You got enough, you don't have to buy any more." We see that Rhoda can repeat this mode of expression in different situations and in different words; this gives us even

---

*This look is parallel to the hurt look Editha gave Rhoda in 2.9, and shows again the importance of this most indirect mode of expression in Rhoda's family.

more reason to suppose that she has been exposed regularly to this type of family interaction and can use it herself.

3.21   TEXT   CUES
R.: ⟨N I-I mean I looked at her one day, ⟩N   Tension: glottalization, hesitation, loo̊ked 'in amazement'.

EXPANSION
As an example of what I mean, ⟨N I had to look at her one day in amazement after she said: ⟩N

INTERACTION
R. initiates narrative of how ⟨‾6‾ she requested E. to help, to show that ⟨‾~AD-E‾⟩ E. does not have the normal competence of an adult member of the household.

3.22   TEXT   CUES
R.: ⟨N She s'd t'me ⟨F "Why—w—you   Tension: condensation,
got enough." ⟩F ⟩N   self-interruption, 'Y-you "got"
                                                                    enough'→. [See Figure 33.]

EXPANSION
R.: ⟨N Editha said to me, ⟨F "Why do you ask me to go to the store? You've really got enough food and I'm surprised you're asking me to go to the store" ⟩F ⟩N

INTERACTION
E. asks R. for information on the reason for her requestion ⟨‾?9‾⟩ and whether or not there is a need for it, thereby ⟨‾~9‾ putting off the request and ⟨‾?AD-R‾⟩ thereby challenging R.'s competence as an adult member of the household.

3.23. Rhoda's response to Editha parallels her response in 2.9. The sharply rising question contour on *That's* **enough**? is shown in Figure 34. Whereas Editha put contrastive stress on *got*, Rhoda responds with contrastive stress on **enough**. There is a direct conflict here over what **enough** is, and a consequent challenge to Editha's judgment.

The mechanism which operates in 3.23 is the same as that in 2.9. Rhoda has made a request on the basis of a need that is assumed to be a matter of shared knowledge. Editha denies this assumption by questioning it or asserting that it is not so (see Rule for Putting Off Requests, Chapter 3, p. 86) with an emphatic intonation contour that is literally a request for confirmation. Since it follows a very clear, highly stressed utterance, this is clearly a request of confirmation of the content rather than the form. Since Editha intended to say what she said, Rhoda's request for confirmation implies that it is hard for her to believe what she has just heard. This aggravated form of a request for confirmation carries with it a strong implication that the other speaker is not competent.

The evaluative points of Rhoda's pseudo-narrative 3.19–3.20 and her real narrative of 3.21–23 are the same. Editha is shown to be incompetent, as Rhoda's look of amazement is intended to convey. If {~AD-E} Editha is not a competent adult member of the household, there is no point in {5} Rhoda asking her for help. We do not know in any of the three narratives told whether Editha finally helped—whether she took a dust rag and dusted around, or went to the store to get milk and bread. The indications of Episode 2 are that Editha withdrew in a huff, and it seems quite likely that she also did so after 3.23. In that case, Rhoda had to go to the store herself. No matter what in fact happened, the point is made: Editha is so childish and aggravating to deal with that it is much easier not to ask her at all. Through the narrative mode of argument, Rhoda has firmly rejected the therapist's suggestion that she solve her problems by turning to Editha for help.

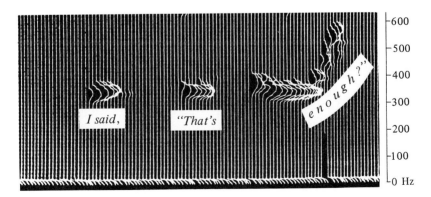

Figure 34. Pitch contour of 3.23, *"That's enough?"*

3.23   TEXT   CUES

R.: ⟨_N ⟨_F *I s'd, "That's **enough**?"* ⟩_F ⟩_N   Derogation: Thaˊt's eˊnoughˊ ↗, 'If that's enough for you, you don't know what you're talking about' (Figure 34).

EXPANSION

R.: ⟨_N I said to Editha, ⟨_F "If you think that's enough, {~AD-E} you don't know what you're talking about." ⟩_F ⟩_N

INTERACTION

R. requests confirmation that 3.22 has occurred, thereby asserting indirectly that it is hard to believe, and asserts simultaneously that anyone who would assert 3.22 is incompetent, thereby asserting again that ⟨ ~AD-E E. is not competent as an adult member of the household, thereby refusing the suggestion that ⟨ ~5 one can ask Editha for help.

EPISODE FOUR
See, I told you so.

At the end of Episode 3, the therapist has reached an impasse. She has tested out a subsidiary form of the basic suggestion and encountered resistance. Rhoda used her knowledge of the everyday situation to demonstrate that it was impractical to turn to her Aunt Editha for help. Since the therapist can only work with the material she is given, she was forced to accept for the moment this evaluation of the situation at home.

As Rhoda returns to the overriding concerns of Episode 1, the therapist takes the opportunity to ask for new material—an account of how Rhoda got into her present predicament. This is the most loaded question of all: who is the blame? In response, Rhoda gives us a long and complicated narrative revealing much more of the interplay among family members, and also showing that Rhoda is not yet ready to answer this question. Some of this material has already been used for contextual expansion in Episode 1; in that same sense, the reader has an advantage over the therapist, since the therapist heard Episode 1 without the hindsight that we have gained by putting together Rhoda's three retellings of the event.

Except for the initial direction and encouragement given by the therapist, this episode seems to be dominated by Rhoda's account. Yet if we pay attention to the larger frame, we will be witnessing interaction between therapist and patient, since Rhoda's way of accounting for the situation is a result of her desire to demonstrate her independence from the therapist; this unfolding of Rhoda's view of her family is largely a product of the therapeutic situation.

4.1. In order to observe how Rhoda moves back into the material of Episode 1, we begin Episode 4 with a bit of material left over from Episode 3. In 4.1, Rhoda continues to attack the competence of her aunt:

4.1[a]   R.: *Like she is—. . . it's like—. . she could be down to one slice of*

4.1

TEXT	CUES
[a] R.: ⟨_EV_ *Like she is—... it's like—..* *she could be down, to one slice of bread an'* ⟨_F_ *then it would **dawn** on her* ⟩_F_ *that well, maybe she'd as' me if she should go get it.* ⟩_EV_	Tension: hesitation, self-interruption, choking. Derogation: *dawn on* = 'slow to learn'.
[b] Th.: *Mmhm.*	

EXPANSION

[a] R.: ⟨_EV_ As an example of {~AD-E} the way E. behaves which {~5} makes it impossible for me to rely on her for help, she would not ask me if she should go to the store and get a loaf of bread until we had only one slice of bread left, while any normal person would have bought the bread before that, and even then she might not ask. ⟩_EV_

INTERACTION

[a] R. gives evaluation of E.'s behavior that ⟨~AD-E⟩ E. does not have normal standards of role performance, thereby refusing again the suggestion ⟨5⟩ that she should express her needs to E.
[b] Th. gives support and acknowledges R.'s argument.

> *bread an' then it would **dawn** on her that well, maybe she'd as' me if she should go get it.*
> [b] Th.: *Mmhm.*

Here we encounter the familiar choking and self-interruption that signals from Rhoda 'It is too much for me, no one could put up with such behavior'. To indicate sarcastically that Editha is very slow to respond to a shortage of bread, she uses the family style expression, *an' then it would dawn on her*.* Again the expansion includes the embedded proposition that Editha is not a competent adult. 4.1 provides a vivid illustration of the way in which someone can be attacked for having deficient standards of role performance. At a point where any normal person would have seen that there wasn't enough bread in the house, Editha still fails to act. It is not that she does not acknowledge her obligation—she is simply not competent to know when role performance should begin. Rhoda has shown us Editha as subnormal in initiating performance in three roles: cleaning the house, preparing the food, and buying provisions. These three tasks are a very large part of the obligations of adult members of the household; the challenge to Editha's competence is complete.

*****Dawn*** is sarcastic here as it normally is in referring to someone else's perception. It implies a long period of darkness and a slow breaking-through of the light.

Rhoda herself seems to have realized that she has come a full circle; when the therapist does not pick up this cue for interruption, Rhoda interrupts herself.

4.2. Rhoda's first move is an abrupt departure from the material in Episode 3, one that she herself promptly censors:

4.2[a]   R.: *See, they have . . . but—*

This is an oblique, almost suppressed reference to the more powerful members of her family: *they*. These are her mother and her married sister who is living in Household 2; they are the members who have taken a superior position in criticizing her for being underweight, for not eating, and for not being able to take care of herself in general. Our expansion completes Rhoda's thought, drawing on information in other parts of the session. The important fact is that Rhoda censors herself and does not pursue her challenge to whatever idea *they* have.*

EXPANSION
[a]   R.: You should understand that my mother and sister have the idea that {~AD-R} I can't get along without my mother because I am not strong enough to be a student and do housework, too, but {~~AD-R} that's not so.

Rhoda makes no backward reference to the problem of Editha; instead, she looks forward with an appeal to the therapist to "see." What is it that the therapist is supposed to understand here? That there is a class of people who are opposed to Rhoda's viewpoint, who deny that she is an adult, who deny that she can get along without her mother. Our expansion obviously draws from the material that follows directly after. The most pressing fact is that *they* must be made to understand that Rhoda is not being dependent on her mother by asking her to come home. Rhoda's hesitation and self-censorship indicate that she has not been able to formulate explicitly the kind of contradiction in which she finds herself; her demonstration of independence can still be interpreted as a sign of dependence.

Before proceeding, we may ask: why does Rhoda decide to change the subject? It must be remembered that it was Rhoda who introduced in Episode 1 the topic of her mother's absence as the major source of her difficulty this week. It was the therapist who turned away from this theme

---

*The reference to a generalized *they* indicates that the speaker feels the weight of forces aligned against her, powerful enough that it is best not to attack them directly. In extreme cases, such references indicate an unreal kind of paranoia; in the more ordinary cases like this, it expresses the polarity of the family and the power relationships which lie behind many of the dynamic developments in anorexia.

4.2 TEXT
[a] R.: ⟨ɪᵥ *See, they have . . . but—*
[b] *—like we were—s-saying—that—* . . .
I can get along—without my mother—
[c] *And I'm—'n—I can but it's just—all
of a **sudden** it seems to have gotten too
much.* ⟩ɪᵥ
[d] Th.: *Mmm . . .*

CUES
Tension: self-interruption, silence.
Tension: hesitation, choking;
extra high pitch on *can*; whine.

EXPANSION

[a] R.: ⟨ɪᵥ You should understand that my mother and sister have the idea that {~AD-R} I can't get along without my mother because I am not strong enough to be a student and do housework, too, but {~~AD-R} that's not so.
[b] As we were saying before, {AD-R} I really can perform normal activities and carry out normal obligations without being dependent on my mother, even though they say the opposite.
[c] And I can perform normal role obligations but {X:STRN} the situation has suddenly gotten too much for me or any normal person to handle. ⟩ɪᵥ

INTERACTION

[a] R. redirects the discussion to relations between herself and her mother (and sister), initiating a challenge to their view but not completing this challenge.
[b] R. asserts again that she is ⟨ AD-R ⟩ an adult member of the household.
[c] And asserts again ⟨ X:STRN ⟩ that external circumstances are the cause of the problem.
[d] Th. reinforces.

---

to consider Editha as a way of coping with her mother's absence, but Rhoda has rejected this suggestion. She now returns to the original topic and theme {AD-R}, that she is an adult member of the household.

> 4.2[b] R.: *—like we were—s-saying—that—* . . . *I can get along—without my mother—*
>
> [c] *And I'm—'n—I can but it's just—all of a **sudden** it seems to have gotten too **much**.*

4.2[b] repeats 1.5[a] and also reproduces its prosodic structure.

> 1.5[a] *I mean I—I—I've proved, I **know** that I can get along without my mother,*

The parallel in paralinguistic cues is striking: Rhoda stammers, chokes, interrupts herself, and then bursts forth with extra heavy stress on the first available verb. She is dealing again with her central concern: to prove that she is independent, an adult, and free to make her own decisions. It's also clear that she feels a powerful pressure from her mother and sister to establish the opposite. As we pointed out in Chapter 1 (p. 10), other studies of anorexia nervosa point to the power struggle within the family as a recurrent problem associated with this syndrome.

It is then not surprising that Rhoda follows with another close parallel, between 1.5[d] and 4.2[c]:

1.5[d] *But it seems that—I have jist—a little too much t'do.*
4.2[c] *And I'm—'n—I can but it's just—all of a **sudden** it seems to have gotten too **much**.*

This restatement sums up Rhoda's basic position, which the therapist must deal with: first, a blanket assertion of her adult status, and, secondly, the transference of any blame away from family members to purely external, neutral circumstances. Rhoda suppresses direct criticism of her family and returns to the vague language of her everyday style, in which "it" or "things" is responsible for her problems rather than "they."

4.3. We observe again the familiar mechanism Rhoda uses to invite intervention from the therapist. The therapist recognizes again that Rhoda is repeating herself in identical words, and that she is prepared to continue this recycling indefinitely until she is interrupted. The therapist then accepts the invitation to intervene by beginning *All right,* which slightly anticipates Rhoda's attempt to continue. There is nothing strident about the overlap: the therapist's utterance has a deliberate fall and rise which indicates a tentative acceptance of Rhoda's argument. The signal concedes the force of what Rhoda has said, but implies that there is more to follow. This reservation recalls the therapist's dissatisfaction with Rhoda's account that she expressed at the end of Episode 1.*

4.3[a] R: *But it's not that—*
   [b] Th: *All right.*
   [c] *If it's "too **much**," then—*

We cannot understand the therapist's tentative beginning without reference to the earlier series of sudden shifts in the therapist's intervention of 2.1. We have expanded the suppressed question with what seems to be the most likely material—a return to the problem that was bothering the therapist in 2.1. What is the source of the guilt that is expressed in Rhoda's

---

*The 2 1 2 contour on *All right* is the same as that used in the mother's heavily expressive *Oh, why?* With strong stress, especially in a question, this signal can be labeled 'heavy implication', or 'There is more to this than meets the eye'. However it might be called 'light implication' in a reinforcing signal which has no heavy stress.

254 EPISODE FOUR

4.3		TEXT	CUES
[a]	R.:	But it's not that—	Implication: 2 1 2.
[b]	Th.:	All right.	
[c]	Th.:	⟨_IV_ If it's "too **much**," then—	

EXPANSION
[a] R.: But it's not that I can't get along without my mother.
[c] Th.: Granted that {AD-R} you can get along without your mother, and that the real problem is that {X:STRN} the situation is too much for you, then why {?E₂} do you still feel guilty about asking your mother for help?

INTERACTION
[a] R. repeats the phrase of 1.10, thereby requesting the therapist to intervene and reevaluate the material of Episode 1.
[b] Th. acknowledges Rhoda's argument again.
[c] Th. interrupts and begins to request information on the reason for Rhoda's hesitation in Episode 1.

---

hesitation? Again the therapist turns away from the temptation to explore this loaded question directly.

4.4 The therapist's next move is in a sharply different direction, as indicated by the discourse marker *now*.

4.4 Th.: *Now—tell me: why is mother staying there so long—I don't understand. It is something the matter there?*

The use of *tell me* is appropriate for a referential situation, in which the therapist is asking for information rather than orientation or interpretation. The therapist sets the stage for a lengthy narrative, but not without some emotional implications, as the paralinguistic cues indicate. Emphatic stress and high pitch on *why* and *stay* might be seen as a challenge to Rhoda's mother, emphasizing that her conduct is inexplicable.*

The break between 4.3 and 4.4 is quite abrupt and cannot be understood without looking ahead. Our interactional statements are limited to an intermediate level of analysis and do not deal with the therapist's deeper

---

*The general principles for the interpretation of stress would differentiate sharply between stress on *why* and stress on the referential items. When *why* is stressed, we find an implication that the action described is inexplicable and therefore unreasonable; but contrastive stress on some referential item like *stay* indicates that some other opposing item might have been entered here. See 1.11 for the operation of this contrastive principle on "Why don't you tell Phyllis that?"

| 4.4 | TEXT | CUES |

Th.: ⟨_{EV} *Now—tell me: why is mother staying there so long—I don't understand. It is something the matter there?* ⟩_{EV}   Tension: extra high pitch on *why* and *stay*. Mitigation: matter there, 'tentative question'.

EXPANSION

Th.: ⟨_{EV} Now explain to me a little more about your original problem: Why is your mother staying at your sister's so very long, four days instead of coming home after two days as she usually does—I don't understand why she is staying longer than usual. Is there something wrong at your sister's house that would justify your mother being absent from your own house so long? ⟩_{EV}

INTERACTION

Th. requests information about ⟨ ?X ⟩ the circumstances which are responsible for Rhoda's difficulty.

---

strategy. She may be making the following connection between 4.3 and 4.4: if Rhoda feels guilty, she may feel that she really is responsible for the present situation, and may indeed have helped to set it up herself. In asking for more information on the everyday life situation, the therapist hopes to clarify for Rhoda the extent to which she is or is not responsible, and what her options in the situation are. Since these narratives often reveal a contradiction between the patient's argument and her behavior, it is possible that we would find Rhoda actually blaming herself in this further account.

At the same time, we can see that the contrastive stresses of 4.4 imply an indirect challenge to the competence of Rhoda's mother. If her behavior is hard to explain, then she would not be acting as the best possible mother. Rhoda's narrative that follows can be understood best as a response to this indirect challenge to her mother—in fact, it finally emerges in 4.17 as a defense of her mother.

Rhoda's Second Account: 4.5

Rhoda's narrative account of the events leading up to Episode 1 begins in 4.5 and is carried out for some time without any direct quotations in family style. There is a marked contrast between the style here and the highly emotional style she used in the preceding discussion. The emotional involvements that produce hesitation, choking, glottalization, and self-interruption are gone; instead, we see Rhoda struggling with the cognitive problem of explicating the situation. The complexity is real, since three households are involved, with many events overlapping in time and space. As Rhoda begins her narrative, we find ourselves plunged in a maze of references to family events and situations that are difficult for the outsider to disentangle. The interaction is primarily one between Rhoda (speaker) and therapist (listener). The problems involved are cognitive rather than emotional; Rhoda becomes entangled in the difficulties of explication and fails to provide the listener with a coherent sequence of events. Since the narrative of everyday events is an important component of therapeutic discourse, this episode will help us to understand the work of using language to portray the many-dimensional textures of social reality.

Rhoda plunges into the narrative with three events, in rapid succession. cession.

 4.5[a] R.: *Well, my brother-in-law's mother fell.*
  [b] *She's—a-an elderly woman*
  [c] *and she broke her leg*
  [d] *and she was in the hospital.*

The normal orientation to a narrative is somewhat truncated here: we are introduced to the person and the events, but the place, and particularly the

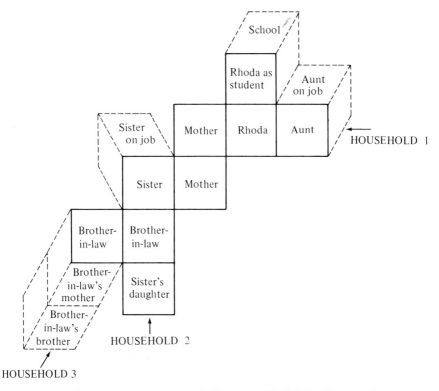

Figure 11″. Further expansion of role sets for Rhoda's family network.

RHODA'S SECOND ACCOUNT   257

4.5	TEXT	CUES
[a]	R.: ⟨N Well, my brother-in-law's mother fell.	Tension release: rapid delivery, no fading, whining or choking.
[b]	She's—a-an elderly woman	
[c]	and she broke her leg	
[d]	and she was in the hospital. ⟩N	

EXPANSION
[a]   R.: ⟨N The reason is that: my mother is staying at my sister's house because my brother-in-law's mother had fallen some time previous to my mother's going there.
[b]   And my brother-in-law's mother is an elderly woman whose bones are easily broken
[c]   and she broke her leg when she fell
[d]   and she was taken to the hospital and was in the hospital on Sunday. ⟩N

INTERACTION
[a]   Rhoda initiates a narrative without an abstract or explicit connection to 4.4 thereby asserting indirectly that the events of the narrative do give ⟨X the information requested.
[a-d]   Rhoda gives information on persons and behavior but not time or place.

time, is missing. The relevance of these events is not immediately clear, because Rhoda does not give the temporal or causal relations to show why these events will provide a reasonable answer to the question: why is her mother staying away so long? However, the Rule of Narrative Response (Chapter 3, p. 107) operates here: once the listener recognizes that Rhoda is engaged in a narrative, it is understood that the evaluative point of this narrative will provide the answer to the request for information. The listener can therefore suspend the demand for a connection if all the intervening steps are afterwards made clear. However, it will be helpful to the reader at this stage to lay out the wider range of social relations that underline the circumstances responsible for Rhoda's problems. Figure 11" is a further expansion of the network of social relations in which Rhoda is engaged.

The basic suggestion of therapy {S} is that Rhoda should make her needs and problems known to relevant others. Who are these relevant others? Figure 11" shows the kind of sociological expertise that is needed to answer this question. We see a third household involved; we do not know how many members it has, or how they are related, but we do know that Rhoda's sister's husband is involved with another set of obligations. He is responsible not only to his wife and daughter in Household 2, but also to

258   EPISODE FOUR

his mother in Household 3, and he apparently has another brother who shares this responsibility.

Figure 11" locates seven other persons besides Rhoda, and names them by their relation to her. The interlocking of the households shows that most of the persons involved have at least two kinds of relations that impose two kinds of role obligations. There are kinship relations, which are permanent, and institutional obligations, which are created by residents in the household, enrollment in school, or employment on a job. Just as Rhoda is responsible to both school and Household 1, her mother is responsible to Household 1 and Household 2, and the issue in dispute is the extent of the claim of Household 2 upon her. We will see that the chain of events that reinforces this claim of Household 2 is brought about by a disturbance in its equilibrium, which is in turn caused by the claim of members of Household 3 on the members of Household 2. Rhoda's sister's in-laws can make no direct claim upon Household 1, and it is indeed an indirect series of circumstances that leads to Rhoda's involvement.

4.6–7. With this background, it will be possible to untangle Rhoda's account though she does not succeed in putting all the events into the clearest kind of temporal order. Her next narrative clause contains a past perfect, which indicates that this event takes place at some time previous to those given in 4.5.

4.6[a]   R.: *We had come home from the bar mitzvah, and—uh—*......

This turns out not to be the case; 4.6[a] took place *after* the hospitalization of 4.5[d], but just *before* 4.6[c], a telephone call about it.

4.6[b]   *My—brother-in-law's brother—couldn't get—something was wrong with my sister's phone an' couldn't get in touch with them.*
   [c]   *And so he called our house.*

Rhoda is dealing with a story that would be difficult for any narrator to handle: two parallel sets of events with different extensions in time. Yet she compounds the difficulty: (1) She does not introduce the persons in the second stream of events but simply refers to them as *we* in 4.6[a]. (2) She refers to the new event, a bar mitzvah, with the definite article *the* as if it had been mentioned before.

A careful study of the whole narrative shows that Rhoda had gone to this bar mitzvah with her mother, her sister, and the sister's husband.* The pronoun *we* in 4.6[a] therefore refers to these four people.

In the cross section for 4.6 we have no paralinguistic cues to help us in deciphering the text; the mode of expression is direct and the obscurity is a

---

*Possibly all members of Household 1 were included, Aunt Editha as well, but this is irrelevant to the main stream of the narrative.

4.6 TEXT	CUES
[a] R.: ⟨_N We had come home from the bar mitzvah, and—uh—..... [b] My—brother-in-law's brother—couldn't get—something was wrong with my sister's phone an' couldn' get in touch with them. [c] And so he called our house. ⟩_N	

EXPANSION

[a] R.: ⟨_N My mother, my sister, my brother-in-law (her husband) and I had come home late Sunday from a bar mitzvah.
[b] My brother-in-law's brother tried to call my brother-in-law and my sister to tell them about the accident to their mother, but something was wrong with my sister's phone and he couldn't get in touch with them.
[c] And therefore my brother-in-law's brother called our house instead. ⟩_N

INTERACTION

R. continues the narrative, but fails to give complete orientation to persons and order of events involved.

---

result of cognitive and referential problems. We do observe hesitation and a 2½-second silence following 4.6[a], This silence is different from the silences in Episode 1: it does not signify tension or the suppression of speech, but rather the time needed for a cognitive recoding. Whenever a person is retelling his experience for the first time, there are certain personal relations which have to be translated into a form that the listener can understand. In ordinary family interaction, Rhoda probably refers to her brother-in-law's brother by his name. She does not have to translate her relation to him into the explicit kinship terminology of 4.6[b], and it takes her three seconds to do this. It is obvious that there are many different kinds of silences.

The expansion and interactional statement of 4.6 does not show the embedded propositions and indirect speech acts that appeared in 4.1–3. There are no personal dynamics involved here, and no conflict has developed which would force mitigation of language with indirect modes of expression and argument. Still, it is not clear what is happening; rather than pursue the expansion of 4.6 in isolation, we will do better to proceed to the next series of events.

4.7[a]   R.: *And we had just happened to walk in.*

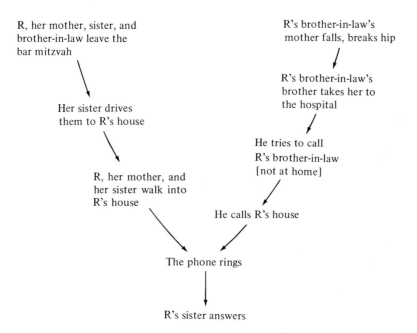

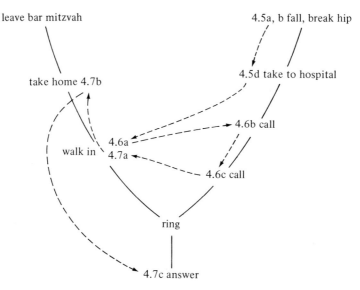

Figure 35. (top) Two separate series of events underlying 4.5–4.7. (bottom) Rhoda's attempt to narrate the events above.

[b] *So naturally my sister took us home,*
[c] *An-nd—ah—she answered the **phone**.*

At this point, we would expect the reader (and the therapist) to have been badly confused because 4.7[b] is placed after 4.7[a] even though it occurred before 4.7[a] and there is no grammatical signal to register this fact. The basic Rule of Narrative Sequencing (Chapter 3, p. 107) indicates that the occurrence of an independent clause with a verb in the past tense is heard as asserting that this event came after the one described in the last such clause. If the event did in fact occur earlier, the past perfect is used. Thus if Rhoda had said, "So naturally my sister *had taken* us home," the listener would have gotten a correct orientation. Rhoda did in fact use the past perfect in 4.7[a], to indicate that the "walking in" took place just before 4.6[c], the "calling up."

The narrative problem here is not a simple one, and Rhoda should not be faulted too severely for failing to cope with it. The sequence of events is explicated in the expansions of 4.5 and 4.7, but it is still not easy to follow. Figure 35 shows the two parallel series of events. Series I involves four persons from Households 1 and 2; Series II involves two persons from Household 3. The events within each series are ordered sequentially, but cannot be ordered with respect to any of the events in the other series until they converge with the ringing of the phone. At bottom we see how Rhoda's narrative traces these events. She begins at the beginning of Series II,

---

4.7	TEXT	CUES

[a] R.: ⟨_N And we had just happened to walk in.
[b] So naturally my sister took us home,
[c] An-nd—ah—she answered the **phone**. ⟩_N

EXPANSION

[a] R.: ⟨_N And my mother, my sister and I had just walked into our house when my brother-in-law's brother was calling.
[b] My sister was with us because she was at the bar mitzvah, too, and because she had a car and we don't, she naturally had taken us home.
[c] And my sister answered the phone just when my brother-in-law's brother called. ⟩_N

INTERACTION

R. continues the narrative, but fails to mark time relations for new orienting information.

and then jumps over to Series I with 4.6[a], *we had come home from the bar mitzvah*. The past perfect does not apply until Rhoda returns to Series II with 4.6[b] and [c]. Then she returns again to the same point in Series I, patching up the confusion of 4.6[a]. Her next reference is backwards in Series I, without the past perfect, which would have made it clear; she then jumps to 4.7[c], which is practically simultaneous with 4.6[c].

The failure in sequencing is less serious than Rhoda's failure to evaluate the events she is describing. Why is it necessary for her to include these details about how the phone call was received? We must infer that she thinks they are important in explaining the force of the obligation on her mother. At the very moment that Rhoda's sister received the bad news and realized she would have to go to the hospital to see her mother-in-law the next day, she also realized that she would need someone to take care of her daughter, and turned to Rhoda's mother to ask for help.

This event shows how kinship relations bind the households together and produce the overlapping set of obligations. It was such a joint activity that brought them all together at the bar mitzvah and was responsible for the crucial fact that when they were found by the brother-in-law's brother, they were all suddenly involved in the problem.

4.8. As Rhoda continues her narrative, the sequencing problems persist, and the problems of interpretation and motivation become even more severe.

4.8[a] R.: *And so my—and so she had to go to the* **hospital** *the next day.*
[b] *It was Washington's Birthday.*
[c] *So her and my brother-in-law* **went.**
[d] *And there was no one to watch the children.*
[e] *So my* **mother** *went.*

Again, our cross sections show no prosodic cues of interest, as the mode of expression is quite direct. The interactional statement is also quite brief, since the narrative has not come to any clear interactional focus. The major contribution of our cross section is in the expansion, which provides coherence to the narrative that would otherwise be missing. It is not immediately clear why Washington's Birthday is relevant in 4.8[b]: our expansion provides the connection. Similarly, we have provided a fuller context for 4.8[e], which is quite elliptical. The *went* of 4.8[c] is not the same *went* of 4.8[e]. The expansion motivates the various details about how the request came in and why Rhoda's mother had to go.

Up to this point, Rhoda has been describing a series of events with no reference to their emotional effect upon her. We are not sure how to evaluate the incoherence of her narrative: is it a purely cognitive problem having to do with the ability to organize a sequential set of events in discourse? It is possible that this reflects an underlying psychological ten-

4.8	TEXT	CUES

[a] R.: ⟨_N_ And so my—and so she had to go to the **hospital** the next day.
[b] It was Washington's Birthday.
[c] So her and my brother-in-law **went**.
[d] And there was no one to watch the children.
[e] So my **mother** went. ⟩_N_

EXPANSION

[a] R.: ⟨_N_ And so my sister found out just then that she had to go to the hospital to see her mother-in-law the next day, Monday,
[b] which was Washington's Birthday when my brother-in-law was home from work.
[c] So my sister and my brother-in-law could go to the hospital together.
[d] There was no one at my sister's house to watch my sister's children if they did go together,
[e] so {10} they asked my mother just then to watch the children and she agreed and so she went with them to my sister's house. ⟩_N_

INTERACTION

R. continues the narrative, giving information on how ⟨ 10 ⟩ her role partner was involved in other obligations and still fails to give full sequencing and evaluation.

---

sion that is clearly shown in the preceding and following sections. However, she shows no sign of this tension in her paralinguistic cues.

4.9. In 4.9, Rhoda begins to add the emotional texture that was missing in the early parts of the narrative.

4.9[a] R.: *And **then-n**, with everything,*
 [b] *my sister wanted to go to **work** again.*
 [c] *So she stayed **Tuesday**.*

She indicates tension and an underlying exasperation by the elliptical phrase *with everything,* which we must expand as "in spite of everything that happened and all the trouble that had been caused at her house and ours." However, the criticism of her sister is muted, and the mode of argument is quite indirect. In our expansion of 4.9[b], we add the fact (which appears later in 4.10) that Rhoda's sister didn't go to work after all. Rhoda plainly feels that she was imposed on by her sister, but she does not

4.9　　　　　　TEXT　　　　　　　　　　　　CUES
[a]　R.: ⟨ₙ *And **then-n**, with everything,*　Tension: *with everything* (ellipsis),
[b]　*my sister wanted to go to **work***　　exasperation.
again.
[c]　*So sh- stayed **Tuesday.*** ⟩ ₙ

EXPANSION

[a]　R.: ⟨ₙ And then, in spite of everything that happened and all the trouble that had been caused at her house and ours,
[b]　my sister wanted to go to work and {10} call on my mother to help some more which was an unreasonable thing to do,
[c]　so my mother stayed at my sister's house one more day, Tuesday, but my sister didn't go to work after all so {~RSNBL-S} she wasn't being reasonable because she had no good reason to {10} have asked my mother to stay. ⟩ₙ

INTERACTION

R. continues the narrative, giving information to show that her mother did not have any obligation to fulfill in Household 2, and asserts indirectly that the circumstances ⟨ X:STRN ⟩ for her problem were caused by ⟨ ~RSNBL-S ⟩ her sister's unreasonable behavior.

---

say so; we have translated her implicit criticism into explicit condemnation in the expansion, but it must be remembered that repression of this explicit criticism has interactional significance.

4.10.　As Rhoda's evaluation of the narrative begins to increase in intensity, she uses the resources of family language in a way that we have not seen before.

4.10[a]　R.: *So my mother s'd, "Well I'll go home Wednesday morning."*
　　　[b]　*She said, "**Oh no**, don't go, I'm gonna work."*
　　　[c]　*And anyway, she didn't work—anyway.*

The derogatory intonation that Rhoda uses in 4.10[b] is sometimes referred to as "sing-song" because it has a repeated pattern of pitch and stress (Figure 36). This intonation contour is normally heard as an editorial type of comment—not intended to represent the intonation Rhoda's sister actually used. Of course, Rhoda is reporting here a family encounter that took place when she was not present, and she must be quoting her mother's version; it is possible that the derogatory intonation is her mother's, and Rhoda is quoting directly. On the other hand, it is most likely that the pejorative intonation is Rhoda's edition, part of her continued criticism of

RHODA'S SECOND ACCOUNT   265

4.10   TEXT   CUES
[a] R.: ⟨_N So my mother s'd, "Well I'll   Derogation: Oh³ no,² don't go,³ I'm³
go home Wednesday morning."   gonna² work, 'This is the kind of
[b] She said, ⟨_F "Oh no, don't go, I'm   ridiculous thing she always says'.
gonna work." ⟩_F   (Figure 36).
[c] And anyway, she didn't   Tension: repetition of 'anyway'.
work—anyway. ⟩_N

EXPANSION

[a] R.: ⟨_NSo my mother said to my sister, "In view of all I have to do at home,
I'll go home tomorrow, Wednesday morning, and I won't be able to help you
any longer."
[b] So my sister said something that was really absurd, ⟨_F "Oh, no, don't
go home, I'm going to work tomorrow and I need you to take care of my
children." ⟩_F
[c] But in spite of what my sister said about going to work, she didn't go to
work after all. ⟩_N

INTERACTION

R. continues the narrative, giving information on claims made on her role
partner, thereby ⟨ ~RSNBL-S challenging her sister as unreasonable, and
thereby requesting sympathy for the injury done to her.

---

her sister. Just as Rhoda directed a relentless criticism against Editha in
Episodes 2 and 3, she now concentrates her efforts in Episode 4 to show
how unreasonable her sister is.

The most damaging fact about her sister's behavior is that she didn't go
to work. When Rhoda gives us this information in 4.10[c], she evaluates it
with a very unusual device—the repetition of *anyway*, with extra stress on

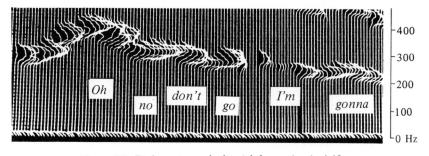

Figure 36. Pitch contour of editorial derogation in 4.10.

any. We expand this as, "in spite of what my sister said about going to work," and add, "she didn't go to work after all." We could argue that this repetition of *anyway* indicates that the sister's unreasonableness is compounded. At a higher level, 4.10 must be seen as a complaint on Rhoda's part (Chapter 2, p. 63)—that is, a request for sympathy. Our paralinguistic cues indicate a sense of personal grievance that might be symbolized as {~RSNBL-S:X:STRN}, but we have not made this complaint into a formal proposition because it doesn't recur. Rhoda will continue to insist {X:STRN} that it was simply circumstances that were the cause of her present difficulties.

4.11: Resolution. Rhoda now completes the answer to the therapist's question, *Why is mother staying there so long?* She does so in a relatively straightforward style, explicating the details of the interaction without hesitation or stumbling.*

4.11[a] R.: *So I thought she'd come home this morning.*
  [b] *So, it ended up that she's not comin' home this morning, 'cause now my sister went to work.*

The phrase *it ended up* in 4.11[b] indicates that this is to be the resolution of the narrative. Rhoda has now provided the information that the therapist asked for in 4.4: she has given the reason why her mother has stayed so long.

With the exception of Rhoda's editorial intonation in 4.10[b], the mode of expression in this narrative has been fairly direct. Rhoda's words, rather than her paralinguistic cues, carry the main message. However, the mode of argument is complex, since the narrative must carry out two distinct functions. (1) Rhoda has to explicate a complicated series of overlapping events to answer the therapist's question. (2) She has to show what general principle these events illustrate, and she has to introduce a new and rather delicate argument: though others have been unreasonable, it is primarily her sister who is at fault and not her mother.†

The first task turned out to be a difficult one since the events were not organized in a single series in time. Rhoda has more success with the second task—the evaluation of the narrative. Rhoda's intonation pattern in 4.10[b] plainly marks the evaluative point of this narrative: that her sister was unreasonable {~RSNBL-S}. This general proposition thus gives the

---

*Rhoda does put the blame for her problem on the unreasonable behavior of her sister, but she does not become as exasperated as she did over Editha's behavior. The editorial comment and her intonation of 4.10[b] make it plain that she disapproves of her sister's behavior, but she does not become choked up or exhibit extreme tension. Her sister may not have been involved in the intense kinds of family interaction described in Episodes 2 and 3.

†The focus on her sister's responsibility may be compared with the indirect implication of *they* in 4.2[a], before the narrative began.

4.11   TEXT   CUES
[a] R.: ⟨_N *So I thought she'd come home this **morning**.*   Tension release: rapid but not condensed.
[b] *So, it ended up that she's not comin' home this morning, 'cause now my sister went to **work**.* ⟩_N

EXPANSION
[a] R.: ⟨_N So since my sister didn't go to work Tuesday *or* Wednesday, I thought that my mother would come home this morning, Thursday morning.
[b] But in spite of all the time my mother had been away, what was actually decided was that she wouldn't come home this morning, Thursday, because now after all that delay, my sister did go to work and my mother had to stay home and take care of the children, all of which answers your question as to why my mother has stayed away so long and produced a problem that I tried to solve. ⟩_N

INTERACTION
R. ends the narrative, giving the information requested by the therapist, and simultaneously defends her mother's behavior ⟨ RSNBL-MO as a reasonable response to her sister's behavior, and challenges her sister's behavior ~RSNBL-S ⟩ as unreasonable.

---

appropriate answer to the therapist's question, *Why is mother staying there so long?* and justifies the expectation under the Rule of Narrative Response that Rhoda's account would answer the question.

The basic issue we are dealing with here is one of the most sensitive in personal interactions: who is to blame? We saw in 4.4 that the therapist's question might attach this blame to Rhoda's mother; 4.10[b] shows that Rhoda's response is to blame her sister.

Ultimately, we must relate this to the basic theme of Episode 1—that Rhoda *did the right thing*. If Rhoda's mother has been unreasonable in this affair, then Rhoda's inability to get her mother to come home is a failure on Rhoda's part. But if Rhoda's mother had a good reason to stay away, and it was her sister's fault, then her mother was correct in saying, *Why don't you tell **Phyllis** that?* and Rhoda could not reasonably have been expected to persuade her mother to come home. It would then follow that Rhoda not only did the right thing, but that she actually did it as well as one could have expected. Rhoda's argument might indicate that we were wrong in assessing her narrative of Episode 1 as an illustration of her communicative incompetence. Fortunately, we now have the opportunity to reassess our

268   EPISODE FOUR

conclusions in Episode 1, since Rhoda continues with a retelling of the events of Episode 1.

The Retelling of Episode 1

Rhoda's narrative does not end with the conclusion of 4.11; as she moves smoothly on, we discover that she is repeating the account that she gave in Episode 1.*

4.12–13. We have already drawn upon this retelling for our expansion of Episode 1, since this version is somewhat fuller than the first. It returns to the mode of expression of Episode 1. Rhoda's style now changes radically from the straightforward narrative style of 4.5–11, and we again hear the rapid, choked, and condensed delivery that we read as evidence of internal tension.

4.12 R.: *So I says t'her, "Are you coming home **tomorrow** morning?"*		TEXT FOR EPISODE 1
	1.8	R.: *An-nd so—when—I called her t'day, I said, "Well, when do you plan t'come **home**?"*
4.13 R.: *So she s'd, "Why-y?"*		
	1.9	R.: *So she said, "Oh, why?"*

If the two accounts are fundamentally the same, the expansions and analyses should match. The expansion of 4.12 is slightly different from 1.8, since in this version Rhoda links her question to 4.11 in the preceding account. Instead of asking her mother if she plans to come home, she specifically refers to *tomorrow* [Friday] *morning*. The stress contrast of *tomorrow morning* can be expanded as, "since you didn't come home *this* morning." Secondly, we find that the expression *plan* is omitted, making the request seem slightly more mitigated. These are relatively superficial differences, part of the work that is necessary to fit this retelling into the preceding context. It seems to us that Rhoda's account in 4.12 and 4.13 is remarkably consistent with the earlier statement, and we provide the same interactive interpretation.

There is no significant difference in Rhoda's report of her mother's reply.

---

*It is not at all obvious that Rhoda would have continued with this narrative. We might have expected an intervention from the therapist at the end of 4.11 since her question was answered. We have seen before that Rhoda seldom brings her account to a full stop to allow the therapist to take a normal sequencing turn. Her usual method is to return to her original statement and keep repeating herself until interrupted. The therapist might have interrupted her as she begins to repeat with 4.12 and 4.13, but the therapist must have realized, as we realize now, that this retelling is significantly different. It is not a repetition in exactly the same words of Episode 1, and in the light of the therapist's puzzled reaction in 2.1, it is understandable that she would listen without interrupting to a retelling of the events.

THE RETELLING OF EPISODE 1

4.12	TEXT	CUES
R.: ⟨_N *So I says t'her, "Are you coming home* **tomorrow** *morning?"* ⟩_N		Tension: rapid condensed, glottalization. Mitigation: tentative question, 2 3 2.

EXPANSION

R.: ⟨_N So when I learned she wasn't coming home today (Thursday), I called her up and said to her, "{3} Your obligations to my sister's household have been fulfilled, since you didn't come home this morning as I expected, and {4} your primary obligations to our household are being neglected, are you coming home tomorrow morning, Friday, {2, S} to give me the help that I need?" ⟩_N

INTERACTION

See 1.8.

4.13	TEXT	CUES
R.: ⟨_N *So she s'd,* ⟨_F *"Why-y?"* ⟩_F ⟩_N		Heavy implication: 1 1 2, "There's more to this than meets the eye."

EXPANSION

See 1.9, EXPANSION (p. 166).

INTERACTION

See, 1.9, INTERACTION (p. 166).

The intonation pattern is slightly different, but it retains the characteristic feature of heavy implication; the initial *Oh* is dropped.*

4.14–15. Rhoda's reply to her mother in 4.14 is given in almost exactly the same words as in 1.10 of Episode 1:

4.14	R.: *A-and—I said, "Uh—well, it's getting a little too* **much.***"*	TEXT OF EPISODE 1
		1.10 R.: *An-nd I said, "Well, things are getting just a little too* **much!** *[laugh] This is— i's jis' getting too hard, and* .... —"

---

*The expression of surprise is omitted here, but see the third retelling in Episode 5, where this feature is emphasized at the expense of others.

4.14	TEXT	CUES
R.: ⟨N A-and—I said, "Uh—well, it's getting a little too **much.**" ⟩N		Mitigation: well, 'temporizing'; *it's a little.* Tension: *too much,* with whine.

EXPANSION

See 1.10, p. 170.

INTERACTION

See 1.10, p. 170.

4.15	TEXT	CUES
R.: ⟨N So she s'd, ⟨F "**See, I told you so.**" ⟩F ⟩N		Tension: very condensed. Implication: 3 2 3 2 ↗

EXPANSION

R.: ⟨N So my mother said to me, ⟨F "You see, I have been right all along: I told you that {~AD-R} you can't take care of yourself as an adult should, and that's why I can't go away." ⟩F ⟩N

INTERACTION

Mother asserts that she was right in the previous conversation, thereby asserting indirectly that R.'s requesting assistance shows that ⟨←~AD-R→⟩ R. is not an adult member of the household, thereby challenging R.'s assertion that she is an adult member of the household.

But at this point, Rhoda departs from her original narrative and inserts new material.

   4.15 R.: *So she s'd, "See I told you so."*

This is the unstated implication we used to expand the original expression of 1.9, *Oh, why?* We take the first account (Episode 1) as likely to be closer to the original events; by Episode 4, Rhoda has had more time to evaluate her mother's indirect mode of expression and to clarify in her own mind the significance of her mother's intonation.* This second account yields three family style expressions in rapid succession: *Oh, why-y? It's getting a*

---

*This situation is parallel to one observed in Episode 3, where Rhoda gives a more explicit version of her interchange with Editha in a second repetition. She may, of course, be giving a more accurate version in this episode, just as it is possible that she actually did force from her aunt an explicit admission that she was the one who felt lonely. It seems more likely that Rhoda is now externalizing her own personal interpretation.

little too much. I told you so. Rhoda shows a good grasp of the family mode of expression, with its complex intonation contours and elliptical forms. The mode of argument is equally indirect. Even when Rhoda makes explicit what was contained in her mother's intonation, the surface forms make implicit reference to other unstated propositions. The speakers are aggressive and at the same time protect themselves by not committing themselves in so many words. Finally, the mode of interaction is also quite indirect, as our cross sections show. This type of indirection seems to be intimately involved with the mechanism of anorexia. There is no opportunity for the child to ventilate her emotions by a direct reply. If she responds to these indirect aggressions overtly, she would be seen as disrespectful, as a bad and ungrateful child. This is the problem of emotional repression that the therapist must cope with, and she will try to do so in Episode 5.

4.16. Since 4.15 was not included in Episode 1, Rhoda's response to it is also missing in the earlier account.

4.16 R.: *But I said, "The other times you've gone away a day or so, and i-it's... nothing, and—"*

This, however, is familiar material. The last clause of 4.16 is Rhoda's comment to the therapist in 1.2: *So—it's nothing.** In this version of the argument between Rhoda and her mother, we can see most explicitly the dynamics of the struggle between mother and daughter. Rhoda's mother makes her choose between being infantilized or being deprived of the support she needs as a student. This situation highlights the importance of Rhoda's disclaimer, *It's nothing.* In 1.2, it appeared as an answer to the therapist's premature sympathy; we can now see that it is part of Rhoda's basic argument with her mother.

To understand expressions such as *it's nothing*, it is necessary to read the interview backwards and forwards, expanding the scope of our interpretation to include the whole therapeutic process. An atomistic interpretation in the fashion of Bales or Lennard and Bernstein would see each use of *it's nothing* as unconnected to the others: in 1.2 it would be viewed as a simple assertion to the therapist, and in 4.16, as a statement made to her mother. In the study of ad hoc small groups, this atomistic approach might be defended more easily; but when speakers have a long history of interaction, there is a large residue of unstated propositions, unresolved arguments, and unsatisfactory interactions that must be understood to give a

---

*We see again that the basic mode of argument in the family transforms quantitative judgments into categorical statements. The mother's position is that "I can't leave Rhoda alone for a minute." In the face of these categorical statements, it is hard for Rhoda to make the quantitative point that a day or two is nothing, but that three or four days is *too much.*

4.16

TEXT	CUES

R.: ⟨_N But I said, ⟨_F "The other times you've gone away a day or so, and i-it's... nothing, and—" ⟩_F ⟩_N

EXPANSION

R.: ⟨_N But I said, ⟨_F "The other times when you said you couldn't go away because of me and I encouraged you to go because {AD-R} I know I can take care of myself, you've gone away only a day or so and it was no problem; I did take care of myself." ⟩_F ⟩_N

INTERACTION

R. asserts that she did perform obligations as an adult member of the household when mother took up other role obligations in the past, thereby asserting ⟨ AD-R ⟩ that she is an adult member of the household, thereby defending herself against her mother's challenge ⟨ ~AD-R ⟩.

---

reasonable semantic analysis. A conversation between therapist and patient or a reported conversation between mother and daughter is an intricately woven fabric, and only part of it is visible at any one time. It cannot be treated like a string of beads, with linear connections that can be added and subtracted. The most challenging and difficult part of our analysis is the assembling of backward and forward references in the expansion, forming the matrix out of which we draw the modes of argument and interaction.

At a later point in this interview, beyond any of the episodes we are considering, Rhoda begins to review her arguments with her mother. She repeats the exact words that she used in Episode 1 when she was evaluating the situation to the therapist:

R.: *I mean, if she goes during intercession when I have off, she can stay two weeks. It really doesn't bother me because I—no—no problems of school, nothing to worry about, on having an exam or something (Mhm.) and—uh—I can—I can go out most of the time, so—it didn't bother me in the least, because she did go away.*

TEXT OF EPISODE 1

1.5[b] R.: *I know that—when I don't have any* **school***, an' she's gone away—she went away for a week, an' a* **half** *an'—i' didn' bother me in the leas'.*

In both cases, Rhoda is discussing this problem with the therapist, but in the later discussion she makes transition to an argument with her mother.

> R.: ...*So why—so I'll see her, like, y'know, if you don't wanna go, say you don't wanna go, but don't use me as an excuse.*
> Th: *Right!*

The situation is now more complex than before, since Rhoda argues that her mother really does not mean that she (Rhoda) is unable to take care of herself, but that her mother is using this as an excuse to avoid doing something she doesn't want to do.

> *Like if she doesn't want to go—to my sister's,—she just needs an excuse—"I can't leave Rhoda."*

We must conclude that Rhoda's account of the situation to the therapist is not manufactured for the occasion of the therapeutic interview; on the contrary, it is woven out of materials that seem to have been consistently used in family interaction.

The Justification

4.17. Rhoda's account now takes a curious turn: instead of continuing her account of how she handled the situation with her mother, she begins to explain that it really wasn't her mother's fault.

4.17	TEXT	CUES

R.: ⟨_N_ *I-it's, not that—it happened that.... the way things turned* **out**, *like, she wasn't prepared—it was unexpected,* ⟩_N_   Tension: self-interruption, incoherence.

EXPANSION

R.: ⟨_N_ The only problem now that makes this case different is that she stayed long, but this wasn't a matter of her choice or mine, it was {X} unexpected circumstance and demands for which she wasn't prepared. ⟩_N_

INTERACTION

R. defends her mother's behavior in taking up role obligations at her sister's house, thereby asserting indirectly that ⟨ RSNBL-MO ⟩ her mother is a reasonable person, thereby ⟨ ~?HEAD-MO ⟩ retreating from her challenge to her mother's competence.

---

274 EPISODE FOUR

> 4.17 R.: *I-it's, not that—it happened that.... the way things turned **out**, like, she wasn't prepared—it was unexpected,*

There is a great deal of tension in the delivery of 4.17, with self-interruptions indicating that Rhoda is not quite sure of her position. She is engaged in a retreat, abandoning the challenge to her mother that she planned to take in 1.7: *Look y'been there long enough!*

4.18 Rhoda now moves backwards in time to give an account of events that occurred before 4.5–4.11. The short narrative that she adds is an account of the negotiations between her mother and her sister, which show that her mother actually refused an earlier request (and therefore did take Rhoda's welfare into account).

> 4.18[a] R.: *like she didn't expect to be going.*
> [b] *My sister said she wanted to go to work, and my mother said, "**Well, yeh**, next week... uh—I don't feel like going this week."*

Rhoda follows a usual mode of narrative argument to make her point, using the Rule of Narrative Response, and gives us a clearer view of interaction between her mother and her sister than we had before. The

---

4.18	TEXT	CUES
[a] R.: ⟨_N_ *like she didn' expect to be going.*		Mitigation: we̊ll, yeh̊, 'reluctant acknowledgment'.
[b] *My sister said she wanted to go to work, and my mother said,* ⟨_F_ *"**Well, yeh**, next week... uh—I don't feel like going this week."* ⟩_F_ ⟩_N_		

EXPANSION
R.: ⟨_N_ As a matter of fact, my mother didn't expect to go to my sister's house at all this week. My sister had said that she wanted to work this week, and so she wanted my mother to come to her house to take care of her daughter. And my mother answered her, ⟨_F_ "See what your need is, and I don't want to refuse it, but I won't come because I don't feel like going this week." ⟩_F_ ⟩_N_

INTERACTION
R. gives a narrative to support her justification of her mother's behavior. R.'s sister states the need for help at her house, thereby ‾10‾⟩ requesting Rhoda's mother to help; Rhoda's mother suggests another time for help, and puts off the request ⟨‾~10‾ .

parallels between this exchange and the conversation of Episode 1 are striking. In each case, a daughter is asking her mother to do something. This is the last of a series of local propositions that connect the various episodes of this interview:

{4}   Rhoda asks her mother to come home.
{6}   Rhoda requests Aunt Editha to help.
{9}   Rhoda asks Editha to go to the store.
{10} Rhoda's sister asks Rhoda's mother to take care of her children.

The interaction between Rhoda's sister and her mother is shown as quite different from that reported between Rhoda and her mother or between Rhoda and her aunt. The separation of the two households has apparently established some kind of equality between mother and married daughter. Rhoda's mother is the head of Household 1 and her sister is (perhaps) the head of Household 2, so neither is in a position to make demands on the other by means of an unmitigated request for action. We are witnessing negotiations in which the sister cannot make a request too insistently and the mother cannot refuse too definitely. It would be an overstatement, however, to say that these two parties are on an equal plane.

We must bear in mind that our view of this interaction is extremely indirect. Rhoda apparently heard about the conversation from her mother, and now she is giving her version of her mother's report to the therapist. But we can see that Rhoda's sister makes the request {10} indirectly, by using a mitigating form of the Rule of Requests—she refers to the need, which is one of the four preconditions. Her mother is quoted as giving a very indirect refusal, typical of the verbal style Rhoda has attributed to her mother throughout.

The first words of her mother's reply are *well, yeh* with a low falling intonation. This is superficially an agreement to do what her daughter has asked, but then her mother proceeds to add *next week*. Rhoda's mother then names another time, so that her action is seen as putting off the request rather than refusing it.

It becomes increasingly evident that there are very many ways in which a person can put off a request. The method employed here is to suggest a different time to carry it out. If the person makes the original request for a time T_0—right now—the second time suggested can be remote enough that something else may very well occur in the meantime that will make it possible to put off the request again.

We could, of course, interpret 4.18 as a neutral account of her mother's feelings at the moment, without reference to her obligations to Rhoda or Rhoda's sister; but that would make it a pointless narrative. Rhoda is engaged in showing that her mother was not willing to undertake the action that eventually caused Rhoda's problem.

4.19. The next step in the negotiations shows Rhoda's sister using a common tactic: Rhoda's sister suggests a time T_2, which is closer to T_0:

4.19[a] R.: *So my sister s'd, "Well, maybe the end of the week."*
  [b] *She s'z, "**Well, maybe**,"*
  [c] *And everything's—um—s—ah—was unexpected.*

Rhoda uses the same paralinguistic cues in 4.19[b] to indicate that her mother was reluctant to go. The low falling intonation on *well, maybe* can be read as a reluctant concession, at best.

There is no difficulty in expanding the elliptical remarks of 4.19[a], [b], once we have set up for 4.18 the underlying request for action {10}. Thus 4.19[a] is expanded as "Maybe you can come to my house at the end of the week." However, 4.19[c] is more difficult. Something was not expected: who didn't expect what? We must first provide the deleted subject of *expect* and then expand *everything*. This is not exactly the same *everything* that we found in 4.9[a], but refers instead to the series of events of 4.5–4.11 and links this short narrative to the longer narrative that began this episode. We can expand 4.19[c] as, "My mother didn't expect all the events that led to her having to go to my sister's house this week." Behind this justification there lie other general social propositions, which we have not expanded here.

Serious accidents like the one that happened to Rhoda's sister's mother-in-law are unexpected, and the obligations they bring about cannot be put off by ordinary excuses. Rhoda's mother is not responsible for this accident, and her response to it was out of her control. The further interactive implications of this justification indicate that Rhoda was agreeing with her mother in the excuse that she gave for not coming home immediately:

1.11 R.: *"Why don't you tell **Phyllis** that?"*

If her mother's answer to Rhoda's request was reasonable, then Rhoda's failure to get her mother to come home was not due to Rhoda's own lack of ability to negotiate. It follows that Rhoda did all that she could and actually "did the right thing" when she called up her mother to make the original request.*

The interactional statement for 4.19 shows one of the most elaborate chains of "thereby" connections used so far. There are many links in this chain, and we cannot say that each of them holds with equal firmness. Still, these connections are made many times throughout the session, as Rhoda returns again and again to her basic argument: that external circum-

---

*It was noted above that the power relations between Rhoda's mother and sister are balanced more evenly than the other dyads involved here. We would expect a difference in verbal style and emotional tension, and Rhoda's accounts show such a difference. This may lead us to put more faith in the way in which Rhoda's narratives reflect the family situation. If the tension in the narratives of Episodes 1, 2, and 3 were due entirely to Rhoda's subjective coloration in the interview situation, we would expect the same verbal style in Episode 4.

THE JUSTIFICATION   277

| 4.19 | TEXT | CUES |

[a] R.: ⟨_N_ So my sister s'd, ⟨_F_ "Well, maybe the end of the week." ⟩_F_
[b] She s'z, ⟨_F_ **"Well maybe,"** ⟩_F_   Mitigation: 3 2 1, 'reluctant concession
[c] And everything's—um—s—ah—was   of possibility'.
unexpected. ⟩_N_

EXPANSION

[a] R.: ⟨_N_ Then my sister said to my mother, "If you can't come now, maybe {10} you can come to my house at the end of the week."
[b] My mother then answered, "Since you're asking me again, it is possible I will come, because I do not want to refuse you, but I'm not promising to come."
[c] And in spite of the fact that my mother had refused twice to go to my sister's house this week, she did have to go because she didn't expect all the events (4.5–4.11) that led to her having to go to my sister's house this week. {X} Everything that did lead to her going to my sister's house was unexpected and she wasn't able to refuse as she had done before. ⟩_N_

INTERACTION

[a] R.'s sister suggests a time T_3 replacing T_2, thereby ⟨ 10 ⟩ reinstating the request again in mitigated form.
[b] Mother does not agree to time T_2, thereby ⟨ ~10 ⟩ putting off sister's request again.
[c] R. asserts ⟨ X ⟩ that her mother's taking up role obligations in Household 2 was beyond her mother's control, thereby asserting that her mother could not have come back to Household 1 of her own free will, thereby asserting ⟨ RSNBL-Mo ⟩ that mother's answer to her own request was reasonable, thereby asserting that her failure to get her mother's help was not due to her own inability, thereby asserting ⟨ 1 ⟩ that she actually did the right thing.

---

stances are to blame for her predicament, that she did the right thing in calling up her mother, and that she has understood and applied the basic suggestion of therapy.

The therapist is not convinced that Rhoda has gained the ability to communicate her needs to others, or to understand the nature of her own emotions. In the next episode, she makes a decision to move into a completely different sphere of interaction, away from the evaluation of social norms and everyday life into the deeper levels of psychological interpretations. In so doing, she will meet with an extraordinary resistance from the patient. The therapist expects this resistance, and her decision to make the move is not taken lightly. But it must be made: the therapist is convinced that the fundamental problems have yet to be faced.

EPISODE FIVE
So there's a lot of anger passing back and forth.

Although Episode 5 follows directly after the last utterance quoted in Episode 4, it has a very different character from anything that has preceded. It begins with a decision by the therapist to turn the discussion into new channels, to begin a new way of speaking about Rhoda's problems, and to take up new subject matter. We have been listening to discussion of what was done, what was said, whether so-and-so can help, or what would happen if you asked X for help. Now we will be listening to a discussion of what people have done to each other and what they feel towards each other.

Episode 5 moves into a sphere that is properly psychological, rather than sociological; the therapist will deal with emotions and responses to emotions, rather than with rights, duties, and obligations. The informally assumed knowledge of social relations will now give way to a fairly explicit understanding of the therapist's competence in dealing with unexpressed emotions. Furthermore, the discussion will show a new kind of complexity in that the therapist will make comparisons between past and future actions of a number of the parties concerned. The complexity of Episodes 1–4 lay in the network of personal obligations and events connecting the people concerned; now we will be dealing with internal actions and reactions and the consequences of these actions upon inner states.

Therapists themselves frequently describe their aims as "trying to put people in touch with their feelings." It is a fundamental postulate of therapy that patients have emotions that influence their behavior, but that are not available for their conscious inspection. In the course of Episodes 1–4, we have been looking over the therapist's shoulder at the various contradictions, incoherencies, and hesitations of the patient. We have seen that the patient's claim to independence and her claim to an understanding

280 EPISODE FIVE

of the basic therapeutic message is not brought out in the events that actually occurred, even if we accept her version at face value. The therapist is alert to these contradictions, although she has not been able to analyze them in great detail, nor to juxtapose the various sections of the interview as we have done here. She has followed Rhoda's exposition through 25 sessions, and has seen the same pattern recur.

The therapist's own actions show that she is sensitive to the small details of behavior that we have been examining. We have seen her avoid direct suggestions and resist the temptation to plunge immediately into the emotional center of the problem. She has been sparing in her interpretations in the first four episodes: her interventions have occurred only at points where she felt an immediate need for clarity. All the therapists who reviewed their work with Fanshel insisted that the patient's exposition should be allowed to flow freely with as little interruption as possible. In Rhoda's case, the therapist is particularly anxious to avoid reinforcing a "harsh superego," which is the product of her past relationship with her mother.

Nevertheless, the therapist now finds it imperative to enter into an emotionally charged area and deal with the question that has aggravated the relations between Rhoda and her family for so long: she raises the issue of Rhoda's weight and her failure to eat, the basic symptom of anorexia nervosa. In the confrontation that follows, we obtain our most direct view of the therapist trying to realize the goals of her therapeutic orientation. We will also witness the most direct resistance of the patient to the basic suggestion and orientation of therapy.

Episode 5 should thus illuminate the question put by many observers: why does therapy take so long? This is the 25th session that Rhoda has spent with the therapist. A commonsense view of the matter might be that it should be sufficient for the therapist to discuss Rhoda's case with her, assemble the facts, and organize them to give Rhoda insight that will guide her future behavior. Therapy does not work this way, and it is not at all obvious why. Episode 5 will give us some understanding of why it is a long and difficult process, and why therapy is such hard work for the therapist.

The Therapist's Intervention

5.1.   At the end of Episode 4, the therapist obtained the full account of why Rhoda's mother stayed away from home. In 5.1, she acknowledges Rhoda's defense of her mother only indirectly—beginning her interpretation with a comment about what *they* are doing.

>   5.1   Th.: (breath) *Well what they are really doing to you is so similar to what . . apparently this goes on in the family—to what you did with them aroun-nd the dieting.*

THE THERAPIST'S INTERVENTION   281

The therapist provides a number of paralinguistic cues that demonstrate her awareness that she is about to take an important and difficult step. There is a sharp intake of breath before she begins. We observe a prolonged hesitation in the midst of the word *aroun-nd,* just before the most heavily loaded term, *dieting;* but the most marked paralinguistic cue is a continued high pitch on *really doing.* This use of *really* refers to the familiar stratification of behavior into overt, superficial description and covert or underlying interpretations involving deep-seated emotions. This deeper interpretation is built on two other interpretations and so represents a very sophisticated analysis of the situation.*

On the surface, Rhoda's mother and sister simply are carrying out their obligations, as older members of the household, to look after a younger member who is not able to take care of herself. However, the therapist's propositions argue that what they are *really doing* is responding emotionally to Rhoda's behavior in the characteristic family pattern. She does not identify the pattern, but draws a parallel between two exemplifications of it. In our contextual expansion, the therapist is seen as stating that two actions were essentially the same with the participants reversed. We can express this parallelism as the first local proposition of this episode:

{11} Rhoda's family overreacted to her claim of independence in the same way that she overreacted to their claim that she ate too much.

This proposition is still stated in a relatively superficial form and does not reflect the full psychodynamics that the therapist intends to bring out. Like many complex interpretations, proposition {11} establishes an analogy: it presents the therapist's analysis of the etiology of the anorexia.

$$\frac{\text{R}\rightarrow\text{FAM ''I am independent.''}}{\text{FAM}\rightarrow\text{R [Withholds all help.]}} = \frac{\text{FAM}\rightarrow\text{R ''You eat too much.''}}{\text{R}\rightarrow\text{FAM [Stops eating altogether.]}}$$

In these episodes and elsewhere, the therapist has obtained a good view of how Rhoda's mother controls her daughter by giving or withholding help. Rhoda's assertion that she is independent is of course the proposition {AD-R} that she has expressed many times in the interview: *I can get along without my mother* (1.5 [a]). Her mother's response to this assertion has been to go away for a long time and not give Rhoda any help at all. The therapist sees this overreaction as parallel to Rhoda's behavior in an earlier situation when she was overweight. In response to her family's suggestion that she eat less, Rhoda stopped eating almost entirely, and her weight

---

*Since the pronoun *they* includes both Rhoda's sister and her mother, it avoids any conflict with Rhoda's interpretation that her sister, and not her mother, is to blame.

| 5.1 | TEXT | CUES |

Th.: ⟨_IV_ (breath) *Well what they are really doing to you is so similar to what . . apparently this goes on in the family—to what you did with them aroun-nd the dieting.* ⟩_IV_

Contrast: rea̋lly doi̋ng, high pitch without fading.
Tension: (breath); hesitation on aroun-nd.

EXPANSION

Th.: ⟨_IV_ In view of what you have told me, {11} what your mother and your sister are doing to you in giving you *no* help when you say you don't need *much* help, is similar to what you did to them in not eating *at all* when they said you should eat *less;* apparently this way of opposing a suggestion is the way you generally behave in your family. ⟩_IV_

INTERACTION

Th. redirects conversation to the topic of ⟨ ~EAT Rhoda's low weight, and gives interpretation of R.'s family behavior by asserting that 11 ⟩ their action in not supporting at home is equivalent to R.'s action in not eating, indirectly challenges ⟨ ~~EAT ⟩ R.'s denial of the claim that she is subnormal in her eating habits.

---

dropped to 70 pounds. For the therapist and anyone else who sees Rhoda, this is a fact. But Rhoda denies this fact and presents it as a claim that her family is making about her. It must therefore be presented as a proposition to be asserted or denied:

{~EAT-R}   Rhoda does not eat enough to stay healthy.*

The family interaction is more than an exchange of assertions. We are observing a struggle in which one side withholds normal role performance until the other side is forced to make a damaging admission. When Rhoda stopped eating, she forced her family to reverse their position and ask her to eat more rather than less. From her point of view, it follows that they were wrong when they asked her to eat less. Unless they can show that Rhoda is now subnormal in her pattern of eating, it would follow that they are not capable of deciding what is best for Rhoda, since they gave her bad advice at the outset. Thus in both cases, a person can use nonverbal behavior to extract some verbal response from others, which can be interpreted as an admission that those others were wrong.

*Since predicate {EAT} is applied only to Rhoda's performance, we will abbreviate the proposition as {~EAT}.

In bringing out this parallel, the therapist is operating on a tacit principle that it is always easier for a person to see unreasonable and aggressive behavior on the part of others towards himself than to see the same pattern when he is the actor. The therapist wants to take advantage of the family's action towards Rhoda to help her recognize the nature of her own actions towards them. Rhoda refuses to see the point. Throughout the first four episodes, Rhoda has presented herself as a reasonable, matter-of-fact person, ignoring the overemotional reactions that she displays towards her sister and Editha; but she has not yet learned how to use this rationalizing style in talking about her emotions.*

The interactive statement for 5.1 must begin with the therapist's action in redirecting the conversation. When we contrast her behavior here with the oscillation and self-interruptions that begin Episodes 2 and 3, it is evident that she has come to a decision. She firmly moves the conversation to the topic with the heaviest emotional load: Rhoda's eating. At a higher level, this action is a kind of confrontation, which challenges Rhoda to examine her own behavior.

When the therapist says, *what you did with them,* she is confronting Rhoda with an analysis of her behavior that has not been brought up before in this session. This analysis assumes that Rhoda *did* something in regard to dieting, and therefore it challenges implicitly her position that she didn't do anything: that is {~~EAT}, it is not true that she stopped eating.

This is a surprising move, and it occupies a crucial position in that portion of the therpay we are reviewing. If we are to answer the basic question, "What is the therapist doing in therapy?" we must keep this decision in mind throughout our study of Episode 5. As far as Rhoda is concerned, it is a shocking move in the literal sense of the word. How is Rhoda to cope with the challenges implicit in this new material, and how is she to relate this to the position she has been taking?

5.2. Rhoda does not answer at all. She does not speak, and therefore does not respond to the therapist's assertion {11} or the therapist's implied criticism of her eating habits.

5.3. The therapist waits 4 seconds before continuing. She then expands on the problem of Rhoda's weight, summing up the history of the situation by relating two propositions.

5.3 Th.: *Y'know, when—when they said you shouldn't be eating so much, you stopped eating entirely.*

---

*In our study of other therapeutic series, we find many patients who have learned to use the same rationalizing, nonemotional style in regard to their own emotions. Rhoda is relatively immature in her grasp of interview style.

284   EPISODE FIVE

5.2   TEXT   CUES
R.: .... [4 sec.]   Reservation: a total repression of
                                     speech.

INTERACTION

R. does not accept her turn to speak, and does not respond to the therapist's assertion ⟨‾11‾ and challenges ⟨‾~EAT‾ , thereby refusing support to the therapist's interpretation.

The two propositions are symmetrical in form, but one is the general proposition {~EAT} and the other is a local fact mentioned in this episode:

{12}   Rhoda's family complained that she ate too much.

This complaint embodies another proposition, that at one time Rhoda did eat too much. In this session, Rhoda does not take issue with this claim, though we have suggested that her anorexia was originally a way of disputing it. At this point all her attention is devoted to contradicting {~EAT}. The therapist's statement is a temporal juxtaposition of {12} with {~EAT}. This implies that there is a close connection between the two: that {~EAT} was a response to {12}.*

The interactional statement shows a hierarchical organization of some depth.

Rhoda's silence presents the therapist with a new problem of interpretation. In terms of the mode of argument, nothing is more indirect than silence. A total lack of response is subject to many interpretations: that Rhoda did not want to answer, did not know how to answer, was not ready to answer, or could not decide between two possible answers. Anything that the therapist says will select among these.

The new statement that the therapist puts forward acts as a clarification: it is a more explicit interpretation of what was said in 5.1. The implication is that Rhoda did not answer because she did not know how: she did not understand 5.1. The new material also contains a more explicit endorsement of {~EAT-R}. This has to provoke some response from Rhoda, because it is closely linked with several other propositions that challenge

---

*There is a striking parallel to the Rule of Narrative Sequencing (Chapter 3, p. 107), which establishes temporal ordering through juxtaposition. We might put forward a Rule of Juxtaposition: If A states that event X was followed immediately by event Y, he is heard as asserting that X was a cause of Y. It is, of course, possible to describe a coincidence: that is, that the juxtaposition of X and Y was accidental. However, this appears to be the "marked" case, which needs special mention, as in "when they said you shouldn't be eating so much, you *just happened to* stop eating entirely."

5.3		TEXT	CUES

Th.: ⟨_IV_ Y'know, when—when they said you shouldn't be eating so much, you stopped eating en**tire**ly. ⟩_IV_   Contrastive stress: en**tire**ly.

EXPANSION

Th.: ⟨_IV_ Even though you don't answer, you know that what I mean is that when your family said {12} you shouldn't be eating as much as you did then, {~EAT} you stopped eating entirely. ⟩_IV_

INTERACTION

Th. responds to Rhoda's silence by giving a more explicit interpretation of 5.1, thereby giving the interpretation that Rhoda's silence was due to her lack of understanding of 5.1: when R.'s family criticized her ⟨ 12 for eating too much, she responded by eating too little; the therapist thereby asserts ⟨ ~EAT that Rhoda is not normal in her eating, and thereby asserts indirectly that ~S-CARE-R ⟩ Rhoda fails to take care of herself and thereby asserts that ~AD-R ⟩ Rhoda is not behaving like an adult.

Rhoda's status as a competent adult and a reasonable person. The link is through the general proposition:

{S-CARE}   A person has an obligation to take care of himself

If Rhoda has not been eating enough to stay healthy, she clearly is failing to observe this general obligation, and therefore {~AD-R} she is not behaving like an adult. The linkage between {~EAT-R}, {~S-CARE-R}, and {~AD-R} applies throughout this Episode and need not be repeated explicitly in each interactional statement.

5.4. At first glance, it seems that Rhoda has ignored the therapist's explanation, since she begins to talk about the *other* half of proposition {11}, her independence from her mother

5.4[a]   R.: *Well, when I said I could get along without my mother, x x x*
   [b]   Th.: *So she—she's making you get along entirely, without her . . .*

The prosodic cues that Rhoda gives us in 5.4 are something quite different from anything we have heard before. She talks in a low mumble, with very lax articulation, to which we give the general caption of "reservation."*

---

*The most complete reservation or repression of speech is silence, and so we have entered the label in the *cues* section of 5.2.

286 EPISODE FIVE

5.4	TEXT	CUES

[a] R.: ⟨_EV_ Well, when I said I could get along without my mother, x x x ⟩_EV_   Reservation: low volume, monotone intonation.
[b] Th.: ⟨_IV_ The other—she—she's making you get along entirely, without her... ⟩_IV_   Tension: strident overlap.

EXPANSION
[a] R.: ⟨_EV_ Well, granted what you say, when I said {AD-R} I could get along without my mother, I— ⟩_EV_
[b] Th.: ⟨_IV_ Your mother is making you get along without her to an abnormal extent {?HEAD-MO} almost entirely. ⟩_IV_

INTERACTION
[a] R. begins to give information to support her assertion ⟨ AD-R that she can get along without her mother, thereby putting off the therapist's challenge. ⟨ ~AD-R .
[b] Th. interrupts with strident overlap, giving interpretation of {12} that when R. asserted {AD-R} she could get along without her mother, her mother overreacted by ⟨ ?HEAD-MO neglecting her primary obligation to support her.

We cannot be sure what argument Rhoda was about to bring forward, since the therapist interrupts her stridently in 5.4[b]. One possibility is that Rhoda was denying the parallelism, pointing out that she had not criticized her mother by saying that she could get along without her, while they had criticized her by saying that she ate too much. Another possibility is that she was turning away from the parallel, emphasizing again that her family was unreasonable. When she said she could get along without her mother, she didn't mean that her mother should go away and leave her to do all the work.

The therapist's overlap completes Rhoda's sentence for her. Rhoda begins in the style of everyday speech, and the therapist finishes in the style of the interview situation, but as the expansion shows, the contents fit together quite well. 5.4[a] is interpreted as the first part of the analogical proposition {11}, and the therapist provides the second part. We can also connect the two interactive statements. Rhoda seems to be turning away from the implications of the therapist's challenge to her adult status, and the therapist, by completing the proposition, goes further along that direction. She has thus expanded all four parts of {11}: the first half in 5.4 and the second half in 5.3. Despite the tension shown in the overlap, the therapist does attempt to achieve some kind of mutuality, perhaps taking advantage of the fact that she and Rhoda have apparently cooperated in expounding this complex proposition. The therapist's next remark is an attempt to capitalize on this mutuality, but it is clear from her hesitancy and mitigating forms that she is aware that she is on shaky ground and that Rhoda has not accepted the interpretation put forward.

5.5 After the therapist finishes her interpretation of the pattern of family interaction, she adds the meta-comment of 5.5[a].

> 5.5[a]   Th.: *An-nd—uh—mayb—y'know—maybe some of this has to be discussed together. Actually it—uh—usually* . . .

There are many ways in which this comment may be understood, depending upon the meaning of *together*. That is, it is possible to read it as meaning Rhoda and the therapist together, Rhoda and her family together, or the two kinds of interaction together. All of these come back to a variant of the basic suggestion of therapy: that participants in interaction can solve their problems by talking together and gaining overt knowledge of their needs and emotions.

The therapist speaks quite tentatively, with a number of pauses and mitigating forms. If we are correct in thinking that she means that Rhoda should discuss with her family the way they behave towards each other, it is a bold extension of the basic therapy. Would they have the competence to make things plainer to each other at the end of such a conversation? The therapist seems to imply that if they did so, they could recognize the truth of her insight in 5.3: that there is a strong parallelism in the way family members deal with each other. She is thus making a further suggestion to Rhoda as to what she might do, and the mitigating forms that she uses are typical of such suggestions. The therapist does not leave the matter at this point; she continues at length, drawing again from her sociological competence to provide Rhoda with arguments to justify her position.

> 5.5[b]   Th.: *Students, who go to college away from the home,* **don't** *attempt to keep house. They either live in a dormitory where most things are done for them, and they, y'know, eat together in a—uh—dining hall, or they live in a sorority house where some of the housekeeping is done for them, and meals are served. It isn't* **contemplated** *that you would carry a* ***whole*** *house, and go to school at the same time* . . .

The therapist expresses these social norms in the language of everyday life. Furthermore, her style is quite impersonal. She refers to the general class of *students* rather than talking about Rhoda personally. The generality and impersonality of her statement is reinforced by the expression "It isn't contemplated..." rather than the more direct "I don't think." This long discussion can be summed up in a single proposition:

> {STUD}   The primary responsibility of a student is to study.

288   EPISODE FIVE

5.5   TEXT   CUES
[a] Th.: ⟨_IV_ *An-nd—uh—mayb—*   Tension: filled pauses, rapid speech.
y'know—maybe some of this has to be Mitigation: *maybe, some of this.*
discussed together. Actually it—uh
—usually ⟩_IV_

EXPANSION

Th.: ⟨_IV_ Maybe some of these different points of view have to be discussed by you and your family together {S} so that you can understand the basic pattern of what is really going on when you deal with each other. ⟩_IV_

INTERACTION

Th. asserts indirectly, in mitigated form, that family members talk together about their mode of interaction ⟨‾S‾], thereby giving support to her assertion in 5.3.

            TEXT   CUES
[b] Th.: ⟨_EV_ *Students, who go to college*
away from the home, ***don't*** *attempt to*
keep house. They either live in a dormitory
where most things are done for them, and
they, y'know, eat together in
a—uh—dining hall, or they live in a
sorority house where some of the
housekeeping is done for them, and meals
are served. It ***isn't*** *contemplated that you*
would carry a whole house and go to
school at the same time . . . ⟩_EV_

EXPANSION

Th.: ⟨_EV_ You should tell your family that {S} you have a right to ask for help because {X:STRN} you have too much to do: students who go to college away from home aren't expected to keep house. Their housekeeping is done for them, and {STUD} it isn't expected that a student would take care of a whole house and go to school at the same time. ⟩_EV_

INTERACTION

Th. gives orientation by asserting the social norm that ‾STUD‾⟩ school obligations are primary and thereby supporting R.'s assertion ⟨‾X:STRN‾ that external circumstances were responsible for her problem, and that {1} she did the right thing in asking her mother for help.

The interactional statement of 5.5[b] shows three steps in the chain of argument:

{STUD}→{X:STRN}→{1}

By asserting that Rhoda's primary obligations are to school, she supports the defense Rhoda made to her mother's challenge in 1.10 and 4.14 and therefore supports Rhoda's basic claim to have done the right thing. The therapist has used her informal sociological expertise to take Rhoda's side against her family: whereas they have indicated in various ways that she is not strong enough to be a student, the therapist treats Rhoda as a normal person with normal rights and claims upon her role partners. One can recognize this tactic of the therapist as part of a continual pattern of circling about the issue, advancing and retreating in response to Rhoda's reactions. Her eventual task is to bring Rhoda to the point where she can recognize some of her own emotions, and this will require a certain solidarity between therapist and patient. Whenever the work the therapist has done leads to a breach in this relationship, she feels impelled to repair that breach and recreate the mutuality that preceded it. She thus turns to the use of social judgments to support Rhoda's claim that external circumstances are responsbile for her problem.

5.6. The effect of this support is that Rhoda begins to talk volubly. After a short pause, she issues a strong complaint against the way her family interprets the situation. She does this in the form of a pseudo-narrative, using the general present tense, in which she repeats the kinds of conversations that have revolved about her. Again, we see that her main criticism is directed against her sister rather than her mother.

5.6 R.: . . .x. . *it seems to my sister that this is*—"*Oh, nothing's* **wrong** *with her,*" *she s'ys t'm'mother,* "*Everything's fine.*"

Rhoda's account is very fluent; the most striking paralinguistic cue is the nasal whine that she uses to signal complaints.

There are several problems in expanding 5.6. First of all, Rhoda does not orient her narratives in time or place, so we must do this for ourselves. We infer that these discussions take place when Rhoda's mother is at Rhoda's sister's house, in response to an earlier request from Rhoda that her mother come home. It is not likely that Rhoda heard this directly and is giving her mother's report, but we should not rule out the possibility that such discussions have taken place in front of Rhoda.* Secondly, we have the prob-

---

*If this is the case, we see that Rhoda's mother and sister would have been talking about Rhoda in the third person in her presence. This is a common tactic that adults use when discussing the problems of children, whom they consider incapable of taking care of themselves.

lem of expanding the pronoun *this* and then completing the sentence that Rhoda breaks off and never finishes herself. It would seem that *this* refers to the predicament we have been discussing—Rhoda's being left alone to run the house and go to school at the same time. The rest of the quotation shows that her sister is saying that this situation is no problem, and we have expanded the statement accordingly.

What kind of action is Rhoda performing in 5.6? On a superficial level, she is initiating a pseudo-narrative, and the Rule of Narrative Response (Chapter 3, p. 109) leads us to believe that the point of this narrative will be a response to the position the therapist advances in 5.5. Our expansion suggests that the position that Rhoda will be putting forward by means of her narrative will show the other side of the situation: "You see it this way, but they don't." Until the narrative is finished, we must suspend judgment on its full interactional meaning.

A debate about one of the preconditions that would make Rhoda's phone call a valid request occurs in 5.6. Does she need help or doesn't she? On the face of it, Rhoda's sister seems to be supporting her by saying that everything is fine. Rhoda herself has said at many points that there is nothing wrong with her. Are we discussing Rhoda's fundamental capacity or the particular situation she finds herself in at the moment? The rest of the pseudo-narrative shows the complexity of Rhoda's position: what

---

5.6   TEXT   CUES
R.: ⟨$_{EV}$ ... x .. *it seems to my sister that   Tension release: rapid and fluent
is*— ⟨$_F$ "Oh, *nothing's wrong with her*,"   speech.
she s'ys t'm'mother, "*Everything's*   Derogation: nasal whine, 'complaint'.
fine." ⟩$_F$ ⟩$_{EV}$

EXPANSION
R.: ⟨$_{EV}$ But even though you can see {X:STRN} that my mother's being away for so long creates a great strain for me, it seems to my sister that this situation is no problem at all. When my mother says that she has to come home to help me, my sister says to my mother, "You don't have to go home, because nothing's wrong with Rhoda. Everything is fine at your house." ⟩$_{EV}$

INTERACTION
R. initiates a pseudo-narrative of the conversations in her family that have influenced the outcome of her action in ⟨__4__ in asking her mother to come home:

    R.'s sister denies that ⟨__STRN__ Rhoda has a problem of role strain, thereby questioning the need ⟨__?4__ for Rhoda's mother to go home.

seems to be support is not support, and those that seem to be for her are really against her.

5.7. As Rhoda continues her pseudo-narrative, it seems that she may be talking about a particular event—perhaps a continuation of the same telephone conversation she has reported in Episodes 1 and 4. This cannot be decided easily, but we will see in 5.8 that she is talking about a recurrent situation, so we may not be dealing with any one conversation. In any case, we now see Rhoda's mother reporting her sister's comments to her.

> 5.7 R.: *My mother says—I says to my mother, "Yeh—everything's **fine**?" I s's, "Things **aren't** so fine." I said, "I'm getting tired."*

Rhoda continues her account fluently, though there is a problem with the uncompleted phrase *My mother says—* If her mother said anything else to her besides reporting her sister's comments, we will never know what that was, and we do not try to reconstruct it. The rest of the expansion is quite simple, because 5.7 repeats themes that we have already dealt with. The word *fine* recurs three times, with sarcastic emphasis. The request for confirmation, *everything's fine?* recalls the parallel requests of 2.8[b], ***That** looks*

5.7   TEXT   CUES
R.: ⟨_EV_ *My mother says—I says to my*   Aggravation: '*everything's fine*',
mother, ⟨_F_ *"Yeh—everything's **fine**?"I*   'incredulous'.
*s's, "Things **aren't** so fine." I said, "I'm*   Emphasis. *I says,* historical present.
getting tired." ⟩_F_ ⟩_EV_

EXPANSION
R.: ⟨_EV_ And when my mother told me what my sister had said, I said to my mother, ⟨_F_ "Am I right in thinking that she said that everything here is fine? She's wrong, the situation in our house isn't fine now that you've been away for so long. I'm getting tired because I have too much to do." ⟩_F_ ⟩_EV_

INTERACTION
Rhoda continues the narrative about her family's discussion of her problem: R.'s mother reports R.'s sister's assertion that there is no need for her to come home, thereby ⟨ ~4 ⟩ putting off again Rhoda's request that her mother come home. R. requests confirmation that her sister has asserted this, thereby asserting indirectly that ⟨ ~RSNBL-S ⟩ her sister is not reasonable. R. asserts that ⟨ STRN ⟩ she does feel strain, thereby asserting that there is a need for her mother to come home, thereby reinstating her original request ⟨ 4 ⟩, thereby carrying out the basic suggestion ⟨ S ⟩.

clean to you? and 3.23, *That's enough?*. It is a common tactic for Rhoda to ask for confirmation of an utterance that she believes is so unreasonable that it cannot be accepted at face value. All this shows the now familiar family style.

In the interactional implications of 5.7 we can also follow a recurrent line of argument: does Rhoda's mother *have* the ability to decide for herself? Perhaps Phyllis *is* the proper person to direct a request to, since she is the one who has been denying the need for Rhoda's mother to go home. Rhoda continues to argue that external circumstances are too much for her and that there is a real need for mother to come home.

Before we pass on to the main point of this pseudo-narrative, it is worthwhile observing the verbal maneuvers Rhoda's mother engages in. We have seen (at least in Rhoda's account) that she uses Rhoda's problem as an excuse for not taking up her obligations at Household 2. We don't know what she herself said in this reported conversation, but it seems that she did report a conversation to Rhoda. In doing so, she presented Rhoda's sister's position, disclaiming any responsibility for the decision herself. Rhoda then found herself arguing indirectly with her sister through the reports her mother gave her of what her sister had said.

5.8. As Rhoda continues her pseudo-narrative, she becomes literally incoherent.

5.8   R.: *I said, "E—but—y'see now, if—I-I wanna s—I-I told my mother this, and* [breath], *now if I wanna s-s-say, "I'm tired," then—I know just the answer I'm gonna get . . .*

The extraordinary number of self-interruptions are signals of considerable internal tension. Rhoda breaks off her references to two events that actually occurred, and sums up her situation by a general statement about what her mother is bound to say to her if she ever confessed {TIRE} that she felt tired.

In this indirect argument, Rhoda shows two ways of not saying what she means. First she interrupts herself, then she makes an oblique reference to the answer she will get without stating it explicitly. Our expansion fills in what "the answer" is, but only by looking ahead to 5.9; the interactive significance of 5.8 similarly depends upon what follows.

"Coming back to that": Eating

5.9. Everything that has been said up to this point reflects the presence of an unstated agenda on which one item always takes priority. This crucial item is Rhoda's weight, and the eating pattern that is connected with it.

In defending herself against the charges that she does not eat enough and take care of herself, Rhoda seems to make a good case. However, the reader must continually bear in mind that Rhoda is a good-sized girl, 5'5",

5.8   TEXT   CUES
R.: ⟨_IV_ I said, "E—but—y'see now, if—I-I   Tension: multiple self-interruption.
wanna s—I-I told my mother this, and
[breath], now, if I wanna s-s-say, "I'm
tired," then—I know just the answer I'm
gonna get... ⟩_IV_

EXPANSION

R.: ⟨_EV_ Whenever I have told my mother in the past that {TIRE} I was getting tired, she would always answer me that {~EAT} it was because I didn't eat, so I know that is what she will say now. ⟩_EV_

INTERACTION

R. gives the evaluative point of the pseudo-narrative by asserting that whenever she says TIRE she feels tired, her mother interprets this as ~EAT→STRN due to her not eating, and this unreasonable behavior on the part of others makes it difficult for her ?S to ask for help.

---

who stopped eating when she was about 140 pounds, and was hospitalized when her weight dropped to 70 pounds. She responded to drug therapy in the hospital, and at this point her weight has risen to 90 pounds. However, she has reached a plateau, and in talking to her the therapist is continuously faced with the visual evidence that the patient is dangerously thin. Her physical appearance contradicts her verbal testimony. Rhoda follows the pattern of other cases of anorexia* reported in the literature (Chapter 1) in claiming that she is in fact normal in her eating habits. She consistently argues that she has been doing everything she possibly can to gain weight and rejects any discussion that starts with the premise {~EAT} that she does not eat enough.

We also have here an explicit reference to arguments about proper standards. Eating is a classic case of behavior that has a threshold for initiation and a cutoff point for termination, and there is serious social concern about defining these points. In our own society, there is great concern about dieting—it is recognized that many people do not possess internalized controls for locating the cutoff point or being governed by a cut-off point already located. The opposite end of the spectrum—showing no ability to locate the threshold for initiating activity, is not a matter of equal concern. If Rhoda had continued overeating, her behavior would not have seemed

*Rhoda's insistent denial that she undereats is characteristic of the anorexia patient's behavior. "... All the physician's prescriptions and recommendations are frustrated by the patient's rejection. From the very first moment, objective judgments and considerations are overshadowed by the sheer conflict of the situation, and it is not long before the shadows are lengthened and obscure sense and reason" (Thomä, 1967).

294   EPISODE FIVE

5.9   TEXT   CUES
[a] ⎧ Th.: x x x   Tension: breath, hesitation.
[b] ⎩ R.: *That's right.*
[c] R.: ⟨$_{EV}$ *If*— [breath] *everything seems to come back—to* **that**, *and like*—..... *uhm*—⟨$_F$ *I* **don't** *eat, and I do eat.* ⟩$_F$ ⟩$_{EV}$

EXPANSION
[c] R.: ⟨$_{EV}$ All the discussions in my family about {STRN} my being tired or showing strain seem to come back to my eating habits. My mother and the others say that ⟨$_F$ {~EAT} I don't eat enough to stay healthy but as I tell them {EAT} I do eat enough to stay healthy. ⟩$_F$ ⟩$_{EV}$

INTERACTION
[c] R. asserts that her family asserts that $\overline{\text{STRN} \rightarrow \sim\text{EAT}}$ she gets tired because she doesn't eat enough, and asserts that $\overline{\text{EAT}}$ she does eat enough thereby denying this proposition.

---

so mysterious to her family. Society does not have available machinery or appropriate social explanations for someone who does not know when to begin eating. Rhoda's behavior seems wilfully wrong to her family—that she is not eating just to spite them. It seems unlikely that they would have the same feeling if she continued to overeat, because then her behavior would be understood as gratifying her own appetites and being unable to restrain them.

In response to Rhoda's oblique reference of 5.8, the therapist fills in with some reference to the charge about Rhoda's eating, but we have not been able to decipher this comment: It is entirely overlapped by Rhoda's agreement.

5.9[a] Th.: x x x
   [b] R.: *That's right.*
   [c] R.: ⟨$_F$ *If-*[breath] *everything seems to come back—to* **that**, *and like*—..... *uhm*—*I* **don't** *eat, and I do eat.* ⟩$_F$

This is a very tense utterance, with a long silence in the middle. It also shows a considerable amount of ellipsis, which we have restored in the expansion. The propositions being argued here are:*

---

*Again, it should be pointed out that these propositions appear in actual conversation in categorical form, without "enough to stay healthy." The full form shows the underlying link to {S-CARE} and {AD}.

{~EAT}   Rhoda doesn't eat enough to stay healthy.
{EAT}   Rhoda does eat enough to stay healthy.

It is not difficult to attribute the first of these statements to Rhoda's family and the second to her. The speech act is superficially a contradiction, but by expanding in the light of other discussion, it plainly appears as a denial.

5.10.   Rhoda now begins a long account of her position that her eating habits are normal, repeating herself over and over again. She is arguing her point simultaneously with her family and with the therapist. We cannot lose sight of the fact that in 5.3 the therapist endorsed the family's viewpoint, and even though the therapist now tries to mitigate this claim, Rhoda realizes that she has one more person to convince.

5.10[a]   R.: *But I don't eat be—their-their—uh—thing is that I don't eat—because—uh—I like the way I am, and that—I'm not tryin' to help myself,*
    [b]   R.: *But I eat! There's nothing I can do, look*
    [c]   R.: *I went away—I proved to them—I went away for a week. I didn't do anything. I* **laid** *around and* **ate***. An' I didn' gain any weight.*

This long argument involves a direct contradiction between Rhoda and her family. After some initial hesitation, she speaks quite fluently and uses many rhetorical devices to convey the impression of her own sincerity and reasonableness. At two points she exhibits the effect of tension by using an extra-high pitch, but in 5.10[c] she speaks slowly and forcibly, a prosodic style we have not observed in her speech before.

Here we see explicit evidence that the family's accusation goes deeper than the claim that Rhoda does not eat enough. She is also accused of being content with the way she is, and even preferring the kind of unreasonable behavior that forces others to worry about her. This is a violation of {S-CARE} (See p. 285 above). As we have noted before, there is a connection between this proposition and the claim to adult status: if someone does not take care of himself in a way that is appropriate to his age and status, he loses the claim to that status. Therefore {~S-CARE} implies {~AD}.

Rhoda has not proved anything about her own desires and personal controls on eating; the claim that she cannot help being thin means that some mysterious external circumstances are responsible. She has refuted the challenge to her claim to be an adult. She is not anxious to take advantage of the prerogatives of a sick person. Rhoda is far more concerned with avoiding the penalties of being sick and losing her claim to decide her own future.

This discussion of the central theme of therapy shows less indirection than anything we have seen before. The modes of expression, argument,

5.10   TEXT   CUES

[a] R.: ⟨$_F$ *But I don't eat be—their-their—uh—thing is that I don't eat—because—uh—I like the way I am, and that—I'm not tryin' to help myself,* ⟩$_F$ Tension: self-interruption.

[b] ⟨$_{EV}$ *But I eat! There's nothing I can do, look*   Tension: eát, dó, extra high pitch.

[c] *I went away—I proved to them—I went away for a week. I didn't do anything. I laid around and ate. An' I didn' gain any weight.* ⟩$_{EV}$

EXPANSION

[a] R.: ⟨$_F$ But my family claims that {~EAT} I don't eat enough, and that I don't eat enough because I like {THIN} being too thin, {TIRE} getting tired, and being a source of concern, and that {S-CARE} I am not trying to help myself be healthy as everyone should. ⟩$_F$

[b] ⟨$_{EV}$ But {~~EAT} they're wrong because I eat more than enough food, and {X→THIN} nothing I can do in the way of eating can affect my weight.

[c] I proved to my family that I'm right in my claim that my weight is not affected by the amount that I eat. I went away for a week. I didn't do any work. I laid around and ate. And I didn't gain any weight. ⟩$_{EV}$

INTERACTION

R. gives information on her family's challenge to herself ⟨ ~EAT and ⟨ ~S-CARE which challenge her status ⟨ ?AD-R and gives information to support her assertion ⟨ ~~EAT and ⟨ S-CARE, thereby challenging her family as being unreasonable ⟨ ~RSNBL-S,MO ⟩

---

and interaction are all quite direct, and we can see that this issue has been debated quite often in Rhoda's family. We also see a mode of argument that goes beyond verbal interaction—where disagreements are translated into actions. This is, in fact, the nature of Rhoda's neurosis. In anorexia, the patient argues by reacting with her own body, converting her anger into actions that injure her family, but also, unfortunately, injuring herself. When Rhoda denies that she is doing this, she is also arguing against the therapist's analogy of 5.1. Whereas the therapist would like to show her that there is some reciprocity involved, Rhoda would destroy half of the comparison. She argues that her family is unreasonable to her, but that there is nothing unreasonable in the way she has behaved. As long as Rhoda makes this claim, it is impossible for the therapist to use the agree-

"COMING BACK TO THAT": EATING   297

ment that they have achieved in discussing the justification of Episode 1—Rhoda's appeal for help—to achieve insight into Rhoda's own behavior.

5.11. In the midst of Rhoda's voluble exposition of her position on the eating question, the therapist interrupts to move the discussion out of the everyday framework to consider Rhoda's verbal behavior in the framework of the interview situation. The topic is no longer Rhoda's eating habits, but rather the way that she presents her position on those habits.

5.11[a] ⎧ R.: *And*—
    [b] ⎨ Th.: x *You also proved it to yourself.*
    [c] ⎧ R.: *Yes.*
    [d] ⎨ Th.: *Because you know, you have a lot of* —*they*
    [e] ⎩ R.:   *Yeh.*
    [f] ⎧ Th.: *They shake your . . . self-confidence.*
    [g] ⎨ R.:   *Yeh, I wonder sometimes, too . . .*

If we simply look at the text of 5.11, it seems that there is a great deal of overlap and competition for the floor, but the paralinguistic cues show that this is not the case. The therapist interrupts Rhoda, but there is only one word of overlap and no indication that Rhoda was about to continue. Rhoda's formal *yes* is pitched to low volume and indicates deference to the therapist's point of view. Lines [f] and [g] overlap, but, again, are pitched at a low volume, indicating that the two speakers are agreeing in completing the same thought.

Section 5.11 is an exercise in redirection. The therapist shows that she has not quite made up her mind as to her next move. In 5.11[d] she hesitates several times and trails off in 5.11[f]. From a structural point of view, this section plays the same role as the therapist's intervention of 2.2, where she considered various tactics before moving on to the substance of Episode 2. The issues of self-confidence and self-doubt that she raises might be elevated to the status of general propositions, but they do not play that role in this episode.

In 5.10, the therapist was faced with a vehement repetition of a position that is, on the face of it, unrealistic. Her basic strategy will be to bring the patient into closer touch with physical and emotional reality. Her tactic is to avoid direct confrontation with the contradictions in Rhoda's position; instead, she follows the tactic of supporting and agreeing with Rhoda. The therapist directs her disagreement to the effect of the situation upon Rhoda herself. In fact, she cannot contradict Rhoda directly, since in 5.10 Rhoda has made a strong case for herself based upon the incidents of everyday life (A-events) in which she is necessarily an expert. However the therapist, whose expertise lies in the area of interpreting emotions, is entitled to call

5.11   TEXT   CUES
[a] ⎧ R.: *And*—
[b] ⎨ Th.: ⟨_IV_ x *You **also** proved it to*   Th. interrupts.
yourself.
[c] ⎧ R.: *Yes.*   Reservation: formal *yes,* low volume,
[d] ⎨ Th.: *Because you know—you have*   non-strident overlap.
     a lot of—they   Tension: Self-interruption, hesitation.
[e] ⎩ R.:   *Yeh.*
[f] ⎧ Th.: *They shake your ... self-*
     confidence.
[g] ⎩ R.:   *Yeh, I won-*
... ⟩_IV   *der sometimes, too*

EXPANSION
Th.: ⟨_IV_ You also proved to yourself that {~~EAT} you know you are right
about your eating and you had to do this because you have a lot of uncertainty
about your position and your family shakes your confidence in yourself.
R.: Yes, you are right; I also wonder sometimes whether I'm right or not. ⟩_IV

INTERACTION
Th. redirects the discussion to R.'s emotions, asserting that Rhoda is uncertain of
the proposition she has just asserted ⟨ ?~~EAT .
R. agrees explicitly by expressing deference and uncertainty.

---

attention to the uncertainty in Rhoda's mode of expression. She makes some headway by blaming Rhoda's family for creating this lack of self-confidence in her. In discussing Rhoda's uncertainty, the therapist has moved into the outer margin of the essential discourse area: Rhoda's emotions. In 5.11[g], Rhoda recognizes for a moment her own feeling of uncertainty and even admits that there is something about her feelings that she does not understand—in sharp contrast with her confident explanations of her own behavior in 5.10. This is achieved through a fairly direct mode of argument about the nature of family interaction and its effect upon Rhoda's verbal behavior.

5.12. Rhoda continues the defense she began in 5.10, but it is not surprising to discover that she shows a great deal more hesitation than she did before. The discussion of her lack of self-confidence is now reflected overtly in her verbal style. Even more significant than the multiple stammering is the suppression of reference to her responsibility:

5.12 R.: *But there was seven—six days proof—that it can't be m—I-I-I mean—I ate **really**. I-I—ate. I know I did.*

THE CENTRAL QUESTION: RHODA'S WEIGHT

5.12 TEXT

R.: ⟨$_{EV}$ *But there was seven—six days proof—that it can't be m—I-I-I mean—I ate really. I-I—ate. I know I did.* ⟩$_{EV}$

CUES

Tension: self-interruption, suppression of *my fault*.

EXPANSION

R.: ⟨$_{EV}$ *But even though I am sometimes uncertain, the fact that I ate so much for six days and didn't gain any weight proves* X:THIN *that it can't be my fault that I don't gain weight.* {~~EAT} *I ate a lot in those six days.* ⟩$_{EV}$

INTERACTION

R. expresses uncertainty in asserting again ~~EAT that her eating habits are normal, thereby challenging again Th's assertion ?~EAT that she is not normal in her eating habits.

Our expansion of 5.12 completes the argument by explicit use of propositions that first appeared in 5.10:

{THIN}   Rhoda is too thin.
{X:THIN} External circumstances are responsible for Rhoda's being too thin.

Of all the propositions that might be disputed, {THIN} is the least likely. It is a matter of cold fact that Rhoda is too thin, but the responsibility for this fact can be disputed. In 5.12 she begins to argue that it cannot be her fault, that some stated circumstance is responsible for her being too thin. The interactional statement shows that she is, in effect, arguing the same case as 5.10, again challenging the therapist's assertion that she is not normal in her eating habits. However, the topic of her weight is coming closer to the surface, and her self-censorship indicates to the therapist that it might be time to press Rhoda once again to examine more basic issues. We have therefore indicated at the beginning of the interactional statement that the principal act of importance for the interaction is the display of uncertainty. Here is a case where the most significant aspect of the verbal exchange is not found in the expansion, but rather in the superficial paralinguistic cues that reflect the state of Rhoda's defenses.

The Central Question: Rhoda's Weight

5.13. The therapist takes a deep breath and launches a major effort to approach the central topic of the therapy:

5.13[a] Th.: (breath) *Yes, but* now *let's us—uh—see if we can separate out two things,*
    [b] Th.: *Does it have anything to do with ... your ... weight?*

The paralinguistic cues of 5.13 are parallel to those in 5.1 but much more striking. They give the clearest evidence of the basic therapeutic dilemma constraining all of the therapist's tactics in conversational interaction with Rhoda. She wants Rhoda to talk about her weight, and she knows that there will be profound resistance to that move. Even the mention of Rhoda's weight is apt to produce a shock, and the therapist uses many mitigating devices to reduce the impact of her inquiry. She approaches the question indirectly, using such vague reference as *two things,* which she does not expand. She continues with another vague reference, *it,* which is equally unclear. Then, as Figure 37 shows, her voice rises to an extra-high pitch while the volume falls to a very low level.* At the same time, the tempo slows, and she pauses for almost two seconds after *with* and pauses again after *your,* before presenting the loaded word *weight.*

In the expansion of 5.13, the analyst faces the same problem that the listener did: how to interpret these vague references. There is first of all a superficial sign of agreement which begins 5.13[a]: *Yes, but ...* Though rules of ellipsis expand this to indicate agreement with Rhoda's position on {~~EAT}, *yes, but ...* is a recognized social convention that illustrates the most marginal concession to the other person's point of view. The problem is complicated by the fact that there is actually no connection between 5.13[a] and [b]; rather, this represents another case where the therapist begins with one approach and changes midstream to another (see 2.2). The same expression—*two things*—recurs in 5.14[b]. A mechanical approach to interpretation might assign them the same referents; but the *two things* of 5.14[b] are Rhoda's school work and her responsibilities at home, which certainly did not require careful examination to be separated. The clue to the expansion of 5.13 is to be found even later on, in 5.17:

... Let's see if we can separate the things that people say from {E} the feelings that lie behind what they say.

This distinction is incorporated in our expansion of 5.13[a], without any claim that this full expansion was available to Rhoda at the time.

The issue is effectively postponed as the therapist continues with 5.13[b], where we have another vague reference to *it.*† We might be no more successful than Rhoda in expanding this if it were not for the fact that the therapist gives us the answer in 5.14[b]. The reference is to the general

---

*Normally, high pitch goes with increase in volume, so that the overall effect of English "stress" depends upon pitch even more than upon volume (Fry, 1955). Therefore an utterance that simultaneously rises in pitch and falls in volume is heavily marked.

†See the parallel problem of *it* in 1.1.

THE CENTRAL QUESTION: RHODA'S WEIGHT

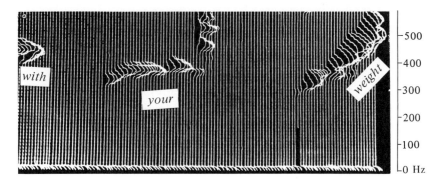

Figure 37. Pitch contour of 5.13: *Anything to do with . . . your . . weight?*

proposition we have summarized as {STRN}: Rhoda's inability to carry out school duties and household tasks at the same time.

The speech action of 5.13 is one of the fundamental mechanisms used for dealing with disputable events. It is frequently referred to as a "Socratic question," after Socrates' technique of posing a long series of yes–no questions that ultimately and necessarily brought the other person to a position agreeing with Socrates' own. The distinguishing characteristic of this ac-

---

5.13	TEXT	CUES
[a]	Th.: ⟨$_{IV}$ (breath) *Yes, but now let's us see—uh—if we can separate out two things.*	Mitigation: *the two things.* Tension: hesitation.
[b]	*Does it have anything to do with . . . your . . .weight?* ⟩$_{IV}$	Mitigation: *it,* low volume, high pitch: 3 4 4 4 4 ↑ (Figure 37).

EXPANSION
[a] Th.: ⟨$_{IV}$ Yes, you may be right about {~~EAT} about your eating, but let's see if we can separate the things that people say from {E} the feelings that lie behind what they say.
[b] Does {STRN} your inability to perform both school duties and household duties have anything to do with {THIN} your dangerously low weight. ⟩$_{IV}$

INTERACTION
Th. agrees with Rhoda's statement about her eating ⟨‾‾~~EAT‾‾ and requests information about Rhoda's position on the relation between ⟨‾THIN‾ her weight and ⟨‾STRN‾ the role strain that she feels, thereby indicating that she is prepared to discuss Rhoda's weight on the basis of her answer.

tion is that it takes the form of a yes–no question in cases where we might otherwise expect a request for more extended opinion. Here we might have, for example, "What has your weight go to do with your feeling tired?" When a yes–no question is used, it sets up the expectation that the answer will provide the basis for further discussion, and in fact shifts the basis for that for discussion to a point different from that which existed before. As a yes–no question, it is, of course, a request for information; but since the question is known to be a disputed one (a D-event), it is understood that the questioner will not accept the answer as if it were a mere matter of fact. The information he gains is not the answer to the question, but the other person's position on this question.

RULE FOR SOCRATIC QUESTIONS
If A directs to B a yes–no interrogative about a D-event, it is heard as a request for information about B's position on this event, which will form the basis for further discussion.

This rule is not a simple rule of production and interpretation but involves consequences for sequencing that move at least two steps ahead—another request and another response.

5.14. In spite of the therapist's precautions, Rhoda responds with a dramatic display of shock. She whispers:

5.14[a]   R.: [*What?*]

Rhoda responds as if she could not find the literal referent of *it* in 5.13. We are aware that she knows that the question of her weight is an essential concern of the therapy, but still she gives the impression of having been caught off guard. The therapist's response deals with external matters: the problem of role strain that we used to expand 3.13[b]. Yet even this fairly neutral subject is delivered in a tentative way, beginning with the vague reference of *two things,* and trailing off with another vague reference to "what else."

5.14[b]   Th.: *Your inability to carry the two* **things***,*
   [c]   Th.: *school . . and . . what else.*
   [d]   R.: *No, I don't* **think** *so!*

Even before the therapist has finished explaining herself, Rhoda replies with a vehement denial in a falsetto squeal (Figure 38).

This violent response is the converse of the repressed [*What*] and illustrates dramatically the strain Rhoda feels in discussing this question. Our expansion and interactional statements follow quite regularly from the discourse rules already given. Rhoda's repressed question, 5.14[a], is a request for information embedded within the larger request for a position of

THE CENTRAL QUESTION: RHODA'S WEIGHT   303

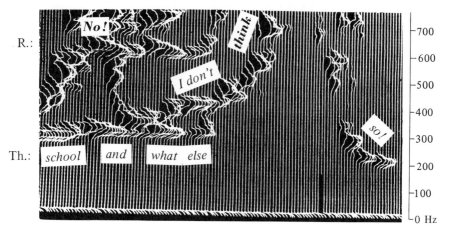

Figure 38. Pitch contour of Rhoda's falsetto response of 5.14[d]: *No! I don't think so!*

5.14   TEXT   CUES
[a]   R.: ⟨$_{IV}$ *What?*   Reservation: low, breathy whisper.
[b]   Th.: *Your inability to carry the two*   Mitigation: *things*.
      things,   Tension: strident overlap.
[c] ⎧ Th.: *school . . and . . what else.*   Th.: Mitigation, hesitation.
[d] ⎩ R.:   *No, I don't think so!* ⟩$_{IV}$ R.: Tension: falsetto squeal (Figure 38).

EXPANSION
[a] R.: ⟨$_{IV}$ What has something to do with {THIN} my weight?
[b] Th.: Your alleged inability {STRN} to perform both school and household duties has something to do with your weight.
[d] R.: No, I don't think my taking on these two duties has anything to do with my weight. ⟩$_{IV}$

INTERACTION
[a] R. requests further information on the referrent of *it*, thereby asserting that she needs this information to answer the request of 5.13, thereby asserting indirectly that ⟨~THIN⟩ she does not know that her weight is connected with any problem.
[b] Th. responds to R.'s request by specifying her original request for Rhoda's position on a connection between Rhoda's household problem and her eating habits, thereby asserting indirectly again that some people believe that ⟨THIN:STRN the problem is caused by Rhoda's weight being too low.
[d] R. gives her response that ⟨~THIN:STRN there is no connection between her weight and her household problem, thereby denying that ⟨~THIN she is too thin.

304   EPISODE FIVE

5.13, and once the therapist provides this information, the request is automatically reinstated (see Rule for Reinstating Requests, Chapter 3, p. 93).

5.15. We are now ready for the second move in the Socratic argument. The therapist has obtained from Rhoda a forcible expression of her position, and she then tries to use this as a basis for further exploration, returning to the one weak point in Rhoda's defense that has appeared so far: her expression of uncertainty in 5.11[g].

5.15   Th.: *All right so, why can't you stay with that?*

The therapist has not abandoned her mitigating techniques. She begins again with a concession to Rhoda's position, *All right*, and then adds the high pitch with falling contour, which we observed in 5.13[b]. Mitigation is certainly appropriate, since the challenge inherent in a second request for information is a sharp one.

In expanding 5.15, we may not do full justice to the challenge implicit in the expression *stay with*. The full force comes out when we examine the presuppositions of the negative question (following the same rules as in our discussion of 1.11, *Why don't you tell* **Phyllis** *that?*).

Why can't you stay with that?
↓
You can't stay with that for some reason.
↓
Someone would have expected you to be able to stay with that.
↓
You should stay with that but you are not staying with that.

These presuppositions follow regularly from the principle that a WH-question presupposes all the information given besides the item questioned, and that a negative presupposition implies the expectation of a corresponding positive. We then see that the therapist is challenging sharply Rhoda's lack of consistent support for her own position. This clearly echoes the reaction she showed to Rhoda's hesitancy in 2.2 (*What's your question?*). It follows that if Rhoda's low weight is not the cause of her problem in maintaining the household, then external circumstances are responsible, and she is more than ever justified in putting the suggestion into effect by calling up her mother and asking her to come home.

This formulation illustrates the great complexity of the therapist's relation with Rhoda. On the one hand, she has given Rhoda support in saying that it is perfectly normal for someone to ask her mother to come home and help after 4 days absence. On the other hand, she is aware that Rhoda does have a special physical problem, tires easily, and her failure to admit this fact shows a certain divorce from reality. As the therapist herself states in a *Playback* session,

	TEXT	CUES
5.15	Th.: ⟨$_{IV}$ *All right so, why can't you stay with that?* ⟩$_{IV}$	Mitigation: Wh${\overset{4}{y}}$ ca${\overset{3}{n}}$'t y${\overset{4}{o}}$u st${\overset{3}{a}}$y with th${\overset{1}{a}}$t?

EXPANSION

Th.: ⟨$_{IV}$ Since you don't believe that {THIN:STRN} your problems in doing school work and housework are due to your low weight, why can't you keep your belief in that idea? ⟩$_{IV}$

INTERACTION

Th. acknowledges R.'s denial ⟨ ~THIN:STRN as the position requested, and on this basis requests information as to why R. does not consistently maintain that denial, thereby asserting indirectly that R. does not maintain her denial, thereby ⟨ ?~THIN:STRN ⟩ challenging R.'s denial.

... BECAUSE THERE IS A *PHYSICAL* REALITY WITH RHODA. SHE COULD WELL BECOME OVERTIRED, COULD START GOING DOWNHILL, SHOW WEIGHT LOSS AGAIN.

The Feeling behind What They Are Saying

5.16. Rhoda's response to the Socratic questioning of the therapist is to contradict immediately the therapist's presupposition that she has not been consistent in her position.

> 5.16[a] R.: *Oh, I'm staying with it,*

She uses the same falsetto squeal we heard in 5.14, but then, surprisingly enough, she turns in the direction the therapist is looking for: a discussion of underlying feelings.

> 5.16[b] *butit'sjustthat—I don't know why, but it jist bothers me when they say that, because they look at me as if—* (breath)
> [c] *Like my sister will say to my mother, "Oh, **Rhoda** should never get tired."*

On the surface, this discussion continues as a criticism of her family. Rhoda begins with the same kind of rapid condensation that we have seen before when she showed us how she had responded aggressively to her aunt (2.6–2.8). As Rhoda then recovers from the shock of the mention of her weight, she continues with an increasingly fluent denuciation of her family. She employs one of the resources of family language: a superimposed intonation that adds a meaning quite different from the literal interpretation of her words. 5.16[c] shows a series of alternating heavy stresses,

5.16

TEXT	CUES
[a] R.: ⟨_IV_ Oh, **I'm staying with it,** ⟩_IV_	Tension: 2 3 2, with falsetto squeal.
[b] ⟨_EV_ butit'sjustthat—I don't know why, but it jist bothers me when they say that, because they look at me as if— (breath)	Tension: condensation, self-interruption. Mitigation: *jist*, 'only, simply'; *bothers*, 'angers me a little'.
[c] Like my sister will say to my mother, ⟨_F_ "Oh, Rhoda should never get tired." ⟩_F_ ⟩_EV_	Derogation: 2 3 2 3 2 3 1 'This is the kind of stupid thing she always says' (Figure 39).

EXPANSION

[a] R.: ⟨_IV_But you are wrong in thinking that my problems aren't caused by my loss of weight; I do commit myself to that idea. ⟩_IV_

[b] ⟨_EV_ The only thing that gives you the impression that I am not committing myself to that idea is that {E₃} my family makes me a little angry when they look at me as if {~AD-R} I was not grown up,

[c] and my sister often says such ridiculous things to my mother as ⟨_F_ "Oh, {TIRE} Rhoda should never get tired!" ⟩_F_ ⟩_EV_

INTERACTION

[a] R. responds to Th.'s request by asserting that by contradicting the presuppostion that she does maintain her denial ⟨~THIN:STRN⟩ thereby defending herself against the therapist's challenge.

[b] R. admits that she does feel an emotion of anger ⟨E₃⟩ caused by her family treating her ⟨~AD-R⟩ as if she were not an adult.

[c] R. gives further information on her family's way of treating her ⟨~AD-R⟩ by quoting her sister's claim that ⟨TIRE⟩ she gets tired more easily than normal people, and simultaneously challenges her sister ⟨~RSNBL-S⟩ as being unreasonable.

---

producing a rhythmic, "sing-song" pattern, which we interpret as ridicule directed at the speech being quoted (Figure 39). Rhoda does not mean to imply that this is the intonation pattern that her sister uses.

As we expand 5.16, we must deal with the pronoun *they*; this seems to refer to Rhoda's mother and sister.* Yet Rhoda's ridicule is directed only at her sister, rather than at her mother, and the mocking intonation is superimposed on a statement attributed to her sister.

Rhoda's mode of expression in this crucial passage is quite indirect: her

---

*We feel that Aunt Editha is not included in *they*, since she is not a major power in the household, and Rhoda does not refer to her remarks anywhere as representing authority or privileged position in respect to herself.

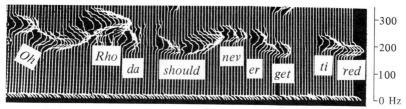

Figure 39. Pitch contour of 5.16[c]: *Oh Rhoda should never get tired.*

feeling comes out through intonation and implication. The overt text, on the other hand, is mitigating. Instead of speaking of her anger, she uses the weaker *bother*. Rhoda further mitigates her expression by adding the word *just*, which can be interpreted here as 'It is not a whole lot of other things that you might want to read into it, it is simply that...'

The proposition that is ridiculed is apparently used quite often in Rhoda's household: {TIRE} *Rhoda gets tired easily.* This is a performance characteristic that implies the general proposition that Rhoda cannot take care of herself, and therefore {~AD-R} is not an adult member of the household. This proposition brings out another concerning Rhoda's emotional reaction to her family:

{E_3}   Rhoda feels anger.

However, it should be noted that Rhoda presents this emotion in a very restricted form: *anger* is reduced to *bother*, and the word appears in the continued criticism of her sister as unreasonable—without mentioning her mother.

5.17. The therapist now makes a major move towards a direct discussion of underlying feelings.

5.17[a]   R.: *An'Is'dt'her—*
   [b]   Th.: *I don't think* **really** *it's the—uh—what they're saying as much, as, that, you, are reading in . . . uhh—the* **feeling** *behind what they're saying.*

The therapist is pressing quite hard, for she enters her turn at the same time that Rhoda begins again.* The therapist shows hesitation and self-interruption in 5.17, indicating that she herself is not entirely sure of what the correct formulation of her thought might be. The commas in 5.17[b] stand for a staccato enunciation that is quite distinct from the hesitations

---

*This is not strident overlap: someone takes a breath, and then at the same time that Rhoda very rapidly begins the narrative, the therapist begins to express her opinion. It takes very close listening to hear what Rhoda said, since her introduction to a narrative of this sort is typically condensed to a single phonological word. While we did not get the impression that the therapist was overriding Rhoda deliberately, it is also clear that she is not anxious to hear more elaboration of the arguments in the family at the same emotional level.

indicated by dashes and periods. Rhoda's resistance to the interpretations already made is a sufficient warrant for this uncertainty. The therapist knows that Rhoda resists direct suggestions, and she is searching for a way of leading Rhoda to interpretations of her own behavior that are natural and acceptable to her.

Our expansion of 5.17[b] specifies more fully what Rhoda's family has been saying and what the feelings are that she is referring to, drawing information from statements that are made before and after. The therapist denies that Rhoda's anger is caused by the fact that her family says that she tires too easily or is too thin $\{E_3:\text{TIRE, THIN}\}$. Instead, she proposes that this anger is caused by some unspecified emotion that Rhoda perceives in her family's reactions. The emotion discussed is not a specific one, and we have reserved the E without subscript for this general proposition. E' indicates emotion felt by Rhoda's family. Looking ahead, we then specify:

$\{E_3:E_3'\}$ The emotion of anger that Rhoda feels is the reaction to the emotion of anger that she attributes to her family.

Even though we know (and we believe that Rhoda knows) what emotion is being specified here, we must not overlook the fact that the therapist is not specific at this point. This fact is captured in our interactional statement by the unsubscripted proposition $\{E:E'\}$: Rhoda's emotion is a response to her family's emotion. The vague referent *it* is then interpreted: "What makes you angry is..."

There are two lexical features of interview style in 5.17 that strengthen the thrust of the therapist's interpretation. *Really* establishes two levels of reality: what we observe on the surface, and what really lies below it. The expression *reading in* indicates that Rhoda attributes an emotion to her family on the basis of their observed behavior, with a strong implication that this is a misperception, at least in part, and may reflect Rhoda's own emotional state more than the reality.

The interpretation the therapist offers in 5.17[b] is set up in the form of a statement as complex as the analogy of 5.1: "What causes you to do X is not so much that M does Y as that M does Z." However, the interpretation the therapist offers is more complex even than this. She wants to point out that the source of emotion in Rhoda is not so much what in fact "they" are feeling, but what Rhoda feels that they are feeling. The therapist establishes *three* levels of phenomena:

1. What Rhoda's mother and sister are saying;
2. What Rhoda's mother and sister are feeling;
3. What Rhoda feels her mother and sister are feeling.

These distinctions point towards one of the goals of the therapeutic session. We have seen that the therapist is first given an account of the

5.17   TEXT   CUES
[a] ⎧ R.: ⟨_N An'Is'dt'her— ⟩_N   Tension: hesitation, self-interruption.
[b] ⎩ Th.: ⟨_IV I don't think **really** it's
the—uh—what they're saying as much,
as, that, you, are reading in . . . uhh—the
feeling behind what they're saying.
[c] R.: . . . .   Reservation: silence.
[d] Th.: What c—what are they feeling
about it? ⟩_IV

EXPANSION

[b] ⟨_IV I am suggesting to you that {~E:TIRE, THIN} what makes you angry is not that your family says that you're tired and thin, but {$E_3:E_3'$} the feeling of anger that you attribute to them in listening to what they are saying. ⟩_IV
[c] R.: [I don't agree.]
[d] Th.: ⟨_IV The important question to you seems to be {E'}: "What is your family feeling about your being underweight?" ⟩_IV

INTERACTION

[b] Th. redirects the discussion to R.'s feelings giving an interpretation of the emotional interaction in the family by asserting that E:E' R. feels an emotion in response to the emotion that she feels that her family feels, and simultaneously questions the E:TIRE, THIN interpretation being unconsciously made by R., thereby supporting her own status as INT-TH an interpreter of emotions and challenging Rhoda's status in this respect ~INT-R .
[c] Rhoda refuses to respond, thereby denying indirectly the assertion ~E:E' that her emotion is a response to her family's emotion.
[d] The therapist requests information on the specific emotion felt by Rhoda's family thereby asserting again indirectly that E:E' this emotion is the cause of Rhoda's emotion.

---

events of everyday life, in a style stripped of emotional evaluation and interpretation. To this are added overt justifications in terms of general social norms and then more personal interpretations of the patient's relations with others. Now the therapist introduces the view that Rhoda's behavior is motivated by underlying emotions.

Rhoda shows total resistance to this direct suggestion.

    5.17[c]   R.: . . . .

Rhoda's silence might be difficult to interpret if the therapist had made a casual remark. But the assertion that the therapist made in 5.17[b] certainly

310   EPISODE FIVE

requires a response, and Rhoda's silence can be interpreted only as a refusal of assent to it.

There is a silence of 4 seconds. The therapist then reformulates her suggestion as a request for information.

5.17[d]   Th.: *What c—what are they feeling about it?**

The proposition referred to here is the same as in 5.15[b]: that Rhoda is reacting to an emotion conveyed by her family and that she should recognize these emotions. Since Rhoda does not respond to the assertions of 5.17[b], the therapist then uses a surface form that is linked to a sequencing rule demanding a response: *requests* must be acknowledged and responded to (Chapter 3, p. 79).

5.18. Rhoda's reluctance to respond continues: There is a 6-second silence. When she does speak, her voice is low in both pitch and volume. Her utterance shows that the request for information is strong enough to produce some kind of verbal response; but it also shows that such a response can be quite superficial, equivalent on an interactive plane to silence.

5.18   R.: . . . .*No-I-I—I don't see the difference.*

When we try to expand this utterance, it appears at first to be incoherent. 5.17[d] was a WH- question, which should be answered in terms of the emotions that Rhoda's family felt. But Rhoda's *No* cannot be expanded as "No, I don't think they are feeling anything." The expansion must locate the complement of *difference*: difference between what elements? The only contrast that has been made is between *feeling* and *saying*, so we must ignore 5.17[d] and reconstruct a response to 5.17[b]: "No, I don't see the difference between what my family is saying and what they are feeling."

Once again we see that the connections between adjacent utterances need not be coherent at a surface level. If we were to abstract the exchange of 5.17[d]–5.18 from context, we would have:

Th.:   *What are they feeling about it?*
R.:   *No, I don't see the difference.*

Can we then say that the sequence 5.17[d]–5.18 is incoherent? The interactional statement for 5.17[d] shows that the therapist is reasserting the presupposition of her WH-question: "What are they feeling about your being underweight?" presupposes {E':~EAT} 'They are feeling something about your being underweight that is relevant to your weight'. Rhoda refuses assent to this presupposition, so her response to 5.17[b] is also a

---

*The therapist's restart gives us very little additional information. It is possible that *are* is being substituted for an original *could* or *can*.

5.18	TEXT	CUES
R.: $\langle_{IV}$............ *No-I-I—I don't see the difference.* $\rangle_{IV}$		Reservation: silence, low pitch and volume. Tension.

EXPANSION

R.: $\langle_{IV}$ No, I don't see the difference between what my family is saying about {~EAT} my being underweight and {E':~EAT} what they are feeling about it. $\rangle_{IV}$

INTERACTION

R. denies that there is a difference between what her family is saying ⟨ ~EAT about her being underweight and what they are feeling, thereby denying indirectly that these emotions are relevant to her being underweight.

---

response to the request for information of 5.17[d]. Under the Rule of Requests, this request for information depends on the precondition that the information is needed, and Rhoda refuses the request on the basis that the information is not needed: she sees no reason to discuss any emotions that lie behind her family's statements.

One might have said that Rhoda ignores 5.17[d]. Yet once we see that the interactive significance of 5.17[d] is to reassert the proposition {E'}, we can see that Rhoda is responding appropriately to both of the therapist's utterances.

5.19. The therapist now is faced with a very direct form of resistance. As she searches for a way around it, she produces another interpretation:

5.19[a] Th.: (breath) *Well, let's see.*
[b] *It—maybe it's similar to the feeling that you had when your sister said, "You're eating too much," and you stopped eating totally,*
[c] *what does that express?*

The therapist uses a number of paralinguistic cues that serve to mitigate the force of the suggestion underlying her interpretation. In the phrase *Well, let's see,* her voice rises to a high falsetto, and then fades in volume, which is the mitigating intonation we have seen used many times before. She conveys an impression of reasonableness and a willingness to listen to counter-suggestions. The therapist thus acknowledges an overt disagreement and invites Rhoda to participate in a discussion that will permit some resolution.

The therapist begins her interpretation in 5.19[b], but immediately corrects herself by inserting *maybe.* She thus retreats one step from the posi-

312 EPISODE FIVE

5.19 **TEXT** **CUES**

[a] Th.: ⟨$_{IV}$ (breath) *Well, let's see.* Mitigation: High falsetto on *let*.
[b] *It—maybe it's similar to the feeling that you had when your sister said, "You're eating too much," and you stopped eating totally.*
[c] *What does that express?* ⟩$_{IV}$ Mitigation: High contour 3 3 4 3, low volume.

EXPANSION

[a] Th.: ⟨$_{IV}$ In relation to your disagreement with my suggestion, let me see if I can lead us to agreement.
[b] Let me suggest again {E_3' =E_3} the feeling behind what your family is saying is similar to the feeling you had when your sister said, "{EAT} You are eating too much," and you {~EAT} began to eat much less than a normal person should.
[c] What {E?} emotion is expressed by your not eating as much as you should? ⟩$_{IV}$

INTERACTION

[a] Th. acknowledges lack of agreement and asks for agreement.
[b] Th. gives interpretation that ⟨$E_3=E_3'$ R.'s feelings about her mother staying away are the same as R.'s feelings about her family's criticism of her eating habits, and asserts again that ⟨~EAT R. is subnormal in her eating habits.
[c] Th. requests information ⟨E?⟩ on the emotion R feels, and in the light of the shared knowledge that she believes ⟨E_3 R feels anger, thereby requests acknowledgement of this proposition.

tion that she took in 5.1, where she said, *What they are **really** doing to you is so similar* ...

So far, the therapist has been referring to "feelings" in general. She now suggests that one feeling is similar to another, so it follows that she must have a fairly clear idea of what these emotions are. Nevertheless, she continues her mitigating tactic of not identifying them directly. In our expansion, we have used the symbols E_3 and E_3', since the text both before and after indicates that this emotion is anger. At the same time, the therapist plainly is determined to get Rhoda to recognize this emotion herself. Instead of identifying the emotion in so many words, she asks Rhoda to identify it in 5.19[c] {E?}.

The superficial form of 5.19[c] is a request for information, and it is shown as such in our cross section. But the Rule of Requests will not recognize this as a *valid* request for information, since it is a matter of shared knowledge that the speaker believes she knows the answer to the question (see 5.21 below). It is therefore a known-answer question. However it is not similar to a test-question, where the goal is to find out if the listener knows the answer: The purpose here is to get the listener to *acknowledge* the answer. This procedure is similar to the pattern of the Socratic yes–no question, in that it projects a further conversation that will be based upon Rhoda's answer.

However, this acknowledgement is not easily given.

Rhoda's Longest Silence

5.20. The mitigating tactics of 5.19 seem to produce no result. Instead, Rhoda's response is more negative than anything we have seen so far: an eloquent silence of 13 seconds.

5.20 R.: ....

One way that we can understand this resistance is to look once again at 5.19—not at the direct assertion, but at the presuppositions in 5.19[b]. In describing the feeling that Rhoda had, the therapist produces this complex grammatical structure (see illustration on page 314). When the therapist characterizes the *feeling*, she does so with a complex determiner involving five embedded sentences. The fifth of these is *You stopped eating totally*. This is the categorical form of expression, which we have found typical of colloquial language, and it is certainly not consistent with the mitigating posture that the therapist adopted in the rest of 5.19[b]. While Rhoda's behavior was extreme, and probably came as close to eating nothing as one could get, the expression *totally* is undoubtedly an exaggeration. The therapist does not assert this proposition explicitly; it is contained in the description of the "feeling," and is only presupposed, but the presupposition is a very strong one and is unacceptable to Rhoda. Rhoda had denied over and over again that she stopped eating; by the use of this presupposition, the therapist now has aligned herself with the position that her family has taken on the facts of the matter.

5.20	TEXT	CUES
R.:	⟨_IV_ .... ⟩_IV_	Reservation: silence [13 sec].

INTERACTION
R. refuses information or confirmation requested, and simultaneously refuses agreement to the assertion of the therapist $\overline{\sim\text{EAT}}$ that she stopped eating.

314   EPISODE FIVE

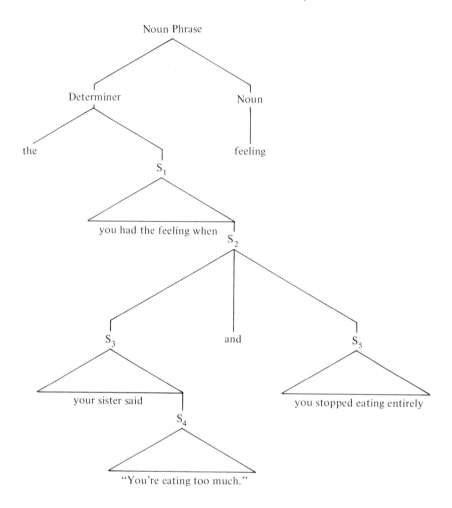

It is not easy to understand the immediate motivation of the therapist's direct expression at this point. She apparently has decided to abandon the hesitant tactics of earlier confrontations. The candor with which she approaches the topic may be seen as a shift of tactics; she asks the patient herself to give the answer to her problem. It is not surprising that the tactic fails, since the fundamental inference is that Rhoda has not been able to express this emotion in words and has converted it into the psychosomatic syndrome of anorexia. It is reasonable to conclude that Rhoda's long silence is her most direct way of refusing assent to the presupposition that she stopped eating totally.

The Recognition of Anger

5.21. When the therapist fails to extract any response from Rhoda, she probes again by reemphasizing the emotional component of the argument:

5.21[a] { Th.: *In terms of how you felt.*
         R.: (*No—*)

This probe serves as a mitigating tactic, which reinterprets Rhoda's silence as a misunderstanding rather than a refusal. By adding a qualififcation or explication and fitting it into the grammatical structure of the original request, the therapist concedes that this request was not as clear as it might have been. It now reads, "What does that express in terms of how you felt?" This in turn provides the favorable interpretation of Rhoda's silence as an inability rather than a refusal to respond. The therapist might have taken a more aggressive interpretation of this silence, for example, "Come on now, how do you feel about this?" or "Why don't you say something?" The pattern followed here is the familiar one of pushing into the area of emotional resistance and then retreating when that resistance is encountered.

In the midst of the therapist's addition, Rhoda introduces a soft *No*, repeating her disagreement in a muted form. Throughout the exchanges of 5.21, Rhoda shows extreme reservation. Her volume remains low, her words are condensed and difficult to follow, and another long silence is heard. Nevertheless, the therapist finally extracts an admission from her:

5.21[b] R.: *Oh, I guess I w's angry, but—*
   [c]   Th.: *Ye-es.*
   [d]   R.:...... (*Yeh.*)

The paralinguistic cues in Rhoda's responses are quite informative. The *Oh* does not have the high contour of surprise we have seen earlier, but the more level intonation expressing the concession of a point without full agreement; in this respect it matches the final *but*. Furthermore, it is surprising to find Rhoda using the expression *I guess* in connection with her own emotions. We have observed before that Rhoda is not the sole authority on her own emotions in the therapeutic situation. The *I guess* is a reluctant concession to a person who is considered to be an expert in the interpretation of emotions.

The therapist's reinforcement is not a simple "Yes." It is the same kind of strong reinforcement that we first heard in 1.6[f] (*Right!*). This is a "recognition" intonation, which is used when something is finally located that has been expected for some time. However this reinforcement does not

316 EPISODE FIVE

	5.21	TEXT	CUES
[a]	{	Th.: ⟨₁ᵥIn terms of how you felt. ⟩ᵢᵥ	Reservation: low volume.
	R.:	(No—)	Reservation: low volume, condensation.
[b]		R.: ⟨ᵢᵥ Oh, I guess I w's **angry**, but—	Reinforcement: 4 4 2, 'recognition'.
[c]		Th.: Yé-es.	Reservation: silence, low volume.
[d]		R.: ......(Yeh.) ⟩ᵢᵥ	

EXPANSION
[b] R.: ⟨ᵢᵥ I didn't think so, but I can see that you may be right: I may have been {E₃} angry though I don't accept this entirely. ⟩ᵢᵥ

INTERACTION
[a] Th. gives orientation, thereby reinstating her request again. Rhoda simultaneously expresses her disagreement with the assertion contained in the request.
[b] R. hesitantly gives acknowledgment ⟨E₃⟩ requested by the therapist that the emotion felt was anger and adds an unspecified partial disagreement.
[c] Th. reinforces R.'s admission.
[d] R. repeats agreement reluctantly, retreating from her partial disagreement.

---

have the desired effect.* Rhoda produces her third silence, this time only 3 seconds, and then a very low, quiet agreement. On the whole, it seems that the therapist has made very little progress in getting Rhoda to recognize her own emotions or those that she reacts to in her family. The reluctant concession of 5.21 provides little more material than the silence of 5.20.

5.22. For the third time, the therapist provides an interpretation she hopes will stimulate Rhoda's reactions and recognition of the emotional realities in her family.

5.22[a] Th.: (breath) *So—then—and for some reason you feel they're angry because you're so, underweight, or*
  [b] *because they—think you're underweight.*

The therapist begins with two conjunctions which she discards before settling on *and* as the right word to introduce her interpretation. But there is nothing tentative about the way in which she states her position. There are

---

*In these and similar reinforcements, the therapist seems to be adopting an adult-to-child relationship to Rhoda, which is probably not deliberate but is called forth by Rhoda's immature style. Though the therapist recognizes that Rhoda wants to be treated like an adult, and wishes to treat her like one, Rhoda keeps giving the cues that prompt responses of this kind.

heavy stresses on *some, angry,* and *think.* The heaviest of all is on *angry,* which is accompanied with a harsh voice qualifier which seems to symbolize the emotion which she is talking about.

Even though the therapist has replaced *so* as an introduction, it is plain that 5.22 is built upon the concessions obtained in the previous Socratic discussion. The therapist now discusses the family's anger, in the light of the fact that Rhoda has conceded that she felt the same emotion.

The therapist's statement assumes the substance of the analogies made before in 5.1 and 5.20—that Rhoda's action in not eating is comparable to her family's action in not giving her support. The therapist now enters more deeply into the motivations that lie behind Rhoda's overreactions, motivations that would account for Rhoda's emotional responses to her family.

Though the therapist has led Rhoda up to the point of seeing a causal explanation in terms of emotional factors, Rhoda's hesitant agreement of 5.21 does not satisfy her. She feels that Rhoda herself must recognize the emotional basis for her responses to her family. Our contextual expansion cannot show all of the implications that might be drawn, but we can complete the argument by comparing this with the original discussion of {STRN}—the emotional strain Rhoda described in Episodes 1 and 4. Until now, this strain has been discussed as the result of objective social factors—the fact that Rhoda has had too much to do. In the therapist's eyes, this subjective reaction on Rhoda's part is due not only to her own inability to fulfill her obligations; it is also the product of the emotional burden created by interchanges of anger.*

We have therefore departed considerably from the socially oriented logic used in the first two episodes, based upon the principles of distributive justice that are involved in role obligations. The therapist has now redefined Rhoda's problem in terms of the anger that she feels.

Even as she recognizes the need for a clear statement about the emotional situation, the therapist also feels the need to mitigate the challenge to Rhoda's position on the facts of the matter. In 5.20, the therapist implicitly endorsed the claim that Rhoda had stopped eating totally; she now adds a mitigating clause that throws doubt upon the accompanying proposition {THIN} that Rhoda is too thin. The pause before *think* gives full emphasis to this insertion and makes it plain that the therapist is dissociating herself from the family's position on this point. In order to bring Rhoda into contact with the realities of the situation, the therapist has performed a complicated series of realignments. She has now balanced her endorsement of the family's claim that Rhoda stopped eating totally with doubt about their claim that she is too thin.

*It is not clear whether the strain is attributed primarily to Rhoda's emotions or to her perception of her family's emotions, or to the complex of both.

318 EPISODE FIVE

5.22   TEXT   CUES
[a]   Th.: ⟨$_{IV}$ (breath) *So—then—and for*   Tension: ***angry***, with strident voice
some reason you feel they're angry because   qualifier.
you're so, underweight, or
[b]   ***because they—think you're***
underweight. ⟩$_{IV}$

EXPANSION
Th.: ⟨$_{IV}$ Since you admit that {E$_3$} you feel anger, we now have to explain that feeling: it is because you feel {E$_3'$} your family is angry with you because they think that you have deliberately made yourself underweight {THIN} and are violating the principle that you should take care of yourself {S-CARE}. ⟩$_{IV}$

INTERACTION
[a]   Th.: Th. gives further interpretation of Rhoda's emotion, and asserts that $\overline{E_3:E_3'}$⟩ Rhoda's anger is a response to her perception of her family's anger against her caused by their feeling that she has deliberately made herself underweight, thereby asserting indirectly that ⟨ THIN Rhoda is in fact underweight.
[b]   Th. attributes the statement ⟨ ~EAT that R. is underweight to her family, thereby retreating from her indirect assertion that R. is in fact underweight.

5.23. With this concession, the therapist seems to have made it possible for Rhoda to speak more freely, but her response is still one of denial:

> 5.23[a] R.: . . . . . . *I'on't—I dunno, I don't—I don't—I never felt like **that**—it's just that . . . no I never thought of it like that and I don't—I don't think I feel **anger** because* . . .

There is none of the agreement that she gave to the social and psychological propositions of Episodes 1–4; here she responds first with silence, then with hesitation, and finally with outright denial, repeated over and over again. This dramatic explosion of resistance to the therapist's ideas is accompanied by a wealth of paralinguistic cues, all of which show severe emotional agitation. We often find that our contextual expansion must be much longer than the actual statement, but here we have the reverse, as Rhoda says the same thing over and over again.

Rhoda then attempts to refute the therapist's proposition in a manner that is now familiar to us.

> 5.23[b] R.: (breath) *I mean I jist get **annoyed**, like I'm not—I don't say I get—angry, but it jist gets **annoying** to hear the same thing.*

She denies a direct statement but admits it in a mitigated form. She uses

5.23   TEXT   CUES

[a] R.: ⟨$_{IV}$ ...... I'on't—I dunno, I don't—I don't—I never felt like **that**—it's just that ... no I never thought of it like that and I don't—I don't think I feel **anger** because ...	Reservation: Silence, low volume. Tension: Whine on *I'on't,* choking and straining, hesitation, self-interruption. Mitigation: *just that I don't think I feel.* Mitigation: *jist, annoyed, annoying,* and *it,* impersonal construction.
[b] (breath) *I mean I jist get **annoyed**, like I'm not—I don't say I get—angry, but it jist gets **annoying** to hear the same thing.* ⟩$_{IV}$	

EXPANSION

[a] R.: ⟨$_{IV}$ I never {~E$_3$} felt angry towards my family; I only get annoyed when my family repeats over and over again {THIN} that I an underweight. ⟩$_{IV}$

INTERACTION

R. denies ⟨‾~E$_3$‾ the therapist's assertion that she feels anger, and admits ⟨‾E$_3$‾ that she feels anger in a mitigated form, and asserts that this emotion is justified by her family's unjustified assertion that ⟨‾THIN‾ she is underweight.

---

the term *annoyed* as a euphemism for 'angry,' just as she uses *bother* for 'anger' in 5.16[b]. The mode of argument here is quite straightforward. The therapist has made an assertion in 5.22. This assertion drew conclusions from an earlier proposition that Rhoda had conceded: that she felt the emotion of anger. Rhoda's outburst is not directed at the therapist's previous remark; but it goes back to deny the concession that was wrested from her before and which is now being used as a presupposition. The Socratic method the therapist had used has not proved effective, because the agreement that had been obtained was not a permanent one. Rhoda is willing to concede the existence of some degree of emotion, but not to allow the therapist to draw the further conclusions that seem to be imminent. Her denial, therefore, follows the pattern of "It is not that X, it is just that Y," where Y is a mitigated form of X.*

At this point, the therapist has succeeded in bringing Rhoda's refusal to

---

*We can see a parallel here to the kind of behavior that Rhoda demonstrates in Episodes 2 and 3, where she denies that she showed any strong emotion towards Editha, saying *All I did was...* She suppresses the reporting of her own requests or actions that might be considered aggressive, as in 2.9[c].

admit anger into the open, and we have a direct view of the devices she uses to deny her anger. It seems clear that mitigated forms of emotion are acceptable in Rhoda's framework. We can see an analogy between Rhoda's emotional behavior and the range of behavior that is considered appropriate in carrying out role obligations. Not to feel any emotion would be wrong, since her family did something that was clearly wrong in her eyes, but to feel *anger* is also wrong. The appropriate range of emotional display reactions to other family members is to be "annoyed" or "bothered." This verbal mitigation is an important element in masking for Rhoda her own feelings of hostility towards her family. We can infer that she has undergone a long history of conditioning to repress anger and convert it to other forms of expression.

How Rhoda's Family Annoys Her

5.24. Now that Rhoda has expressed the emotion that she feels in a form that is acceptable to her, she is encouraged to justify it at length. The anger or irritation that she feels recalls the many expressions of irritation in Episodes 2, 3, and 4, when she endorsed the general proposition that her sister and her aunt were {~RSNBL} not reasonable at all. She now introduces a pseudo-narrative to support her position, the style of narrative response that is already familiar to us.

> 5.24[a] R.: *I mean, the first thing if I say I have a pain in my finger—right away, it's because "Oh, you're **thin!**"*

This anecdote reintroduces the fluency of earlier episodes, as Rhoda freely expresses herself in family style. The preposing of *the first thing* is an element of local colloquial style: our expansion restores it to its position in the second clause. There is a great deal of ellipsis throughout 5.24[a], which we have restored in the expansion, but not without loss of force.

The underlying proposition here is that Rhoda's family is not reasonable. In explaining her emotion, Rhoda argues that the situation is not a symmetrical one. In this argument, she sees her family as unreasonable and herself as reasonable. Therefore the therapist's elaborately constructed parallel of 5.19 cannot stand; our interactional statement shows that Rhoda rejects the notion that her family behaves to her as she behaves towards them.

Rhoda retreats: she restates her emotion in mitigated form, and then suggests that perhaps, after all, it is not justified.

> 5.24[b] R.: *I mean, after awhile it gets annoying to hear and I-I know that—*
> [c] Th.: *Yes.*

HOW RHODA'S FAMILY ANNOYS HER

5.24   TEXT   CUES
[a] R.: ⟨_EV_ I mean, ⟨_F_ the first thing if I   Derogation: *the first thing, right away.*
say I have a pain in my finger—right   Emphasis: thín.
away, it's because "Oh, you're **thin!**" ⟩_F_   Mitigation: *annoying.*
[b] I mean, after awhile it gets annoying
to hear and I-I—know that—
[c] Th.: Yeh.
[d] R.: I guess—maybe I should let
it—not bother me. ⟩_EV_

EXPANSION

[a] R.: ⟨_EV_ As an example of how they keep saying over and over again that {THIN} I am underweight, if I say I have a pain in my finger, the first thing that my family will say, without seeing what actually caused it, is that it's because I am too thin, and this is the kind of ridiculous thing that they always do.
[b] And this is why I am right in being angry {E_3}
[d] but I should not become angry. ⟩_EV_

INTERACTION

[a] R. gives information ⟨~RSNBL⟩ on her family's failure to follow appropriate norms of behavior, thereby challenging the therapist's interpretation of 5.19 that her emotions are parallel to those shown by her family.
[c] Th. gives support to R.'s assertion that ⟨ E_3 ⟩ her anger is justified.
[d] R. asserts hesitantly that ⟨ $\simeq E_3$ ⟩ she should not feel anger, thereby retreating from her assertion and challenge of 5.24 [a], and simultaneously denies the basic suggestion {S} that she should express her emotions.

[d] R.: *I guess—maybe I should let it—not bother me.**

The notion that she is expressing here—that it is wrong for her to be angry—contradicts {S} the basic suggestion of the therapist, which Rhoda has endorsed in 1.6: *If I keep it in what's bothering me, then nobody else knows and everybody thinks everything is fine and good and I end up—hurting myself.* It is not an absolute contradiction: Rhoda could believe that she should express only those emotions that are appropriate. Yet she has expressed over

---

*Her retreat shows considerable syntactic confusion. She vacillates from *I know* to *I guess* and *maybe.* She then finds herself in a most peculiar syntax when she begins with a positive expression *I should let it* and then finds that she has to add a *not* yielding "I should let it not bother me" instead of "I shouldn't let it bother me."

and over again that her feeling of anger (mitigated to "annoyance") is justified and appropriate, and it follows that she is denying the basic suggestion of the therapist.

The therapist has given Rhoda some reinforcement, sympathetically reacting to her expression of anger, but this reinforcement has led to a retreat from that expression and a denial of the fundamental suggestion. We have seen a great many advances and retreats in the course of Episode 5, but this would be a retreat that the therapist is not prepared to accept.

5.25. Rhoda begins a new anecdote, presumably to support the charge that her family is unreasonable, but the therapist will not permit her to turn back to the events of the everyday world again. Instead, she insists upon a direct confrontation with the question of who is feeling what emotion.

5.25[a] R.: *I mean, I went to the doctor last week—*
  [b] Th.: *But why do **they** keep repeating it?*
  [c] R.: *I don't know . . . . .*
  [d] Th.: *What are **they** feeling?*

The therapist's interruption of Rhoda is quite insistent and shows a certain amount of impatience. The interactional statement of 5.25[b] shows a request for interpretation. This is no more a request for information than were the Socratic questions that preceded. We have already seen that the therapist is defined here as an expert in the interpretation of emotions, and she does not need help from Rhoda in this respect. This is therefore a known-answer question, a request for acknowledgement similar to 5.19[c] and 5.17[d]. We might project a further discussion in which Rhoda would acknowledge the explanation already foreshadowed. However Rhoda refused to do so: In a low and breathy voice she says that she simply does not know.

The therapist now uses a tactic that is part of the arsenal of Socratic interrogation. She supplies a more specific question, which gives enough information so Rhoda cannot continue her claim that she does not know the answer.

The Rule of Socratic Specification that is operating here can be formulated as follows:

If A makes a request for information of B, and B refuses to answer on the ground that he does not have the ability, and A makes another request for information, which is more specific, then A is heard as asserting that this specific information is part of the answer, thereby disallowing further refusals on the same account.

If B now answers the second request, it will appear that he has accepted the

| 5.25 | TEXT | CUES |

[a] R.: ⟨_N *I mean, I went to the doctor last week—* ⟩_N
[b] Th.: ⟨_{IV} *But why do they keep repeating it?* — Irritation: interruption.
[c] R.: *I don't know.....* — Reservation: low volume, breathy voice.
[d] Th.: *What are they feeling?* ⟩_{IV}

EXPANSION

[a] R.: ⟨_N As another example of {E_3} of how annoying my family can be to me, I went to the doctor last week— ⟩_N
[b] Th.: ⟨_{IV} But disregarding these other stories, if your family's {~EAT} criticism of your eating is unjustified and makes you angry {E_3}, why do they keep repeating it as you say?
[c] R.: I don't know why my family keeps repeating their criticism of me.
[d] Th.: What emotion {E'} do the other family members feel which makes them criticize you so much? ⟩_{IV}

INTERACTION

[a] R. initiates a narrative to give more information on the family's behavior, thereby justifying her anger towards them.
[b] Th. interrupts and requests interpretation from R. on the reasons for her family's behaving in a way that makes her angry.
[c] R. responds that she is not able to give the interpretation requested, thereby refusing the therapist's request.
[d] Th. requests information on ⟨?E'⟩ the feelings of family members towards R., and in the light of R.'s refusal to answer the previous question, asserts indirectly that she is supplying the information that R. needs to answer the question, thereby reinstating her request for interpretation of 5.25[b].

---

underlying assertion that the more specific information contained in this request was part of the answer to the first. Therefore if Rhoda should answer 5.25[d], she will also be admitting that the reason that the family keeps repeating their charge that {~EAT} she does not eat is the emotion that they feel rather than their perception of the real situation.*

*The relation between the questions of 5.25[b] and [d] can be seen somewhat more clearly if we look at the presuppositions of the question form. *Why do they keep repeating it?* implies "They keep repeating it for some reason." The question *What are they feeling?* implies "They are feeling some emotion." It is then implied that the emotion in the second question is the reason of the first question.

The questioning of 5.25 is the obverse of the systematic reinforcement the therapist uses in 1.6 and elsewhere. In the one case, there is a crescendo of cues that promote the verbal production of the patient. In the other case, there is a series of increasingly insistent questions, which have the reverse effect. There is certainly a danger that Rhoda would retreat into the stubborn silences that she used before. Rhoda does not retreat: instead, she produces a sudden outburst of information on family interaction that gives the therapist a clearer view of the situation.

5.26. After five restarts, Rhoda gives us an indirect quotation from her family, which seems to be very close to the words that they actually use.

> 5.26 R.: . . . . . *that I'm doing it on purp—like, I w's—like they . . . well—they s—came out an' tol' me in so many words that they worry and worry an' I seem to take this very lightly.*

There is a great deal of tension evident at the beginning of Rhoda's outburst; this is rather similar to the slow beginning of 5.23. She interrupts herself, hesitates, and adds a whine to reinforce her complaint against her family.

In this answer of Rhoda's, we return to the fundamental issue of her claim to adult status and her family's denial of it. It is possible to see just how serious an issue this is and how much emotion revolves around it. Rhoda finally says, in characteristic family language, that her family is angry with her: *They came out and told me.* The expression *came out* implies that they had already conveyed the message in many indirect ways before they said it *in so many words.* In our expansion, we have enlarged the idea of *take this very lightly* to show that Rhoda is seen to be in violation of the basic principle that each person has an obligation to take care of herself: she is placing an undue burden on the other members of the household by not doing so.

We now encounter a new set of social norms that concern the rights and obligations of the sick. The family's criticism of Rhoda seems to reflect the general hostility that members of society often show towards sick people.* The sick person is allowed to play a very special role, withdrawing from normal responsibilities; although members of a family will express love and affection towards this person, and great concern for their well-being, there are also ways in which they convey a sense of social strain. The patient is

---

*Parsons (1951) sets out four expectations society sets up for someone filling the role of a sick person. First is the exemption from normal social role responsibilities; secondly, he must be "taken care of," so that his condition can be changed. The third expectation is that he must see the state of being ill as undesirable and want to "get well." Finally, the sick person is obliged to seek technically competent help and cooperate with him in the process of trying to get well.

5.26

TEXT	CUES
R.: ⟨_EV_ ..... *that I'm doing it on purp—like, I w's—like they ... well—they s—came out an' tol' me in so many words that* ⟨_F_ *they worry and worry an' I seem to take this very lightly.* ⟩_F_ ⟩_EV_	Tension: self-interruption, hesitation, whine.

EXPANSION

R. ⟨_EV_ The family feels {~EAT} that I am not eating on purpose. They told me explicitly {E_3'} they are angry with me because even though they worry a great deal about my losing weight, I seem not to care about my health as I should {S-CARE} and therefore I am not behaving like an adult {~AD-R} ⟩_EV_.

INTERACTION

R. responds to Th.'s request by giving the family's criticism of her as ⟨—~AD-R⟩ not behaving like a responsible adult.

---

made aware of the fact that there are greater obligations placed upon other members of the family since the patient cannot perform his share. He gives up certain rights in determining his own future, and places himself under a strong obligation to do everything possible to resume the original role of healthy adult.

The moral dimension is dominant in almost all the family arguments that we have seen reflected in the therapeutic session: each person seems to be struggling to define himself as a good person in the sense that he fulfills the obligations that society puts upon him. In the other interviews examined in the *Playback* series, we find reports that family members have accused the patient of selfishness, and neglecting his basic responsibilities, just as Rhoda is accused of malingering. These charges produce violent emotions in all parties concerned, and the therapist is aware that the anger Rhoda must experience from her family interaction is quite intense. She is also aware of how difficult it is for Rhoda to express these emotions even when she perceives them.

Charging that a person is being willfully sick or irresponsible, or that he is not trying to alleviate the burden put on others, is a very serious charge indeed. It is an allegation of bad faith, and it is therefore more than a question of denying adult status to Rhoda: it is a question of denying that Rhoda is a good and moral person.

5.27. At this point, it might seem that the major goal of the session has been achieved. After many efforts, the therapist has gotten from Rhoda the most important kind of statements about interaction in the family—the nature of the arguments about Rhoda's weight and the blame that she has received for her behavior. One might expect that she would be ready to explore these emotions in some detail and help Rhoda achieve greater insight into her emotions. Yet, the interpretation the therapist now provides is not asserted with any dramatic force. Again we find the mitigating contour with a high initial pitch and low volume that conveys the impression that "this is only a suggestion."

5.27[a] Th.: *So they get **angry** at you.*
 [b] R.: *Yes . . . they do, yes.*
 [c] Th.: *So there's a lot of **anger** passing back and forth.*
 [d] R.: *. . . . . Yeh . .*
 [e] Th.: *(Mm.)*

Since this is a very direct statement, our expansion and interactive description follow quite readily. There is no deep layering of one action upon another since the therapist is asserting plainly what she believes to be the central facts of the case. Even though her intonation contour is a mitigating one, she does not use any other form of mitigation in asserting that the family feels anger towards Rhoda and that she, in turn, expresses anger to them.

The cost of this direct statement from the therapist cannot be avoided. Instead of the stream of speech Rhoda has produced in other episodes, we again note a repression of speech. Rhoda has nothing further to say at this point. She is willing to admit the therapist's assertions, but the fact that she does not add anything to the discussion shows that her acceptance is very limited. We might anticipate a further exploration of these emotions now that this one insight has been achieved, but Rhoda's further responses indicate that she is not ready for such an advance. On the contrary, she retreats into the minimal responses that indicate that she will not produce any further evidence for the therapist and her to explore together.

Episode 5 has thus come to a full stop. After Rhoda makes this admission, she returns to the anecdote that she started in 5.24 about her going to the doctor last week, trying to show again that everything is fine with her and that her family is mistaken. The therapist does not try to push further into the emotional area at this time. She moves away from the entire topic and returns once again to the external matters of family obligations that would justify Rhoda's request to her mother in Episode 1. The therapist calls Rhoda's request "very realistic," and then pursues the question as to why Rhoda's mother said that Rhoda should have talked to Phyllis.

We could continue the analysis of this therapeutic session, adding more

5.27

	TEXT	CUES
[a]	Th.: ⟨_IV_ So they get **angry** at you.	Mitigation: 4 3, with low volume.
[b]	R.: Yes... they do, yes.	Reservation: low volume, silence.
[c]	Th.: so there's a lot of **anger** passing back and forth.	
[d]	R.: ..... Yeh..	
[e]	Th.: (Mm.) ⟩_IV_	

EXPANSION

[a] Th.: ⟨_IV_ So your family's explicit statement means that $\{E_3'\}$ they get angry at you.
[b] R.: Yes, my mother and sister do get angry at me.
[c] Th.: So $\{E_3, E_3'\}$ you are often angry at your family and they are often angry at you.
[d] R.: Yes, we are often angry at each other. ⟩_IV_

INTERACTION

[a] Th. asserts explicitly that $\overrightarrow{\_E_3'\_}$ the family feels anger towards R.
[b] R. agrees hesitantly.
[c] Th. asserts that $\overrightarrow{\_E_3\_}$ R. feels anger towards her family as well as the family feels anger towards R.
[d] R. agrees very hesitantly to 5.27[c].

---

and more examples of the fundamental patterns that are exhibited here; but the sequence from Episode 1 and Episode 5 seems to reveal the fundamental pattern of the therapeutic operation. We have seen what the therapist is trying to accomplish—to move from discussion of everyday events and the overt norms recognized by society into the area of deeply felt emotions. We have also seen the kinds of resistance that the patient is capable of showing and the difficulties the therapist has in moving to her final goal. We have not been arbitrary in terminating Episode 5 at this point. It represents a local maximum, the therapist's furthest penetration into the area of deeper emotional reactions.

10

WHAT HAS HAPPENED IN THIS SESSION

The preceding six chapters have presented a comprehensive discourse analysis of five episodes from a single therapeutic session. The analysis of the text is formalized in a series of cross sections; some of these are linked into longer sequences that display the deeper levels of coherence. The various episodes exhibit particular aspects of the therapeutic work and exhibit various answers to the question: "What is the therapist trying to do?"

In this chapter, we will approach the question by examining the five episodes together, as an example of one kind of therapeutic practice.

The therapy we have been studying was carried out by a highly experienced social worker in an agency that specialized in the sustained treatment of individual cases. The therapist had been exposed to the psychoanalytic tradition through many formal and informal educational channels. She and her colleagues were participants in that tradition and were well versed in such modern developments as ego psychology. They shared among them a certain ideological orientation towards the causes of human failure: profoundly seated emotions that originated in earlier family relationships. This orientation is consistent with the view that emerges from our analysis of the therapeutic work in this session. In the course of daily life, these deep emotions are usually masked by a variety of social and psychological mechanisms and are not always recognized by the actors involved. However, their effects can be seen by the continued disturbance of family relationships and the neurotic behavior that interferes with the life goals of the family members.*

The session begins with the presentation of material from everyday life. In trying to understand this material, the therapist elicits a larger body of

---

*Chapter 1 cites a number of recent references indicating the psychoanalytic thinking that has had the most influence upon the therapist and her colleagues (cf. Chapter 1, p. 12).

information about complex family networks. In the course of the discussion, the therapist brings to bear her informal sociological expertise to present commonly accepted norms and suggest the obvious resolution of certain family problems. Throughout this discussion, she gives many indications that she is also thinking about other questions involving the feelings that family members have towards each other; in Episode 5 she finally engages in a direct discussion of those feelings. She presents an opposition between what people are *saying* and what they are *feeling*, and she indicates plainly that she believes that feelings are more fundamental. This mode of argument has been discussed at many points throughout the five episodes, and does not require further elaboration here. The overall shape of the therapeutic conversation is dictated by the theory that insight is to be gained by moving from a discussion of superficial matters (social interaction) to fundamental causes (feelings).

There are, of course, many other orientations towards therapy, and some of these reverse the pattern just outlined. There are social workers who begin by observing the expression of violent emotions and gradually try to elucidate the structural situation and the financial problems within the family, which they see as the underlying causes—or at least the causes they can remedy. If we examine the literature on anorexia nervosa, we find many approaches to treatment (see Chapter 1, pages 8–12). Some therapists believe that it is best to deal directly with the family as a whole, to observe and correct, if possible, the unbalanced power relationships. But face-to-face interviews with the patient alone still represent the predominant mode of treating this and most other psychological problems. Our analysis applies most directly to this orientation, though the general principles of the study of discourse apply to any conversation. The answer to the question, "What is the therapist trying to do?" must be answered in relation to the particular orientation of this therapeutic session. Chapter 11 will deal with more general issues in the application of our method to the study of conversation.

THE FIVE EPISODES AS A WHOLE

In the course of the analysis, we have set up a number of units, a necessary device for any close examination. The grammatical units of word and sentence have been useful, and we also have found it convenient to group one or more sentences in a single cross section. On a larger scale, we find that narratives provide natural units that are clearly marked in their beginnings and endings. The most important structural unit in our therapeutic session is the episode. Each of the five episodes is marked by two features: (1) they deal with a distinct topic drawn from everyday life or from emotional issues, and (2) the major initiative for conversation is the

THE FIVE LESSONS AS A WHOLE   331

therapist's intervention in this area. Thus Episodes 2 through 5 are dominated by the following initiatives:

Episode 2:   *Now what about Aunt Editha, she doesn't help you in the house?*
Episode 3:   *Well, what would happen if you—um—you know—tried to arrive at some working relationship with her—*
Episode 4:   *Now—tell me: why is mother staying there so long—I don't understand. Is it something the matter there?**
Episode 5:   *Well what they're really doing to you is similar to what . . . . . to what you did with them around the dieting.*

The therapist's role in re-directing the session is natural enough, since we have seen that Rhoda tends to stay on the same subject, repeating herself until she is interrupted. We do not know if this pattern is characteristic of her conversation in general; but it is consistent throughout the therapeutic sessions.

The topics and ranges of these first four episodes are related in a symmetrical way. We can show their structural relations by two sets of enclosing circles:

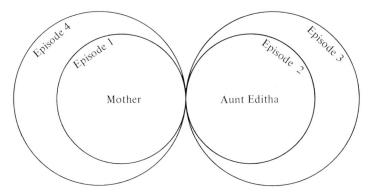

Episodes 1 and 4 are cyclical initiatives revolving about mother, and Episodes 2 and 3 are focused in a similar way on Editha. Episode 3 is seen as an enlargement of Episode 2, and Episode 4 enlarges upon Episode 1. Another view of these relative domains can be seen in Figure 40, which lcoates these narratives in the structure of family relationships that we have developed in Figure 11". Episode 1 deals with only three members: Rhoda, her mother (in roles in two different households), and indirectly Rhoda's sister. Episode 2 is also confined to a narrow context: it deals only with

---

*It should be noted that Rhoda is the one who actually shifts the topic in this case, away from Aunt Editha and back to her relations with mother. But it is the therapist who provides the initiative for the main narrative of Episode 4.

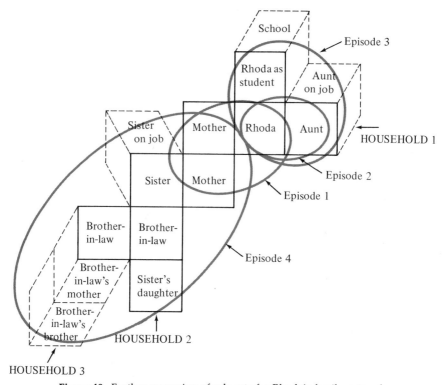

Figure 40. Further expansion of role sets for Rhoda's family network.

Rhoda and her aunt as members of Household 1. Episode 3 enlarges this view to show us the consequences of the fact that both Rhoda and her aunt work, adding two more roles, and so we see the conflict between their obligations at work and at home. Episode 4 has the widest range: it includes at least six persons: Rhoda, her mother, her sister, her sister's husband, his mother, and his brother. Furthermore, we now see Rhoda's sister in two roles: mother and worker, so this conflict is added to the social motivations of behavior.

Episode 5 contracts, focusing more narrowly upon Rhoda, her mother, and her sister. However, it is differentiated more sharply along another dimension: it marks a sudden turn away from the discussion of everyday social interaction into the area of feeling. Thus the episodes fall into two widely separated groups. The first four deal with social interaction in everyday life {S}, and the fifth deals with the psychological interpretation of actions and emotions {E}. At first glance, this appears to be an abrupt and sudden movement, and even though we see that the therapist showed several indications that she was thinking of making this move, it is not immediately clear why she was more prepared for it at the beginning of

Episode 5 than she would have been at the beginning of Episode 2. This is a fundamental question we must attempt to answer in this chapter.

TWO SURFACES AND TWO INTERIORS

Throughout these chapters, we have made a systematic contrast between the surface structure—what is actually said—and various levels of underlying structure that represent what is done in conversation. There are many ways in which these speech actions can be seen as more fundamental or more central to human behavior. We have argued that the fundamental coherence of conversation is reflected in connections between actions rather than connections between utterances. The relationship we have shown above between the exterior discussion of social interaction and the interior discussion of emotions can be replicated on both these planes. Given the framework of the therapist that emotions are central and fundamental to the behavior being studied, we can show two such concentric circles.

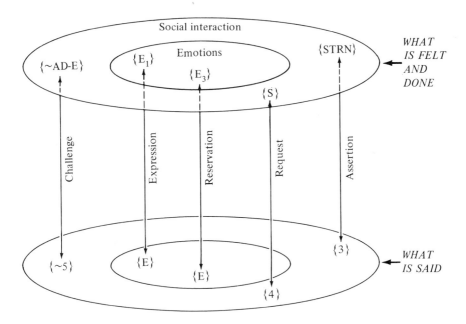

The arrows connecting these two planes are familiar symbols for the rules of production and interpretation we have seen in a number of diagrams above. Another way to look at these rules is to think of them as the actions themselves, which locate in the interactive plane the longitudinal propositions that are extracted from the conversation as a whole. Since this is a static view of the relation of these planes, we can insert on the upper plane several of these propositions to illustrate the structure that remains as a result of the conversational interaction. Particular utterances may represent *assertions* of these propositions, but we also find the propositions involved in *challenges, retreats, supports,* and *denials.* There is a sense in which the longitudinal propositions represent the underlying content, which is manipulated by the speech act being performed.

The social propositions refer to structural facts, and they can be thought of as neutral on the affective plane. Not everyone wants to be an adult, or a student, or head of a household—these are social facts that can be coupled with almost any emotional state. On the other hand, we find a rather restricted series of emotions in the underlying center of the therapeutic session we are studying:

{E_1} Rhoda feels frustration.
{E_2} Rhoda feels guilt.
{E_3} Rhoda feels anger.
{E_4} Rhoda feels loneliness.

Not all underlying emotions are negative. People have many indirect ways of showing such profound emotions as love, pity, admiration, and gratitude. In some therapeutic sessions, the patient appears unable to express these positive emotions. However they are not a central problem for this therapy: the ultimate focus is on anger, frustration, guilt, and loneliness. The therapist is trying to deal with the psychopathology that underlies Rhoda's self-destructive behavior, and it is not likely that she will find it in positive emotions that bind people together.

It should also be noted that not all of these emotions are located far below the surface. Some topics are so loaded with emotion that they evoke a very marked reaction when they occur in surface structure. For example, there is no simple way to refer to Rhoda's weight without disturbing the smooth flow of conversation (see 5.1 ff.). On the other hand, the various devices that people use to disguise, mask, and mitigate emotion are so effective that it is possible to listen to very long stretches of conversation without picking up any obvious signs of what people are feeling. (See the first half of Episode 4.)

MASKING AND RESISTANCE

One of the first questions we raised in regard to therapy is why the process often takes so long. We are studying the 25th in a series of weekly sessions between Rhoda and the therapist. We have seen many examples of the phenomenon that therapists call *resistance.* If the patient could express simply and clearly what she felt and could give a perfectly accurate view of her relations with others, the therapist's problem would be simple. Then no psychopathology would be involved. The most difficult problem for the therapist is, therefore, to see through the many forms of masking and mitigating behavior that prevent the patient from seeing her own problem clearly and explaining it to others.

First of all, it would be unreasonable to expect everyone to tell the full truth at all times. It is normal for people to give only the part of the truth that favors their point of view, and without lying directly, they are capable of denying a large part of the reality that determines the success or failure of their actions. Rhoda is able to report the interaction with her mother without recognizing explicitly that she failed to get her mother to come home. She reports that her aunt took offense for no obvious reason, and she even denies explicitly that she insulted her. We noted that she was entitled to deny an insult conveyed by intonation alone, (2.9: *I didn' yell and scream.*). At the same time, she is denying something very real that occurred in social interaction, which would explain for her, if Rhoda were willing to recognize that fact, why her aunt behaved as she did. To this extent, Rhoda is not in full contact with the factual reality of her everyday situation.

Secondly, all participants in the conversations we have studied use a rich variety of mitigating devices, which transform the surface appearance of the speech actions they are performing and the propositions that they are using. Without such devices, interaction would be too abrasive to be maintained. Goffman has alerted us to the extraordinary amount of work that must be done to maintain the *face* necessary for continued social interaction.

> The person shows respect and politeness, making sure to extend to others any ceremonial treatment that might be their due. He employs discretion; he leaves unstated facts that might implicitly or explicitly contradict and embarrass the positive claims made by others. He employs circumlocutions and deceptions, phrasing his replies with careful ambiguity so that the others' face is preserved even if their welfare is not [Goffman 1967: 16–17].

Let us examine briefly the range of mitigating devices Rhoda uses in the therapeutic session.

(a) *Euphemisms.* Rhoda substitutes one lexical item, which refers to a milder or a mitigated form of emotion, for another, which is more direct: *bother* for *anger* (2.3, 5.16), *annoyed* for *angered* (5.23, 5.24).

(b) *Vague reference.* Rhoda uses a series of vague and abstract terms to refer to her family problems: *jistalittle.. situation* (1.1), *things are getting just a little too much* (1.10), *it's getting a little too much* (4.14).

(c) *Intonation.* When Rhoda wants to express aggressive feelings, she usually does not convey her message explicitly. Instead, she uses words that are neutral or ambiguous, and the aggressive intent is conveyed by prosodic features. Thus the message 'You're crazy if you think that' is superimposed on *You call that clean?* by the intonation contour of Figure 25. A different technique is illustrated by 2.5, where Rhoda conveys the message 'How can she be so unreasonable?' by many interruptions and choking effects accompanying her description of her aunt's peculiar behavior. The omission of the aggressive words is a mitigating and masking device, although the intonation is aggravating.

(d) *A narrative response.* In many situations, Rhoda responds to a request for information or action with a message that is quite aggressive: 'That wouldn't work because she is so unreasonable,' or 'My mother is away so long because my sister is behaving selfishly.' However these propositions are never stated. Instead, Rhoda gives the narratives of Episodes 2 and 4, in which the evaluative point is conveyed by the narrative as a whole. Thus the mode of narrative response is a mitigating device because the aggressive message (the evaluative point) is never stated directly.

One of the most obvious forms of mitigation is to leave things unsaid. But from these examples we see that there is a great deal of elaboration involved, too. Rhoda omits a number of direct statements and direct connections, but then expands at length with other conversational devices. On the whole, she is quite verbal in this session, but the use of these masking and mitigating devices means that the therapist has to do a great deal of work to decipher what she "really" means and validly assay her inner states.

The examples of verbal interaction are drawn from Rhoda's interaction with the therapist and from her reports of her interaction with members of her family. Rhoda shows that other members of her family use some of the same devices, but not all of them. They appear to share with her the family pattern of the rich use of intonation contour. Presumably they also use euphemisms; but Rhoda does not show us other family members using vague reference, hesitation, and narrative response in the way that she does. On the other hand, they appear to make a greater use of complex indirect speech acts to mitigate and mask their intentions. This appears quite clearly if we list all of the quotations from other family members that occur in these five episodes:

1.9   Mother: "Oh, *why-y*?"
1.11 Mother: "Well, *why don't you tell* **Phyllis** *that*?"
2.7   Editha: "Oh-I-I—it looks *clean* to me,"
3.5   Editha: "You don't like to eat alone."
3.11 Editha: "Well, not that I get lonesome, but I don't like to eat alone."
3.20 Editha: *"**Why** do you need it?"*
3.22 Editha: *"Why—w-you got enough?"*
4.10 Mother: "Well I'll go home Wednesday morning."
      Sister: "Oh no, don't go, I'm gonna work."

4.13 Mother: *"Why-y?"*
4.15 Mother: *"See, I told you so."*
4.18 Mother: *"Well, yeh, next week... uh—I don't feel like going this week."*
4.19 Sister: *"Well, maybe at the end of the week."*
Mother: *"Well, maybe,"*
5.6 Sister: *"Oh, nothing's **wrong** with her. Everything's **fine**."*
5.16 Sister: *"Oh, **Rhoda** should never get **tired**."*
5.24 *"Oh, you're **thin!**"*

From these quotations, we can see that there is a common character to the style of family interaction, but there also seem to be individual differences. In Rhoda's quotations, her sister and mother speak quite fluently, and the editorial intonations that Rhoda superimposes on them do nothing to disturb this effect. They are in a superordinate position in relation to her, and the devices they use for masking and mitigation reflect this security.

SOURCES OF INSIGHT FOR THE THERAPIST

We must now look at this conversation from the therapist's point of view, especially if we want to provide some answers to the question, "What is the therapist trying to do?" First of all, her task is to find out what is going on: to uncover the etiology of the disorder and the psychodynamics that maintain it. The therapist has to discover how family members deal with each other and how they respond emotionally to each other. In the characteristic interview situation, she is talking to one person only. She knows that Rhoda, like any competent speaker, has the ability to adjust her point of view and way of accounting for herself to the person she is dealing with. How can the therapist read through the effect of the interview situation to the basic situation that has produced Rhoda's anorexia? This is a fundamental problem for any interview situation where the interviewer wants to know how the person behaves when she is not being interviewed.*

At first glance, it seems that Rhoda presents an effective screen to any attempt the therapist might make to penetrate her many defenses. Throughout the first four episodes, we see that Rhoda is engaged in long exercises in self-justification. Furthermore, she seems to have a great ability to avoid the central issues. She denies the strong emotions the therapist suspects lie behind her failure to eat. On the surface, this seems to be a very unlikely source of information for solving the problem.

Earlier in this chapter, we asked if there was any perceptible movement in the first four episodes. Has the therapist learned anything about Rhoda's

---

*There is a close parallel here to the Observer's Paradox in sociolinguistic studies, which provides the central motivation for the many techniques developed in community studies (Labov, 1972a, Chapter 8).

problem from these discussions? In the final episode, Rhoda shows a more profound form of resistance, and it is not clear what the therapist has learned from her direct inquiry into emotions. The therapist seems to have come to this inquiry with a certain amount of knowledge: where has she obtained it?

1. Factual Contradictions. There are many points at which Rhoda's statements can be weighed against factual situations, and Rhoda's contact with reality can be assessed by the way in which her statements fit in with those facts. The striking thing about Rhoda's verbal behavior is that it shows such a poor fit with the factual background the therapist has at her command.

(a) *Rhoda's success in dealing with her mother.* Rhoda presents herself in Episode 1 as carrying out the therapist's suggestion by asking her mother for help, and she seems to feel that she did a good job, but the fact remains that she did not obtain that help.

(b) *Rhoda's success in dealing with her aunt.* Rhoda explains in Episode 2 why her aunt is no help to her, but the fact remains that she still has too much housework to do, and has not been able to get her aunt to help.

(c) *Rhoda's weight.* Rhoda claims that she eats a normal amount, but her weight is still so low that this seems very unlikely: This pattern is consistent with the history of other anorexia cases.

The therapist cannot solve Rhoda's problem just by observing such contradictions. They only sharpen the problem by directing her attention to inconsistencies where Rhoda's own account must be considered suspect. The therapist must then discover what psychological defenses are operating at this point, and what emotional problems lie beneath the failure to achieve the stated goals.

2. Emotional Displays. In order to solve the puzzles presented by such contradictions, the therapist must search for evidence of the actual psychodynamics that produce them. The Episodes are not undifferentiated in this respect: In each one, there are one or two points where intense emotion is displayed—emotion that is frequently masked or denied, but that is, nonetheless, in evidence. These are concentrated at the quotations from family interaction, which we have frequently identified as centers for the most complex kind of speech acts. These quotations from Family Style show the mechanisms by which family members deal with each other and the verbal style that appears to prevail in the family.

We have given above a list of quotations from other family members concentrated at a few points in the session. However, the actors are not speaking for themselves: how can the therapist believe that Rhoda is giving

SOURCES OF INSIGHT FOR THE THERAPIST

her a true account of how other family members have dealt with her? It is true that Rhoda superimposes her own editorial intonation on a number of these utterances. Yet there is good reason to believe that these quotations reflect social reality: that they are not created by Rhoda as projections of her own inner states. They provide the mechanism that explains the contradictions in Rhoda's own accounts, and they show why she is not getting the results that she thinks she should get.

The most striking example is the primary data of this session: Rhoda's attempt to get her mother to come home. The accounts of Episodes 1 and 4 reveal that Rhoda's mother successfully put her off in such a way that Rhoda was left with an accounting that showed that her mother was not to blame. Rhoda's narratives indicate that her mother challenged her motivation for making the request and seemed to resent the underlying criticism that came with the request. She then put forward the excuse that it was really up to Rhoda's sister to decide and managed to get Rhoda to accept that excuse. The acceptance is superficial: there is plenty of evidence that Rhoda holds a resentment towards her mother's treatment of her, even though she is not free to express it to her directly (... *Now—when I see— that she says, "Oh!" so I said, "What you mean 'Oh'?"*).

When roles are reversed, and Rhoda shows herself dealing aggressively with her aunt, we find a similar case of strong emotion generated in response to the family style of verbal interaction. Rhoda's own account shows her insulting her aunt and denying the insult (2.6–2.8). The result is an emotion the aunt does not feel free to express (*Sh' short of gave me a funny look as if I—hurt her in some way*). From such an episode, the therapist can grasp the ways in which family members injure each other and generate long-lasting emotions that continue to interfere with their expressed goals.

If we did not have direct access to the therapist's reactions, we still would be able to infer them from the way in which she uses this knowledge in her later dealings with Rhoda. Fortunately, the *Playback* sessions give us a direct documentation of the therapist's sensitivity to these critical displays of verbal interaction. Furthermore, these *Playback* sessions were carried out shortly after the actual treatment session, when the events were fresh in the therapist's mind, and long before we had done any analysis of the conversational interaction. Some of the therapist's comments are spontaneous; others were responses to Fanshel's immediate reactions to issues quite distinct from those we have been considering here. The therapist was quite sparing in her comments during the *Playback* of this session: it is all the more striking that two of her most extended reactions were produced at the two points we have been considering. During the second account of Rhoda's attempt to get her mother to come home, the therapist shows her great sensitivity to the key utterance, "Oh, why?" and particularly to the intonation contour:

4.15 *"See, I told you so."*

340 WHAT HAS HAPPENED IN THIS SESSION

DF: A KIND OF ONE-UPMANSHIP SEEMS EVIDENT THERE. IN RHODA'S EXPRESSING HER NEEDS, WHAT IS REVEALED IS LABELLED AS A KIND OF WEAKNESS.
TH: YES, WEAKNESS. AND YOU SEE SHE MIMICS HER MOTHER. YOU CAN JUST HEAR HER. SHE SAYS, "ARE YOU COMING *HOME* TOMORROW?" (THERAPIST USES EXAGGERATED INTONATION HERE TO IMITATE RHODA.) AND THE MOTHER SAYS, "OH, WHY?" (THERAPIST AGAIN USES EXAGGERATED INTONATION) AND WAITS. AND YOU ALMOST KNOW THIS IS THE WAY THE MOTHER WAS BAITING IT. AND NOW IT'S COMING OUT. MOTHER IS GIVING HER TIME TO THE SISTER WHICH SHOULD BE PUT INTO HER OWN HOME.
DF: AND THE WAY THE MOTHER HANDLES RHODA'S NEED HAS A DESTRUCTIVE QUALITY TO IT.
TH: YES, SHE'S VERY SARCASTIC... SHE SAYS, "OH, I THOUGHT YOU DIDN'T NEED ME."

It is important to note that the therapist is quite willing to accept the intonation contour attributed to her mother by Rhoda and to interpret it as something mother actually said. Figure 19' compares Rhoda's rendition of this contour with the therapist's imitation of it. The therapist is interested in extracting the meaningful aspect of this contour, and she exaggerates its features for this purpose. If we compare the interpretation that she gives

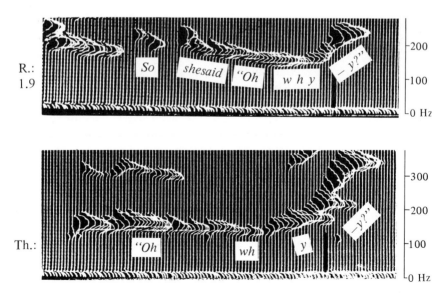

Figure 19'. Comparison of the intonation contour for "*Oh why-y*" reported by Rhoda in 1.8 and 4.13 and mimicked by the therapist in the *Playback* session.

SOURCES OF INSIGHT FOR THE THERAPIST 341

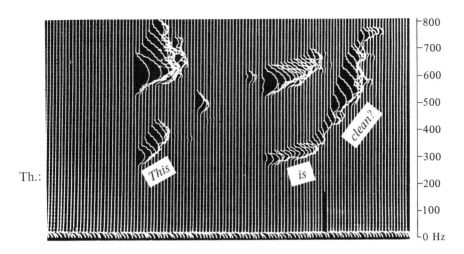

Figure 25'. The therapist's imitation of the intonation contour for 2.8, *That looks clean to you?* in the *Playback* session.

with our expansion of 1.9 (Chapter 5, p. 166) and 4.13 (Chapter 8, p. 269), we can see that the therapist's quick and intuitive response to this utterance has captured the essence of our more painstaking analysis.

The therapist shows the same keen sensitivity to intonation contours in her discussion of the interchange with Editha. It is all the more remarkable, since she reviews this at a much later period in the session, in response to a comment by Rhoda that she is not used to speaking out. The therapist remembers Rhoda's intonation contour and reproduces it in an exaggerated form to bring out its significance. Again, we have an opportunity to compare two versions of the same utterance reported by Rhoda (in 2.8 and 2.9) with the therapist's imitation. Figure 25' may be compared to Figure 25 on page 201 to show that the therapist has brought out the salient characteristics of Rhoda's utterance.

In one sense, the first four episodes remain at a constant distance from the emotional center of Rhoda's problem, as the therapist sees it. In another sense, they give us accumulating evidence on the emotional consequences of this style of family interaction. Figure 41 shows how the therapist gains insight into the emotional consequences of these interactions.

The first four episodes follow each other on the periphery of a circle. The second half of Episode 4 overlaps Episode 1 as Rhoda returns to her original theme. At one or two points in each episode, we have entered the emotional displays that give the therapist insight into the emotional dynamics of the family: the arrows point inward from the behavioral situa-

Fanshel picked up this indication that Rhoda was in the process of learning something:

DF: RHODA SEEMS TO BE REFLECTING RATHER OBJECTIVELY ABOUT HER AUNT AT THIS POINT IN THE SESSION—SHE SEEMS TO BE SEEING HER ALMOST FOR THE FIRST TIME.
TH: BUT SHE SAW, VERY CORRECTLY SO, THAT SHE WAS BEHAVING WITH AUNT EDITHA THE WAY HER MOTHER BEHAVES WITH HER. SHE WAS TREATING HER AUNT LIKE A HELPLESS CHILD. HOW HELPLESS AUNT EDITHA REALLY IS WE DON'T KNOW.

2. Interpretation. In discussions of the technique of the psychoanalytic process, a great deal of attention is given to the act of interpretation. It is not always easy to separate these acts from the main body of the conversation, but many can be recognized by the special topic (discussion of feelings) or their special structure (parallels and analogies). The critical question is when an interpretation is to be put forward, and this is closely connected to the phenomenon of resistance.

> Whenever it is clear to the analyst that the patient almost grasps such a connection of repetition, or almost perceives the meaning of the constellation of events, when, in short, the patient shows that he knows something but doesn't realize that he knows it—at such a point the analyst may intervene in the process like an accoucher assisting in the delivery of a baby [Menninger and Holzman, 1973, p. 125].

There is no reason to think that the patient will automatically accept such an interpretation, and considerable attention has been given to the various forms of response. Bordin (1974) summarizes a number of such studies: for example, Speisman (1959) found that in actual therapeutic interviews "interpretations rated as slightly beyond the patient's current level of awareness were more likely to be followed by a decrease in resistance than interpretations which either fell more within or further beyond the patient's level of awareness."

Once the therapist has made the decision to introduce an overt interpretation, we have reached a conversational level where the modes of expression, argument, and interaction are quite direct. However, the propositional content may be quite complex itself, as we have seen:

5.1 Th.: (breath) *Well what they are really doing to you is so similar to what ... apparently this goes on in the family—to what you did with them aroun-nd the dieting.*

It is sometimes simpler to see such propositions expressed as analogies, as we did in Chapter 9:

$$\frac{\text{R}\rightarrow\text{FAM ''I am independent.''}}{\text{FAM}\rightarrow\text{R [Withholds all help.]}} = \frac{\text{FAM}\rightarrow\text{R ''You eat too much.''}}{\text{R}\rightarrow\text{FAM [Stops eating altogether.]}}$$

3. Direct suggestion. There is a wide range of attitude among therapists towards the use of direct suggestions. None of the therapists we have contacted would like to be considered "directive," though they are not in the "nondirective" tradition of Rogerian therapy. We have made it abundantly clear that the therapist is quite cautious in making any direct suggestion for Rhoda, since her history shows that she reacts strongly against such suggestions. In any case, a suggestion does not take the form of direct advice for the person to do something, but rather is a suggestion that such and such may be the case. This may be part of the process of putting the patient into touch with her own emotions, and those that surround her.

> 5.22   Th.: (breath) *So—then—and for some reason you feel they're **angry** because you're so, underweight . . .*

It is not accidental that the therapist can be heard to take a breath before each of the interventions we have just quoted. The placement of this interpretation is an important decision for her, and her suprasegmental cues show that she is aware that she is taking a chance. If the patient shows extreme resistance to the suggestion, it may be a backward step for the course of therapy.

Our own analysis is not designed to evaluate the therapist's interpretations or speculate on their success or failure. We are interested in the process by which the therapist and patient interact in conversation, gain insights, and move the course of therapy to new topics and new levels of discussion.

THE ROLE OF MITIGATION AND THE PARADOX OF MICROANALYSIS

At a number of points in our analysis, we have called attention to the fact that our expansions and interactional statements exaggerate the aggressive character of verbal interaction. When we separate the mitigating devices from high-level speech acts, we present those speech acts without the mitigated guise that was actually used. Our interactional statement has the ring of reality in one sense—it seems to represent what was actually done. In another sense, it plays false to the actual events because it projects a level of conflict not experienced by the participants. There is every reason to feel that this conflict existed and that it did motivate the events that occurred. On the other hand, it was mitigated successfully and did not lead to a breach of social relations, which would have occurred if the speech acts had been carried out in a more direct form. In other words, mitigating devices do indeed mitigate conflict.

It is necessary to confront directly the paradox of microanalysis: the more deeply we analyze the underlying speech actions that motivated these sequences of events, the further we remove ourselves from the conversation as it was actually experienced.* Most of our analysis has been directed to the question "What did she *really* mean?" in the sense of "What was the fundamental action that she was performing?" An understanding of the whole process means that this act of analysis must be followed by a synthesis, in which we address the question "Did she *really* mean it?"

This second question approaches the problem of meaning in the sense of *intent*, which we have not addressed directly. Our analyses show how participants interpreted their exchanges, as we construct a model that would explain the obvious coherence of the interaction for participants. To make any statement about the actual intent and understanding of the speaker, one would have to know the level of his awareness of the underlying speech actions and the operation of the mitigating devices. All we can do here is to call attention to two distinct problems: (1) What kind of formal linguistic mechanism could we use to recombine the underlying propositions and actions with the mitigating device to produce the direct combination of semantic and affective factors? and (2) To what extent is the speaker influenced by his own use of masking and mitigating devices? We have seen that mitigation operates to reduce conflict between speakers in different social roles: does it also disguise a person's meaning from himself? Rhoda is reluctant to face her own anger, and when she says that she is just a little *bothered* or *annoyed*, it is reasonable to think that she does not realize that she feels angry. When she argues that she didn't *yell* and *scream* but only said, *That looks **clean** to you?* she may also have succeeded in disguising from herself the aggressive nature of her behavior. We cannot decide this issue from the evidence we have, but the therapist must contend with this ambiguity and resolve it if her interpretations are to be accepted, and if she is to win new insight for the patient.

THE OUTCOME OF THE THERAPY

As we studied the overall pattern of this session and the therapy as a whole, we were increasingly impressed with the skill with which the therapist dealt with a problem of this severity and complexity. Some readers do not share this impression when they are first exposed to the close analysis of the text. The paradox of microanalysis applies to the

---

*This problem was insightfully noted by the authors of *The First Five Minutes* (1960) in the ninth of the general principles that we quoted in Chapter 1: "One must not mistake the five-inch scale model for the fly itself."

evaluation of the therapist as well as to the study of the patient. When the technique of the therapist is exposed in detail, the analysis produces the illusion that the therapist is manipulating the patient in a crude and obvious way. This is an inevitable product of the analytical study of spontaneous interaction.

Listeners can develop a hypercritical attitude towards the methods the therapist uses to reinforce the patient's responses, to mitigate her own suggestions, and to model appropriate behavior for the patient. These reactions often fail to take into account the sense of mutuality that has developed in this series of therapeutic sessions, and the special relationship between a young adult and a mature therapist. In any case, this illusion of mechanical and directive behavior disappears when one becomes more familiar with the materials and enters into the delicate problems of therapy from the therapist's point of view. In the course of this analysis, we became convinced that the therapist had gained great insight into the problem and was dealing with it in a sensitive and professional manner.

The outcome of the therapy was successful. The sessions continued for some period after the one analyzed here, and were terminated by the consent of both parties. We learned from the therapist 5 years later that Rhoda had returned to normal weight; she had married and was raising children in a home of her own.

11

DIRECTIONS FOR THE MICROANALYSIS OF CONVERSATION

Our study of therapeutic discourse has been motivated by two interests: the desire to discover what takes place in the conversation between a therapist and her patient, and the desire to extend the scope of linguistic analysis to conversation as a whole. These interests are quite general today among psychoanalysts, psychologists, anthropologists, and linguists; even the combination of the latter two interests is now an established tradition. In our first chapter, we quoted extensively from Pittenger, Hockett, and Danehy, whose study of the first 5 minutes of another therapeutic session provided a set of 9 principles that have been further confirmed in our own work.

The union of these two interests also represents a union of theory and practice. Students who are beginning their training in therapeutic work are anxious to gain some understanding of this process, and those who are already skilled are aware of how much they can gain from each advance in self-awareness. Many of the training programs that now exist and the manuals now in print are aimed at a high level of abstraction, and look quite beyond the details of conversational interaction. Trainees typically write narratives that summarize their overall impressions of what has happened or give oral reports of their impressions. Even when tape recordings are made available, students have no way of orienting themselves to the problem of analysis.

Since conversation is a multifaceted and complex human activity, it is plain that there will be many approaches to an understanding of it. No one technique could say very much of what could be said about a conversation. At the same time, we find that the most sophisticated approaches to conversation have an unpredictable character. Given a body of text, there is almost no way of saying what features will arouse the interest of the analyst, and once he has found a structural point of interest, it is very difficult to say in what direction his interest will carry him.

The most systematic approach to verbal interaction has been the Interaction Process Analysis of Bales (1950), whose categories and concepts are frequently found in more recent work. We have already commented on the limitations of this utterance-by-utterance form of immediate categorization, but Bales' division of speech actions into cognitive, affective, and instrumental types is reflected in our own statements of interactional analysis.

In recent years, the work of Sacks, Schegloff, and Jefferson has given a systematic character to the study of sequencing (1974). Their work on turntaking will inevitably play a larger role when our own approach to discourse analysis is applied to multiperson conversations. If we are to make serious progress in the study of conversation, several different approaches must converge.

The central innovation of our own approach is the view that sequencing rules operate between abstract speech actions, and that they often are arranged in a complex hierarchy. There are no necessary connections between utterances at the surface level, though sequencing patterns may take such surface structure into account.

The concept of hierarchical organization is plainly derived from the linguistic analysis of phonology and grammar. During the period that we have developed and applied this approach to therapeutic discourse, from 1966 to 1975, there has been a great deal of parallel activity in extending linguistic analysis beyond the sentence. Much of this has been done with introspective materials, and the examples quoted have been from conversations that the analyst imagined as possible or persuasive. We do not believe that we could have imagined this therapeutic session or constructed conversational interaction with this type of multilayered hierarchical activity. Some analysts have found it useful to look at conversations imagined by playwrights (Watzlawick, Beavin, and Jackson, 1967), but we are not convinced that the productions of the playwright are a strategic research site for the understanding of natural conversation.

There is one advantage in working with imagined exchanges or making up entire conversations. We then know everything there is to be known about the characters, their factual knowledge, and their histories. The problem of correct interpretation is therefore simplified. There are no references or allusions that might escape us and no hidden connotations from past history that might be more meaningful to the participants than they are to us. Working with real conversations of real speakers poses a profound and perhaps insoluble problem for the external observer, and we may refer to this as the "problem of correct interpretation."

THE IMPORTANCE OF HISTORICAL AND FACTUAL CONTEXT

In principle, the problem of correct interpretation cannot be solved entirely. We can never hope to have all the knowledge that the participants shared among themselves; but we can approximate a solution to this problem by various strategies, and the convergence of all of these strategies will ultimately provide a solution for the problem.

The first step is to be aware of the seriousness of the problem and the likelihood of making gross errors in interpretation in the study of isolated texts.

We have many examples of conversations that have been studied for some time with incorrect interpretations of words and gestures, until someone who had a better knowledge of the history and factual background of the speakers arrived.*

In the therapeutic sessions we have been studying, the therapist gradually accumulates a great deal of information about the patient's history and background. Our entire study documents the need for this contextual information. In another *Playback* session, the same therapist was dealing with a husband and wife who were having problems in their marriage. At one point, the husband said that it might be time for them to have their first child. This would mean losing the wife's income. The wife began to object, in a whining tone of voice, that she would have to give up her housekeeper, the beauty parlor, and so on. The husband then said, *Have a match*. Though Fanshel had heard several sessions with this couple, he simply could not understand this cryptic comment. The therapist had already learned from a much earlier session that this was a private way of

---

*A striking example was provided recently in a seminar devoted to the study of conversation through the observation of video tape recordings. Many members of the class adhered to the principle that no background information was needed for the interpretation of conversations other than what could be observed in the recording itself. One member who held this view began to provide some background information as he introduced a video recording he had made of a family gathered in their kitchen. He was challenged to withhold all of that information until the seminar members had studied the interaction by itself. The discussion was thus turned into a test of the claim that no background information was needed for the systematic study of conversation.

At one point in the conversation, a wife said to her husband, *You don't say that blood is thicker than water!* The husband then turned his head away from his wife and the group as a whole. Members of the seminar discussed this scene for some time with the common interpretation that the wife's statement was heard as an insult, and that the husband had withdrawn from the conversation with a gesture that symbolized repressed anger. When the member who was familiar with the history of the family began to discuss this situation, however, it appeared that he had the reverse understanding: the wife's statement was a compliment to the husband—he shared her concern for her own family—and the gesture was interpreted properly as a modest turning aside in the face of a compliment.

referring to the story of the little match girl, who froze to death, and the husband had chosen this way of saying that his wife was exaggerating her problems by pretending to suffer like the poor little match girl.

Many investigators feel that data of this kind are much too particular to be relevant to their analyses. Since their rules are written at a level of great generality, it is not clear to them why they must be involved with the particular histories of the speakers. This position seems to hold for certain general mechanisms of turntaking, and other sequential patterns of conversation that are close to the level of surface structure; but when a rule relates an element of surface structure to some more abstract speech action, it is important to decide whether or not this is the speech action that actually was utilized in that exchange.

The discourse rules we have presented in Chapter 3 are quite general. They make no reference to the particular histories of any speakers; but the rules do refer to knowledge shared by the speakers, and the analyst must know whether certain assumptions, beliefs, or propositions were actually part of that shared knowledge in order to know whether that rule was used in a particular context.

In many cases, the evidence of the immediate response shows us the interpretation that a speaker made of an utterance he had just heard. In other cases, several exchanges occur before we can see what speakers have made of each other's contributions to the conversation. But as we have noted above, there are many crucial cases where the evidence of the immediate context does not show us how speakers are interpreting what others are saying. We may have to bring together many parts of the conversation, including many widely separated utterances, in order to get the information we need to account for the behavior of the speakers. This kind of longitudinal search may be required even when we are studying particular rules of production and interpretation that apply in a single exchange. It is even more true when we turn to the study of larger patterns of interaction, such as those discussed in the previous chapter.

RESEARCH SITES FOR MICROANALYSIS

One way of attacking the problem of correct interpretation is to use conversations among speakers who are very well known to the analyst. An obvious choice is the analyst's own family. Several students have shown us transcriptions of analyses of conversations in family gatherings, and we have been impressed by the depth of the analysis, and the close approach to a solution of the problem of correct interpretation, but another consideration makes it clear that much of this work may have only limited interest for the general study of conversation. We have already noted that microanalysis magnifies the aggressive mechanisms of conversation and effectively cancels the work done by the mitigating devices. Even if all of the identifying names are changed, it would be very difficult to publish such material without causing serious damage to the personal relationships involved. If we add to the analysis a detailed statement of shared history and beliefs, it appears that very few analysts will be able to use the results of such work in actual publication. It is possible to spend several years analyzing a conversation and then find that only the most general statements can be made in publication.*

The converse possiblility is to study conversations among strangers, who do not share any knowledge among themselves that the analyst himself does not possess. Such conversations frequently occur when people meet for the first time, traveling on planes or taking vacations. It is not impossible to obtain recordings of such conversations and use them with the permission of the speakers. The exchanges are usually quite guarded and polite, and the speakers do not have a great deal at stake in the speech actions being exchanged. This is the strategy followed by Bales and others who continued in his tradition of experimental work with small groups. In order to control the variable of degree of shared knowledge, such groups are usually assembled from students who do not know each other before.

The strategy of assembling ad hoc groups may show us some general mechanisms of conversation, but it may be limited in depth and give us a misleading idea of the simplicity of the hierarchical relations of the speech acts involved. Rules of requests, responses, narrative sequencing, and turntaking may be illustrated, but these conversations may show few speech acts at the more abstract level of challenges, retreats, and defenses, which characterize the conversations of those who have more tightly structured personal relations. As Chapter 3 indicates, those who study conversations only in the abstract have written versions of the Rule of Requests which omit reference to rights and obligations—the most heavily charged part of the personal dynamics involved. For all these reasons, it is likely that the most penetrating studies of conversation will continue to focus upon intimate exchanges between people who share personal histories.

It is certainly no accident that many of the systematic studies of conversation have focused upon therapeutic sessions. As we noted in our first chapter, there is an important social need to understand the conversational exchange that takes place in therapy. These conversations are often quite extended, so we have access to a great deal of information about the speakers. The participants become involved in tense and emotional interchanges, which present some of the most difficult problems for the understanding of the mechanism of conversation and its coherence. This emotional climate is

---

*One student submitted to us a half-hour tape recording of a dinner party with two couples present, including her and her husband. According to her recollection, there would be nothing in this conversation that would prevent it from being used as an example for analysis in a seminar. After two hours' discussion, she was horrified at the aggressive mechanisms revealed, and she insisted that all copies be withdrawn immediately and destroyed.

also an advantage in diminishing the observer effect. There is no doubt that speakers never lose their awareness that the conversations are being recorded, but their involvement in the emotional dynamics of the exchanges reduces the amount of attention that can be given to the monitoring of their speech (Labov, 1972a, pp. 94–98). There is no reason to confine the study of conversation to therapeutic sessions, but for all the reasons just given, it seems likely that therapy will continue to serve as a strategic research site for our understanding of conversation.

COMPREHENSIVE DISCOURSE ANALYSIS

The method that we have introduced in this book is intended to be *explicit* and *comprehensive*. By *explicit*, we mean that the procedures are stated as plainly as possible so that anyone else who would like to use them may find it possible to do so. By *comprehensive*, we mean that we have made ourselves accountable to an entire body of conversation, attempting to account for the interpretations of all utterances and the coherent sequencing between them. We have tried to build upon previous studies of conversation; but we find that most of these studies are either global or fragmentary. Some writers quote large sections of conversation and make a few summary statements about them; this is particularly common in the psychoanalytic tradition. Other analyses extract particular elements from a conversation in unpredictable ways. Quantitative studies extract nonfluencies, pronouns, type-token ratios, or propositions and perform arithmetic operations on these. These tabulations may show some long-range trends, but they are very far from the conversational mechanisms we have studied here and have little value for the practising therapist.

The analyses that have had more influence upon our thinking are qualitative studies focusing upon particular interchanges and constructing statements of the knowledge that speakers would need to respond to each other in this way.

Among the few comprehensive studies of conversation, *The First Five Minutes* seems to provide the firmest foundation on which to build. The authors wrote in a tradition which focused on the problem of giving an explicit notation for paralinguistic cues, without instrumental help. In our terminology, their perspective was confined largely to the interrelation of the text with the paralinguistic cues. They did not deal with the hierarchical structure of propositions and speech actions, which is the major focus of this book. Yet the general principles they developed emerge with equal force from our more abstract analysis.

Throughout this study, we have intended to emphasize interpretations based on objective evidence whenever possible. In different areas of the analysis we have made varying degrees of progress. We can assay the state of the art in nine stages of this comprehensive discourse analysis.

I. The Recording. The first step in any such study is obviously a mechanical recording that can be preserved and reviewed an indefinite number of times. The original *Playback* recordings were not made with high-quality equipment. The Wollensak 1500 would certainly be replaced today with higher fidelity equipment. But since the therapist's office was a quiet, carpeted, and well-furnished room, the problems of noise and reverberation were not serious.

Other studies have been done with film or video tape (McQuown *et al.*, 1971, Scheflen, 1973), and today there is increasing emphasis on the importance of the visual record. Our own work with video tape has convinced us that we are missing a great deal of valuable information that we would have obtained if we had a visual record of this session. At the same time, there is a great deal of redundancy between auditory and visual cues. We do not know how great the loss is or what corrections might be made in an analysis as a result of studying the visual information; no studies have been made that would establish this contrast. As a next step in an over-all research design, we would certainly suggest the application of this technique to a video tape. At the same time, there are two characteristics of video tapes that must be taken into account: The observer effect is heightened, and the increase in the complexity of the information makes the problem of data reduction very severe.

II. Editing. An important part of any microanalysis is the preparation of an accurate version of the text—that is, of the words and other segmental units. It has been noted before that this is an open-ended process, and after 9 years we find that we still are making corrections that are by no means trivial on repeated listenings. Even though the process of improvement continues, the text after four or five editings presents a reasonably objective input to the analysis.

III. Fields of discourse. The divisions of the field of discourse in this analysis are specific to the therapuetic session. They correspond to the analysis of the contextual styles in sociolinguistic interviews (Labov, 1972a, Chapter 3). These divisions are presented as persuasive and interpretive devices, rather than inevitable consequences of objective evidence. We have not provided reliability tests for the divisions into fields of discourse, and we do not feel that very much depends upon any particular decision. The relation of fields of discourse to the overall definition of the interview situation helps to explain some of the violent fluctuations of style within the interview and helps us focus our attention upon a small subset of paralinguistic cues that carries the most information.

IV. Paralinguistic cues. The division between text and paralinguistic cues seems to be reasonably clear. Some of the borderline cases involve lexical items that are intimately involved with idioms and intonation patterns. We have kept in mind from the very beginning that the system of impressionistic notation based upon four or five levels has been proved defective (Lieberman, 1965). Even if the authors of *The First Five Minutes* were quite reliable among themselves in four-level pitch notation, it does not seem that this notation conveys accurate information to other linguists or to readers in general. We hope that our photographs of the display produced by a spectrum analyzer have been reasonably successful in providing objective evidence that can be assimilated and interpreted by any reader. There are limitations in this display,* but on the whole, these figures seem to be quite closely correlated with the subjective impressions from repeated listening, and they allow one to follow directly the rise and fall of the voice.

Other paralinguistic cues, such as voice qualifiers of whine or rasp, remain impressionistic and probably vary in the amount of information they convey to readers. "Choking" is not difficult to interpret but "glottalization" may not be informative without a tape recording to illustrate this feature.

The assignment of semantic values to the paralinguistic cues is one of the more problematic and less objective parts of this analysis. The labels that we have used are reasonably consistent within the five episodes that we have studied, but the same physical signals can have radically different interpretations in different contexts, and we are not sure that this battery of signals could be transposed easily to other conversations.

V. Expansion. Like editing, the expansion of the text is an open-ended process. We terminate at a certain point only because it satisfies the needs of the particular analysis to follow. We have attempted in two respects to add some systematic character to the expansion. First, we methodically examine all pronouns and pro-forms such as *thing, do so,* and so on, and attempt to give them explicit form. We attempt to complete all referentials, including indexical references to time and place. Secondly, we introduce material from other sections of the text, searching for all parallel and repeated utterances that allow us to complete ellipses and supply other missing material. In many cases, we find that these systematic procedures allow us to complete a very substantial part of the expansion.

VI. Propositions. More abstract than the expanded text are the propositions, those general statements which are said to recur implicitly or explicitly in many parts of the session. These propositions provide the firm skeleton for the surface that confronts us. Some propositions are objec-

---

*Particularly in the 100 millisecond memory period in the mode of analysis we use, which leads to some lag and distortion whenever pitch changes rapidly.

tively supported by the text itself; other propositions are never stated explicitly by the participants, but they can be supported by parallel studies in the literature. We have attempted to provide such support for all the propositions dealing with anorexia nervosa, for the rights and duties associated with households, and for the fundamental propositions of therapy itself.

VII. Rules of discourse. These rules, as summarized in Chapter 3, are of great generality, but they are not a part of the conscious knowledge available to speakers, and they are never represented explicitly in the text. Some of the lower-level rules of discourse are supported by the parallel observation of other students of speech acts: particularly, the Rule of Requests. In general, we cannot claim a very close correlation between objective evidence and this large body of abstractly stated rules. We have given great attention to breaks in the coherence of surface structure, which provide objective evidence that some relationship more abstract than the surface relations must be found to account for the continued flow of conversation; but we would not be suprised if future studies altered the forms of all the rules of discourse presented in Chapter 3.

The major research strategy in establishing such a body of abstract rules is the emphasis on simplicity and economy. In the initial stages of analysis, the number of rules grew rapidly; as we neared the end of the study of these five episodes, the number of rules that had to be added declined. If the number of discourse rules were to grow at the same rate as the number of conversations studied, there would be very little to be gained from such an analysis. We hope that the rules that we have presented here will provide a reliable core that can be used repeatedly in analyses of many kinds of conversations.

The rules of discourse provide explicit connections between forms at various levels of abstraction, providing a model of how speakers might go about producing and interpreting these hierarchical structures of speech actions. This is a characteristic problem for linguistic analysis, and there is no doubt that linguists will have the greatest interest in the specific forms of these rules. Our cross sections and diagrams are stated in such a way that it is possible to dispense with the specific forms of rules if this kind of connection is not a major concern of the reader.

VIII. Interaction. The core of the cross sectional analysis is a statement of interaction, which combines the underlying propositions with chain sequences of speech actions. These chains of actions, connected by *thereby*, are the central theoretical construct of this analysis. The fundamental distinction between *what is said* and *what is done* is a common concern of all students of speech acts. We have attempted to give specific form to this general distinction and to marshal all of the evidence at our disposal to support these chains of speech actions. Since the interactional statements are necessarily the most abstract, the evidence is always indirect, but these statements provide an account of what the speakers are doing in verbal interaction and so approach the description of the meaning of the speech.

IX. Sequences. Many discussions of conversation focus entirely upon the problem of sequencing, but in our analysis, only a minority of rules refer to connections between utterances. The major attention is upon the abstract basis of these connections; much of the sequencing follows automatically from the nature of the speech actions involved. Challenges are followed by defenses or admissions; requests are followed by compliance, put-offs, or refusals. However, some of the sequencing that we have noted is much more complex, and we have constructed a number of elaborate sequences that cover large sections of the episode. We have not formalized principles governing these sequences, in part because they are relatively few in number; the next stage in the formal analysis of such conversational structures is to search for the principles that unite sequences such as Figures 20, 22, 24, 26, and 31. The large sequential diagrams of Chapter 10 are specific to this therapeutic session, and the generalizations that govern these patterns would flow from the study of other types of therapeutic and interview situations.

The major aim of formal linguistic analysis is to discover the sets of options available to speakers at any given point in the development of the linguistic structure. Phonological units form relatively small closed sets, and at the level of sentence structure we can still see the possibility of developing such a closed set of options. But when we come to the relationship of speech acts to sentences, such closed sets are more problematic. We have not attempted to provide a closed set of speech acts, though other writers have attempted to circumscribe this field at the level of illocutionary acts (Searle, 1969; Sadock, 1974). Once we have established such a finite set of speech acts, it is not clear how they will be related to the set of syntactic options.

At this point, there is even less reason to think that there is a definable set of ways in which the higher-level speech actions can be carried out—that is, insults, challenges, retreats, and so forth. A very large portion of the social structure enters into the construction of such speech actions, and, at the present time, a comprehensive grammar of insults or challenges seems to be quite out of the question.

We would conclude, therefore, that the general aims of the comprehensive analysis of conversation cannot reasonably be focused upon a model that would generate conversations mechanically. Our aim is to provide a reasonable accounting, after the fact, which will embody as many general principles as we can find.

Many of the mechanisms proposed here are subject to experimental testing. The interpretation of paralinguistic cues is context-sensitive—but within controlled contexts it is possible to carry out laboratory experiments. Current operations with digitalized speech signals make it possible to alter the pitch contours of natural speech and to reconstitute speech signals that differ only by their intonational patterns. One can also begin with synthetic speech; Sag and Liberman have recently established that different intonation contours can produce significant differences in the interpretation of synthetic sentences as requests for information or requests for action (1974).

Variations in surface syntax can be controlled more easily, and it would be possible to provide objective evidence of the effect of various mitigating and aggravating devices. Experiments have been carried out which test the effect of sustained silences or repeated interruptions in counseling situations (Saslow and Matarazzo, 1959). There is no doubt that testing the more abstract rules of discourse requires more ingenuity, but we are confident that the principles of interpretation developed here can be the objects of experimental design.

DIRECTIONS

The microanalysis of this therapeutic session has led us to an appreciation of the richness and inexhaustible complexity of conversation. In this respect, our experience is similar to that of others who have attempted microanalysis of ordinary conversation. We have spent a number of years studying these five episodes; a large part of this time was devoted to defining and developing the method of comprehensive analysis we have just outlined. As we apply this method to new materials, we find that the analysis goes much more quickly. At the same time, an analysis of 5 minutes of conversation at this level of detail will require an investment of many hours.

Since microanalysis can lead to deep involvement and consume a great deal of time, we expect that only small sections of any extended conversation can be studied in this way. The sections of the extract may or may not be critical: some sections seem to show more interpersonal dynamics than others (as in Episode 3), but the analysis of long monologues can be equally revealing (as in Episode 1).

One advantage of the systematic and comprehensive character of this approach is that it is available to analysts with a wide range of technical backgrounds. We can see such analyses developing in two different directions. On the one hand, many students of conversation are more interested in the substance of interpersonal exchange than in the rules and structure of conversation. The rules of discourse may have only incidental interest for them. For many students of psychotherapy, a major concern will be the isolation of the underlying propositions that govern therapy in different settings, and this method will allow them to show how such propositions are embedded in the conversational exchange itself. In a wider range of social settings, it will be necessary to isolate a very different set of underlying propositions, and it may be necessary to develop independent sources of evidence to validate them.

The other direction of development is a more technical one: the separation and identification of paralinguistic cues, the codification of methods of expansion, and the systematic development of rules of discourse. This is the natural area of interest for linguists who have been involved in formal analysis at lower levels of organization. We have noted also that some of the most important tactical developments have been introduced by sociologists, psychologists, and students of communication. Our own analysis shows the influence of linguistics and the emphasis on a structured hierarchy, and the interaction of rules of production and interpretation with rules of sequencing. This technical development can quickly become an end in itself, and a separate discipline for the study of the conversation of rules can be created.

If there is sufficient convergence on the basic principles, and a fundamental set of rules, such a separate study might well be justified, but given the complexity and many-sided character of conversation, it does not seem likely that this convergence will be reached quickly. At this stage, it would be unrealistic to foresee a science of the study of conversation, or even the foundations of one. It seems to us that the main justification for the microanalysis of conversation is the immediate benefit it gives us in enriching our understanding of human relations, and the ways in which people deal with one another.

In the last chapter, we talked about sources of insight for the patient and the therapist. An analyst also gains insight through microanalysis. Some of this knowledge will be grounded on objective evidence and some on more subjective evidence. It may be harder to get interpersonal agreement for some of these insights than for others. But we cannot escape the strong conviction that we know more about Rhoda and the therapist than we would have gained from a simple reading of their conversation. We have a greater appreciation of their problems of communication and the subtle skills they need to resolve them.

Some speakers are convinced that they use very little indirection and limit themselves to plain and direct expression. But even a brief analysis of our own conversations shows us that we deal with others at roughly the same level of complexity and indirection as the therapeutic sessions analyzed in this book. We also use a wide range of mitigation and aggravation in modifying our utterances; we also construct long chains of indirect speech actions. We also use our intimate knowledge of rights, duties, and obligations to support, put-off, defend, or retreat from our actions in the course of conversation. The study of conversation is engrossing for us because we are all participants in the same practice. For better or for worse, conversation is the human way of dealing with human beings, and we find in it a fundamental expression of our humanity.

APPENDIX A
The Text of the Five Episodes

EPISODE 1

1.1[a] R.: *I don't.. know, whether... I—I **think** I did—the right thing, jistalittle.. situation came up......... an' I tried to uhm...... well, try to ....use what I—what I've learned here, see if it worked.*
 [b] Th.: *Mhm.*
 [c] R.: *Now, I don't know if I did the right thing.*

1.2[a] R.: *Sunday.. um—my mother went to my sister's again.*
 [b] Th.: *Mm-hm.*
 [c] R.: *And she usu'lly goes for about a day or so, like if she leaves on Sunday, she'll come back Tuesday morning. [Hm] So—it's nothing.*

1.3[a] R.: *But—she lef' Sunday, and she's still not home.*
 [b] Th.: *O—oh.*
 [c] R.: *And... I'm gettin' a little nuts a'ready.*

1.4[a] R.: *I's... I haven' been doin' too much school work*
 [b] *because—here this has to be done, here that has to be done,*
 [c] *and..... I really—I'm getting tired. It-it's—I have too much to do, an' I can' con'trate on any one thing.*
 [d] Th.: *Mhm.*

1.5[a] R.: *So..... it's in—it's **not** that I—... I mean I—I—I've proved, I **know** that I can get along without my mother, it isn't that—I—I can't get along with**out** her, but it—*
 [b] *I know that—when I don't have any **school**, an' she's gone away—she went away for a week, an' a **half** an'—i' didn' bother me in the leas'.*
 [c] Th.: *Mhm.*
 [d] R.: *But it seems that—I have jist—a little too much t'do.*

363

1.6[a] R.: *So at first, I wasn' gonna **say** anything. Then I remembered—that—if I keep it **in** what's bothering me*
  [b] Th.: *Mhm.*
  [c] R.: *then nobody else knows an' everybody thinks everything is fine, and good*
  [d] Th.: *Mhm.*
  [e] R.: *and I end up—hurting myself.*
  [f] Th.: *Right!*

1.7[a] R.: *Which would be that if I kept letting her **stay** there and didn' say, "Look—uh—I mean y'been there long enough," I'd jus' get tired, an-nd I-I'm not doing my school work right,*
  [b] Th.: *Mhm.*

1.8 R.: *An-nd so—when—I called her t'day, I said, "Well, when do you plan t'come **home**?"*

1.9 R.: *So she said, "Oh, why?"*

1.10 R.: *An-nd I said, "Well, things are getting just a little too **much**! [laugh] This is—i's jis' getting too hard, and ...... I—"*

1.11 R.: *She s'd t'me, "Well, why don't you tell **Phyllis** that?"*

1.12 R.: *So I said, "Well, I haven't talked to her lately."*

1.13 R.: *And—uh ... I'm just gonna **tell** her.*

1.14 R.: *Now ..... I **think** I did the right **thing**, I think that—*

EPISODE 2

2.2[a] Th.: *Yes, I think you did, too.*
  [b] *Well, **what's** your **question**?*
  [c] *You know, you have a lot of **guilt** about it,*
  [d] *You have a **very full** schedule at school ..*
  [e] R.: *Yes, it's a little—*
  [f] Th.: *Now **what** about Aunt Editha, she doesn't help you in the house?*

2.3[a] R.: *No like*
  [b] *she'll go .... sh—I dunno, like the **house** could—like my mother wasn't home for a week, and the house gets **dusty** ...*
  [c] *Now **she** could **sit** there an' the dust could be **that thick** and doesn't **bother** her*
  [d] *But yet it bothers me, I mean if I .... I—n-not—not that I-I run around the house **cleaning** ev'ry-ev'ry time,*
  [e] *But it's jis' that I know if I see the house getting dirty, it sort of **bothers** me, I 'on't like to live in a dirty house but*
  [f] *—she could sit, the dust could be that—*

2.4[a] Th.: *Well, what would happen if you **said** something to her—*
[b] *too—since* (R.: *Well you know, sh—*) *we're in the, in the business* (R.: *Yes.*) *of **talking**, yes.*

2.5[a] R.: *She—looks, well—w—once I said sumpin' to her, and she . . . looked sort of funny, like then—she—r-realizes it,* (breath) *and then . . . .*
[b] *It's like I **hurt** her, in some way . . . It's like—I-I dunno, I can't explain it, but I—*

2.6[a] R.: *I said t'her* (breath) *w—one time—I asked her—I said t'her,*
[b] *"Wellyouknow, wdy'mind takin' thedustrag an'justdust around?"*

2.7 R.: *Sh's's, "Oh-I-I—it looks **clean** to me," . . .*

2.8[a] R.: *An' then I went like **this**,*
[b] *an' I said to her, "**That** looks **clean** t'you?"*

2.9[a] R.: *And she sort of . . . . I d'no—sh'sort of gave me a funny look as if I—hurt her in some way,*
[b] *and I mean I didn' **mean** to, I didn' **yell** and **scream**.*
[c] *All I did to her was that "**That** looks **clean** to you?" . . . .*
[d] Th.: *Mmm.*

2.10[a] R.: *An' like—if I—y'like, she'll go t'th'**store** and get little **things** but . . . . um . . .*
[b] *Uh—she . . . like iflaskhertobuyonething . . . she'll always come back w'something else. If I ask her t'get—this—a **small** one, she'll come back with a **large** one—or . . .* (breath)
[c] *She . . . I d'no, she jist doesn't do it **right**. It's just she—*

2.11[a] Th.: *She **presents** herself as **very** helpless and needing to be waited on hand an' foot.*
[b] R.: *Yes.*
[c] Th.: *An' she's really used to this in her relationship with **mother**.*
[d] R.: *Yes.* (breath)

EPISODE 3

3.1[a] Th.: *But what would happen if you—um—you know—tried to arrive at some working relationship with her—*
[b] *To say—you work all day an' I go to school all day—*
[c] *Maybe when we . . . uhm . . get to the point where we have t'have some—uh—effort made about dinner and so on that it could be joint, you know, let's figure out what **you** should do an' what I should do.*

3.2[a] R.: *Sso-like-las' night—like, on Wednesday night is my late—one o' my late nights—*

4.4   Th.: *Now—tell me: why is mother staying there so long—I don't understand. It is something the matter there?*

4.5[a] R.: *Well, my brother-in-law's mother fell.*
  [b]   *She's—a-an elderly woman*
  [c]   *and she broke her leg*
  [d]   *and she was in the hospital.*

4.6[a] R.: *We had come home from the Bar Mitzvah, and—uh—.....*
  [b]   *My—brother-in-law's brother—couldn't get—something was wrong with my sister's phone an' couldn't get in touch with them.*
  [c]   *And so he called our house.*

4.7[a] R.: *And we had just happened to walk in*
  [b]   *so naturally my sister took us home,*
  [c]   *An-nd—ah—she answered the **phone**.*

4.8[a] R.: *And so my—and so she had to go to the **hospital** the next day.*
  [b]   *It was Washington's Birthday.*
  [c]   *So her and my brother-in-law **went**.*
  [d]   *And there was no one to watch the **children**.*
  [e]   *So my **mother** went.*

4.9[a] R.: *And **then-n**, with everything,*
  [b]   *my sister wanted to go to **work** again.*
  [c]   *So she stayed **Tuesday**.*

4.10[a] R.: *So my mother s'd, "Well, I'll go home Wednesday morning."*
  [b]   *She said, "Oh no, don't go, I'm gonna **work**."*
  [c]   *And anyway, she didn't work—anyway.*

4.11[a] R.: *So I thought she'd come home this **morning**.*
  [b]   *So, it ended up that she's not comin' home this morning, 'cause now my sister went to **work**.*

4.12   R.: *So I says t'her, "Are you coming home **tomorrow** morning?"*

4.13   R.: *So she s'd, "Why-y?"*

4.14   R.: *A-and—I said, "Uh—well, it's getting a little too **much**."*

4.15   R.: *So she s'd, "**See**, I **told** you so."*

4.16   R.: *But I said, "The other times you've gone away a day or so, and I-it's ... nothing, and—*

4.17   R.: *I-it's, not that—it happened that .... the way things turned **out**, like, she wasn't prepared—it was unexpected,*

APPENDIX A 369

4.18[a] R.: *like she didn't expect to be going.*
   [b] *My sister said she wanted to work, and my mother said, "**Well, yeh**, next week... uh—I don't feel like going this week."*

4.19[a] R.: *So my sister said, "Well, maybe at the end of the week."*
   [b] *She s'z, "**Well, maybe.**"*
   [c] *And everything's—um—s—ah—was unexpected.*

EPISODE 5

5.1 Th.: (breath) *Well what they are really doing to you is similar to what.. apparently this goes on in the family—to what you did with them aroun-nd the dieting.*

5.2 R.: ....

5.3 Th.: *Y'know, when—when they said you shouldn't be eating so much, you stopped eating entirely.*

5.4[a] R.: *Well, when I said I could get along without my mother,* x x
   [b] Th.: *The other—she—she's making you get along entirely, without her...*

5.5[a] Th.: *An-nd—uh—mayb—y'know—maybe some of this has to be discussed together. Actually it—uh—usually...*
   [b] Th.: *Students, who go to college away from the home, **don't** attempt to keep house. They either live in a dormitory where most things are done for them, and they, y'know, eat together in a—uh—dining hall, or they live in a sorority house where some of the housekeeping is done for them, and meals are served. It isn't **contemplated** that you would carry a **whole** house, and go to school at the same time...*

5.6 R.: ... x.. *it seems to my sister that this is—"Oh, nothing's **wrong** with her," she s'ys t'm' mother, "Everything's **fine**."*

5.7 R.: *My mother says—I says to my mother, "Yes—evrything's **fine**?" I s's, "Things **aren't** so fine." I said, "I'm getting tired."*

5.8 R.: *I said, "E—but—y'see now, if—I-I wanna s—I-I told my mother this, and* [breath], *now if I wanna s-s-ay, "Im tired," then—I know just the answer I'm gonna get...*

5.9[a] Th.: x x x
   [b] R.: *That's right.*
   [c] R.: *If—*[breath] *everything seems to come back—to **that**, and like—..... uhm—I **don't** eat, and I do eat.*

5.10[a] R.: *But I don't eat be—their-their-uh-thing is that I don't eat—because—uh—I like the way I **am**, and that-I'm not tryin' to help myself,*

　　　　[b]　*but I eat! There's nothing I can do, look*
　　　　[c]　*I went away—I proved to them—I went away for a week. I didn't do anything. I **laid** around and ate. An' I didn'* gain any weight.

5.11　[a]　R.: *And—*
　　　[b]　Th.: x *You **also** proved it to yourself.*
　　　[c]　R.: *Yes.*
　　　[d]　Th.: *Because you know, you have a lot of—they*
　　　[e]　　　　　　　　　　　　　　　　　　　　R. *Yeh.*
　　　[f]　Th.: *they shake your ... self-confidence.*
　　　[g]　　　　　　　　　　R.: *Yeh, I wonder sometimes, too ...*

5.12　R.: *But there was seven—six days proof—that it can't be m—I-I-mean—I ate **really**. I-I—ate. I **know** I did.*

5.13[a]　Th.: (breath) *Yes, but now let's us—uh—see if we can separate out two things,*
　　　[b]　*Does it have anything to do with ... your ... weight?*

5.14[a]　R.: *(What?)*
　　　[b]　Th.: *Your inability to carry the two **things**,*
　　　[c]　Th.: *school .. and .. what else.*
　　　[d]　R.:　　　　*No, I don't **think** so!*

5.15　Th.: *All right so, why can't you stay with that?*

5.16[a]　R.: *Oh, **I'm staying** with it,*
　　　[b]　*butit'sjustthat—I don't know why, but it jist bothers me when they say that, because they look at me as if—* (breath)
　　　[c]　*Like my sister will say to my mother, "Oh, **Rhoda** should **never** get **tired**."*

5.17[a]　R.: *An'Is'dt'her—*
　　　[b]　Th.: *I don't think **really** it's the—uh—what they're saying as much, as, that, you, are reading in ... uhh—the **feeling** behind what they're saying.*
　　　[c]　R.: ....
　　　[d]　Th.: *What c—what are they feeling about it?*

5.18　R.: .... *No-I-I—I don't see the difference.*

5.19[a]　Th.: (breath) *Well, let's see,*
　　　[b]　*It—maybe it's similar to the feeling that you had when your sister said, "You're eating too much," and you stopped eating totally,*
　　　[c]　*what does that express?*

5.20　R.: ....　　　　　　　　　　　　　　[13 sec]

5.21[a]　Th.: *In terms of how you felt.*
　　　　　　　R.: *(No—)*
　　　[b]　R.: *Oh, I guess I w's angry, but—*

[c] Th.: *Ye-es.*
[d] R.: ...... (*Yeh.*)

5.22[a] Th.: (breath) *So—then—and for some reason you feel they're **angry** because you're so, underweight, or*
[b] *because they—think you're underweight.*

5.23[a] R.: ...... *I'on't—I dunno, I don't—I don't—I never felt like **that**—it's just that ... no I never thought of it like that and I don't—I don't think I feel **anger** because ...*
[b] (breath) *I mean I jist get **annoyed**, like I'm not—I don't say I get—angry, but it jist gets **annoying** to hear the same thing.*

5.24[a] R.: *I mean, the first thing if I say I have a pain in my finger—right away, it's because "Oh, you're **thin**!"*
[b] *I mean, after awhile it gets annoying to hear and I-I-know that—*
[c] Th.: *Yes.*
[d] R.: *I guess—maybe I should let it—not bother me,*

5.25[a] R.: *I mean, I went to the doctor last week—*
[b] Th.: *But why do **they** keep repeating it?*
[c] R.: *I don't know.....*
[d] Th.: *What are **they** feeling?*

5.26 R.: ......*that I'm doing it on purp—like, I w's—like they ... well—they s—came out an' tol' me in so many words that they worry and worry an' I seem to take this very lightly.*

5.27[a] Th.: *So they get **angry** at you.*
[b] R.: *Yes ... they do, yes.*
[c] Th.: *So there's a lot of **anger** passing back and forth.*
[d] R.: ..... *Yeh..*
[e] Th.: (*Mm.*)

REFERENCES

Austin, J. L. *How to do things with words*. London: Oxford, 1962.
Bahner, F. Fettsucht und Magersucht. *Handbuch der Inneren Medizin* 7(1). Berlin: Springer, 1954.
Bailey, Charles-James N. A new intonation-theory to account for pan-English and idiom-particular patterns. *Working Papers in Linguistics* 2(3): 171–254. Honolulu: University of Hawaii, 1970.
Bales, Robert F. A set of categories for the analysis of small group interaction. *American Sociological Review* 15:257–263, 1950.
Bales, Robert F., F. Strodtbeck, T. M. Mills, and M. E. Roseborough. Channels of communication in small groups. *American Sociological Review* 16:843, 1951.
Bateson, Gregory, Don D. Jackson, Jay Haley, and John H. Weakland. Toward a theory of schizophrenia. *Behavioral Science* 1:251–264, 1956.
Blitzer, J. R., N. Rollins, and A. Blackwell. Children who starve themselves: Anorexia nervosa. *Psychosomatic Medicine* 23:369–383, 1961.
Bolinger, Dwight L. A theory of pitch accent in English. *Word* 14:109–149, 1958.
Bolinger, Dwight L. *Generality, gradience, and the all-or-none*. The Hague: Mouton, 1961.
Bolinger, Dwight L. Intonation as a universal. *Proceedings of the Ninth International Congress of Linguists*. The Hague: Mouton, 1964. Pp. 833–848.
Bordin, Edward S. *Research strategies in psychotherapy*. New York: John Wiley, 1974.
Borgatta, Edgar F., David Fanshel, and Henry J. Meyer. *Social workers' perceptions of clients*. New York: Russell Sage Foundation, 1960.
Brown, Roger, and A. Gilman. The pronouns of power and solidarity. In T. Sebeok (Ed.), *Style in language*. New York: Wiley, 1960. Pp. 253–276.
Cole, Peter, and Jerry L. Morgan. *Syntax and semantics*. Vol. 3: Speech Acts. New York: Academic Press, 1975.
Davidson, P. O., and C. G. Costello. *N = 1: Experimental studies of single cases*. New York: Van Nostrand Reinhold, 1969.
Davitz, Joel R. *The communication of emotional meaning*. New York: McGraw-Hill, 1964.
De Groot, A. Structural linguistics and syntactic laws. *Word* 5:1–12, 1949.
Deutsch, Felix, and William F. Murphy. *The clinical interview*. Vol. 2: Therapy. New York: International Universities Press, 1960.
English Language Research Group. Discourse analysis of a union meeting. Working Paper No., Birmingham.
Ervin-Tripp, Susan. Is Sybil there? The structure of some American English directives. *Language in Society* 5:1–128, 1976.

Fanshel, David, and Freda Moss. *Playback: A marriage in jeopardy examined*. New York: Columbia University Press, 1971.
Fanshel, David, and Eugene B. Shinn. *Children in foster care: A longitudinal investigation*. New York: Columbia University Press, 1977.
Farquharson, R. F., and H. H. Hyland. Anorexia nervosa: The course of 15 patients treated from 20 to 30 years previously. *Canadian Medical Association Journal* **94**:411–419, 1966.
Fraser, Bruce. Hedged performatives. In Cole and Morgan 1973. Pp. 187–210.
Freud, Sigmund. On psychotherapy. *Standard edition*, **7**:257–268. Original edition, 1905. Reissued, London: Hogarth, 1953.
Fry, Dennis B. Duration and intensity as physical correlates of linguistic stress. *Journal of Acoustic Society of America* **27**:765–768, 1955.
Garfinkel, Harold. *Studies in ethnomethodology*. Englewood Cliffs: Prentice-Hall, 1967.
Garvey, Catherine. Requests and responses in children's speech. *Journal of Child Language* **2**:41–63, 1975.
Gill, Merton, Richard Newman, and Frederick C. Redlich. *The initial interview in psychiatric practice*. New York: International Universities Press, 1954.
Glover, Edward. *The technique of psycho-analysis*. New York: International Universities Press, 1955.
Goffman, Erving. *Asylums*. New York: Aldine, 1961.
Goffman, Erving. *Interaction ritual*. Chicago: Aldine, 1967.
Goffman, Erving. *Relations in public*. New York: Basic Books, 1971.
Goffman, Erving. *Frame analysis*. New York: Free Press, 1975.
Gordon, David, and George Lakoff. Conversational postulates. In *Papers from the Seventh Regional Meeting of the Chicago Linguistic Society*. Chicago: Chicago Linguistic Society, 1971. Pp. 63–84.
Gottschalk, Louis A. (Ed.). *Comparative psycholinguistic analysis of two psychotherapeutic interviews*. New York: International Universities Press, 1961.
Gottschalk, Louis A., and Arthur H. Auerbach (Eds.) *Methods of research in psychotherapy*. New York: Appleton-Century-Crofts, 1966.
Gottschalk, Louis A., and Goldine C. Gleser. *The measurement of psychological states through the content analysis of verbal behavior*. Berkeley: University of California Press, 1969.
Gottschalk, Louis A., Carolyn N. Winget, and Goldine C. Gleser. *Manual of instructions for using the Gottschalk–Gleser content analysis scales: Anxiety, hostility and social alienation—personal disorganization*. Berkeley: University of California Press, 1969.
Grice, H. P. Meaning. *Philosophical Review* **66**:377–388, 1957. Reprinted in D. Steinberg and L. Jakobovits (Eds.), *Semantics*. Cambridge: Cambridge University Press, 1971.
Grice, H. P. Logic and conversation. In P. Cole and J. Morgan (Eds.), *Syntax and semantics*. Vol. 3: Speech Acts. New York: Academic Press, 1975. Pp. 41–58.
Grimes, Joseph E. Kinds of information in discourse. *Kivung* **4**:64–74, 1971.
Grimes, Joseph E. The thread of discourse. Technical Report No. 1. Ithaca: Cornell University, 1972.
Gunter, Richard. On the placement of accent in dialogue. *Journal of Linguistics* **2**:159–179, 1966.
Gunter, Richard. *Sentences in dialogue*. Columbia, South Carolina: Hornbeam Press, 1974.
Haley, Jay. *Strategies of psychotherapy*. New York: Grune and Stratton, 1963.
Harris, Zellig. *Structural linguistics*. Chicago: University of Chicago Press, 1951.
Hartmann, Heinz. *Essays on ego psychology*. New York: International Universities Press, 1964.
Hymes, Dell. The ethnography of speaking. *Anthropology and human behavior*. Washington, D.C.: Anthropological Society of Washington, 1962. Reprinted in J. Fishman (Ed.), *Readings in the sociology of language*. The Hague: Mouton, 1968.
Jaffe, Joseph. Dyadic analysis of two psychotherapeutic interviews. In L. Gottschalk (Ed.), *Comparative psycholinguistic analysis of two psychotherapeutic interviews*. New York: International Universities Press, 1961. Pp. 73–90.

Kadushin, Alfred. *The social work interview.* New York: Columbia University Press, 1972.
Karttunen, Lauri. Some observations on factivity. *Papers in Linguistics* 4:55–70, 1971.
Kaufman, M. Ralph, and Marcel Heiman (Eds.). *Evolution of psychosomatic concepts: Anorexia nervosa: A paradigm.* New York: International Universities Press, 1965.
Kiparsky, Paul, and Carol Kiparsky. Fact. In M. Bierwisch and K. Heidolph (Eds.), *Progress in linguistics.* The Hague: Mouton, 1970. Pp. 143–173.
Klima, Edward S. Negation in English. In J. Fodor and J. Katz (Eds.), *The structure of language: Readings in the philosophy of language.* Englewood Cliffs: Prentice-Hall, 1964.
Kris, E. The development of ego psychology. *Samiksa* 5, 1951.
Kutner, Bernard, David Fanshel, Alice M. Togo, and Thomas S. Langner. *Five hundred over sixty.* New York: Russell Sage Foundation, 1956.
Labov, William. The social motivation of a sound change. *Word* 19:273–309. 1963.
Labov, William. *The social stratification of English in New York City.* Arlington: Center for Applied Linguistics, 1966.
Labov, William. The study of language in its social context. *Studium Generale* 23:30–87, 1970a.
Labov, William. *The study of non-standard English.* Champaign, Illinois: National Council of Teachers of English, 1970b.
Labov, William. Finding out about children's language. In D. Steinberg (Ed.), *Working papers in communication.* Honolulu: Pacific Speech Association, 1971.
Labov, William. *Sociolinguistic patterns.* Philadelphia: University of Pennsylvania Press, 1972a.
Labov, William. *Language in the inner city.* Philadelphia: University of Pennsylvania Press, 1972b.
Labov, William. On the grammaticality of everyday speech. In W. Labov (Ed.), *Quantitative analysis of linguistic structure.* New York: Academic Press. (Forthcoming)
Labov, William, Paul Cohen, Clarence Robins, and John Lewis. *A study of the non-standard English of Negro and Puerto Rican speakers in New York City.* Report on Cooperative Research Project 3288. New York: Columbia University Press, 1968.
Labov, William, and Joshua Waletzky. Narrative analysis. In *Essays on the verbal and visual arts.* Seattle: University of Washington Press, 1967. Pp. 12–44.
Laffal, Julius. *Pathological and normal language.* New York: Atherton, 1965.
Lakoff, George. *Linguistics and natural logic.* Ann Arbor: University of Michigan, 1970.
Lakoff, Robin. Some reasons why there can't be any *some-any* rule. *Language* 45:608–615, 1969.
Lasegue, E. C. On hysterical anorexia. In M. R. Kaufman and M. Heiman (Eds.), *Evolution of psychosomatic concepts.* New York: International Universities Press, 1964. Pp. 141–155.
Lennard, Henry L., and Arnold Bernstein. *The anatomy of psychotherapy.* New York: Columbia University Press, 1960.
Lieberman, Philip. On the acoustic basis of the perception of intonation by linguists. *Word* 21:40–54, 1965.
Lipton, Earle L., Alfred Steinschneider, and Julius B. Richmond. Psychophysiologic disorders in children. In L. Hoffman and M. Hoffman (Eds.), *Review of child development research,* Vol. 2. New York: Russell Sage Foundation, 1966. Pp. 169–220.
Litwak, Eugene. Geographic mobility and extended family cohesion. *American Sociological Review* 25:385–394, 1960a.
Litwak, Eugene. Occupational mobility and extended family cohesion. *American Sociological Review* 25:9–21, 1960b.
MacKinnon, Roger A., and Robert Michels. *The psychiatric interview in clinical practice.* Philadelphia: W. B. Saunders, 1971.
Mahl, George F. Measures of two expressive aspects of patient's speech in two psychotherapeutic interviews. In L. Gottschalk (Ed.), *Comparative psycholinguistic analysis of two psychotherapeutic interviews.* New York: International Universities Press, 1961. Pp. 91–114.
Mahl, George F., and Gene Schulze. Psychological research in the extralinguistic area. In T.

Sebeok, A. Hayes, and M. C. Bateson (Eds.), *Approaches to semiotics*. The Hague: Mouton, 1964. Pp. 51–124.

Marsden, Gerald. Content-analysis studies of therapeutic interviews: 1954 to 1964. *Psychological Bulletin* **63:** 298–321, 1965.

Mayer, John E., and Noel Timms. *The client speaks: Working class impressions of casework*. New York: Atherton, 1970.

McQuown, N. E., G. Bateson, R. Birdwhistell, H. Brosen, and C. Hockett. *The natural history of an interview*. Microfilm Collection of Manuscripts in Cultural Anthropology. Chicago: University of Chicago Library, 1971.

Menninger, Karl A., and Philip S. Holzman. *Theory of psychoanalytic technique*, 2nd edition. New York: Basic Books, 1973.

Parsons, Talcott. *The structure of social action*. Glencoe, Illinois: Free Press, 1951.

Pike, Kenneth. *Phonemics*. Ann Arbor: University of Michigan Press, 1947.

Pittenger, Robert E., Charles F. Hockett, and John J. Danehy. *The first five minutes*. Ithaca, New York: Paul Martineau, 1960.

Rogers, Carl R. *Client-centered therapy*. New York: Houghton Mifflin, 1951.

Ross, John R. On declarative sentences. In R. Jacobs and P. Rosenbaum (Eds.), *Readings in English transformational grammar*. Waltham, Massachusetts: Blaisdell, 1970.

Sacks, Harvey. An initial investigation of the usability of conversational data for doing sociology. In D. Sudnow (Ed.), *Studies in social interaction*. New York: Free Press, 1972a.

Sacks, Harvey. On the analyzability of stories by children. In J. Gumperz and D. Hymes (Eds.), *Directions in sociolinguistics*. New York: Holt, 1972b.

Sacks, Harvey, Emanuel A. Schegloff, and Gail Jefferson. A simplest systematics for the organization of turn-taking for conversation. *Language* **50:**696–735, 1974.

Sadock, Jerrold. Queclaratives. In *Papers from the seventh Regional Meeting of the Chicago Linguistic Society*. Chicago: Chicago Linguistic Society, 1971. Pp. 223–232.

Sadock, Jerrold. *Toward a linguistic theory of speech acts*. New York: Academic Press, 1974.

Sag, Ivan, and Mark Liberman. The intonational disambiguation of indirect speech acts. In *Papers from the Eleventh Regional Meeting of the Chicago Linguistic Society*. Chicago: Chicago Linguistic Society, 1975.

Saslow, George, and Joseph D. Matarazzo. A technique for studying change in interview behavior. In E. Rubinstein and M. Parloff (Eds.), *Research in psychotherapy*. Washington D.C.: American Psychological Association, 1959. Pp. 125–159.

Satir, Virginia. *Conjoint family therapy*. Palo Alto, California: Science and Behavior Books, 1964.

Scheflen, Albert E. *Communicational structure: Analysis of a psythotherapy transaction*. Bloomington: Indiana University Press, 1973.

Schegloff, Emanuel. Sequencing in conversational openings. *American Anthropologist* **70:**1075–1095, 1968.

Schegloff, Emanuel. Notes on a conversational practice: Formulating place. In D. Sudnow (Ed.), *Studies in social interaction*. New York: Free Press, 1972.

Searle, John. *Speech acts*. London: Cambridge University Press, 1969.

Sebeok, Thomas A., Alfred S. Hayes, and Mary C. Bateson (Eds.). *Approaches to semiotics*. The Hague: Mouton, 1964.

Shatz, Marilyn. Towards a developmental theory of communicative competence. Unpublished University of Pennsylvania dissertation, 1975.

Shatz, Marilyn, and Rochel Gelman. The development of communication skills: Modifications in the speech of young children as a function of listener. *Monographs of the Society for Research in Child Development* **38,** 1973.

Shopen, Tim. A generative theory of ellipsis: A consideration of the linguistic use of silence. Reproduced by the Indiana University Linguistics Club, January 1972.

Skinner, B. F. *Verbal behavior*. New York: Appleton-Century-Crofts, 1957.

Soskin, William F., and Vera P. John. The study of spontaneous talk. In *The stream of behavior*. New York: Meredith, 1963.

Speisman, J. C. Depth of interpretation and verbal resistance in psychotherapy. *Journal of Consulting Psychology* **23**:93–99, 1959.

Stennes, Leslie. The identification of participants in Adamana Fulani. Unpublished Hartford Seminary Foundation dissertation, 1969.

Stockwell, Robert P. The place of intonation in a generative grammar of English. *Language* **36**:360–367, 1960.

Sudnow, David (Ed.). *Studies in social interaction*. New York: Free Press, 1972.

Szasz, Thomas S. *The ethics of psychoanalysis*. New York: Delta, 1965.

Thomä, Helmut. *Anorexia nervosa* (translated by Gillian Brydone). New York: International Universities Press, 1967.

Trager, G. L., and H. L. Smith. *An outline of English structure* (Studies in Linguistics: Occasional Papers 3). Norman, Oklahoma: Battenburg Press, 1951.

Truax, Charles B., and Robert R. Carkhuff. *Toward effective counseling and psychotherapy*. Chicago: Aldine, 1967.

Wald, Benji V. Variation in the system of tense markers of Mombasa Swahili. Unpublished Columbia University dissertation, 1973.

Watzlawick, Paul, Janet Beavin, and Don Jackson. *Pragmatics of human communication*. New York: Norton, 1967.

Weinreich, Uriel. Notes on the Yiddish rise-fall intonation contour. In *For Roman Jakobson*. The Hague: Mouton, 1956.

Wheeler, Alva. Grammatical structure in Siona discourse. *Lingua* **19**:60–77, 1967.

INDEX TO DISCOURSE RULES[1]

Admitting Presupposition, Rule for, **103,** 174
Challenging Propositions, Rule for, **97,** 124–125
Confirmation, rule of, **100,** 228, 236–237, 241
Delayed Requests, Rule of, **94,** 95, 161
Disputable Assertions, Rule of, **101–102,** 179
Embedded Requests, Rule of, **90–92,** 99, 165–166
Forward Reference, Rule of, **106**
Implicit Responses, Rule of, **99,** 242
Indirect Requests, Rule for, 66–67, 79, **82–86,** 87, 90, 151, 158–159, 194, 275
Juxtaposition, Rule of, 284
Narrative Orientation, Rule of, **106,** 109, 131, 217, 242, 245
Narrative Response, Rule of, **107,** 257, 274, 290
Narrative Sequencing, Rule of, **107,** 261, 284
Overdue Obligations, Rule of, **96,** 151, 161, 198, 203

Putting Off Requests, Rule for, **86–88,** 173, 199, 202–203, 244, 246, 311
Redundant Responses, Rule of, **92,** 166
Reinstating Requests, Rule for, **93,** 171, 201, 304
Reinterpretation, Rule of, **227**
Relayed Requests, Rule of, **88,** 194
Repeated Requests, Rule of, 66–67, **95,** 214–215
Requests for Information, Rule of, **88–90**
Requests, Rule of, 2, 75, **77–82,** 90, 94, 102, 158–159, 162, 187, 198, 203, 214, 275, 290, 311, 312, 353, 357
Socratic Questions, Rule for, **102,** 302
Socratic Specification, Rule of, **103,** 322

[1] Boldface type indicates defining statements.

INDEX TO PARALINGUISTIC CUES

aggravation, 47, 192, 202, 204, 291
breathiness, 42
choking, 46, 191, 250, 252, 255, 319, 356
condensation, condensed, 115, 119, 126, 141, 198, 205, 210, 219–220, 221–222, 269, 270, 305, 314–315, 319
contention, 195
derogation, 47, 193, 210, 224, 225, 229, 233, 236, 248, 264–265, 290, 306, 321
doubt, 222, 242
emphasis, 221, 291, 321
exasperation, 47, 144, 183, 191, 210, 219–20, 224, 264
formality, 47, 136, 211
glottalization, 42, 46, 115, 128–129, 168, 170, 191, 193, 196, 245, 247, 255, 269, 356
hesitation, 46, 115, 119, 126, 128–129, 139, 144, 170, 177, 191, 193, 195, 196, 210, 250–251, 255, 259, 281–282, 287, 294, 295–296, 304, 307, 319
implication, 166, 199, 218, 221, 233, 253–254, 269, 270
incoherence, 273
informality, 47
irritation, 323
laughter, 42, 170, 191, 193, 234
mitigation, 47, 161–162, 183, 187, 191, 192, 193, 195, 197–198, 206, 213–215, 221, 255, 269, 270, 274, 277, 287, 288, 301, 303, 305–306, 307, 311–312, 313, 319, 321, 326–327, 335
neutrality, 47
overlap, strident, 221, 225, 286, 307
reinforcement, 47, 128–129, 131, 136, 137, 139, 141, 144, 145–147, 152, 205, 217, 218, 221, 234
reservation, 284, 285, 286, 298, 303, 309, 310–311, 313, 314, 316, 319, 323, 327
self-interruption, 115, 119, 126, 145, 168, 191, 193, 195, 196, 222, 240, 244, 250, 252, 273, 292–293, 296, 298, 299, 319, 325
silence, 168, 170, 196, 252, 259, 283–284, 285 fn, 310–311, 313, 316, 358
stammering, 205
stress, contrastive, 222, 254, 282, 285
surprise, 166
sympathy, 47, 136, 137
tension, 46, 47, 115, 119, 126, 139, 141–142, 144, 168, 170, 177, 183, 191, 193, 195, 196, 197, 198, 205, 210, 217, 220, 222, 225, 230, 234, 240, 244, 250, 252, 255, 269, 270, 273, 276 fn, 282, 286, 288, 292–293, 294, 295–296, 298, 299, 301, 303, 306, 309, 310, 318, 325
tension release, 129, 144, 152, 178, 230, 231, 232, 234, 257, 267, 290
whine, 42, 46, 191, 219, 222, 289–290, 324–325, 356

INDEX TO PROPOSITIONS:[1]

LOCAL

{1}, 59, 66–67, **121,** 125–126, 129, 147, 150–152, 161, 166–167, 174, 175–176, 178–179, 183–184, 189, 267, 288–289
{2}, 54, **150–152,** 156–157, 162, 170, 269
{3}, 54, **150–152,** 156–157, 161, 162, 269, 333
{4}, 54, 59, 66, 126, 150–152, 156–161, 170, 173, 174, 176, 177, 178–179, 183, 269, 275, 290, 291, 333
{5}, 184, 193, 195, 198, 205, 210, 211, 241, 242, 243, 246, 248, 250
{6}, **196,** 198, 199, 202–207, 247, 275
{7}, 196, **197,** 205
{8}, 218, **219,** 220, 221, 222, 224, 225, 229–231
{9}, **243,** 244, 247, 275, 333
{10}, **263,** 274, 275, 276, 277
{11}, **281,** 282, 284, 286
{12}, **284,** 285, 286

GENERAL

{AD}, 55, 66–67
{AD-E}, **192,** 193, 196, 202, 204–205, 210, 211, 215, 233, 234, 236, 242, 246–247, 248, 250, 333
{AD-R}, 52, 55, 57, **135,** 136, 142–143, 144, 149–151, 155, 164, 165, 166–167, 170, 171, 183, 192, 193–194, 199, 201, 202, 244, 251, 252, 254, 270, 281, 285, 286, 295, 296, 306, 307, 325
{AUT}, 54, **195**
{CLEAN}, 56
{COOP}, 54, 215, **216,** 233, 234–235, 236, 244
{E}, 54–55, 183, 300, 312, 332, 333
{E'}, **308,** 309, 319–311, 323
{E_1}, 54, 138–139, 142, **185,** 333, 334
{E_2}, 54, 183, **185,** 189, 254, 334
{E_3}, 54, 57, 306, **307,** 308, 312, 316, 318, 319, 321, 323, 325, 327, 333, 334
{E_4}, 54, 55, **218,** 224, 225, 229–231, 233, 334
{EAT}, 56, **140, 282,** 283, 284–286, 293–296, 298, 299, 300–301, 310–311, 312, 313, 318, 325
{HEAD-Mo}, 52, 55, 59, 149–152, 157, 166–167, 273, 286
{INSIGHT}, 54, **189**
{INT-E}, 55, **125,** 126, 220, 221
{INT-R}, 225, 227, 231, 309
{INT-Th}, 225, 227, 241, 309
{RSNBL}, 321

{RSNBL-E}, 204–205, 211, 220, 229, 320
{RSNBL-Mo}, 267, 273, 277, 296
{RSNBL-R}, 55, **192,** 193
{RSNBL-S}, 264, 265, 267, 291, 296, 306, 320
{S}, 54, 59, 66–67, 97, **121,** 122–124, 126, 144, 147, 152, 155, 160, 162, 166–167, 173, 174, 176, 177, 183, 184, 189, 191, 193, 194, 195, 196, 205, 208, 211, 215, 233, 234–235, 237, 242, 243, 269, 287, 288, 291, 293, 321, 322, 332
{S-CARE}, 57, **165, 285,** 295, 296, 318, 324–325
{SICK-R}, 165
{STRN}, 56, 59, 66, 135–136, **137,** 140, 141, 142–143, 152, 161, 162, 166–167, 170, 185, 194, 195, 290–291, 293, 294, 301, 303, 305, 306, 317, 333
{STUD}, 55, **287,** 288–289
{THIN}, 56, 296, 299, 301, 303, 305, 306, 308–309, 318, 319
{TIRE}, 56, **140,** 141, 143, 144, 152, 292, 296, 306, 307, 308–309
{X}, 183, 185, 255, 257, 277, 299
{X:STRN}, 56, 57, 144, **168–170,** 183, 187, 237, 240, 252, 254, 264, 266, 288–289, 290

[1]Boldface type indicates defining statements.

INDEX TO INTERACTIONAL TERMS

acknowledge, acknowledgment, 61 **64,** 110, 144, 222, 231, 233, 240, 250, 254, 305, 312–313, 316
admit, admission, 59, 61, **64,** 65, 98, 150, 230, 233, 235, 241, 242, 282, 306, 319, 358
agree, agreement, 174, 176, 182, 183, 211, 225, 231, 233, 277, 298, 301, 327
aggravate, 61, **65,** 206
ask for, See "Request"
assert, assertion, 61, **62,** 65, 101, 124, 126, 127–129, 141, 144, 147, 149, 150, 152, 166–167, 170, 173, 174–175, 177, 178–179, 183, 187, 189, 192, 194, 202–203, 205, 210, 220, 222, 224, 225, 227, 229, 233, 234, 236, 242, 248, 252, 257, 264, 270, 273, 277, 282, 284, 285, 286, 288, 289, 291, 293, 294, 296, 298, 303, 305, 306, 309, 312, 313, 318, 319, 321, 323, 327, 333
attribute, 318
carry out, See "Perform"
challenge, 25, 26, 58, 59, 61, **64,** 65, 93–98, **96–97,** 105, 124, 126, 127, 150, 152, 161, 164, 166, 168, 170, 176, 182, 183, 184, 186, 189, 192, 193, 199–200, 202, 205, 209, 215, 216, 220, 221, 222, 224, 225, 229, 230, 231, 234, 236–237, 241, 242, 244, 247, 252, 265, 267, 270, 282, 284, 289, 295–296, 299, 304, 305, 306, 309, 321, 333, 358
continue, 61, **62,** 65, 67, 139, 147, 225, 230, 234, 259, 261, 264, 265, 291
contradict, 202, 306
counterchallenge, 203, 225
defend, defense, 58, 61, **64,** 98, 175–176, 202, 203, 225, 230, 231, 267, 273, 289, 306, 358
deny, denial, 144, 176, 193, 195, 199, 202–203, 205, 216, 224, 230, 282, 290, 294, 303, 305, 306, 309, 311, 318–319, 321, 334, 337

end, 61, **62,** 267
express, 61, **62,** 124, 126, 183, 189, 215, 224, 233, 299, 316
fail, 176
give confirmation, 61, **64,** 193, 225, 236, 242
give evaluation, 61, **63,** 139, 141, 144, 147, 149, 152, 205, 222, 231, 242, 250, 293
give information, 59, 61, **62, 64,** 65, 67, 110, 139, 141, 149, 174, 175–176, 177, 178, 193, 194, 198, 202, 208, 218, 220, 225, 230, 240, 257, 264, 265, 267, 286, 296, 306, 321
give interpretation, 61, **63,** 210, 225, 228, 282, 285, 286, 309, 312, 318
give orientation, 17, 61, **63,** 218, 244, 259, 261, 288, 315
give re-interpretation, 61, **63**
give support, 61, **63, 64,** 129, 136, 139, 147, 183, 189, 208, 210, 221, 231, 236, 250, 274, 288, 309, 321, 334
huff, 61, **65,** 88, 205, 247
identification, 209
initiate, **60,** 61, 123, 126, 135–136, 198, 218, 244, 247, 252, 257, 290, 291, 323
interpret, **60,** 61, 209
interrupt, 184, 189, 194, 195, 208, 210, 218, 221, 222, 224, 225, 242, 254, 286, 323
mitigate, mitigation, 61, **64,** 65, 190, 194–195, 198, 206, 212, 213, 215, 229, 230, 231, 244, 317, 320, 336, 345–346
perform an action, 61, **64,** 110, 215–216, 291, 358
put off, 61, **64,** 86–88, 105, 110, 165, 176, 244, 247, 274, 275, 277, 286, 291, 358
question, 61, **63, 64, 97,** 124, 126, 182, 190, 290, 309
re-direct, **60,** 61, 64, 183, 184, 186, 187, 190, 252, 282, 297, 298, 309

382

refer, 61, **62,** 123, 126, 127
refuse, refusal, 61, **64,** 87, 110 fn, 111, 173, 175–176, 193, 194, 196, 199, 205, 208, 210, 248, 250, 284, 309–310, 313, 323, 358
reinforce, reinforcement, 110, 128–*136, 141, 143, 152, 207, 217, 218, 252, 316*
reinstate, 61, **64,** 175–176, 202–203, 291, 315, 323
reinterpretation, 241
repeat, 61, **62,** 221, 230, 236, 254, 315
request for acknowledgment, 312, 322
request for action, 24, 59, 61, **63,** 65, 79–81, 91–93, 94–95, 110–111, 150, 152, 157–162, 166–167, 175–176, 177, 178, 184, 187, 192, 194, 196, 198, 208, 216, 274
request for agreement, 61, **63,** 233
request for approval, 147
request for confirmation, 61, **63,** 101, 184, 187, 202, 204, 222, 224, 227, 229, 230, 236, 241, 242, 246, 248, 291, 292

request for evaluation, 61, **63,** 101, 194, 254
request for help, *See also*{S}, {5}, {6}. 150, 175–176, 195, 198, 208, 215, 247, 293
request for information, 24, 25, 26, 59, **61,** 63, 65, 66, 67, 78, 88–93, 98, 102, 156–159, 165, 166–167, 168, 173, 176, 183, 187, 189, 195, 196, 198, 213, 215, 216, 225, 227, 243 n, 244, 247, 254, 255, 301, 302–303, 304, 305, 309, 312, 322, 323
request for interpretation, 61, **63,** 322, 323
request for support, 17
request for sympathy, 61, **63,** 265
respond, 60**,** 61, 105, 139, 168, 170, 196, 198, 205, 225, 230, 284, 285, 303, 306, 323, 325
retreat, 58, 61, **64,** 174–176, 188, 203, 205, 210, 211–212, 273–204, 316, 318, 320, 334, 358
signal completion, 61, **62,** 178, 194, 208, 254
suggestion, suggestion, *See also* {S}. 198, 213–215, 218, 227, 233, 234–235
withdraw, 61, **62, 64**

INDEX TO UTTERANCES[1]

1.1, 33, 41, 44, 105, 106, **113–130,** 131, 141, 179, 335
1.2, 39–40, 106, **130–136,** 137, 138, 271
1.3, 36, **137–139**
1.4, **139–141,** 155, 161
1.5, 45, **139–144,** 147, 155, 214, 252–253, 272, 281
1.6, **145–147,** 155, 178, 214, 315, 322, 324
1.7, 50, 95, **147–153,** 155, 160, 162, 178, 274
1.8, 48–49, 50, 52, 59, 65–67, 71, 92, 95, 104, **155–162,** 165–168, 175–176, 232
1.9, 48–49, 52, 71, 92, 104, **162–168,** 170, 175–176, 199, 243, 253, 270, 336, 339, 342
1.10, 164, **168–171,** 175–176, 269, 270, 289, 335
1.11, 168, **171–173,** 174, 267, 276, 304, 336, 342
1.12, **173–176**
1.13, **177–178**
1.14, 109, **178–179**
2.1, 181, 211–212, 253
2.2, 95, 109, 114, 124, **182–190,** 192, 194, 195, 211–212, 297, 304
2.3, 41, **190–194,** 211–212, 335
2.4, 95, 106, **194–195,** 211–212
2.5, 106, **195–197,** 203, 211, 335
2.6, 83, **197–199,** 204, 206, 211, 305, 320 n, 339
2.7, 87, **199–200,** 204, 206, 211, 336, 339
2.8, 95, 199, **200–201,** 206, 211, 291, 339, 341, 342
2.9, **201–207,** 211, 245 fn, 246, 335, 341
2.10, **208,** 211
2.11, **208–212**
3.1, 95, 99, 107, 194, **215–216,** 217, 227, 244
3.2, 99, 107, **216–217,** 227
3.3, **218–219,** 227–228
3.4, **219–220,** 227
3.5, **220,** 227, 336
3.6, **220–221,** 227

3.7, **221–223,** 227
3.8, **221–223,** 227
3.9, **221–223,** 227, 229, 235
3.10, 224, 227, **228–229,** 342
3.11, 227, **229–231,** 336
3.12, 227, **231–232**
3.13, 227, **232–233,** 302, 342
3.14, 108, 128, 227, **233–235**
3.15, 100, **235–237**
3.16, **238–239**
3.17, 100, **239–241**
3.18, **241**
3.19, **241–245,** 336
3.20, **241–245**
3.21, **245–246,** 336
3.22, 95, 200, **245–246,** 292, 342
3.23, 246–248
4.1, **249–251**
4.2, **251–253**
4.3, 253–254
4.4, 90, **254–255**
4.5, **255–258**
4.6, **258–262**
4.7, **258–262**
4.8, **262–263**
4.9, **263–264**
4.10, **264–266,** 336, 342
4.11, 266–268
4.12, 108, 164, **268–269**
4.13, 108, 164, **268–269,** 337, 341, 342
4.14, 108, 164, **269–271,** 289, 335
4.15, 108, 164, **269–271,** 337, 339
4.16, **271–273**
4.17, 273–274
4.18, **274–275,** 337
4.19, **276–277,** 337
5.1, **280–283,** 284, 296, 300, 308, 312, 317, 334, 344

5.2, **283–284**
5.3, **283–285,** 287, 295
5.4, **285–287**
5.5, **287–289,** 290, 343
5.6, **289–291,** 337
5.7, **291–292**
5.8, 291, 292
5.9, 56, 291, **292–295**
5.10, **295–297,** 298
5.11, 99, **297–298,** 304
5.12, 99, 199, 298–299
5.13, **299–302,** 304
5.14, 300, **302–304,** 305, 319, 335
5.15, **304–305,** 310
5.16, **306–307,** 337
5.17, **307–310,** 322
5.18, **310–311**
5.19, 57, **311–313,** 320, 322
5.20, 199, **313,** 315, 317
5.21, **315–316,** 335
5.22, **317–318,** 335, 345
5.23, **318–320,** 324
5.24, **320–322,** 326, 337
5.25, 103, **322–324**
5.26, **324–325**
5.27, **326–327,** 342

[1]Boldface type indicates cross-sectional analysis.

AUTHOR INDEX

A

Ashby, M., 24
Auerbach, A. H., 3
Austin, J. L., 23, 58, 71

B

Bahner, F., 9
Bailey, C. J. N., 43
Bales, R. F., 16, 17, 38, 60, 116, 271, 348
Bolinger, D. L., 43, 46
Bateson, G., 20, 22, 48
Beavin, J., 348
Bernstein, A., 17, 121, 271
Birdwhistell, R., 20
Blackwell, A., 9
Blitzer, J. R., 9
Borgatta, E. F., ix
Brosen, H., 20
Brown, R., 59

C

Carkhuff, R. R., 3
Cohen, P., ix
Cole, P., 58
Costello, C. G., 8
Coulthard, M., 24

D

Danehy, J. J., 5, 7, 20, 21, 344, 347, 352
Davidson, P. O., 8

DeGroot, A., 48
Deutsch, F., 2, 14, 15, 33

E

English Language Group, 59
Ervin-Tripp, S., 76

F

Fanshel, D., ix, 4, 5
Forsyth, I., 24
Fraser, B., 23, 71, 79, 81, 84, 87
Frazier, S. H., 11
Freud, S., 10, 16
Fry, D. B., 115, 300

G

Garfinkel, H., 51
Garvey, C., 24
Gelman, R., 24
Gill, M., 14, 20
Gilman, A., 59
Gleser, G. C., 17
Glover, E., 2, 13, 14
Goffman, E., 26–27, 30, 32, 34, 36, 73, 88, 94, 96, 111
Gottschalk, L. A., 3, 13, 17
Grice, H. P., 23
Grimes, J. E., 23
Gordan, D., 24, 71, 72, 75, 78, 81
Gunter, R., 23

H

Haley, J., 32
Harris, Z., 38
Hartman, H., 12
Hockett, C. F., 5, 7, 20, 21, 344, 347, 352
Holzman, P. S., 31
Hymes, D., 30

J

Jackson, D., 348
Jaffe, J., 19
Jefferson, G., 25, 62, 73, 76, 110, 348
John, V. P., 18

K

Karttunen, L., 23
Keparsky, C., 103
Keparsky, P., 103
Klima, E. S., 86
Kris, E., 12
Kutner, B., ix

L

Labov, W., ix, 5, 12, 24, 31, 41, 71, 78, 90, 104, 335, 352, 353
Laffal, J., 2, 76
Lakoff, G., 23, 24, 71, 72, 75, 78, 81
Lakoff, R., 85
Langner, T. S., ix
Lasèque, E. C., 9, 11
Lennard, H., 17, 121, 271
Lewis, J., ix
Liberman, M., 86, 357
Lieberman, P., 43, 354
Lipton, E. L., 9, 10, 11

M

MacKinnon, R. A., 1, 3, 15, 34
Mahl, G. F., 19, 116
Marsden, G., 38
Matarazzo, J. D., 357
McQuown, N. E., 20, 353
Menninger, K. A., 31

Meyer, H. J., ix
Michels, R., 1, 3, 15, 34
Mills, T. M., 17
Morgan, J. L., 58
Morton, R., 9
Moss, F., 5
Murphy, W. F., 2, 14, 15, 33

N

Newman, R., 14, 20

P

Parsons, T., 323
Pike, K., 38, 43, 47
Pittenger, R. E., 5, 7, 20, 21, 344, 347, 352

R

Redlich, F. C., 14, 20
Robins, C., ix
Rogers, C. R., 32
Rollins, N., 9
Roseborough, M. E., 17
Ross, J. R., 23

S

Sacks, H., 24, 25, 26, 62, 65, 72, 73, 75, 76, 104, 105, 110, 151, 156, 172, 348
Sadock, J., 58, 71, 82, 83, 86, 356
Sag, I., 86, 357
Saskin, W. F., 18
Saslow, G., 357
Satir, V., 3
Scheflen, A. E., 20, 353
Schegloff, E., 24, 25, 26, 62, 72, 73, 76, 92, 104, 110, 156, 172, 348
Schulze, G., 19, 116
Searle, J., 58, 71, 77, 81, 121, 356
Shatz, M., 2, 24, 86
Shinn, E. B., ix
Shopen, T., 23
Sinclair, J., 24
Skinner, B. F., 121
Smith, H. L., 43
Stennes, L., 23

Stockwell, R. P., 43
Strodtbeck, F., 17
Stubbs, M., 26
Sudnow, D., 72
Szasz, T. S., 10

T

Thomä, H., 9, 10, 11, 293
Togo, A. M., ix
Trager, G. L., 43
Truax, C. B., 3

W

Wald, B. V., 23
Waletsky, J., ix, 104
Watzlawick, P., 3, 348
Weinreich, U., 46, 95, 200
Wheeler, A., 23

Y

Yaeger, M., 110

SUBJECT INDEX

A

A-events, 62–64
AB-events, 63, 80, 101, 122 f.n.
Abstract, 105–106, 217
Acoustic displays of voice, 43
  variable-persistence oscilloscope, 44–45
  real-time spectrum analyzer, 45–46
Action, defined, 76
Actions, speech, *see* Speech acts
Adjacency pairs, 65, 74
Adult status and rights, 52, 55, 67, 135
  challenge to, 96
  in question, 155
  self-care, 295
Aggravated requests, 63
Aggravation, 65, 84–86, 149
Ambiguity in discourse, 177
Anaphoric references, 117, 118
Anorexia nervosa
  nature of illness, 8–12
  symptoms of, 9, 11, 280, 282, 293
  causes, 9, 10, 53
  mode of family expression, 271
  mode of argument, 296
Arrowheads (in cross-sections), 65, 66, 98, 127
Atomic units of coding, 18
Autonomy of patient, 195

B

B-event, 10
  requests for confirmation, 227
"Baiting questions," 90

C

Challenges, 64, 74, 93–94, 124–125
  defined, 124
  to competence, 96
  as speech acts, 97
Coda, 109, 178
Codes and scales, 16, 17, 18
Coherence in discourse, 26–27, 98–99
Concatenation, 341
Condensation, morphological, 140
Conditional relevance, 172 n.
Constitutional predicates, 56
Content analysis, 17
Contextual information, 73
Contradictions, 336
Constrastive stress, 254 n.
Conversation
  nature of, 30, 347–348
  empirical studies of, 24–27
  sociological studies, 24–26
Conversational implicatures, 23
"Correct interpretation," 73, 348–350
Countertransference, 13, 14
Critical requests, 93
Cross-sections, 27, 37, 127
  component parts, 40, 67
  synthesis of, 69
Cues, 5, 42–49, 353
  interpretation of, 46
  nature of paralinguistic cues, 114–117

D

D-events (disputable), 62, 101, 179
Definition of the situation, 26

389

Discourse
  coherence in, 6, 26, 48, 98
  rules, 75, 355
  rules and sentence grammar, 72
  earlier versions of rules, 23–24
  fields of, 42
  analysis within linguistics, 4
Discourse analysis, comprehensive, 29–70, 352–357
Double bind, 48

E

Editing of interview, 353
Elipses
  expansion of, 23, 98–99, 354–362
Episodes, 38–39, 328–331
Euphemism, 34
Evaluation, 63, 101, 108–109
  "external evaluation," 147, 207
Expansion of meaning, 49–53
Expansion of text, 119

F

Family of patient
  network of obligations, 131, 262–263
  role sets, 132–135, 187
  appeals for help, 229
Fields of discourse, 5, 35–37, 42, 128–130, 353
  interview style, 35
  everyday style, 35
  narrative style, 35
  family style, 36, 197, 336–337
First harmonic, 46, 49
Formality, 47
"Free goods," 89
Fundamental contour, 46, 49

H

"Heavy implication" and cues, 47
"Historical present," 107
Histories of speakers," 350
"Huff," 65, 88, 201–202

I

Identification, 209
Idioms, 42
Illocutionary acts, 356
Imperative, 77
Implicit propositions, 51
Implicit responses, 99
Incoherent discourse, 76
Indexical quantifiers, 191
Indirection in conversation, 48, 49, 65, 68, 69, 127
Interaction, 58–60, 123–128, 355–356
  defined, 58, 59
  terms, 60
Interaction Process Analysis (Bales), 16–17
Interchanges, remedial and supportive, 111
Interpretation, 63
  problems of, 25
  resistance, 342
  reinterpretations, 227
Interview
  general characteristics, 30–31
  codes and scales, 17–18
Intonation
  patterns, 5
  contours, 36, 43, 46
  codes, 43
Intuition in linguistics, 72

L

Lexical choice, 42
Linguistic theory, 6
Listener's evaluation, 109–110
"Look," as indication of hurt, 245

M

Markers, in discourse, 156, 185, 189, 254
Meaning, problems of defining, 21, 43, 123, 344
Meta-actions, 60
Meta-propositions about therapy, 57
Methodology, 4–8
Microanalysis, 19–23
  paradox of, 344

Microscopy, dangers of, 22, 51
Mitigation, 34, 51, 63, 65, 84–86, 151, 187
　paradox of microanalysis, 343–344
Mode of argument
　defined, 53, 67
Mode of expression, 48, 120, 271
　defined, 51, 67
　indirect mode, 243 n.
Mode of interaction, 67
Mutual evaluation, 27

N

Narratives, 73, 104–105
　defined, 105
　general propositions, 105
Narrative sequencing, 107–108
Negative statements, conditional relevance of, 104
"Nonfluencies in speech," 116
"Now" as discourse marker, 189, 254

O

Observer's Paradox
　in linguistic studies, 335 n.
O-event, 101
"Oh," to indicate surprise, 199
"Operators," 57
Organization of the study, 27–28
Orientation, as mechanism for initiating narratives, 106–107
Oscilloscope, 44–45
Overdue obligations, 96

P

Paradox of therapy, 32
Parallels and analogies in family behavior, 287, 342
Paralinguistic cues, *see* Cues
Pauses, treatment in text, 41
Performatives, analysis of, 23
Pitch, 42
　contour, 43, 45
Philosophy of language, 23–24, 71

Playback, discussions with therapist, 5, 7, 123, 147, 223, 305, 337, 338, 342
Preconditions, 81–82
Presuppositions, structure of, 23
Production, rules of, 6, 37, 71, 74
Pro-forms, 117–118
Propositional behavior, 17
Propositions, 51–58, 66, 121–123, 354–355
　defined, 52
　longitudinal nature of, 332
　psychological, 54–55
Prosodic cues, 46, 47, 115, 191
"Pseudo-interruptions," 221
Pseudo-narrative, 208, 241–242, 319
Punctuation, 41–42
Put off, 64
Putting off requests, 165
　with requests for information, 90–91

Q

Question, 64
Quantification
　of speech acts, 19

R

Real-time spectrum analyzer, 45–46
Recording of interview, 353
Recurrence, principle of, 7
Redundant responses, 92
Reinforcement, 47, 62
　intonation contours, 127–128
Relayed requests, 88, 94–96
Remarks, 101
Requests, 63, 65, 73, 74, 77
　precondition for valid requests, 24, 88
　for action, 24, 77, 78, 80
　distinguished from jokes, 158
　for information, 24, 88–90
　refusal of, 110
　for display, 89
　repeated, 67, 215
　reinstating, 93, 171
"Reportability," 105
Representations, 62, 104
Resistance, 3, 13, 34, 342
　masking, 332–335

392 SUBJECT INDEX

Responses, 65
Reticence, 34
Retreat, 64
Rhoda, background of patient, 8–12
Role
   performance, cut-off points, 56
   strain, 56
   competence, 94
Rules, in linguistics, 74

S

S: basic suggestion, 67, 122
Self-interruptions, 117
Sequencing in conversation, 24–25, 37, 110–111
Silence, 34, 283, 313–314
"Sincerity conditions," 75 n., 78
Single case, study of, 8
"Sing-song" intonation, 264, 306
"Slips," 13
Social stratification of English, 5
Sociolinguistic variants of New York City speech, 42, 115 n.
Socratic questions, 102–103, 301–302, 321–322
Spectographic displays, 117
Speech act, 6, 29–30, 58, 76, 104
   defined, 59
   hierarchical organization, 59
   completion of, 62
   connectedness of sentences, 23–24
Speech disturbances, 19
Stigma of therapy, 32
Strain, 67, 170
Support, 64

T

Tension cues, 46
"Test questions," 90

Text, 40–41
   full text of therapy session (first 15 minutes), 361–369
Therapeutic interview, 12, 30–35
   nature of, 2–3
   as site of research, 351–352
   as speech event, 30
Therapist, background of, 12
Therapy, paradox of, 32
"Thereby" statements, 65, 276
Turntaking, 76, 348

U

Units and unitizing, 38–40

V

Valid requests for action, 159
Visual record, 20–21
Voice qualifiers, 42
Volume, 42

W

"Well," as discourse marker, 156, 182, 189
Wh- question, 102, 103, 172
When question, 49

Y

Yiddish, "rise–fall" intonation, 46, 95, 200
"You know" as discourse marker, 185, 189

GENERAL PROPOSITIONS

{AD-X}	X is an adult member of the household.
{AUT}	The therapist does not tell the patient what to do.
{CLEAN-X}	X does help clean the house.
{COOP}	Role partners should cooperate to solve mutual problems.
{E-X}	X feels an emotion.
{E_1-X}	X feels confused or frustrated.
{E_2-X}	X feels guilt.
{E_3-X}	X feels anger.
{E_4-X}	X feels loneliness.
{EAT-X}	X eats enough to stay healthy.
{HEAD-X}	X is a competent head of the household.
{INSIGHT}	The patient should gain insight into his or her own emotions.
{INT-X}	X interprets the emotions of others.
{RSNBL-X}	X is a reasonable person.
{S}	One should express one's needs and emotions to relevant others.
{S-CARE}	A person should take care of himself.
{SICK-X}	X is sick.
{STRN}	X's obligations are greater than his capacities.
{STUD-X}	X is a student whose primary responsibility is to study.
{THIN-X}	X is thinner than he should be.
{TIRE-X}	X tires more easily than others.
{X:STRN}	External circumstances are responsible for role strain.